FITTING PREDICTING AND FIXING THE UNITED STATES ECONOMY

BARRY BRUCE

ISBN-13: 978-1-7351367-0-7

Book Cover Design: Elisabeth Heissler
Copy Editor: Rebecca Collins

Published by Barry Bruce
Barry Bruce
1021 Washington Street
Huntingdon, Pennsylvania 16652

Table of Contents

Acknowledgements

This monograph is the result of thousands and thousands of hours of work in which I was able to develop a set of six coupled differential equations along with two algebraic coupling equations that allows a fit to the United States Economy. This thread of macroeconomics is based on the work of some giants who came before. It is based on the work of Karl Marx, Richard Goodwin, Hyman Minsky, and Steve Keen. If their work had not preceded mine, this work would not have been done. It is really the work of all of us, and probably others of whom I am not aware.

Preface

This monograph covers the material of a textbook, but it is not a textbook. It is a running description of a macroeconomic journey, which is intended to be read in order just like a novel.

The *Prelude* is an essential part of the book; it was written after the economic journey was completed. It presents some significant material and macroeconomic principles while it sets the stage for the economic journey. The rest of the book is presented in the order of development and constitutes the macroeconomic economic journey.

Barry Bruce
June 2020

Prelude

This monograph originally started out as an article which included the first four chapters of this book. At that time, I was sending my work out to economic journals in the hope of communicating to economists that it was possible to fit and predict the United States Economy with a set of coupled differential equations. My hope was that the publication of this work, as an article, would stimulate economists to develop the work further. I knew that economists would be better able to develop this approach than I, a physicist, could. I believe it is essential for us to come to understand our economy so that we can learn how to control our economy such that we can prevent severe economic disasters in the future.

While trying to communicate with economists through economic journals, I extended the work by using the coupled macroeconomic differential equations to create a sample solution to the enormous debt problem facing the United States. While the results of this solution seemed reasonable, I also thought the results were almost certainly solid even though every fit I had done to that point had started in 1980. I found it hard to believe that a set of differential equations would fit the United States Economy on some kind of weird fluke. However, because the differential equations worked in current dollars, I had always found it troubling that the equations used the relationship that the output of the economy divided by the productivity equaled the employment level. So, in order to understand, I found myself needing to explore further.

As I discovered, it is often difficult to grasp the nature of macroeconomic variables. It was a continual learning process for me, and I made mistakes in interpretation along the way. I have kept these misinterpretations in the text. I have done so because I think it will make it easier for the reader to see the how and the why of a more correct interpretation of various results as they come into view.

The main macroeconomic variable that presented difficulty was the employment level. The employment level and its relationship with the intimately associated macroeconomic variables, the productivity and the average wage rate, took much exploration in order for me to bring forth the relationship of these variables to each other and to the economy as a whole.

What we will come to see is that the scale of the human being in the economy is not represented in the equations that describe an economy. The equations know nothing about our needs, wants, or desires. The equations do not know how much food or rest we need to sustain ourselves. Thus, as we will see, the equations will not know what will be the scale of our society relative to the output of the economy. We have to input this.

Our macroeconomic differential equations include the macroeconomic variables for the output of the economy, the total debt in the economy, the total investment into the real economy, the average wage rate in the economy, the total profit in the economy, and the productivity in the real economy. We have to input the scale of society through a differential equation that produces the population of our society. Once we have solved our economic equations, we can relate these results to the employment level through the relation that the employment level equals the output of the economy divided by its productivity.

During later explorations with productivity, it will be shown that productivity can be expressed in current dollars rather than in the usual physical terms of output of product per hour of work. This concept of productivity then allows a connection to Bivens and Mishel's work on the separation between wage growth and productivity growth. Bivens and Mishel's work shows that the typical worker's pay has not kept pace with productivity growth, while the elite worker's pay has outpaced productivity growth (Bivens and Mishel, 2015). We will come to see that this income inequality phenomenon is tied to structural changes that occurred in the Federal Income Tax.

The income tax structure, when the top marginal tax rate is low, can be associated with the unleashing of greed in people because it allows people to gamble to gain unlimited wealth. This ability to gamble for unlimited wealth, along with the ability of banks to be able to both lend into the real economy and to lend for speculative purposes, creates a situation in which people can gamble with the Wealth of the Nation for personal gain. Both conditions were present in the lead up to the Great Stock Market Crash in 1929, which led to the Great Depression of the 1930s. Also, both conditions obtained in the lead up to the crisis in the economy in 2008–9.

In this monograph, we set up a scenario in the United States Economy in which the Federal Reserve increases interest rates at three-quarters of a percent per year for seven years, starting in 2017. Starting in 2019, using the Government's sovereign power to create money, we set up a policy in which the Government helps to pay part of the debt and part of the investment of every entity in the United States Economy. We will see that such a policy can fix the huge debt problem, while at the same stabilizing the banks and fixing the slow GDP growth rate. However, this scenario will not completely fix the wage rate problem in our society.

A sample, Constitutional Federal Income Tax structure, and a Constitutional livable wage rate, both based on the output of the United States Economy, are presented that would allow us to fix all the above problems. Also, it is noted that a Social Security Payroll Tax that is a fixed percentage of all income, from whatever the source, would also fix the Social Security funding problem because the funding would be based on the whole economy and not on the demographics of the population at a particular time.

Our Country was set up to secure the rights of the People. One of the rights of the People is the right to life. Thus, the People have a right to a livable wage. Because the Government was instituted to secure the rights of the People, it is the job of the Federal Government to secure this right. A livable wage is definable in terms of the whole economy.

It turns out that one half the GDP per capita is a livable wage for a single person. A livable wage for a small family of three to four is more than three-fifths of the GDP per capita. It is not an easy or pleasant existence for a family, but it is doable and allows for an independent existence that allows the family a sense of self-worth.

For example, in 2018, the GDP in the United States, according to the Bureau of Economic Analysis (BEA), was equal to 20.494 trillion dollars. Because the population in July 2018 was equal to 327.167 million people, this means that the GDP per capita was $62,640.792. So, this single person livable wage of one half the GDP per capita turns out to be $31,320.40 per year.

I have had several jobs in my life where I had to punch a time card. In these jobs, I was allowed two weeks of vacation time per year, but I was not paid during the vacation, so I will assume that during a year a person works 40 hours per week for 50 weeks. That is, I will assume a person works 2000 hours per year in order to calculate the single person livable hourly wage rate. If we set the livable hourly wage rate for 2019 by using the statistics from 2018, we would have an hourly livable wage rate of

$$\text{2019 livable wage rate} = \frac{\$31320.40}{2000} = \$15.62 \text{ per hour.}$$

If we repeat this procedure to find the livable wage rate for 2018 and 2017, we find the results shown below:

$$\text{2018 livable wage rate} = \frac{\frac{1}{2}\$59637.64}{2000} = \$14.91 \text{ per hour}$$

$$\text{2017 livable wage rate} = \frac{\frac{1}{2}\$57646.77}{2000} = \$14.41 \text{ per hour.}$$

These simple calculations show how quickly setting a fixed livable wage becomes an unlivable minimum wage. Therefore, one should define the livable wage, yearly, with respect to the macroeconomic nature of the economy and not in some fixed arbitrary way that works for only an instant of time.

In Figure 1, we display the single person livable wage rate from 1947 to 2017, as calculated above, and the Federal Minimum Wage Rate that was established by law.

We can see from Figure 1 that the Federal Minimum Wage was a livable wage from 1947 to about 1980 for a single person. During the time from 1950 through the early of the 1960s, I was aware that some people in my hometown were raising families while earning on or about the minimum wage rate. My father earned about 1.6 times the yearly minimum wage. There were several people poorer than us in town. At the time, our state's minimum wage and the Federal Minimum Wage were the same. So, I know the Federal Minimum Wage was a livable wage for a small family back then.

By livable, I mean that a family could afford to buy a house by financing with a mortgage. They could afford a car for transportation to work, to pay for doctor visits, and to pay for operations and a brief hospital stay. Moreover, college was affordable for those children that chose to go to college. The child might have to help pay for college by working, but they could do it.

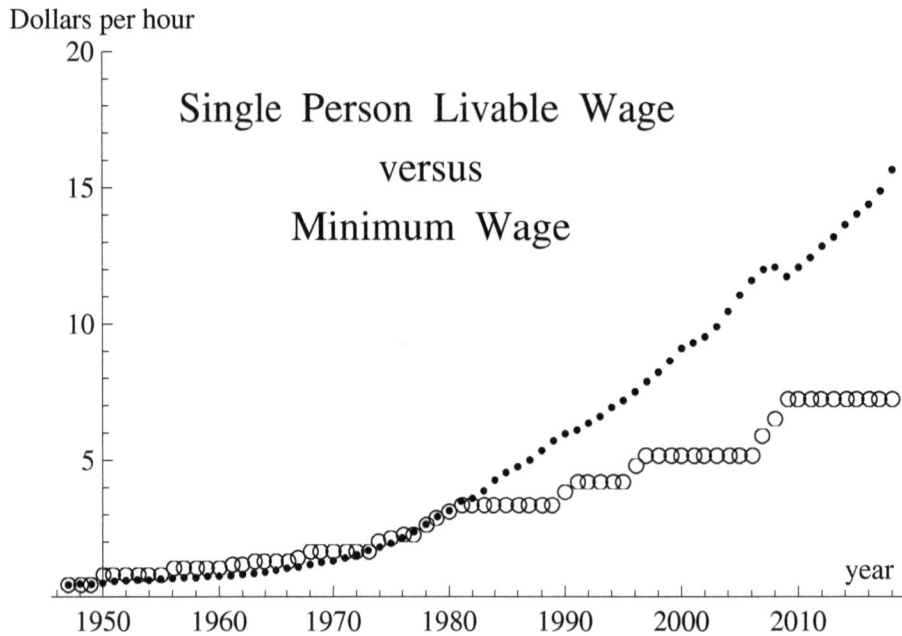

Figure 1: This figure displays a comparison of the livable wage and the Federal Minimum Wage. The single person livable wage is displayed as points and the Federal Minimum Wage Rate is displayed as open circles.

We can also see from Figure 1 that from about 1983 to the present, the livable wage for a single person was systematically above the Federal Minimum Wage. I was a graduate student in physics from the late 1980s to the mid-1990s. My teaching assistant position paid me an income, including a separate summer TA, about equal to a yearly equivalent of five dollars per hour. My income was above the Federal Minimum Wage but below the single person livable wage at the time. It was only with special conditions that this was "livable". The university paid for my medical needs at the school clinic and university hospital. They provided student rental housing units at below the going market rates in the area. Moreover, the units were close enough that I could walk to campus, so I had no transportation costs. I had no car, telephone, TV, or computer. I never went out to eat; it was a bare-bones existence. So I know the single person livable wage is not extravagant.

Next, in Figure 2, we present a comparison of the small family livable wage and the Federal Minimum Wage. The small family livable wage was calculated as 0.65 times the GDP per capita.

In Figure 2, one can see that a small family could live on the Federal Minimum Wage during the 1950s and 1960s. Congress during that time was attentive to raising the minimum wage high enough so that it was always big enough for a small family to live on. When one looks carefully at Figure 2, one sees that from 1950 through 1963, the Federal Minimum Wage grew slightly faster than the rate at which 0.65 times the GDP per capita grew.

If we look closely at Figure 2, we see that the small family livable wage started to pull away from the Federal Minimum Wage in 1968. We also see from Figure 1 that the Federal Minimum Wage even starts growing a little slower than the single person livable wage after

Dollars per hour

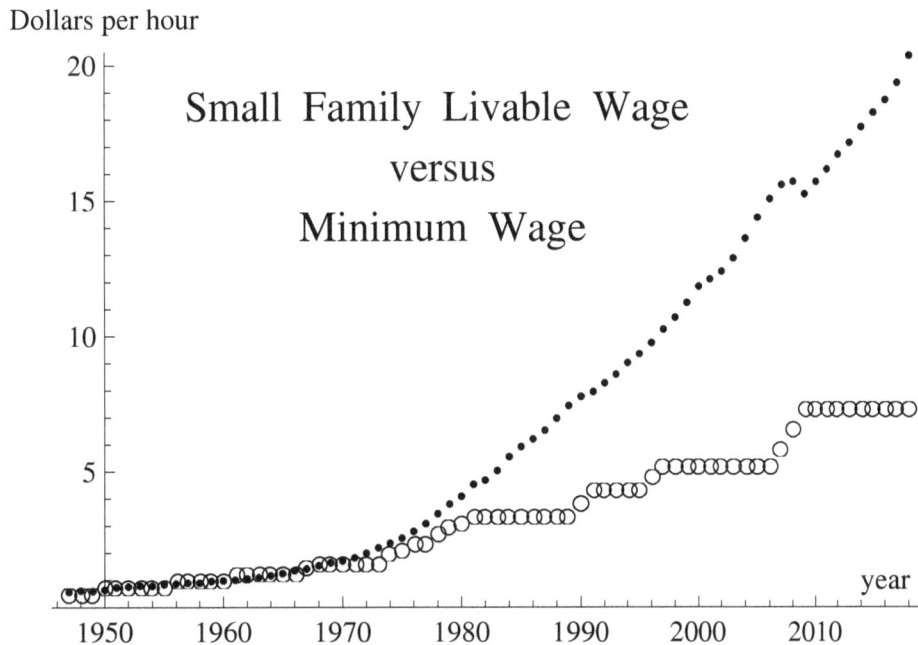

Figure 2: This figure displays a comparison of the livable wage for a small family of three to four people and the Federal Minimum Wage. The livable wage is displayed as points and the Federal Minimum Wage Rate is displayed as open circles.

1968. After 1981, Congress decreased the average growth rate of the Federal Minimum Wage even further. Thus, after 1981, we see in both Figure 1 and Figure 2, the livable wage pulling rapidly away from the Federal Minimum Wage. We will revisit this period when the livable wage separated from the minimum wage in several contexts later in our development.

We have seen that we have been able to set a livable wage using the macroeconomic quantities of the total output of the United States and the population of the United States. We formed the normalized quantity, the GDP per capita, in order to have a measure of what the economy would support per person. This measure of what the economy can support is "independent" of the GDP size of the economy or the population size of the economy. So, once we have identified a livable wage in terms of the GDP per capita in some year, we will know it in any year for which we know the GDP per capita. Defining the livable wage in terms of macroeconomic quantities illustrates the principle that it is more effective to solve a global problem with a macro solution rather than with a micro or meso solution. The Constitutional principle that we are all equal under the law all but requires us to do this.

There is a result of cumulative productivity increases that is making its way into our consciousness. This result is that much of our work is starting to be done by artificial intelligence (AI) and robots. I have not seen these results being connected with productivity increases. However, they clearly are because a productivity increase is just the measure of how the output per hour of work has increased over time. Furthermore, it is clear that with AI and robotics that there will be a decrease in the number of human hours of work needed to produce a given output of a product.

As we will see, productivity increases faster than the population. Therefore, there will come a time when our society will be able to produce all that is needed with a much-reduced number of work hours. This presents a problem for society as to how we should handle this situation. The principle that we are all equal under governance handles this situation in a fair manner. The solution is simple. We reduce the workweek!

If we reduce the workweek from 40 hours per week to 30 hours per week—that is, to five six-hour days—then everybody shares in the work and everybody shares in more free time. It also clears up our hidden unemployment problem, which exists, because, in reality, our unemployment rate is somewhere between twenty and twenty-five percent, the way it used to be counted.

Another solution for our economic problems, Universal Basic Income, is being pushed by some elites. It is an enticing solution that has been taken up by others who have the interest of all people in their hearts. However, this solution would break up society into three main groups: the rich elites, the workers, and an underclass of non-workers. Thus, this solution would stratify our society into a caste system leading to unequal opportunity—inconsistent with the principles of Our Country's founding.

The solution to every economic problem we have rests on the ability of our country to solve its huge debt problem. If our economy falls apart, we can not solve our medical care problem or our livable wage problem. We will be living in a disaster, a disaster of our own making, a disaster that came about by our lack of understanding. Our present situation did not have a single genesis. There were many missteps along the way.

To fix the enormous debt problem while keeping the economy upright, we will need to understand what we are doing. To do this, we will need to know and trust that our macro-economic coupled differential equations accurately represent the reality of our economy. To test this, we have run a series of fits to the United States Economy with a second starting date, far from the starting date of our original fits.

This is a true test because we know that if the coupled differential equations represent the economic reality of the United States Economy, then these equations ***must*** give the same results and same predictions as a different set of fits, which begins at a different starting date. A set of fit parameters was found, for fits beginning in 1964, which allowed the continuation of a fit beyond 2017. This allowed this set of fits to predict the economy under the assumption that the Federal Reserve would raise interest rates at three-quarters of a percent per year.

The result of this test was that the predictions made from these fits for the Federal Reserve rate hike scenario were consistent with each other, for the various fits that began in 1964. The same was true for the fits, which began in 1980. Yet, all the predictions and some aspects of the fits, themselves, were not consistent when the starting time of the fits differed. However, when a term was added to the output differential equation that takes into account periods of high inflation, then all the fits themselves and their predictions became consistent with one another irrespective of the starting time of the fit. This result all but proves that our coupled differential equation model really does represent the economic reality of the United States Economy. And thus, we have a way to fix our economy, without a collapse, if we are bold enough to act on our knowledge.

Part I

FITS THAT BEGIN IN 1980

Chapter 1

Introduction

In 2015, for reasons of my own, not relevant here, I was trying to get an understanding of the United States Economy. I started out by reading Hyman Minsky's book, *Stabilizing an Unstable Economy* (Minsky, 2008). This led me to Professor Steve Keen's book, *Debunking Economics* (Keen, 2011). This is a book with an unfortunate off-putting title and attitude. This is very unfortunate because Professor Keen really has a lot that is worthwhile to say. In particular, he presents an economic model of a pure credit economy (Keen, 2011, pages 362–377). I searched his website in order to learn how to set up the model and play with it (Keen, 2010). I learned much in playing with it. However, more to the point, I found an article on his website, "A Monetary Minsky Model of the Great Moderation and the Great Recession" (Keen, 2013), in which he applies this model to the economic crisis of 2008–9. In addition, he introduces two other models in this article. It is from these models that I have taken my approach.

The first model that Professor Keen presents is:

$$
\begin{aligned}
\frac{dL}{dt} &= L\left(\frac{1 - \frac{w}{a}}{v} - \gamma - \alpha\right) \\
\frac{dw}{dt} &= (-c + d * \lambda) * w \\
\frac{da}{dt} &= \alpha * a \qquad\qquad \text{Keen's (1.1)} \\
\frac{dN}{dt} &= \beta * N
\end{aligned}
$$

These are Keen's equations (1.1) (Keen, 2013, p. 224). These equations are essentially Richard Goodwin's equations that he presented in 1965 at the "First World Congress of the Econometric Society" (Goodwin, 1965). Professor Keen has added the depreciation of capital goods, γ, in the first equation. The last equation states that the time rate of change of the population is equal to a constant, β, times the population N. Goodwin related the growth to the labor population. The third equation relates the time rate of change of the productivity,

a, to the product of a constant, α, and the productivity itself. The second equation equates the time rate of change of the wage rate, w, to the product of the wage rate times a linear relation in the employment rate λ, $-c + d * \lambda$. This relation, when integrated, produces what is known as a Phillips curve. It was created and used to model a competitive type relationship in which the competitive quantities are expected to have exponential-like growth and to be sticky to lowering, such as the wage rate and its competitive quantity, the employment level. The product of the two competitive quantities in their respective equations often causes a cyclic behavior in the quantities. The first equation states that the time rate of change of the employment level (number of workers) is equal to the employment level times the quantity one minus the wage rate divided by the productivity all divided by the capital stock to output ratio, v; minus the sum of the depreciation rate of the capital stock, γ, and the productivity rate, α. Professor Goodwin did not add the depreciation rate to his equation. This relation can be derived from a capital stock equation, $dK/dt = I - \gamma * K$, where K is capital stock and I is investment (Keen, 2013).

Professor Keen's second model (Keen, 2013, p. 224) adds one more macroeconomic system variable by adding the debt equation $dD/dt = I - \Pi$, where I is investment and Π is profit. Professor Keen also added debt interest payments to the definition of profit, $\Pi = Y - w * L - r * D$, where Y is the output of the economy and r is the interest rate paid on the debt (Keen, 2013, equation 1.4, p. 225). This seemingly innocuous addition to the profit equation is important because it keeps the financial system out of the real economy while at the same time keeping its influence in the equations describing the real economy. Compare this with Professor Minsky's struggle to set up an appropriate system of variables and equations (Minsky, 2008, pages 160–171). Thus, Keen's five equations of his second model are:

$$\frac{dY}{dt} = \left(\frac{I\left(\frac{\Pi}{vY} \right)}{v} - \gamma \right) * Y$$

$$\frac{dw}{dt} = P_H(\lambda) * w$$

$$\frac{dD}{dt} = I\left(\frac{\Pi}{vY} \right) * Y - \Pi \qquad \qquad \text{Keen's} \quad (1.5)$$

$$\frac{da}{dt} = \alpha * a$$

$$\frac{dN}{dt} = \beta * N$$

These are Keen's equations (1.5) (Keen, 2013, p. 226). Note that in these equations, $I(\Pi/vY)$ represents a nonlinear Phillips curve relation. Note also, that Professor Keen has changed from the employment level, L, to the output, Y, using the productivity times the number of workers equals the output, that is, $Y = a * L$. The expression $P_H(\lambda)$ in the wage rate equation represents a Phillips curve relation as expressed in the modified Goodwin Growth Model presented in Professor Keen's first model in his equations (1.1) (Keen, 2013, p. 224).

1.1 Eight Macroeconomic Equations and Their Rationale

Professor Goodwin's equations were essentially trying to capture the spirit of a two economic entity, a capitalist versus worker, economic system. In this idealized system, a predator-prey set of differential equations governing the economic system might be expected. However, our economic system has grown more complex than that over the years. The government, in particular, has grown to oversee and regulate the nature of allowed economic interactions within our society. Thus, our system has moved away from the idealized two-sided economic battleground of the past. Those tendencies are still there, but they are now mixed with other tendencies that have arisen in our more complex economy.

In order to deal with our more complex economy, we will try to use equations where we do not require any particular behavior of the macroeconomic variables. In particular, we will not require that the investment variable, I, be of the form of a Phillips curve relation. Instead, we will create a sixth macroeconomic differential equation; an investment equation in the form, the change of investment in time equals some function of the economic system variables, that is, $dI/dt = f(economic\ variables)$. In order to do this, we will want to create an equation that possesses the qualitative properties that both Minsky (Minsky, 1982) and Keen (Keen, 2011) have explained. To wit, we want our equation to reflect the properties that:

1. At times in which the economic prospects look very positive, the business owner will want to invest more in his or her business than their profit alone will allow. They do this in an attempt to maximize their profit in the long run. We will call the term in the investment equation that does this, the Businessman's Term.

2. At times when the debt owed the banker starts to become large, and the banker begins to fear that the borrower might not be able to pay back their loans, the banker will want to be able to put the brakes on making loans. We will call the term in the investment equation that does this, the Banker's Term.

Thus, our investment equation will have the form:

$$dI/dt = \Pi + Businessman's\ Term + Banker's\ Term.$$

A business owner is likely to look at his or her profit and compare it with the business's output. The more profit owners see relative to output, the more likely they would be willing to invest while incurring some debt. That is, the more they would be liable to invest. An expression that would do this is $\Pi * (\Pi/Y)$. Because we do not know what the propensity to invest is relative to risk associated with an unknowable future, we add a coefficient, c_1, to the Businessman's Term in the investment equation.

As we have thought of the banker, we think of him as wanting to put the damper on excess investing because bankers do not want a borrower to default and not pay the loan back with interest. The banker looks at the amount of the debt with respect to the amount of the capital goods when assessing a loan going bad, because if the loan goes bad, he or she can recoup their lost loan by the sale of the capital goods belonging to the borrower. Thus, a reasonable Banker's Term doing what we expect in the investment equation is $-\Pi * (D/(v*Y))$, where $v * Y$ is equal to the capital goods K. Again, because we do not know the propensity of the banker to dampen borrowing, we add a coefficient, c_2, to the Banker's Term in the investment equation.

Our final investment equation is:

$$\frac{d}{dt}I = \Pi + c_1 * \Pi * \left(\frac{\Pi}{Y}\right) - c_2 * \Pi * \left(\frac{D}{v*Y}\right). \tag{1.1}$$

The constants c_1 and c_2 need to be found by fitting the economy. After the coefficients are fitted with the economy, they may change due to special circumstances in the economy that necessitate a change in either banking behavior or business behavior. The profit, as it will be calculated, is defined as $\Pi = Y - w * Y/a - r * D$ because $Y/a = L$. Thus, the investment equation is quite nonlinear because it contains a mix of the products of several system variables. Note that the Businessman's Term and the Banker's Term are both the result of rational thought. However, the thought is by different groups of people who have different and, at times, competing interests. Thus, these terms introduce the possibility of inherent instability into the economic system consistent with Minsky's instability hypothesis. The product of system variables explicitly present in the investment equation once the definition of profit is substituted into the equation makes this mathematically clear.

The coefficients c_1 and c_2 in the investment equation represent the business persons' and bankers' intended policies. If the profit in the economy at a given time is positive and the intention of business people is to spend a little more on investment than their profit alone would allow, then the Businessman's Coefficient, c_1, would be positive. If at the same time, the bankers' intent is to retard loaning to some extent, then the Banker's Coefficient, c_2, would be positive. What if during this time the economy's profit was positive but small and then suddenly the economy's profit moved into negative territory, without the knowledge of either the bankers or the business people, in such a case, we must require the investment equation to keep their policy intentions. The Businessman's Term will do this because the profit is squared in the Businessman's Term so that the product will not change sign when the profit switches from positive to negative. However, in the Banker's Term, the economy profit is multiplied by a positive debt term, $c_2 D/(vY)$, meaning that the sign of the Banker's Term will change when the economy's profit goes from positive to negative, contrary to the will of the bankers.

We fix this problem in the implementation of the investment equation by multiplying the Banker's Term by the function $Sign(\Pi)$, whose value is plus one when the economy's profit is positive and minus one when the profit is negative. That is, our implemented investment equation will be

$$\frac{d}{dt}I = \Pi + c_1 * \Pi * \left(\frac{\Pi}{Y}\right) - Sign(\Pi) * c_2 * \Pi * \left(\frac{D}{v * Y}\right). \qquad (1.1^*)$$

This fix will keep the bankers' intentions irrespective of whether the economy profit is positive or negative.

Among the equations that we will use in our calculations will be a wage equation. The wage equation states that the time rate of change of the average wage rate equals a constant times the economy profit-to-GDP ratio times the productivity. That is, our wage equation will be

$$\frac{d}{dt}w = m * \left[\frac{\Pi}{Y}\right] * a, \qquad (1.2^*)$$

where m is a constant that allows a fit to the economy. This constant will be found by trial and error.

Let us discuss the rationale for this equation. If we put ourselves in the position of an employer and ask ourselves the question: On what basis can we change the total wages per year paid to our employees? The primary or central basis for making a change in employee wages that would be staring us in the face would be the company's profits. Additionally, we assume that as profits rise, employers would likely be more willing to raise the pay of workers. Similarly, we assume that employers would seek to lower the pay of employees as profits fall. Thus, the change in total wages, ΔW, paid by an employer in a year might be expected to be proportional to the company's profit, π, in a year. That is, for a single employer, we might expect

$$\frac{dW}{dt} = k\pi,$$

where k is a constant.

However, we are seeking a macroeconomic wage equation, not a microeconomic equation. Professor Keen's expression for the profit equation,

$$\Pi = Y - w * L - r * D, \quad \text{Keen's (1.4)},$$

will help us proceed. For this to be a macroeconomic equation, each term in the equation must be a macroeconomic term speaking to the whole economy. Therefore, Π must stand for the total profit in the economy per year, and Y must be the total output of the economy per year. For $w * L$ to be the macroeconomic expression for the total wages in the economy when L is the employment level in the economy, then w must be an average wage rate, the average income per year, in the economy. For completeness, we note that r must be the average interest rate per year and D the total debt in the economy.

Since the average wage in a company is always the total wages W divided by the number of employees in the company l, no matter how those wages are distributed, then the time rate of change in average wage per year in the company is

$$\frac{d}{dt}\left(\frac{W}{l}\right) = k\frac{\pi}{l}.$$

The simplest and cleanest connection with this microeconomic differential equation would be the macroeconomic differential equation

$$\frac{dw}{dt} = m\frac{\Pi}{L}, \tag{1.2}$$

where m is a constant and w is the average wage per year. Substituting the relation that employment level equals the output divided by the productivity, $L = Y/a$, gives us Equation 1.2*.

In addition to these equations, we add four fairly classical equations:

$$\frac{d}{dt}N = \beta * N, \tag{1.3}$$

the population equation;

$$\frac{d}{dt}a = \alpha * a, \tag{1.4}$$

the productivity equation;

$$\frac{d}{dt}Y = \frac{I}{v} - \gamma * Y, \tag{1.5}$$

the output equation; and

$$\frac{d}{dt}D = I - \Pi, \tag{1.6}$$

the debt equation. Finally, we connect all the macroeconomic differential equations, the unstarred equations, with two coupling equations, the employment level equation,

$$L = \frac{Y}{a}, \tag{1.7}$$

and the economy profit equation,

$$\Pi = Y - w * L - r * D. \tag{1.8}$$

The economy profit equation will used in our calculations in the form

$$\Pi = Y - w * Y/a - r * D. \tag{1.8*}$$

1.2   Auxiliary Equations and Fitting

In addition to these equations, we create equations that will allow us to try to fit the economy when there are changes to the economy that could never be predicted from any equation, a priori, such as the repeal of Glass-Steagall or the response to the economic crisis of 2008–9. We will also linearize the average interest rate so that when it is multiplied by the total debt, the product gives the interest payment. I have not been able to find any such average interest rate anywhere, so I have used my best guesstimate, which I have plotted from 1980 to 2017 in Figure 1.1.

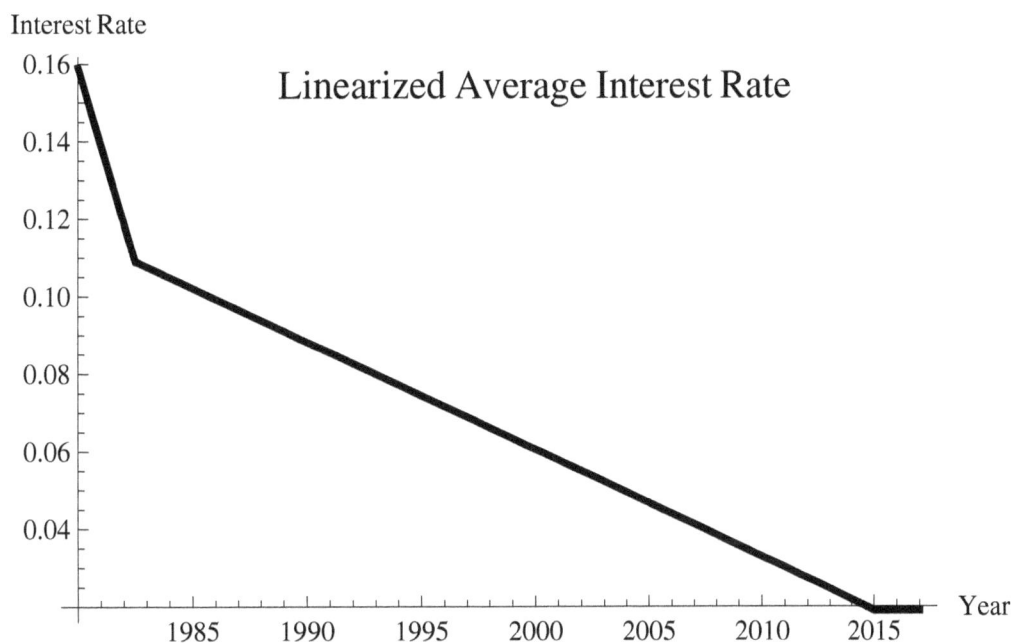

Figure 1.1: This graph displays the estimated average interest rate that was used in fitting the United States Economy between 1980 through the end of 2016 in both the rough, smooth fit and the more fine-grained, refined fit that tried to match the variations in the GDP data.

The variables in these equations are macroeconomic variables. These variables are often not what one expects them to be, given their names, at least not what I expected them to be. For example, the number of workers must include people who are paid from the creation and sale of a product, yet at the same time, these people had no real direct or indirect part in the manufacture or sale of the product. The overall government (Federal, State, and local) collects taxes directly from businesses. Part of the money the overall government takes in goes to pay people who have done little or no work, such as people on Social Security, welfare, or disability. Some of the tax receipts go to pay government workers who also have done no work in the manufacture or sale of the product. All of this "pay" must be included in wages and thus in the average wage rate because macroeconomic equations speak to the whole economy, and because there is nowhere else to put this "pay" within our limited set of equations. No economic statistic that I am aware of has tried to measure this macroeconomic number of workers. Therefore, accurate estimates of the number of "workers" and the average wage rate lack good, independent estimates.

A lot of taxes received by the overall government come from workers who have done work related to the manufacture or sale of products. Their contribution to overall government "pay" is really a transfer of wages from workers who contributed to the manufacture or sale of products to people who did not. That is not to say that the people who receive this transfer have not contributed to our society. Postal workers deliver mail and packages, and police help to keep our society orderly. Social Security recipients have paid into their retirement and contributed to our society at an earlier time. They are now retrieving a maintenance income, for their earlier contributions, from the Federal Government's retirement insurance plan. Taxes complicate the analysis of such things as productivity because it is the workers who actually contribute to the business's work plus some mythical workers that could be associated with the actual tax the business pays. Because business tax is paid on net income, this should mean that the number of mythical workers is small compared to the actual number of workers in the business. Thus, the calculations of productivity should be close to correct when the actual number of workers is used to calculate productivity.

Population should be an easy matter. However, even here, there are complications. The population usually quoted is United States citizens born in the United States. For example, the link

http://www.uspopulations.com/
LiveChart/CensusPopulationChart/COUNTRY/USA/
COUNTRY/USA/CENSUS_SIMPLE/TOTAL_AMERICAN_INDIAN

provided the following information for 2015:

US citizens born in the United States	321,418,944
US citizens by naturalization	2,985,937
Foreign born	43,290,372.

Thus, at the present time, the population of the United States, from which workers are drawn, is about forty million people larger than the population of the United States, as it is usually given in economic statistics. In 1980, the starting date of the fit to the United States Economy, the discrepancy was much less.

The population projection from the differential equation $dN/dt = \beta * N$ will be the same in all calculations. The only consistent United States population data given is for the United States citizen population. Economic data was not needed to find the fit parameter β. The result of the fit projection compared with the United States population data is shown in Figure 1.2.

The data for the United States citizen population follows the trend of the exponential fit to the population growth. However, the fit is not perfect as the population growth is sometimes faster and sometimes slower than that predicted by the exponential fit. Such a fit is complicated by the fact that immigration to the United States would not be expected to grow exponentially. Population growth by immigration should be expected to be more episodic.

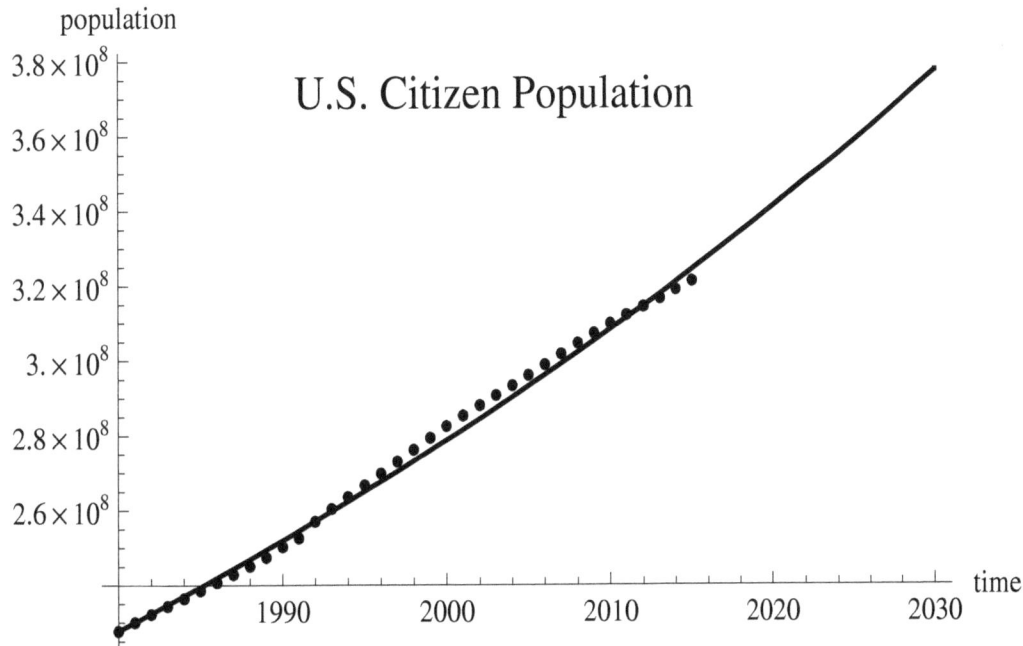

Figure 1.2: This graph shows the projected United States citizen population. However, as mentioned earlier, this is not the population from which workers are drawn. The discrepancy is larger now than it was in 1980.

The output, that is the GDP, should be well estimated on a yearly basis. It is probably the best statistic we have at least when measured in terms of the dollar at the time of the measurement. Because our money is almost entirely created when people, businesses, and the government borrow from financial institutions, an estimate of the amount of investment made per year should be at least in the ballpark. The same should be true of the amount of debt in the economy. Unfortunately, the Federal Reserve in St Louis discontinued putting out this basic statistic for the total debt in the economy—public and private—after the third quarter of 2015.

1.2.1 Fit Details

In order to solve the six macroeconomic differential equations, Equations 1.1 through 1.6, describing the United States Economy, we need to eliminate the profit, Π, from these equations. We do so using Mathematica. This is complicated by the coefficient equations and the equation representing the average interest rate. However, Mathematica handles this easily and allows the creation of six, coupled differential equations that can be numerically integrated. One way to do this is to use Mathematica's NDSolve. NDSolve uses a Runga-Kutta integration, by default, and produces six interpolating functions as the solution. These interpolating functions can be called for any date through which the set of equations was integrated. Doing so produces the value of the macroeconomic variable represented by the interpolating function at the date for which it was called. These interpolating functions can also be plotted, giving a visual representation of economic variables through time.

Plotting the interpolating function representing a particular economic variable over the plot of the economic data points collected from the economy for that particular economic variable creates a visual fit. This visual fit allows one to easily judge the goodness of a particular set of fit parameters, $\{v, \gamma, c_1, c_2,$ and $r\}$. One then adjusts the parameters one by one, slowly zeroing in on a better and better fit. This process is somewhat tedious, but it gets the job done. The fitting was done in three stages, from 1980 to 1997, from 1997 to 2008, and from 2008 to 2015.

From 1980 to 1997, only a smooth fit was attempted. The purpose of this was to find coefficients c_1 and c_2, which allowed a good smooth fit to the data so that they might be considered coefficients, which would provide a reasonable fit during the normal running of the economy. We will call the values of c_1 and c_2 that allowed this smooth fit, the "natural" values of c_1 and c_2.

The second period, from 1997 to 2008, would not quite connect well to the first without altering some of the parameters. The "internal" parameters $\{v$ and $\gamma\}$ were left alone. Only the parameters c_1 and c_2 of the investment equation were changed. The interest rate was continually changing, but the interest rate function creating that change was not altered. Two fits were done for this period. One fit attempted to obtain a smooth overall fit without trying to match the small variations of the output during this time period. The second fit tried to match the small variations along the trajectory of the GDP curve.

During the third period that included the crisis of 2008–9, we tried to fit the crisis and the relatively smooth period following the crisis. We matched the crisis period by adjusting only the parameter values c_1 and c_2 of the investment equation. Then we tempered the fit by adjusting the coefficients c_1 and c_2 about their natural values so that the output would flow through the GDP in 2010, 2011, and 2012. Furthermore, we adjusted our tempering such that during the smooth period beyond 2012, the GDP would be well fit using the natural values of c_1 and c_2.

These natural values are assumed to be close to the values necessary to represent the ordinary running of the economy. Thus, this fit has set up the conditions so that one can run predictive trials for the United States Economy. We do so by assuming no change in interest rates in the period following 2016. Then, we compare the resulting projected economic curves with the results that would be predicted to occur if the Federal Reserve were to follow its stated policy of raising the interest rates by seventy-five basis points per year during the period following 2016.

Chapter 2

A Fit to the United States Economy

We will fit the United States Economy in two ways. In the first way, we will fit the output (GDP) of the economy with a smooth curve, but we will not try to match all the small variations along the GDP data curve. We will adjust the parameters until we also get a ballpark fit to the investment and total debt in the economy. In the second way, we will try to fit the small variations in the GDP curve of the United States Economy over the interval from 1997 to 2008. The period from 1980 to 1997 will use a smooth fit.

Our purpose in doing both a smooth fit and a more fine-grained refined fit is to see how much difference the finer-grained fit makes in predicting the economy into the future.

Once a satisfactory set of values for the constants α, β, and m were found by extensive playing with the data and equations, the values for the set of constants, $\{\alpha = 0.0201, \beta = 0.0101,$ and $m = 1.1\}$, has not been changed for any calculation presented in Part One. In addition, the values for the constants γ and v, lie in the ranges $0.014 \leq \gamma \leq 0.021$ and $2.65 \leq v \leq 2.85$ for the results of all calculations presented in this book. Unless stated explicitly elsewhere, the following initial values were used as the 1980 initial values for all numerical integration calculations: population, $N_0 = 227.726 \times 10^6$; productivity, $a_0 = 30,727.3$; output, $Y_0 = 2.8625 \times 10^{12}$; debt, $D_0 = 4.501 \times 10^{12}$; average wage rate, $w_0 = 19,275.55$; and investment $I_0 = 6.71 \times 10^{11}$. This should make it possible for anyone, with some work, to verify all results if they are so inclined.

2.1 Smooth Fit to the United States Economy

In Figures 2.1 and 2.2, we have pictured the coefficients c_1 and c_2 that allowed us to make our rough, smooth fit to the United States Economy. These piecewise linear and relatively simple coefficients produced a smooth and reasonably accurate trend to the United States Economy over more than thirty-five years.

We see that over much of the time of the fit to the United States Economy, the coefficients c_1 and c_2 have had the same values, yet this has allowed us to make a reasonably smooth fit to the United States Economy.

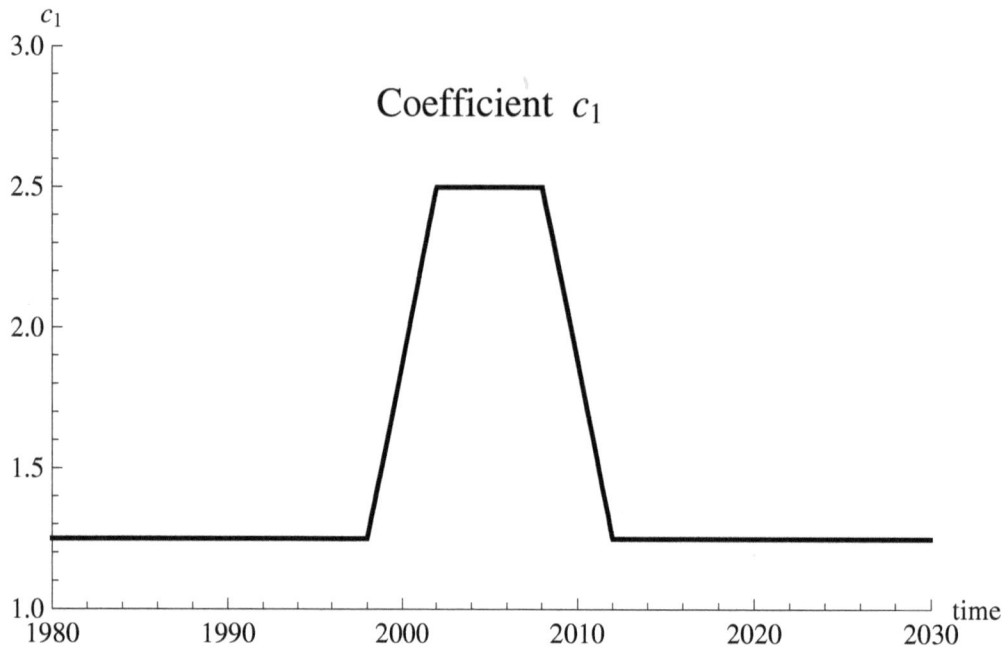

Figure 2.1: This graph shows the simple function governing the coefficient c_1 in the rough, smooth fit to the United States Economy.

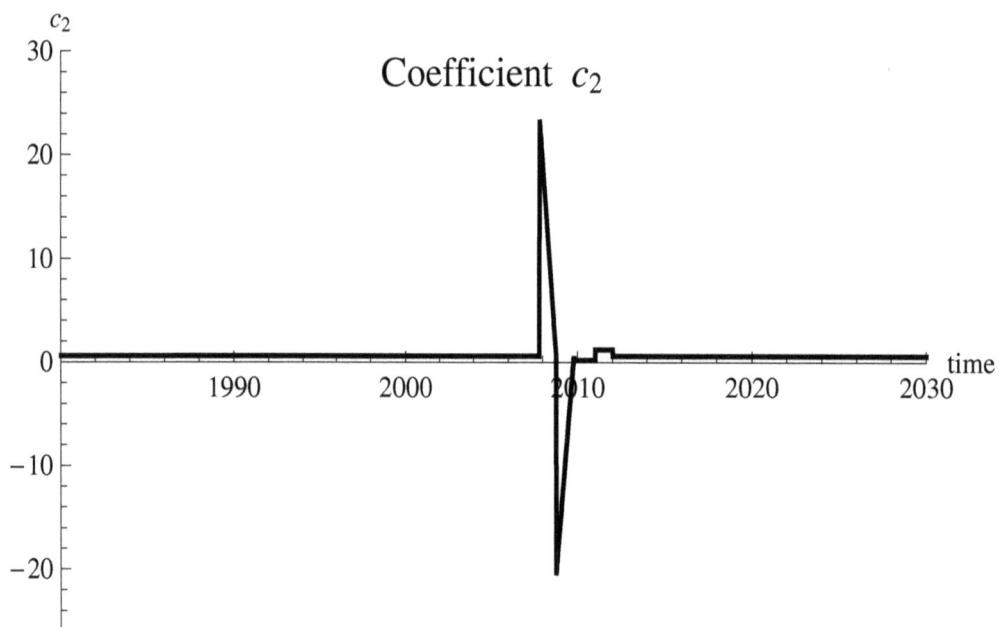

Figure 2.2: This graph shows the Banker's Term Coefficient c_2 used in creating the rough, smooth fit to the United States Economy. The sharp upward spike created the sudden downturn in the economy in the 2008–9 crisis. The almost as sharp downward spike created the quick recovery in 2009–10.

The smooth fit to the United States Economy produces a fit to the United States GDP, as shown in Figure 2.3. This fit is developed by keeping the coefficients in the investment equation simple.

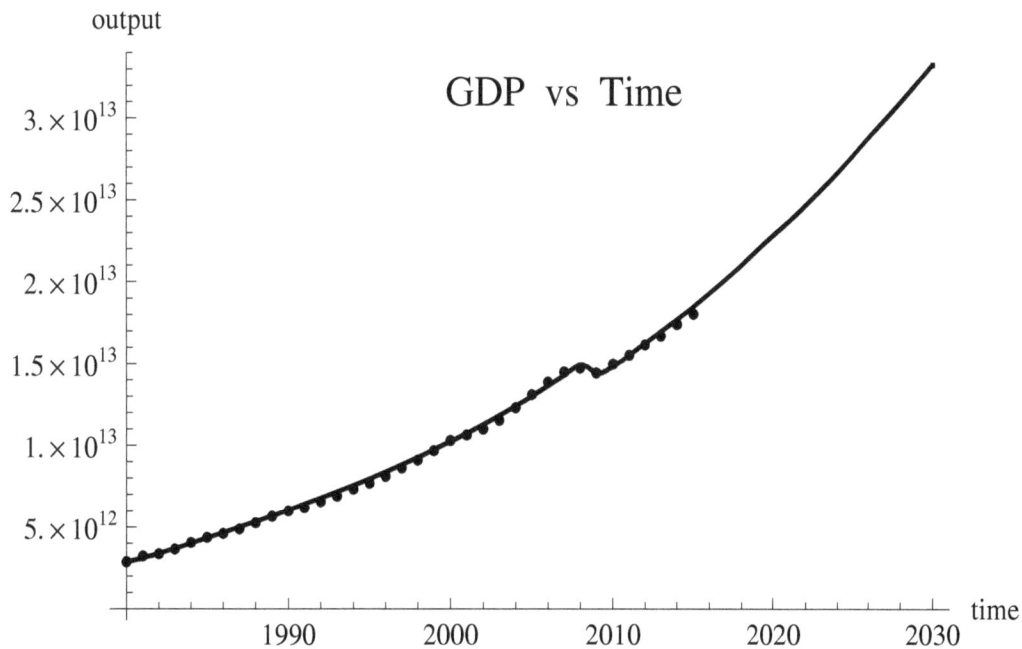

Figure 2.3: Here, we can see that the smooth fit to the United States GDP data produced by the macroeconomic equations is quite good, although we can see small variations of the data from the smooth curve.

Note, no attempt was made to optimize the fit by varying all the parameters and using some statistic such as chi-squared. Instead, we varied the parameters in the equations until a good fit was seen between the output curve and the GDP data. At the same time, we tried to get the investment curve to fit into the range given by the data. This was a trial-and-error procedure, which slowly eliminated values for the various parameters that did not allow this. Eventually, a set of coarse ranges was found that seemed reasonable. Then, more purposeful tweaking and by eye fits were compared, which slowly improve the fits. However, even now, slightly better fits can be easily had.

Figure 2.3 shows our first satisfactory output fit curve that resulted from the above procedure plotted over the GDP data.

The smooth fit output curve for the economy follows the trend of the GDP data for the United States Economy, but it does not follow the finer-grained variations of the data with time. The projection of the output curve beyond the end of 2016 has assumed no change in policy or economic circumstance.

Returning to the topic of tweaking the fit: Clearly, a slightly better fit to the above output curve can be made to the 2013 to 2015 data points. A better fit can be achieved simply by ever so slightly tweaking the c_2 coefficient in the 2008–10 interval. This tweak would allow us to slightly flatten the output curve in the 2013 to 2015 range along with the rest of the curve extended to 2030. However, the choice shown in Figure 2.3 was made in order to let the economy represented by the fit run slightly hot so that the effects caused by the Fed's interest rate policy could not be attributed to the fit representing the United States Economy being weaker than it actually is.

The debt curve overlaying the total economy debt data as compiled by the Federal Re-serve in St. Louis is seen in Figure 2.4.

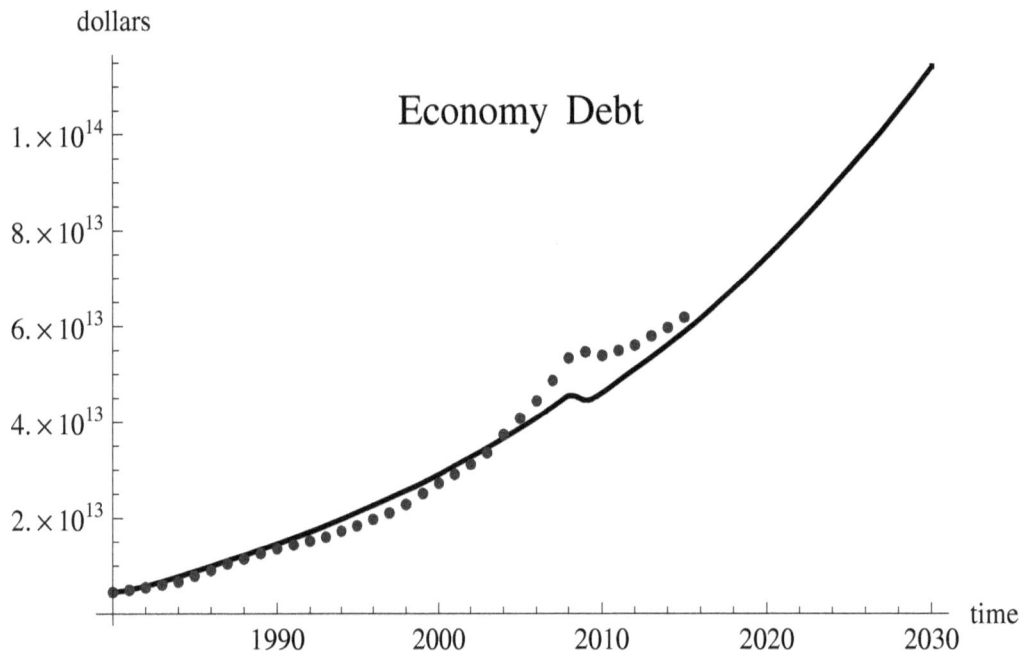

Figure 2.4: Here, the predicted fit from the macroeconomic debt equation is shown plotted over the debt data. While the fit is in the ballpark, it is not anywhere near as close as the fit of the output equation.

I suspect that the more rapid increase in the rate of debt that seems to begin in the data about 1990 might be the result of the slow increase in the use of credit cards. I had not considered credit card interest rates when I was trying to estimate the average interest rate. Because credit card interest rates are higher than the rates that companies borrow at for investment, this might explain the apparent increase in the rate of debt growth. Note also, that the debt data decreased during and after the crisis of 2008–9. During this time, consumers were said to have been reducing their debt. This might mean that consumer debt is not wholly represented by this macroeconomic model.

During much of the fitting period, investment is said to have been fluctuating between twenty and twenty-five percent of GDP. The visual correlation between the predictions of the macroeconomic differential equations and the investment-to-GDP data is shown in Fig-ure 2.5. The employment rate is shown in Figure 2.6.

The fit curve of the investment-to-GDP ratio follows the general trend and level of the investment-to-GDP data. The period from 1990 to the crisis of 2008–9, again, forms a slight discrepancy between the data and the fit curve. Consumer spending using a credit card adds to the overall debt, but it is not investment. In addition, credit card consumptive spending adds to the price of goods sold because the retailer must pay a few percent to the credit card company for each transaction. This means retailers must raise the price over that which they would charge if all transactions were in cash. Thus, credit card use sucks money out of the real economy without adding income to the worker or seller. I have no idea how all this is

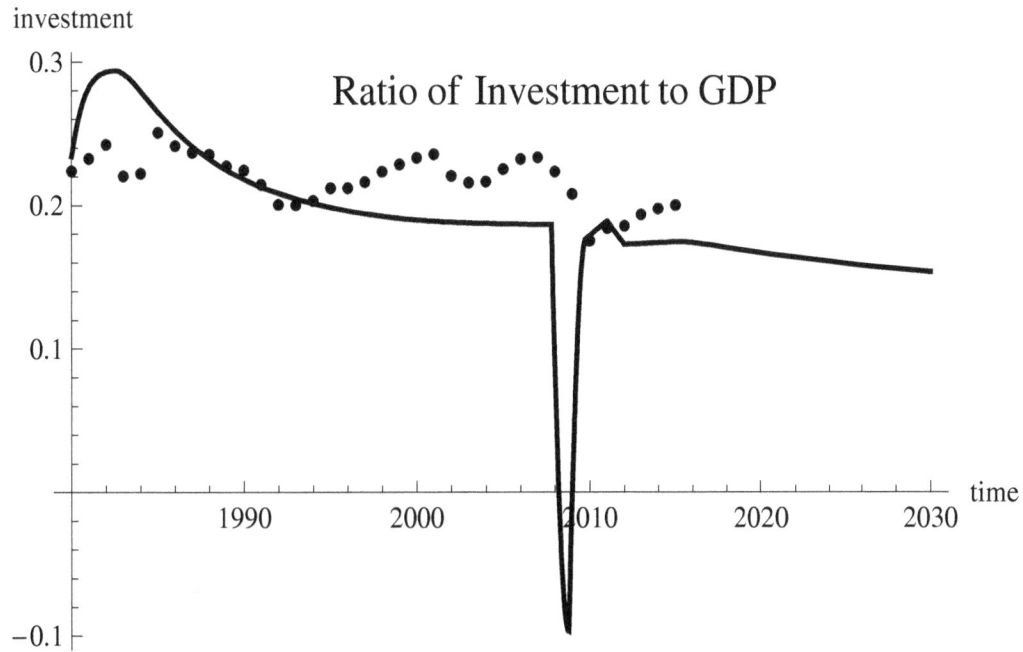

Figure 2.5: The investment-to-GDP ratio is in the ballpark set by the data. The trend is similar, but the average value of the fit curve looks to be hair low.

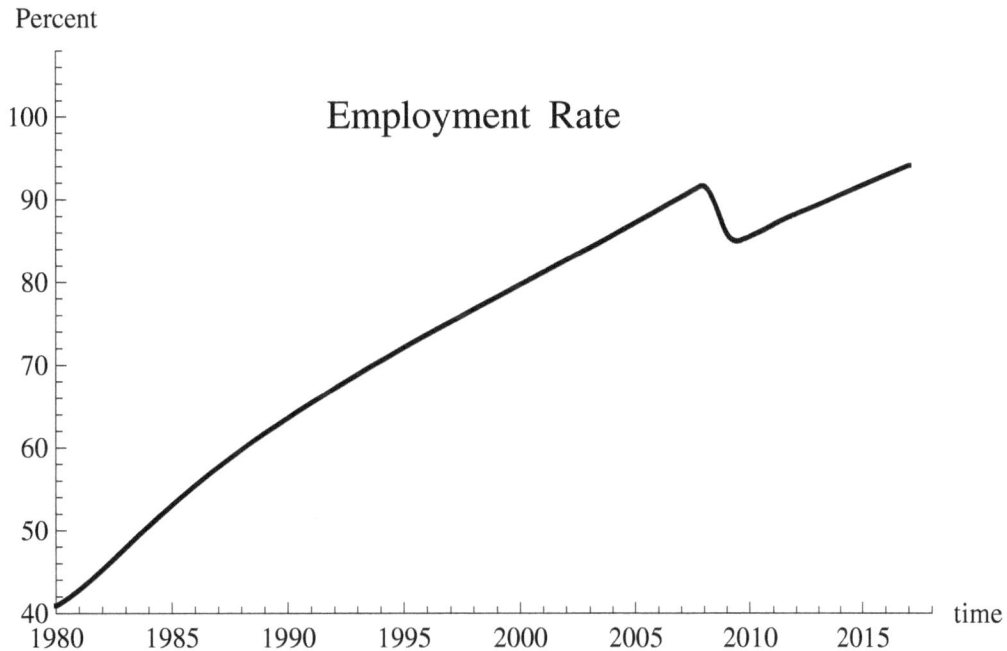

Figure 2.6: This graph shows that the macroeconomic employment rate stays under 100 percent of the United States citizen population throughout the fitting period of the United States Economy when the initial average wage rate in 1980 was taken to be 19,275.55 dollars per year.

handled in the economic statistics, but in my opinion, it makes it less likely that the statistics are actually macroeconomic.

As shown in Figure 2.6, the macroeconomic employment rate peaks at about ninety percent. Even this rate seems too high until one realizes that the citizen population was about forty million people shy of the effective population of the United States in 2015. Using the actual population rather than the citizen population would instead make the macroeconomic employment rate peak at something just short of eighty percent. This rate seems more reasonable when one realizes that the macroeconomic employment rate will include all people who receive pay indirectly from the output of the United States. This realization means we have a kind of qualitative internal consistency.

2.2   Comparing Predictions Made by the Smooth Fit

We will run the smooth fit to project forward two scenarios for the United States Economy during the period from the very end of 2016 to 2030. In one scenario, we will assume that no structural or significant policy changes are made during the period from the end of 2016 to 2030. In the other scenario, we will assume that the Federal Reserve executes its stated intention of increasing the interest rate by seventy-five basis points per year and that no other significant economic change occurs during that time.

In Figure 2.7, we display the average interest rate for the two scenarios. During the projection period from 2017 to 2030, the average interest rate has been created by just tacking the proposed Federal Reserve interest rate hikes onto the guestimated average interest rate shown in Figure 1.1 on page 15, starting at the beginning of 2017. The no rate reference scenario is created by keeping the average interest rate the same as it was at the end of 2016.

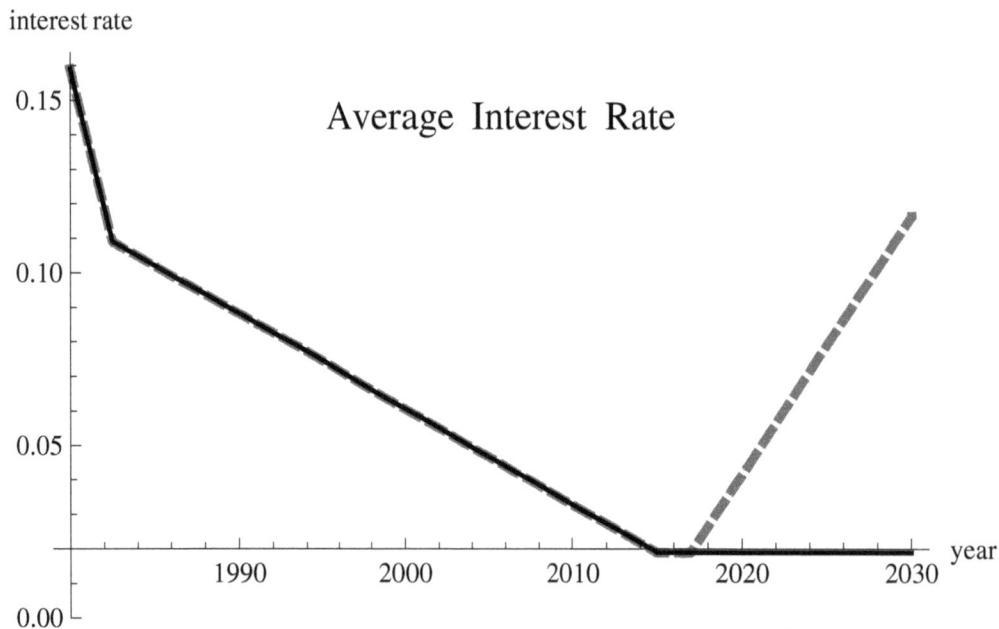

Figure 2.7: This figure shows the average interest rate for the Federal Reserve no rate hike scenario—black line—and the Federal Reserve rate hike scenario—thick dashed gray line.

The rate hike scenario average interest rate will go up too rapidly because there was a long period of 8 years before 2017 in which the interest rate for new loans was very low. Thus, the higher rates for new loans will have to pull up the average from all the previous low rate years. However, in the no rate hike scenario, the average rate should be close to its real average because the interest rates on new loans will keep roughly the same rate as they have had during the previous eight years.

First, in Figure 2.8, let us look at how these two scenarios affect the economy's output. In this plot and all the others to follow, the dark gray dashed curve will represent the United States Economy under the assumption that the Federal Reserve is raising interest rates by three-quarters of a percent per year. The black line represents a policy in which the Fed does not change the interest rates from what they were just after the election in 2016.

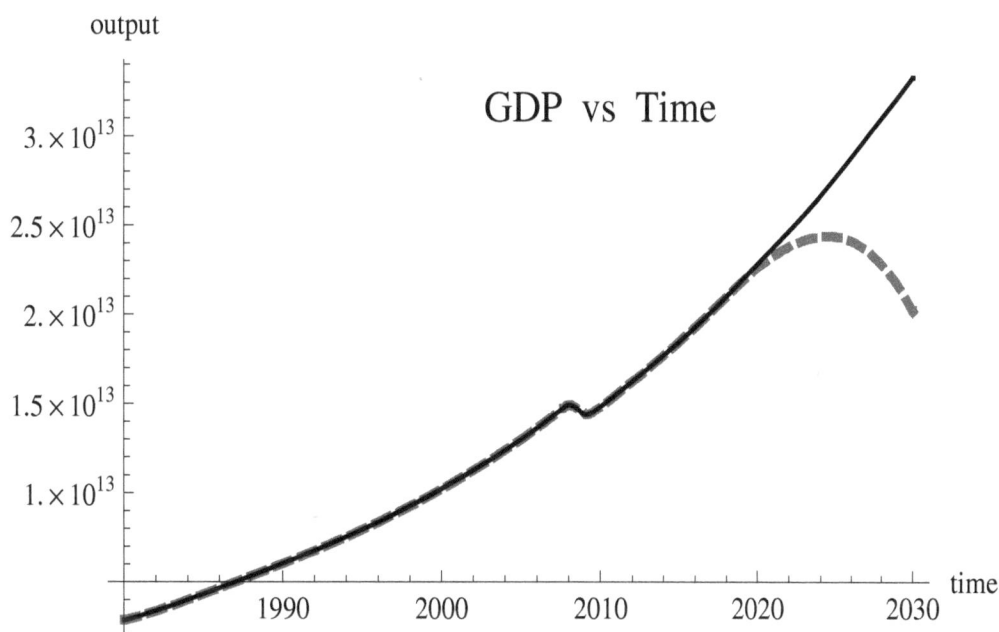

Figure 2.8: The dashed curve in this graph shows that the Federal Reserve policy of increasing interest rates at three-quarters of a percent per year causes the output of the United States to decline relative to what it would be when leaving interest rates as they were in mid-November of 2016.

We can see from Figure 2.8 that raising the interest rates causes a slow loss of output relative to not raising interest rates, taking about four years before there is a tiny sliver of white space between the lines. More important is the fact that the slope of the interest rate scenarios's projected output curve almost immediately becomes concave down, with the slope continually becoming less and less positive and finally becoming negative about seven years after the start of the rate increases. However, the most obvious visual result is that the United States Economy will crash because of the interest rate rises, with the crash, when it comes, quickly becoming severe.

Next, we present what is projected to happen to total debt within the economy under these two scenarios. To do so, in Figure 2.9, we plot the results of not changing the interest rates and the results of raising interest rates by three-quarters of a percent per year.

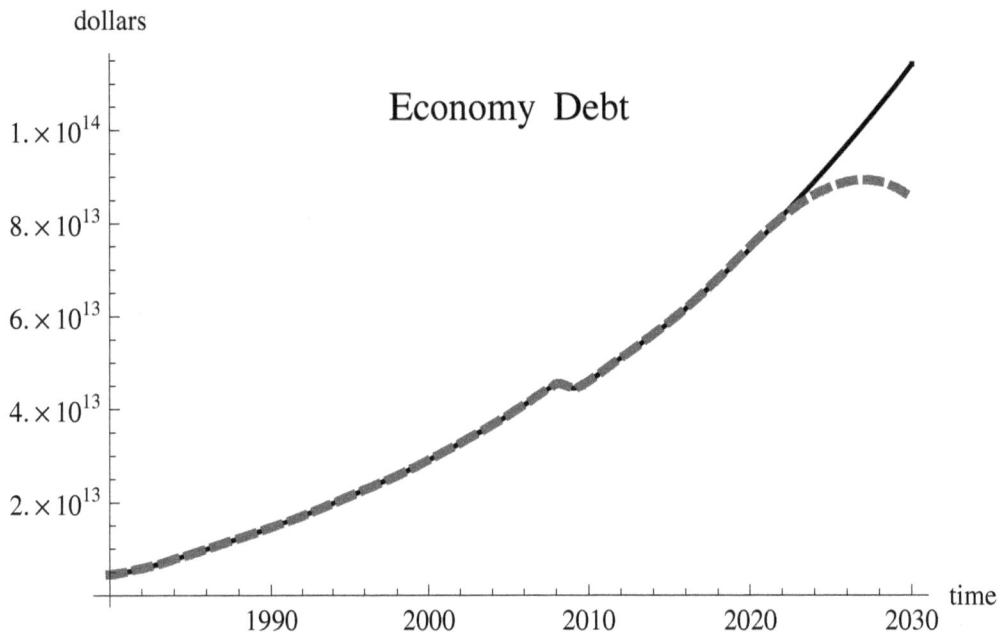

Figure 2.9: Here, we see that the raising of interest rates by three-quarters of a percent per year will eventually cause the total amount of debt within the economy to go down.

As seen in Figure 2.9, at first, the debt in the economy rises ever so slightly faster under the policy of interest rate rises than it does under a policy of no interest rate rises. Then, after several years, the debt under the policy of raising interest rates starts to fall relative to the rate of debt increase under a policy of no interest rate changes. The difference between the two curves slowly becomes greater and greater. Eventually, about two years after the start of the crash of the economy output, debt starts to crash slowly.

Next, in Figure 2.10, we compare how total investment fares in the economy under the two scenarios.

When it comes to investment, we see a relatively dramatic and significant difference between the two scenarios. With no change in interest rates, investment continually rises with time. However, if the Fed continues its stated policy of increasing interest rates at 0.75 percent per year, investment will reach a peak before 2019. Investment would then start to crash. This rapid disintegration in investment is almost certainly going to affect the economy in some dramatic way. We have already seen a dramatic crash in GDP and a less dramatic crash in debt. We need to look at other macroeconomic variables to see how they change.

We start by looking at the macroeconomic employment rate. We can calculate this easily; first, we divide the output by the productivity to get the employment level, then we divide the employment level by the population to get the employment rate. When we do this, we get the results shown in Figure 2.11.

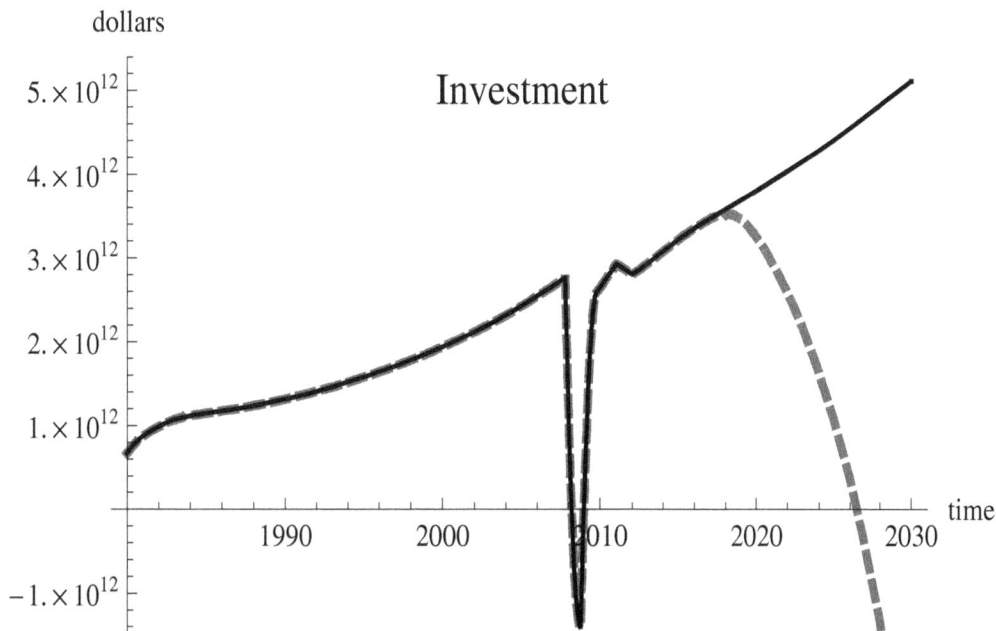

Figure 2.10: Here, we see that the difference in the amount of investment between the two scenarios is dramatic. When interest rates are raised by three-quarters of a percent per year, investment quickly starts to crash. However, if no change is made in interest rates, then investment keeps steadily rising.

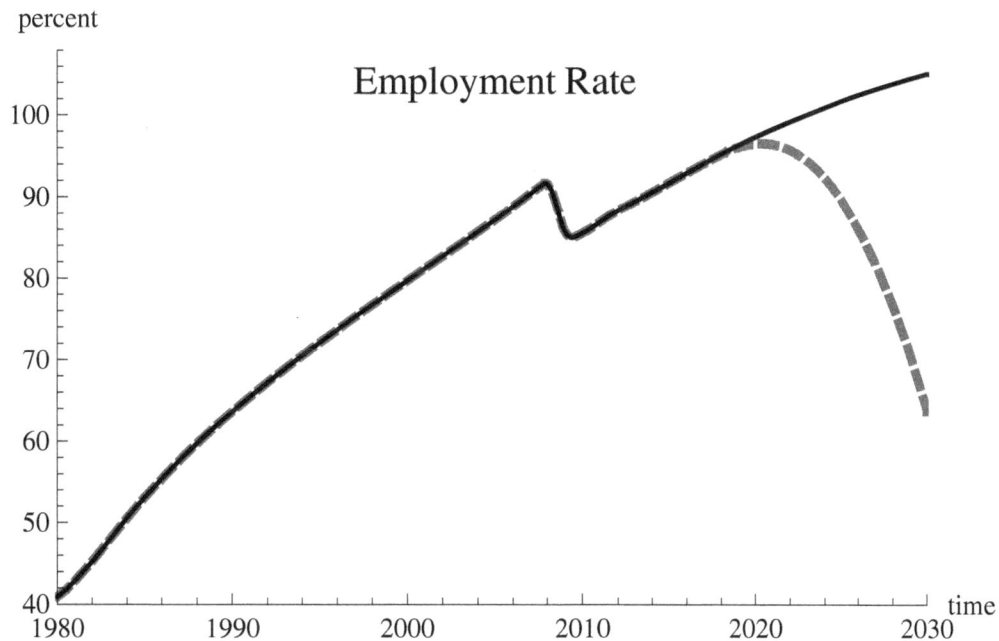

Figure 2.11: Here we see a result that is similar to the investment comparison. The employment rate change between the two scenarios is fairly dramatic. When interest rates are raised by three quarters of a percent per year, the growth rate in the macroeconomic employment rate quickly starts to slow and then starts to decline sharply a little after 2020.

While the two macroeconomic employment rate curves look quite different after the start of interest rate rises at the very end of December 2016, the projections of the macroeconomic employment rate remain quite close until about 2020. Then, soon after 2020, in the rate hike scenario, the employment rate starts a very sharp decline. This would be a dramatic and very noticeable effect. However, even here, while the visual difference is quite dramatic, the real, on the ground, economic effect would take a few years to become apparent.

Next, we move on to the average wage rate to see if there are other dramatic effects. Even though we do not have a real handle on the macroeconomic wage rate, when we compare the effects of the two scenarios we will have a qualitative understanding of the relative effects of the two scenarios; one with no change in the interest rate and the other with three-quarters of a percent per year interest rate increase. Figure 2.12 shows the comparison between the average wage rates.

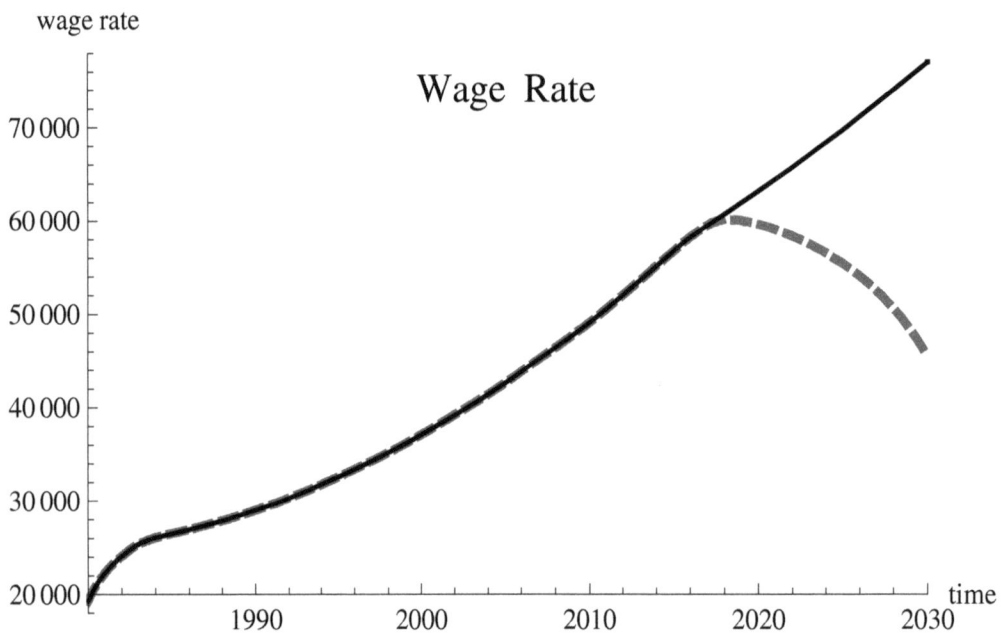

Figure 2.12: Here, the difference between the two scenario curves is less dramatic than in the employment rate comparison. Under the Fed's interest rate raising hypothesis, the wage rate appears to peak in early 2018. The average wage rate then begins a slow decline at a slowly increasing rate.

From the graph, we see that the average wage rate continues to increase at a steady rate when the Fed makes no change in the interest rate. However, fairly quickly, about a year and a half after the start of the policy of raising rates, the macroeconomic wage rate starts to decrease when the Fed continues to raise interest rates at three-quarters of a percent per year.

If we compare the scenario curves for the macroeconomic employment rate with scenario curves for the macroeconomic wage rate, we see that the average wage rate decline starts before the decline of the employment rate. However, once the employment rate decline begins, it is much sharper than the wage rate decline, and soon overtakes it.

Finally, we plot the comparison between the total profit curves within the economy in Figure 2.13.

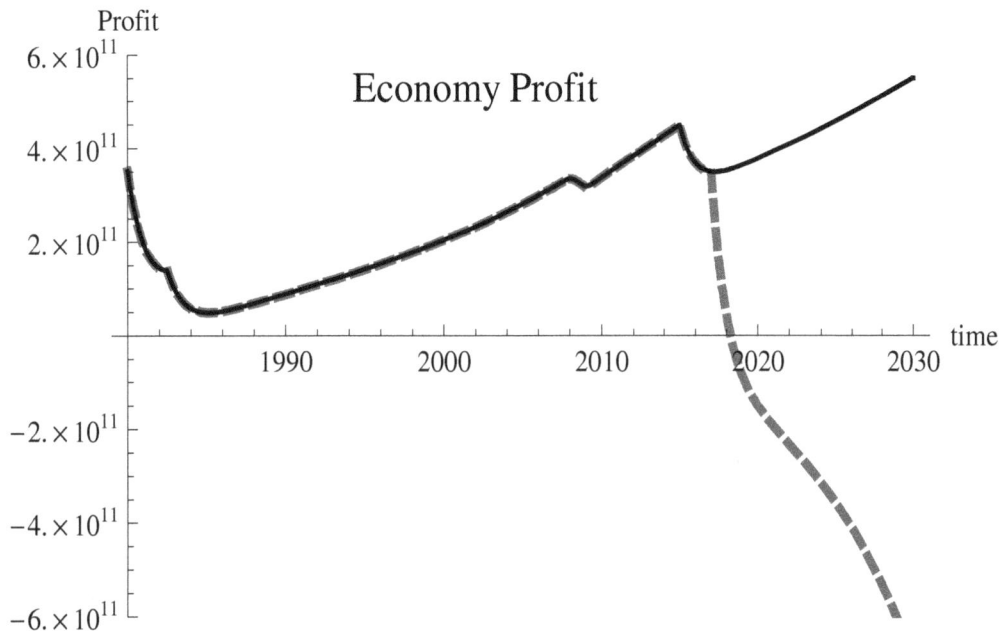

Figure 2.13: The economy profit shows the most dramatic change of any of the macroeconomic variables. The profit drops like a stone almost as soon as the rate increases start. In fact, the total profit reaches zero at about the beginning of April 2018.

The comparison plot indicates that the economy profit, calculated from the economy profit equation, Equation 1.8, becomes zero toward the end of March or the beginning of April 2018. The economy profit then becomes negative, and the total profit in the economy continues to get more and more negative.

The crash in economy profit would indicate that a relatively large number of businesses, many of them likely small businesses, would moderately quickly come under financial hard times. Small businesses, when losing money, often hold on for a while. However, in the end, if things do not pick up, such businesses would have to shut. In such a time, businesses that have to close are, in effect, changing the economic conditions and, therefore, the assumptions made for the models used in projecting the United States Economy forward.

Another caveat needs to be stated for a second time. In the economy, at the present time, the amount of debt is very large. The total economy's profit equation, $\Pi = Y - w * (Y/a) - r * D$, needs to calculate the value of average interest times debt, $r * D$, using the present value of the average interest, r, times the present debt, D, in order to determine the correct value of total profit in the economy. Because it is usually the case that new interest rates do not apply to old loans, our method of just tacking on the Federal Reserve interest rate changes onto the average interest rate will produce incorrect results.

In reality, the effect of the higher interest rates will be delayed somewhat from the predictions made by our macroeconomic equations. If it were approximately true that the average business loan is for 3.9 years, as I have read, then I would guess that the forecasting from these models would be about two years premature.

The prediction from this model, if the Federal Reserve continues interest rate rises of three-quarters of a percent per year, would be that the real economy will "crash". However, the results also say that the "crash" would have a different genesis and evolution than the Great Depression of the 1930s.

Chapter 3

A More Refined Fit to the United States Economy

In this chapter, we will adjust the coefficients c_1 and c_2 in order to create a refined fit to the United States Economy during the period between 1997 and 2008. In this period, we will make adjustments in c_1 and c_2 so that we can match the slight variations in the GDP that were not represented in the smooth fit. One of our main purposes in doing this is to test whether or not fitting the small variations is critical in making an economic model for an economy that would be useful in predicting an economy forward under hypothetical assumptions.

3.1   Creating a Refined Fit

Again, no real attempt was made to optimize the refined fit to the United States Economy. A by hand, chi-squared was used to establish the best c_2 coefficient during the interval from 1997 to 2008, given the previous values for the rest of the parameters. This c_2 optimization only used output data. No debt or investment data was used.

The linearized average interest rate estimate shown in Figure 1.1 on page 15 was used in the refined fit. The coefficients c_1 and c_2 used in the refined fit are shown in Figures 3.1 and 3.2, respectively. Note that the c_1 coefficient is not quite the same as the c_1 coefficient used in the smooth fit (my mistake), but the natural values of both c_1 and c_2 are the same.

One notes from these coefficient curves that only c_2 was needed in order to make the relatively fine-grained adjustments in the refined fit to the output curve of Figure 3.3. This is because the Banker's Term has much more of an impact on the economy than the Businessman's Term. There are two major reasons for this. First, debt, which is used by the bankers as a guide to making loans in our economy, is a much larger fraction of the output than profit, which would be used by business owners as a guide to taking out loans. Second, banks and other financial institutions act much more in concert, under the aegis of the Federal Reserve, than a diverse group of small, mid-sized, and large companies can practically and by law act.

Mathematically, one can create similar fits using the Businessman's Coefficient c_1. When

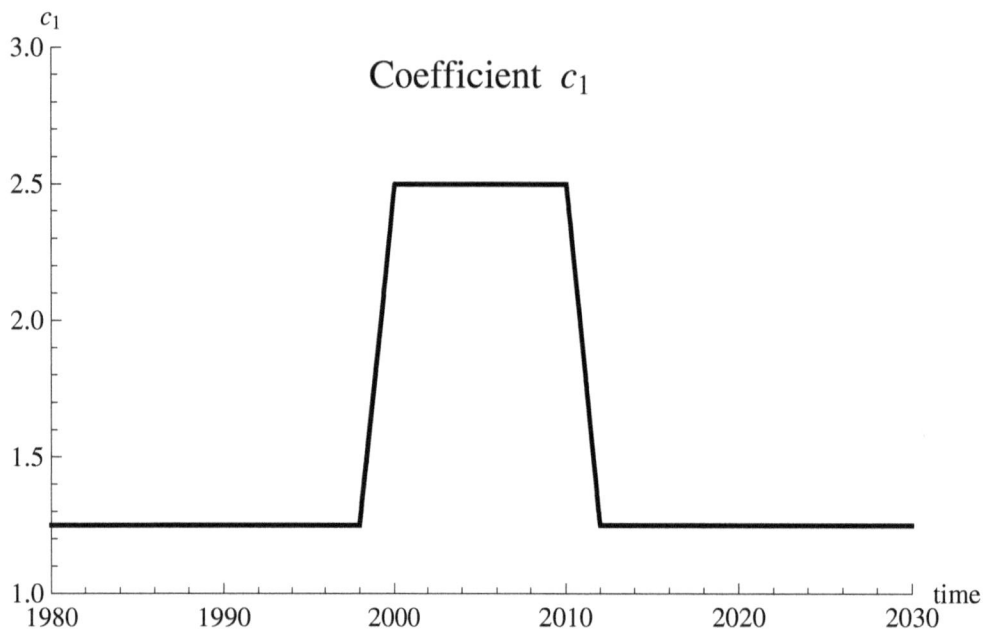

Figure 3.1: When compared to the smooth fit, almost no change has been made to the coefficient, c_1, of the Businessman's Term during the making of the refined fit.

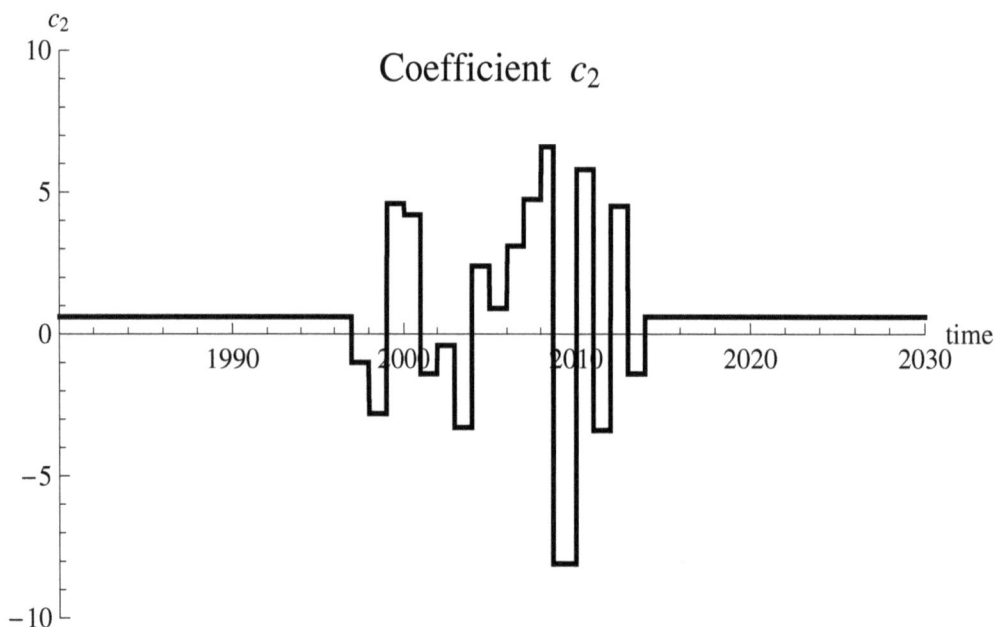

Figure 3.2: Here, we show the coefficient c_2. It has been constructed so that it is less impulse-like in order to spread the "force" that changes the investment curve more evenly over time. This results in noticeably lower amplitudes for the rectangular impulses when compared to the triangular impulses used in the smooth fit.

one does so, one finds the magnitudes of the variations in the coefficient c_1 are much much larger than the amplitudes of the Banker's Coefficient. To create such large c_1 coefficients, almost all business owners would have to collude in order to act in concert. This is unlikely and also against the law. In addition, at times, they would all have to act against their own

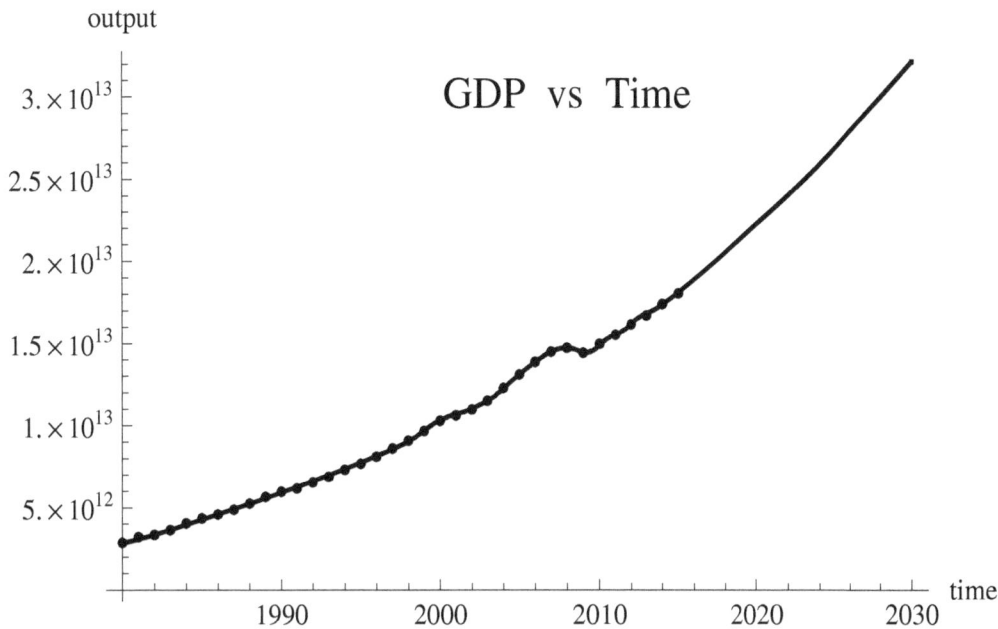

Figure 3.3: Here, we see a refined fit to the output of the United States created by adding variations in the Banker's Coefficient c_2 to the smooth fit of the same period created by the simple changes made in Businessman's Coefficient c_1.

interests. Thus, while it is likely that during the 1997 to 2008 period, during which the refined fit was made, the Businessman's Coefficient c_1 changed somewhat as conditions changed. The influences of these changes were almost certainly small when compared to the bankers' affect on the refined fit. It is only in extraordinary times, such as a panic or the euphoria of a rapidly expanding economy, that the Businessman's Term is a relatively large contributor to the change in the path of an economy.

We see from the fit shown in Figure 3.3 that we can fit well the variations in the output of the economy by varying the bankers' propensity to loan or not to loan, while at the same time fitting the general trend of the economy by the business owners' willingness to invest.

Next, we plot the total debt in the United States Economy as represented in the refined fit in Figure 3.4. We overlay the debt data over the debt curve created by the refined fit.

The refined fit to the output has slightly improved the fit to the debt data in the period of the refined fit. The fit of the macroeconomic equations can never be perfect because they use an average interest rate function of time, which, if multiplied by the total debt at a particular instant would give the debt interest repayment at that instant. Such an average interest rate function would require extraordinary care in order to gather a complete set of data and can, with present data collection, at best, only be roughly estimated from present and past rates.

Figure 3.5 shows the investment-to-GDP curve resulting from the calculations that led to the refined fit to the GDP. We see that the investment-to-GDP curve, which results from the refined fit, generally tracks roughly through the investment-to-GDP data. However, the deep downward spike that appeared in the smooth fit, during the crisis of 2008–9, also appears in the more refined fit.

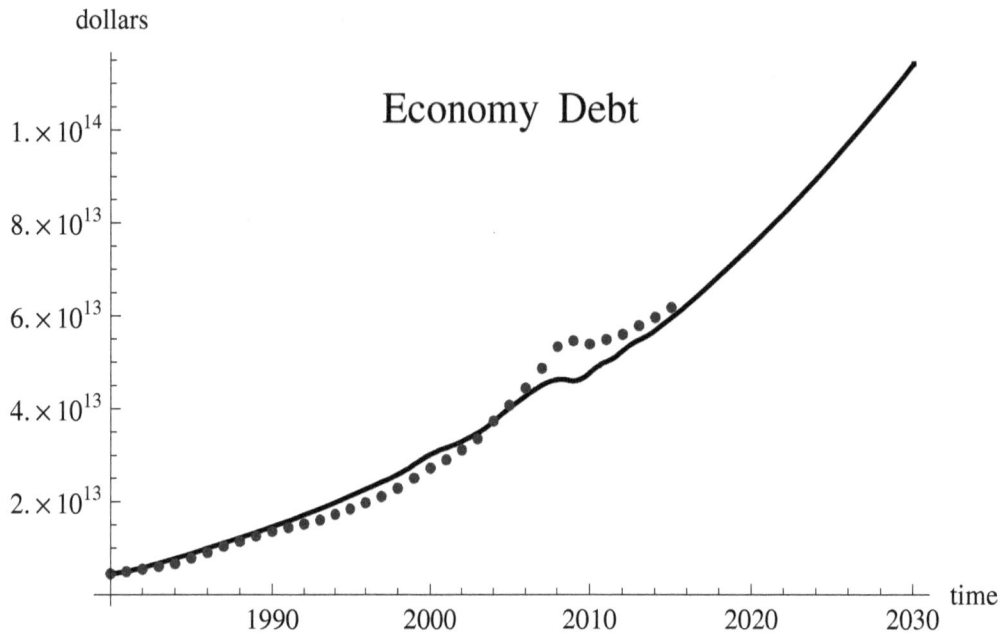

Figure 3.4: Here, we see that the refined fit results in a slightly better fit to the debt data compiled by the Federal Reserve in St. Louis. The fit clearly follows the same general trend as the debt data and is always in the ballpark.

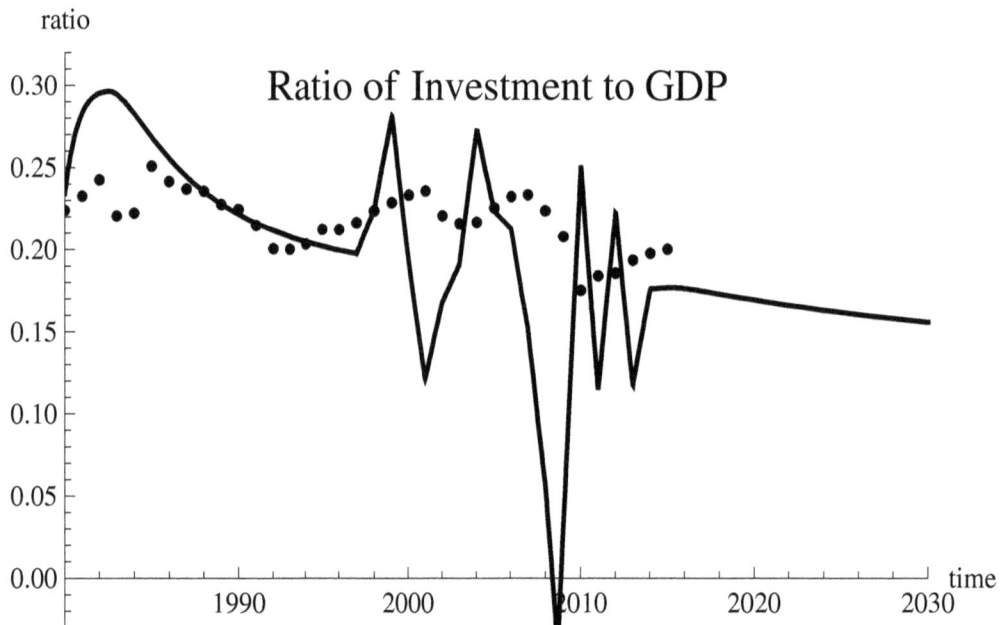

Figure 3.5: The investment-to-GDP curve that results from the refined fit to the GDP is seen to be in the ballpark presented by the investment-to-GDP data.

Unlike the smooth fit, there is no sharp large magnitude spike-like impulse in the coefficient c_2 during the refined fit that we might try to blame as the cause of the large downward spike in the investment curve. This almost certainly means that investment really did plummet when the output suddenly fell in the crisis of 2008–9 and, it rebounded just about as suddenly when the output suddenly stopped crashing and quickly started to grow again. This implies that it was the bankers' sudden and very drastic changes in the propensity to loan that caused the crash and rebound in the output of the United States Economy in the crisis of 2008–9.

Note in this regard that if the investment had stayed relatively constant when the output took a sudden sharp tumble during the crisis of 2008–9, then the investment-to-GDP curve would have actually spiked upward rather than downward.

It was at this point in my writing that I wondered, "How good is the economic data that we have?" The above investment-to-GDP data, shown in Figure 3.5, was taken from the Quandl website at the link:

$$\texttt{https://www.quandl.com/data/ODA/}$$
$$\texttt{USA\_NID\_NGDP-United-States-TotalInvestment-of-GDP}.$$

This investment-to-GDP data and the Bureau of Economic Analysis GDP data were found before similar data was found at the Federal Reserve Bank's St. Louis website. However, once the Federal Reserve GDP and investment data were found, investment-to-GDP data was created and then displayed over the investment-to-GDP curve pictured in Figure 3.6.

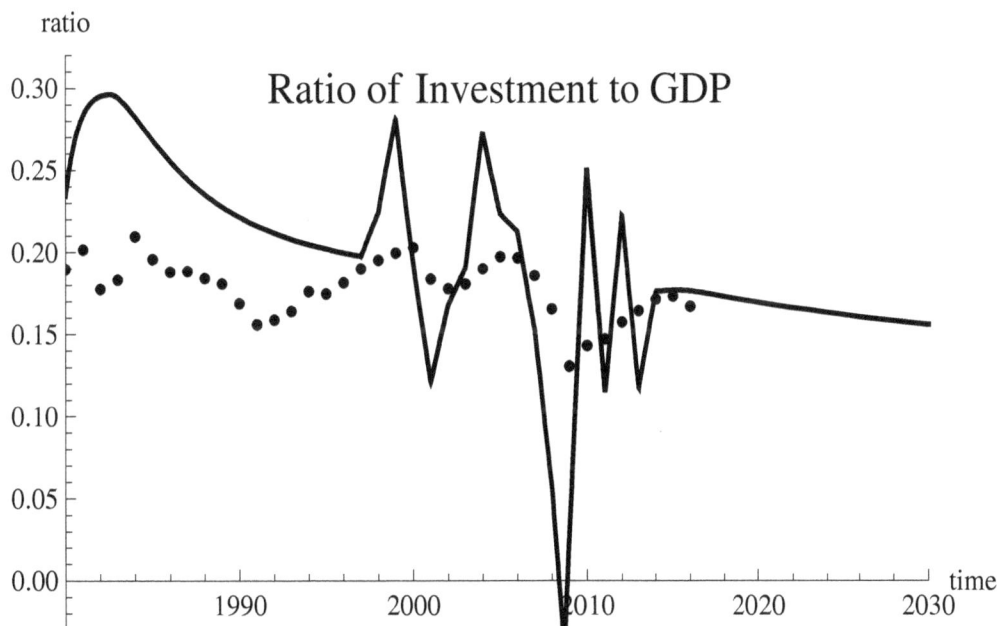

Figure 3.6: The data pictured here was taken from the Federal Reserve website in St. Louis. The data from the Quandl website gives investment-to-GDP data that is some twenty to thirty percent greater than the Federal Reserve data.

When comparing the Quandl data in Figure 3.5 with the Federal Reserve in St. Louis data shown in Figure 3.6, we see that there is a noticeable difference in the magnitude of the investment-to-GDP data in the United States Economy as stated on these two economic data websites. However, the GDP data given on various economic websites seems to be much more consistent—with the greatest differences between GDP values being in the two to three percent range. This would seem to indicate that investment data is ballpark data

3.2   Comparing Predictions Made by the Refined Fit

Just as we did for the smooth fit, we will run the refined fit to predict two scenarios for the United States Economy during the period from the very end of 2016 to 2030. In one scenario, we will assume that no structural or significant policy changes are made during the period from the end of 2016 to 2030. In the other scenario, we will assume that the Federal Reserve executes its stated intention of increasing the interest rate by seventy-five basis points per year and that no other significant economic change occurs during that time.

As we did earlier, we first look at how these two scenarios affect output. In all our comparisons the dark gray dashed curve will represent the United States Economy under the assumption that the Federal Reserve is raising interest rates by 0.75 percent per year, while the black line represents a policy in which the Fed does not change the interest rates from that which they were just after the election in 2016.

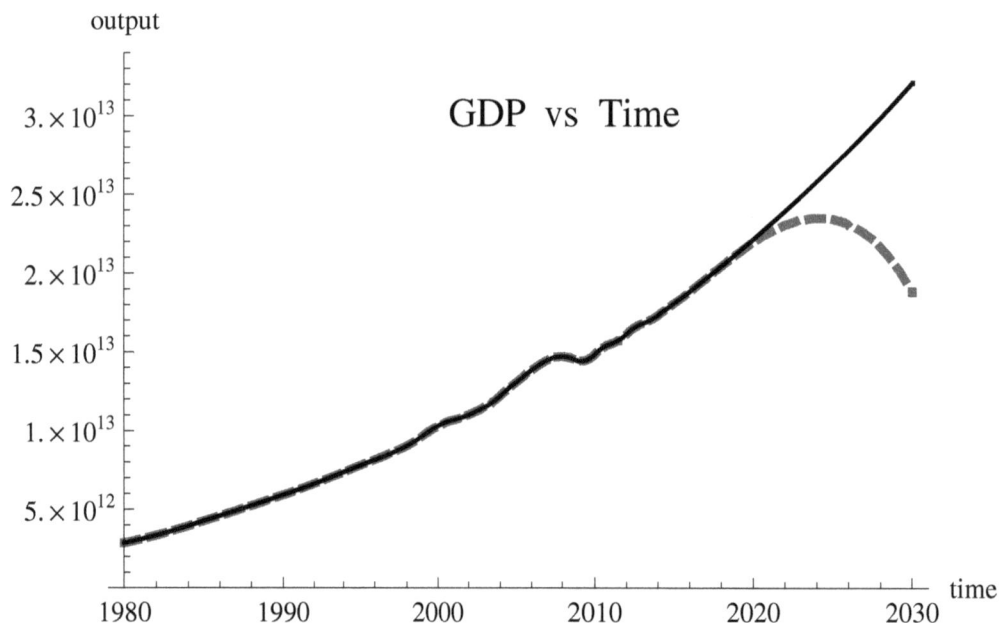

Figure 3.7: Here, we see in the refined fit, when the Fed increases interest rates by three-quarters of a percent per year, the output of the economy starts to slow and then to crash relative to a Federal Reserve policy of no interest rate hikes.

The graph of output versus time refined fit comparison, shown in Figure 3.7, looks almost exactly the same as the smooth comparison shown in Figure 2.8 on page 25. The increase in interest rates at three-quarters of one percent per year causes a slow but steadily increasing deterioration in the rate of growth of GDP. The deterioration in the rate of growth of GDP in the refined fit, just as with the smooth fit, has turned the projected GDP curve concave downward. Then finally, after a little more than seven years of interest rate rises, the output of the economy begins to crash. This is precisely the same result that was predicted by the smooth fit projection.

Next, we present what is projected to happen to total debt and total investment in the United States Economy under these two scenarios. These debt and investment comparisons are shown in Figure 3.8 and Figure 3.9, respectively.

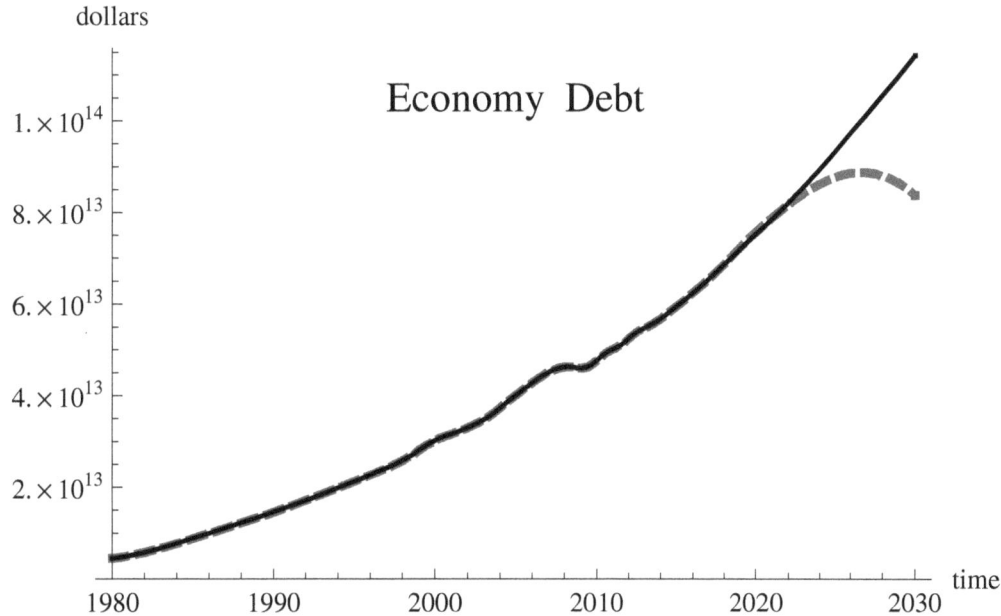

Figure 3.8: The total economy debt in the comparison, under the two Fed scenarios, looks almost exactly the same as it did when a cruder smooth fit was used.

Both the total economy debt comparison and investment comparison, which we have done in order to test the economic effect of two Federal Reserve interest rate scenarios, show all but imperceptible differences in their economic predictions irrespective of whether they are run under the smooth fit or the refined fit.

In both the refined fit and smooth fit debt comparisons, we first see the debt in the rate hike scenario rise slightly above the debt in the no rate hike scenario as the Federal Reserve starts to raise interest rates. Then, after a short time, the economy debt in the interest rate hike scenario falls below that of the scenario in which the Fed leaves interest rates alone.

This behavior is the result of investment taking some time to separate in the two scenarios. Initially, the investment fit curves are very close together in the two scenarios. Therefore, because the interest rate on the new investment is higher in the rate hike scenario, the rate hike curve will be piling up debt faster. However, after a while, the investment curves have separated far enough so that even though interest rates are higher in the rate hike scenario, the investment is enough lower so that the new debt created is greater in the no rate hike scenario.

However, the most noticeable thing about the plot in Figure 3.8 is the debt in the rate hike scenario begins a slow crash at what looks to be after the middle of 2026. We expect that

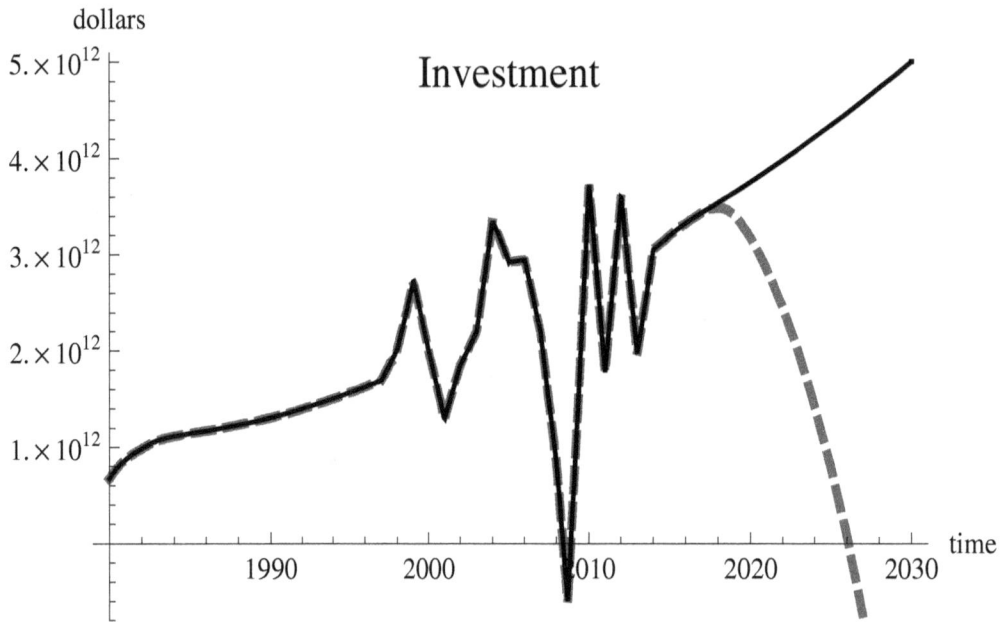

Figure 3.9: Any difference between the effects of the refined fit and the smooth fit is all but un-noticeable during a forward projection of the investment under the two scenarios.

debt should peak and then start to crash when investment equals profit, $I = \Pi$, because, in this case, $dD/dt = I - \Pi = 0$, is the condition for a maximum.

In Figure 3.9, we see that the investment curve in the rate hike scenario crashes with the investment becoming zero at the beginning of 2026. If we compare this to the smooth fit comparison plot in Figure 2.10 on page 27, which we ran slightly hot, we see that the investment reaches zero in that comparison about two months later than the present fit does.

Next, in Figure 3.10, we have plotted a comparison of the total profit in the economy as we did earlier for the smooth fit.

We see that the economy profit will crash in exactly the same manner under the refined fit as it did in the crude smooth fit shown in Figure 2.13 on page 29. There is a very slight difference in timing when looking at the numbers. The refined fit has the economy profit becoming zero about one month before the smooth fit. However, because this macroeconomic model applies the newly instituted interest rate onto the existing total debt, any effect predicted is almost certain to be delayed by about two years as we stated in our discussion of the smooth fit prediction. Thus, the real crippling of the economy would likely not take full effect until at least late 2019 or early 2020 in the Federal Reserve interest rate hike scenario.

Also, note from the profit curve shown in Figure 3.12 and the investment curve in Figure 3.9 that $I = \Pi$ at about -4.7×10^{11} dollars. This equality occurs in mid-summer of 2026 just as the economy debt crests. This result confirms the prediction we made during our discussion of when dD/dt equals zero.

In Figures 3.11 and 3.12, we look at the employment rate and average wage rate comparisons for the two Federal Reserve interest rate scenarios.

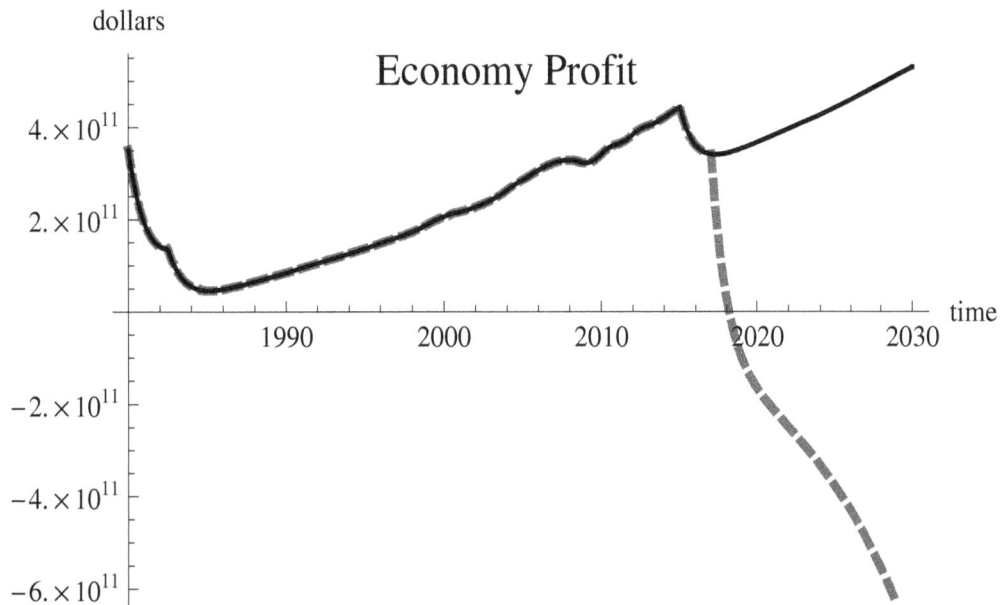

Figure 3.10: In this plot, we see that the Fed's policy of increasing interest rates by three-quarters of a percent per year will quickly kill the profit in the United States Economy without some other intervention that would mitigate the effect of the interest rate hikes.

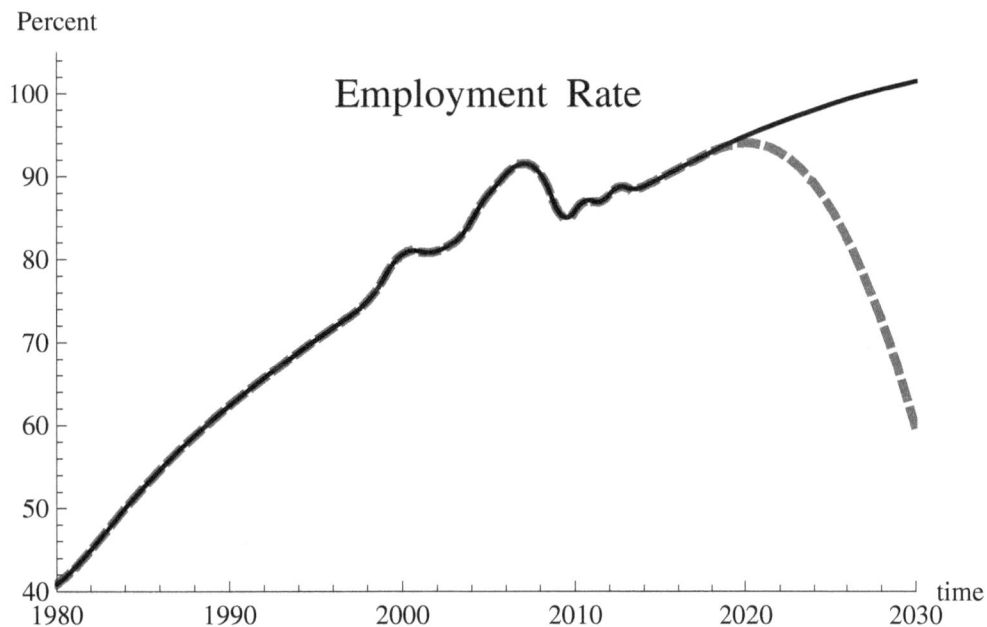

Figure 3.11: The employment rate in the two scenarios diverges fairly quickly once interest rate hikes kick in, with the interest rate hike, scenario curve diverging downward, and starting to crash.

In the corresponding smooth fit comparisons of the employment rate and the average wage rate in Figure 2.11 and Figure 2.12 on page 28, we saw that the interest rate hike scenario caused the two scenario curves to diverge fairly quickly. Moreover, in the rate hike

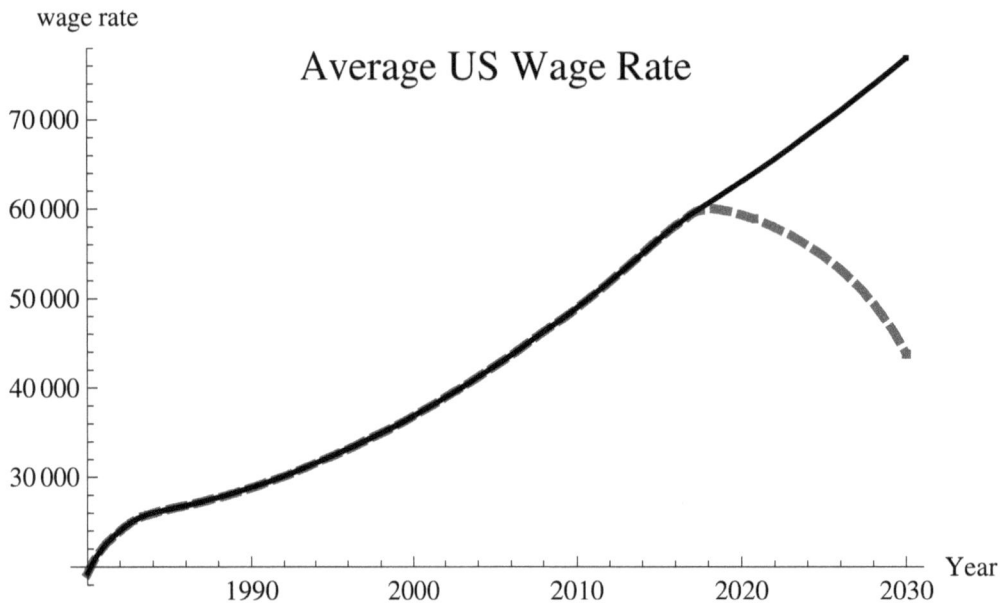

Figure 3.12: Here, we see that the average wage rates in the two scenarios diverge fairly quickly once interest rate hikes kick in, with the interest rate-hike scenario curve diverging downward and starting to crash.

scenario, both the employment rate and wage rate curves almost immediately began to turn downward. We see exactly the same thing in the refined fit comparison plots.

We can notice that both the employment rate and the wage rate increase steadily in the no rate hike scenario. However, there is a difference; the employment rate projection is concave downward while the wage rate projection is concave upward. That is, the growth in the macroeconomic employment rate is slowing, while the growth rate of the average wage rate is increasing.

In the rate hike scenario, we see that both the employment rate and the average wage rate projections are concave downward. Furthermore, both the employment rate and the wage rate start to crash within one to three years after interest rates start to be hiked at three-quarters of a percent per year when the economy is projected forward with the refined fit. These same results were obtained when the cruder smooth fit projected the economy forward.

Note, in the no rate hike scenario, that the average wage rate grows more rapidly than the employment rate. In other words, the employment rate seems to more sticky relative to new hires than the average wage rate is to wage increases. While in the Federal Reserve's rate hike scenario, we observe the opposite. That is, for decreases, the average wage rate seems to be more sticky than the employment rate.

Chapter 4

Addendum

4.1   Other Investment Data

When we compared the investment data from the Quandl website with that of the Federal Reserve in St. Louis, in Figures 3.5 and 3.6 on pages 34 and 35, we found a relatively large discrepancy in the data. Because there was such a large discrepancy in the investment data, in this section a fit has been made using the Federal Reserve data, to see if it would affect the fitting process and the resulting predictions. The initial Quandl investment data point used in the calculations is thirty-three percent larger than the initial investment data point using the Federal Reserve data. However, the Bureau of Economic Analysis GDP data, used originally, is only two to three percent larger than the GDP data from the Fed. Switching to the Federal Reserve GDP and investment data has allowed an easy fit to the economy as the following fits to GDP and investment graphs show in Figure 4.1 and Figure 4.2.

We state, explicitly, that the initial values used in the numerical integration calculations in this "Other Investment Data" section have been changed. The new values for the initial values in 1980 are: output, $Y_0 = 2.7965 \times 10^{12}$ and investment, $I_0 = 5.301 \times 10^{11}$. All other initial values remain the same. After this section, we will revert to the BEA and Quandl data.

We have used the cruder smooth fit procedure to obtain all the results shown in this section. We present an abbreviated, but representative, series of graphs that will be sufficient to show any difference in the quality of the fits, if such difference exists. We start with the output fit to the Federal Reserve data. The result of the calculations is shown in Figure 4.1.

The smooth economy output curve, shown in Figure 4.1, is seen to fit the Federal Reserve GDP data just as well as the economy output curve, shown in Figure 2.3, is seen to fit the Bureau of Economic Analysis GDP data. In addition, we note that the Fed data, shown in Figure 4.1, includes a 2016 GDP data point that was not available when the original economic data was gathered off the Internet.

Examining the GDP data, we see that there was a slight downturn in the rate of growth in the economic output from 2015 to 2016. It seems reasonable that the quarter of a percent increase in the interest rate that was announced in December of 2015, which was integrated

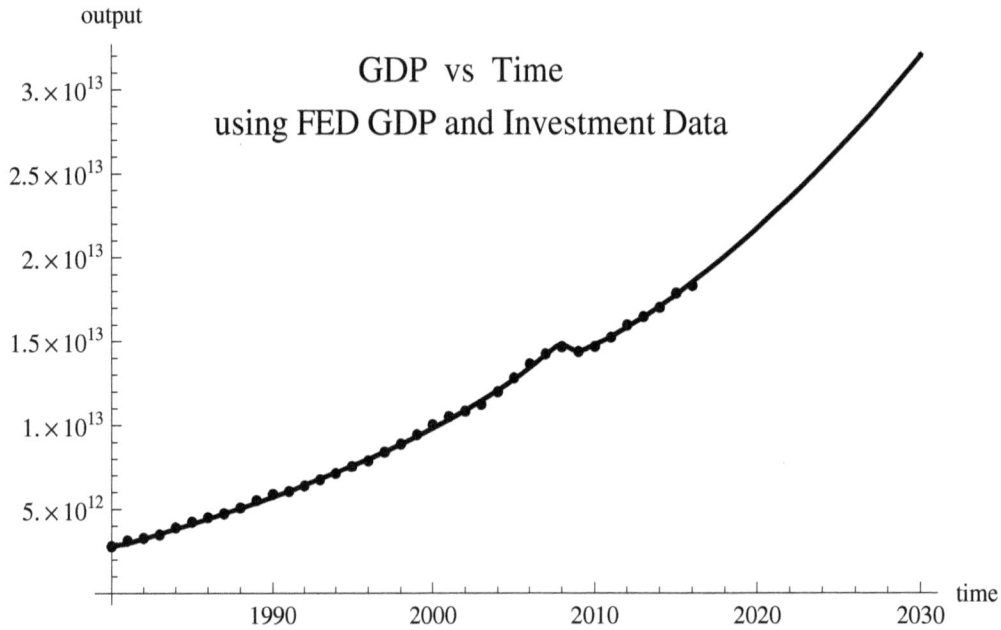

Figure 4.1: This graph shows a smooth fit of the economy output using the Federal Reserve's GDP and investment data. No essential difference in the nature of the fit is noticed in comparison to the smooth fit of Figure 2.3 on page 21, which used non-Fed GDP and investment data.

into the loan rates over the next couple of months, caused a slight decrease in investment relative to output. This slight decrease in investment relative to output over 2016 might be expected to cause a slight decrease in the rate of growth in GDP; thus, this would at least partially explain the drop in growth rate seen in the GDP data.

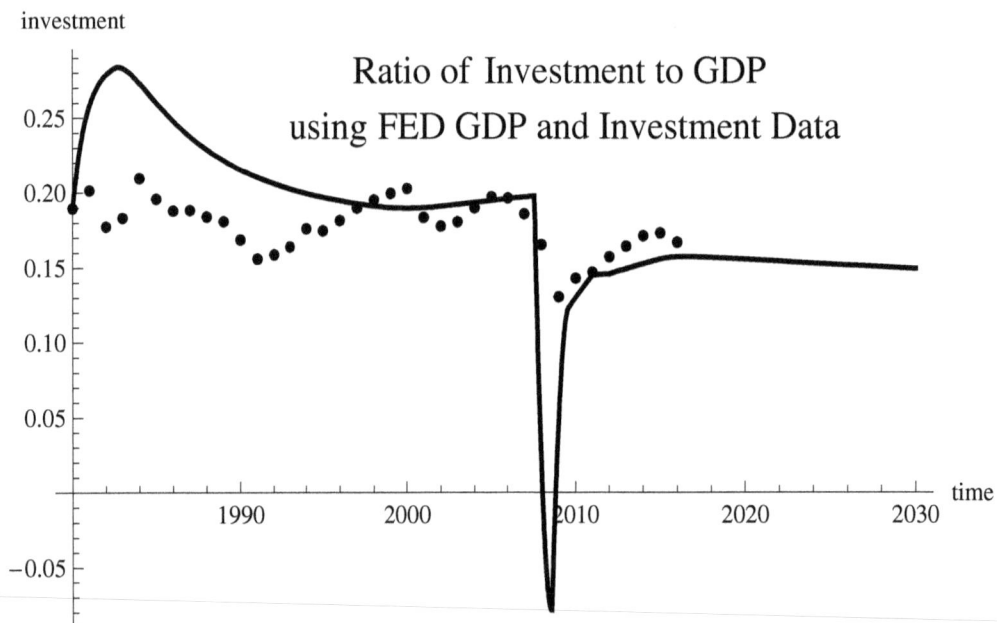

Figure 4.2: Here we show the investment-to-GDP curve that was calculated when we used the Federal Reserve's GDP and investment data to find a good fit for the Fed GDP data. Compare with Figure 2.5 on page 23.

Because we found a large discrepancy in the investment data, we are interested in seeing how the results of the calculations from our model are effected. Furthermore, we would like to see if our reasoning that the Fed's small interest rate hike that started at the end of 2015 would cause a decrease in investment relative to output is confirmed. We present the results of the investment-to-GDP calculation in Figure 4.2.

In Figure 4.2, we see that the investment-to-GDP fit using the Fed data is better in the latter part of the time interval than the fit shown in Figure 2.5 that used Quandl data. While the investment-to-GDP fit is better in the early part of the time period using the Quandl data.

In addition, we note that the final, 2016, investment-to-GDP data point is lower than the 2015 investment-to-GDP data point, just as we hypothesized in our discussion of the small interest rate hike introduced at the end of 2015.

Finally, we show the economy profit comparison graph calculated using the Fed data.

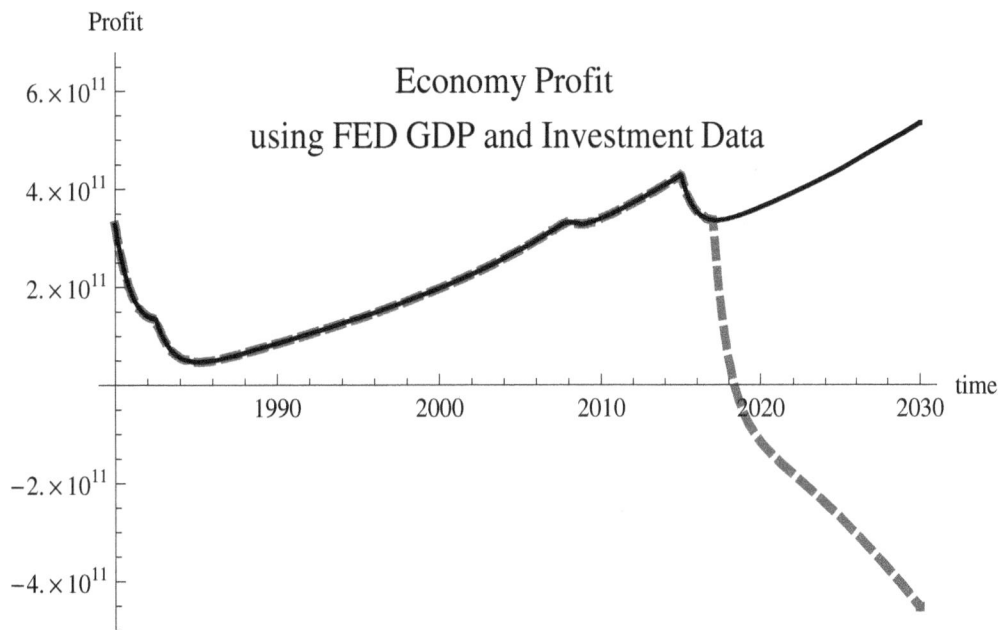

Figure 4.3: Here, we see that the predictions made for the United States Economy are essentially the same when we use the Federal Reserve GDP and investment data as they were in the original predictions that were made using noticeably different investment data.

In Figure 4.3, we see that the economy profit curve calculated from the very different Fed investment and GDP data has produced the same crash in the profit that was predicted earlier with other data. Just as with the other predictions, the profit becomes zero in the Spring of 2018.

4.2 A Qualitatively Better Interest Rate Function

In all of our investment-to-GDP graphs, Figures 2.5; 3.5; 3.6; and 4.2, we see that each of the curves rises smoothly from 1980 to 1983 and then smoothly falls, while the investment data does not do this. The investment-to-GDP data rises from 1980 to 1981, falls in 1982 to a local minimum, keeps roughly that level to 1983, and then rises to 1981 levels in 1984, for a qualitatively very different look. When we look at the Federal Reserve prime interest rate data for the period between 1980 and 1985, we see that Figure 4.4, below, forms a much better qualitative fit to the shape of the prime interest rate data than does our average interest rate function shown in Figure 1.1.

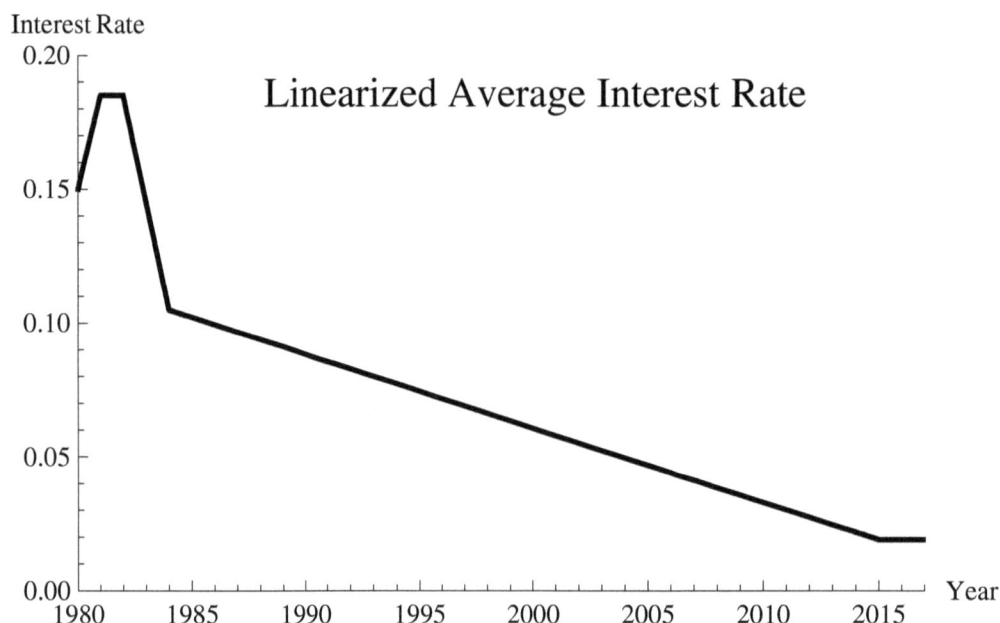

Figure 4.4: The graph above shows a guesstimate to the average interest rate between 1980 and 2017. The shape of the piecewise linearized average interest rate function has a noticeably better fit to the shape of the prime interest rate data, between 1980 and 1985, as published by the Federal Reserve in St. Louis.

The results presented in this section use the same refined fit functional forms that were used in the refined fit of Chapter 3. The investment-to-GDP curve calculated from this qualitatively improved linearized average interest rate function is shown in Figure 4.5, below.

Comparing Figure 4.5 to Figure 3.5 on page 34, which used the same functional form for c_2 to fit the United States Economy, one sees that the Investment-to-GDP graphs are very similar except that the curve using the more realistic looking average interest rate function produced a qualitatively better fit to the data between 1980 and 1985. During this period, the calculated curve introduced a dip in the investment-to-GDP ratio, just as we observe in the investment-to-GDP data.

Furthermore, when we use the average interest rate function pictured in Figure 4.4, it created no difficulty in being able to fit the GDP of the United States Economy. See Figure 4.6, below.

Moreover, the predictions made by using the more realistic looking average interest rate function are fundamentally the same as all the other predictions. All the predictions made for the economy in this book so far have been extrapolated forward from 2017. Furthermore,

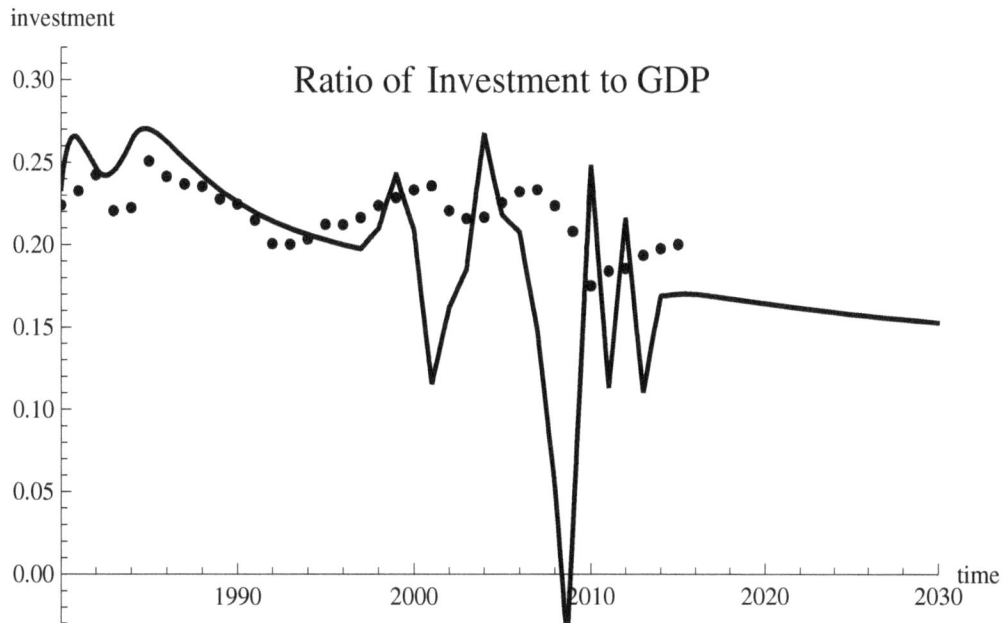

Figure 4.5: This investment-to-GDP plot was created from a fit of the output equation to the GDP data using the average interest rate function pictured in Figure 4.4.

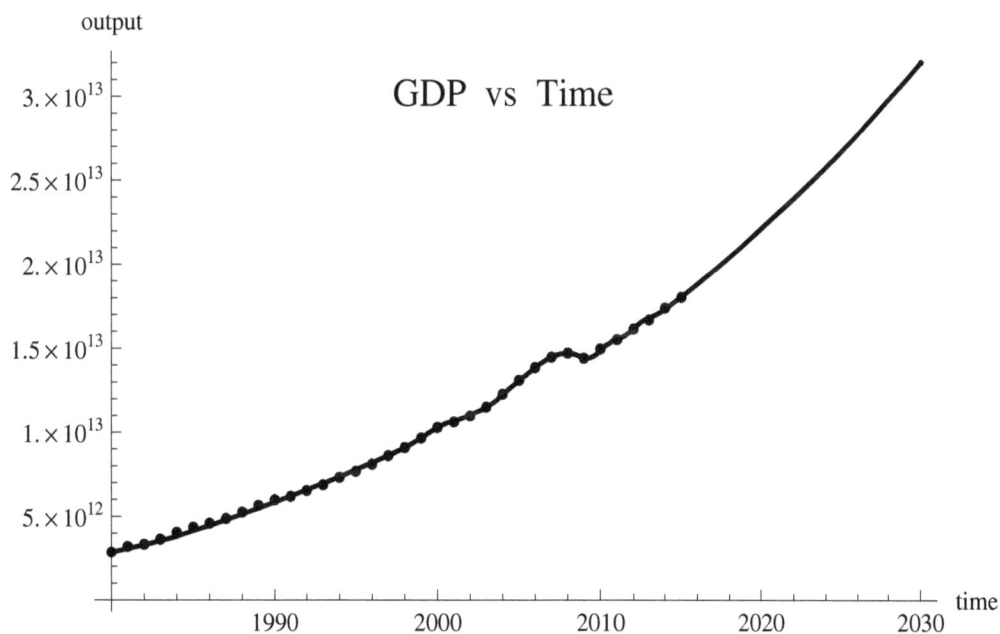

Figure 4.6: This output curve was calculated using the average interest rate function pictured in Figure 4.4. We also adjusted the coefficient c_2 between 1997 and 2017 in order to produce a more refined fit during that time period.

for each scenario, during the time from 2015 onward, the average interest rate functions have had the same values in all comparisons. The representative "Total Economy Profit" curve is shown in Figure 4.7.

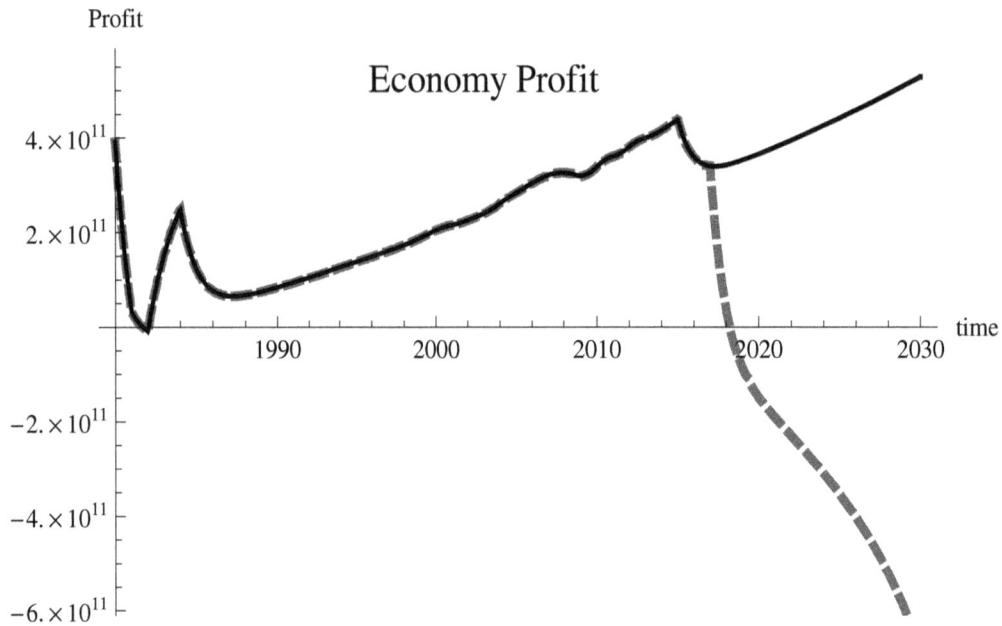

Figure 4.7: The prediction made here, which uses the fit created by the more realistic looking interest rate function shown in Figure 4.4, shows that the total economy profit becomes negative in early spring of 2018.

The predictions made by the economy profit curves have a very sharp intercept with zero total profit. This allows a reasonable estimate for the uncertainty in the predictions caused by the various fits when using the actual numerical values for the intercepts. Using the economy profit zero intercept, we estimate the uncertainty for all the different fits that have been created in our investigations is a little less than ± 2 months. In addition to fit uncertainty, there will be a systematic uncertainty because interest rate payments are being calculated from a guesstimated instantaneous average interest rate for the economy. Because interest rate payments for most loans are not calculated from the interest rate at the time of the payment, but instead are calculated from the interest rate at the time the loan was made, the interest rate payments will be systematically in error, where the amount of the systematic variation is a function of the past loan history within the economy.

The prediction of when the total economy profit becomes negative is likely to be later than predicted. Because of this, the total profit would more likely become negative in the last half of 2019, or sometime in 2020. This prediction assumes no other change in the economy. One likely change would be that businesses would start to fold, further reducing the output and the employment rate within the economy. This change would occur when neither the Government nor the Federal Reserve steps in to change economic policies affecting the economy. Thus, without intervention, the "crash" predicted is likely to be steeper than predicted, but still somewhat later than would be indicated by the total economy profit curve of Figure 4.7.

We have seen in this section that the change in the shape of the average interest rate, by itself, can cause a change in the investment-to-GDP ratio. Also, we have seen in the comparisons of the two Fed scenarios that the raising or lowering of interest rates can cause all the macroeconomic variables to change relative to keeping interest rates fixed. Even though we also know that neither the interest rate value nor the interest rate change caused the crisis of 2008–9, it would be wise to develop a better average interest rate function. If we did so, then we should be able to gain a more intimate knowledge as to what the effects of interest rates, banks' propensity to loan, and businesses' propensity to invest are on the health of our economy. Right now, we do not have that concrete knowledge, and we need that concrete knowledge in order to regulate the economy more effectively.

4.3 An Average Interest Rate for Fed Rate Hikes

We have been forced several times to discuss the fact that the timing of the predictions concerning the results of the Federal Reserve raising interest rates are very likely not accurate and that the predictions we have made based on their stated intentions are probably too early. All of this is nebulous and not as satisfying as it could be. We should be able to get a firmer handle on things if we create an average interest rate function using the projected Federal Reserve interest rate hikes, and the known past Federal Funds interest rates.

Because we do not know the distribution in time of the loans outstanding, we can not expect to create an accurate average interest rate function. We would expect that many loans are short term because both borrowers and lenders are more certain of the near future rather than a more distant future. This expectation is consistent with the statement that I have read that the average business loan is for 3.9 years. We also expect a long tail to the distribution because of the commonness of fifteen and thirty-year mortgages. Furthermore, we expect debt to be front-loaded because debt has been continually increasing for decades. If we follow this simple pattern in creating an average interest rate function, we can not fail to improve upon the completely front-loaded model of just adding the Federal Reserve's rate hikes directly to the 2017 average interest rate.

In order to create an average interest rate function, we need to use the interest rate at the time the loan was made, not the average interest rate at the time the loan was made. We do this because the interest rate of a loan is the rate tendered by a bank or other financial institution at the time the loan is created. We can make a simple sample weighted average whose distribution is front-loaded by:
1. Choosing the first sample at the instantaneous present time, weighted at say 24 percent.
2. Choosing the second sample one year earlier, weighted at 22 percent.
3. Choosing the third sample two years earlier, weighted at 20 percent.
4. Choosing the fourth sample three years earlier, weighted at 18 percent.
5. Choosing the fifth sample four years earlier, weighted at 16 percent.
The implementation of this front-loaded average interest rate extension of the Federal Reserve rate hikes is shown in Figure 4.8.

In general, this averaging is a sample averaging at a few discrete points spaced one year apart. However, because the Federal Funds Rate was essentially constant from 2009 to

2017, ignoring the twenty-five basis point rise implemented at the end of 2015 to the very beginning of 2016, means that the averaging is also an interval averaging over the yearly intervals. We use the Federal Funds Rate as a guide to creating the average interest rate because it is known and because we assume the average borrowing interest rate at a given instant in time is approximately "pegged" to the Federal Funds Rate as a result of borrowing practices.

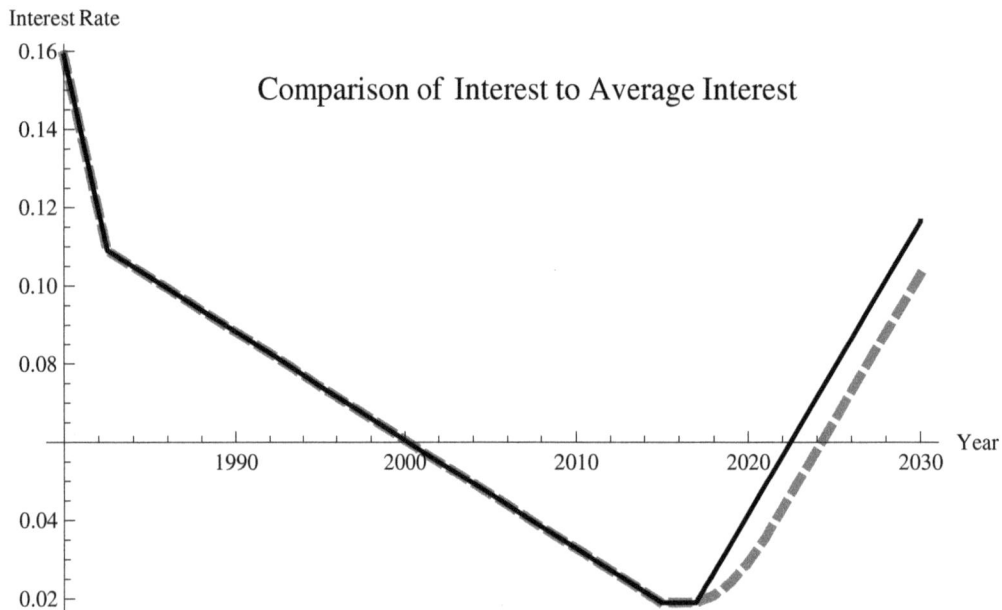

Figure 4.8: In this plot, the solid black line onward from 2017 is the result of adding the Federal Reserve's three-quarters of one percent per year rate hike to the average interest rate at the beginning of 2017. The gray dashed line is the simple sample weighted averaging we created for the value of the average interest rate during the Fed's rate hikes from 2017 onward.

In Figure 4.8, we see that creating a simple weighted average in order to add the Federal Reserve's interest rate hikes into the economy has resulted in the value of the average interest rate used in calculating the interest on the outstanding economy debt has been delayed. The value has been delayed almost two years when we compare it to the value of the average interest rate calculated by merely adding the Fed's rate hikes to the average interest rate in 2017. To see this, observe the spacing between the two curves along the time axis. When we look at the actual numbers, this delay turns out to be almost exactly 1.8 years.

Note, from Figure 4.8 that both methods of creating the average interest rate to use during the Federal Reserve rate hike scenarios have the same average rate interest rate during the fitting of the economy. That is, we always have the same fit no matter how we apply the Fed's rate hikes.

How does this averaging method of applying the Federal Reserve's rate hikes affect our predictions? We look at the averaging method's improved predictions for total economy profit and the average wage rate in Figures 4.9 and 4.10, respectively. In these improved predictions, we have used the smooth fit of the economy in Section 2.1.

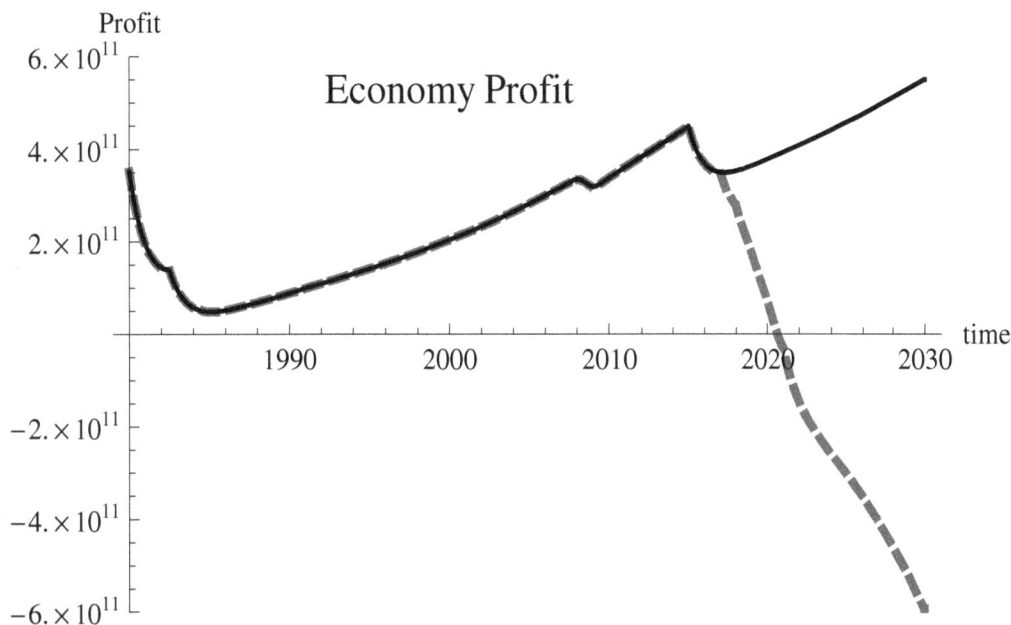

Figure 4.9: Here we see that creating an average interest function to use when applying the Federal Reserve's planned interest hikes will delay the crash of the economy's profit by about two years when compared to the overly-simplified method of just adding the interest rate hikes directly to the average interest rate obtaining when the rate hikes started.

We see in Figure 4.9 that economy profit crashes to zero in the middle of 2020 instead of the early spring of 2018 as it did with our previous method of just tacking the Federal Reserve's rate hikes onto the average interest rate that existed at the time the rate hikes started. When we use the actual numerical results, we find that the total economy profit would be scheduled to become zero during the middle of August in 2020—a delay of 2.4 years.

Previously, we saw that the average wage rate was a vulnerable economic statistic that also succumbed to the Federal Reserve's rate hikes. When we compare the wage rate graph in Figure 4.10 with its smooth fit counterpart in Figure 2.12 on page 28, we see that the present fit's gray dashed curve takes noticeably longer to separate from the no rate hike curve before actually turning downward. This means that there will be a noticeable delay in feeling the effects of the Federal Reserve's rate hike policy than would be indicated by the more simplistic projection method. When we look at the numerical results of the calculations, we find that the average wage rate reaches its maximum value in the middle of August 2020.

This peak occurs precisely at the same time that the economy's profit becomes zero. This is a general result of the equations we are using to fit the economy. Our wage equation, Equation 1.2* on page 13, states that dw/dt is proportional to the economy's profit. Thus, when the economy profit is zero, $dw/dt = 0$, which is the mathematical condition for a maximum or minimum. This result may seem strange until we recall that this change in wage rate is the change of the average wage rate in the economy, not the change in the wage rate of an ordinary worker whose wages we are accustomed to thinking about.

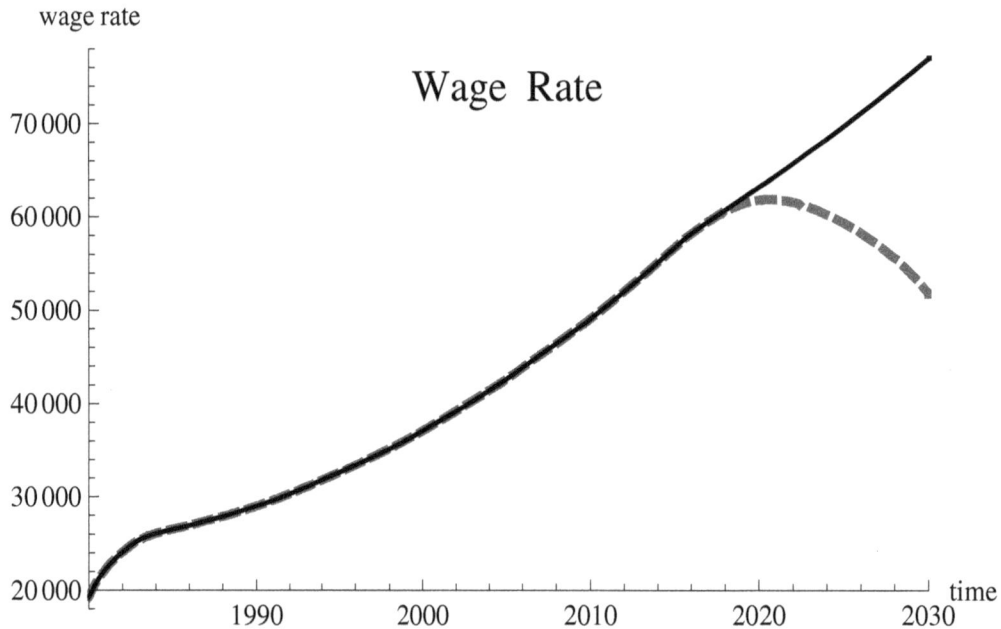

Figure 4.10: When one looks at the effect of the Federal Reserve's three-quarters of a percent per year rate hike on the average wage rate, one sees that the wage rate change will be less abrupt and more gentle than the change predicted by the more simplistic and less accurate implementation of the rate hikes in the smooth fit shown in Figure 2.12 on page 28.

We can see by this example that it is essential to know the average interest rate in order to be able to make accurate predictions of the future of the economy. However, to know the average interest rate, we need to know the distribution of interest rates of the debt as a function of time. This distribution would be a knowable economic statistic. Because each financial institution must know the date, the duration, the interest rate, and the amount of a loan in order to create the loan; all that would be needed in order to create an average interest rate function is for each financial institution to transmit this data to the Federal Reserve at the time of every loan or loan modification. Then, the Federal Reserve could easily compile all this data on a computer. Once compiled, a simple calculation would give the average interest rate on the debt outstanding as a function of time. This average interest rate would allow the Federal Reserve or other economists to have a good idea about the workability of a particular interest rate policy that the Fed might have in mind. In our present situation, this would allow the Federal Reserve to plan an interest rate policy that would safely allow them to raise the interest rates to a high enough level so that they could intervene in a recession, should one arise.

In this section, we have seen that even when we implement the Federal Reserve's rate hike policy in a more accurate way, eventually, after some time, the rate hikes would crash the real economy. In fact, the model we have developed speaks directly only to the running of the real economy. The equations of our model reflect the influence of the financial system, but the model does not describe the workings of the financial system. Thus, our model can only predict how our economy will run given certain economic conditions and, in particular, whether it will falter and crash under these conditions. However, for completeness and a realistic orientation, we should mention that this is not the only way for the real economy to crash.

If the financial system were to crash, then the real economy would crash because the financial system creates the money in our nation upon which the real economy runs. This was the nature of the crisis in 2008–9. In the crisis of 2008–9, the Government bailed out the financial system. This bailout allowed the Federal Reserve to buy up toxic assets from banks so that they could keep creating money by lending for investment.

If a speculative asset bubble were to crash and this speculative bubble was large enough relative to the health of the financial system, then the banks would also crash. This financial system crash would then cause the real economy to crash because the banks create the money on which the real economy runs. This was the nature of the crash that caused the great depression of the 1930s.

Chapter 5

Fixing the United States Economy

In all the comparison plots we did in both the smooth fit in Section 2.2 and the refined fit in Section 3.2, we saw that the Federal Reserve's rate hike scenario would cause a crash of the United States Economy if the rate hikes were continued for a decade or more. Why is this the case; when the higher interest rate hikes of the 1970s and early 1980s did not cause or even come close to causing such a crash? This is clearly an indication that our economy is now fundamentally weaker. What is fundamentally different about our economy now than what it was back then?

According to the Federal Reserve in St. Louis, the Federal Funds rate rose from 4.61 percent on January 1, 1977, to 13.78 percent on December 1, 1979—an interest rate rise of over nine percent in less than three years. It would take the Federal Reserve more than twelve years at three-quarters of a percent per year to raise interest rates that much. So, what is the difference in the economy now and the economy then? Well, there is much more debt now than then. However, the economy now is much larger than then. If we take the ratio of debt to GDP, then we will have a "normalized" economic quantity representing an economy's debt that is not affected by the size of the economy nor by inflation. It is not influenced by inflation because the inflation factor is present in both the numerator and denominator. Similarly, it is not influenced by the size of the society because the debt per capita divided by the GDP per capita is equal to the debt-to-GDP ratio.

Using the Bureau of Economic Analysis's GDP data for 1977 and the Fed's data for the total debt in the United States Economy in the same year, we find that the economy debt-to-GDP ratio in 1977 was 1.46. Because the Federal Reserve discontinued the total debt in the United States Economy statistic in the third quarter of 2015, we will use the projected fit value for the economy debt-to-GDP ratio in 2017. The projection from the refined fit is shown in Figure 5.1. A by-eye estimate puts the value of the debt-to-GDP ratio at the start of the Fed's rate hike policy at about 3.3, while the numbers put it at 3.327. This debt-to-GDP value for 2017 means that the increase in the "normalized" real debt has more than doubled.

The real increase in economy debt is probably a significant factor in the weakening of the United States Economy. To begin our effort to fix the United States Economy, we will set up a scenario in which the Government will help to pay off the debt in the United States

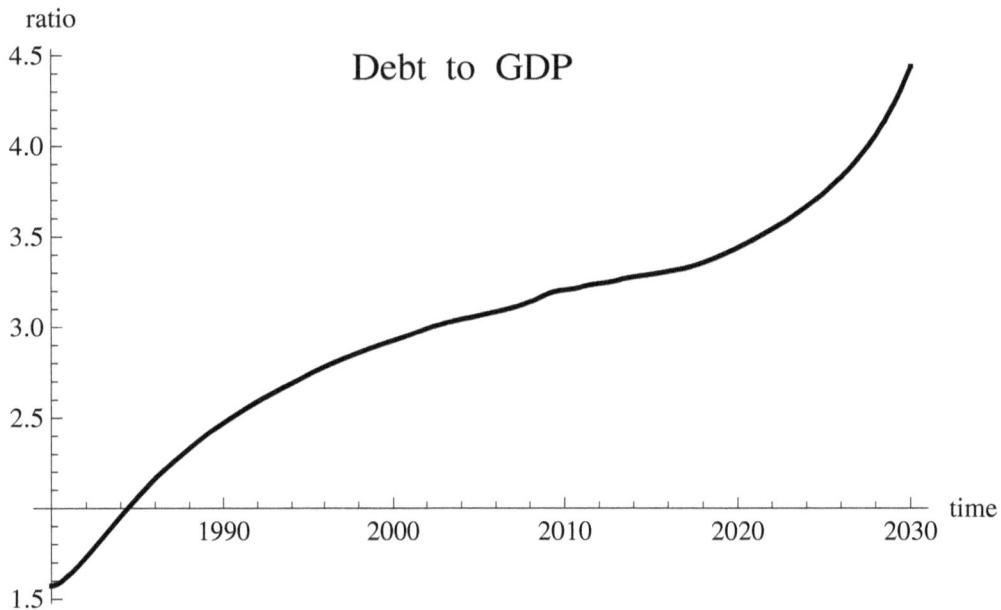

Figure 5.1: This figure shows the debt-to-GDP ratio created by the refined fit of Section 3.2, including the Federal Reserve's three-quarters of a percent interest hike scenario's GDP crash. One might note that the debt-to-GDP ratio increases very rapidly during the crash, as has been observed by some in real crashes.

Economy, using the Government's sovereign power to print money. We will do so in the hope that this simple policy will fix our economy.

5.1 A More Realistic Fed Scenario without Government Intervention

The Federal Reserve may be raising interest rates in order to get ready for the next recession. They might do this on the belief that interest rate policy is their best tool to control the ebb and flow of the economy. The Fed's thinking is: raising the price of a commodity lowers the demand for the commodity while lowering the price of a commodity increases the demand for the commodity. The commodity, in this instance, being money for investment. The price of money being borrowed increases when interest rates for a loan increase while the price of money being borrowed for investment decreases when interest rates decrease. Thus, under this theory, the Fed wants to be in a position where they can lower interest rates to stop a recession—dropping interest rates enough so that investment increases, re-invigorating the economy.

Consistent with this interest rate hike theory, we will have the Fed institute their three-quarters of a percent per year rise for seven years and then stop. During this time, the Fed will have raised interest rates five and one-quarter percent, leaving them with the ability to drop interest rates far enough to stop a recession, should one occur. In this section, we will explore the influence of the Federal Reserve's three-quarters of a percent per year rate hike policy on the United States Economy when the Government does not intervene to prevent the unintended consequences of the interest rate hikes. The average interest rate function used in the calculations is shown in Figure 5.2.

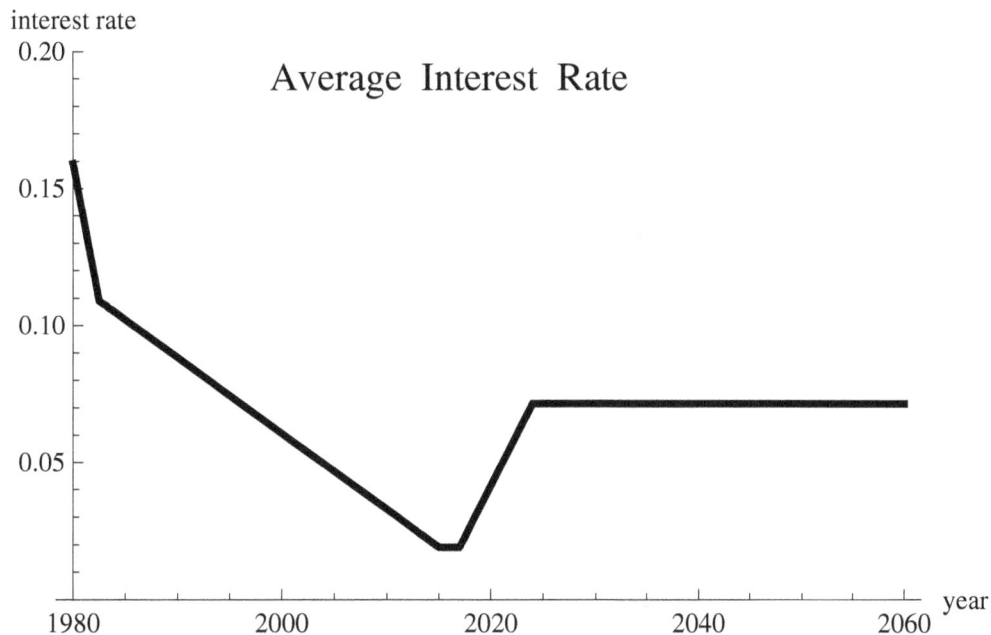

Figure 5.2: The average interest rate during the Fed's rate hike scenario has been created by just adding the Fed's rate hike to the average interest rate at the end of 2016. This sets the average interest rate beyond 2024 at 7.4 percent.

We present the various economic responses en masse and talk about them below. We have extended the timeline out to 2060 in order to be able to show more clearly the effects of the Fed's policy and possible Government interventions on various aspects of the economy. The gray dashed line in the comparison plots again represents the Fed rate hike scenario.

In Figure 5.3, we see that the Federal Reserve rate hikes would severely damage the growth of the output in the United States, but at the same time, we see in Figure 5.4, the rate

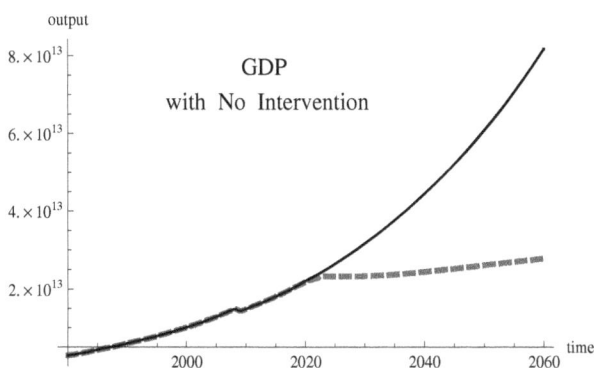

Figure 5.3: GDP growth has severely weakened.

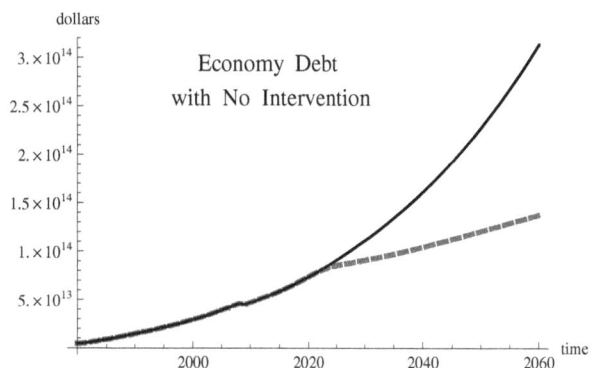

Figure 5.4: The growth of economy debt has slowed.

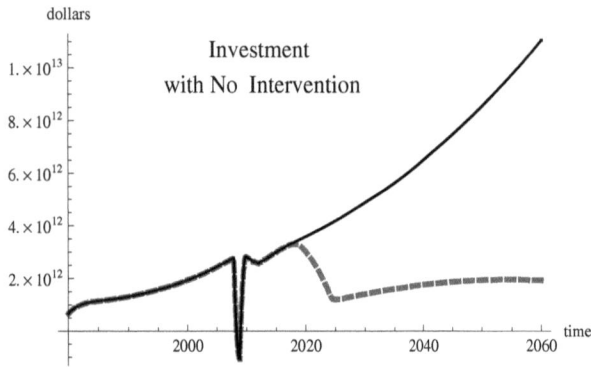

Figure 5.5: Investment has been reduced, and its rate of growth slowed and almost stopped.

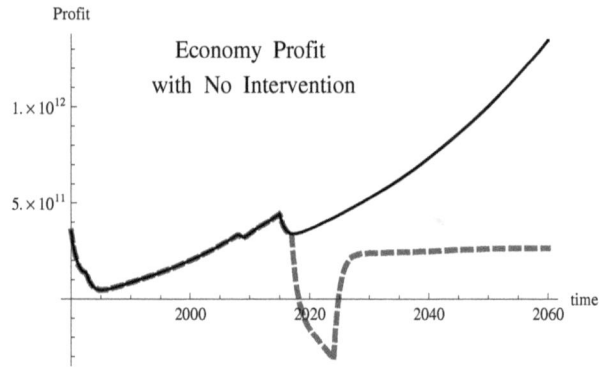

Figure 5.6: The total economy profit has been reduced, and its rate of growth has all but stopped.

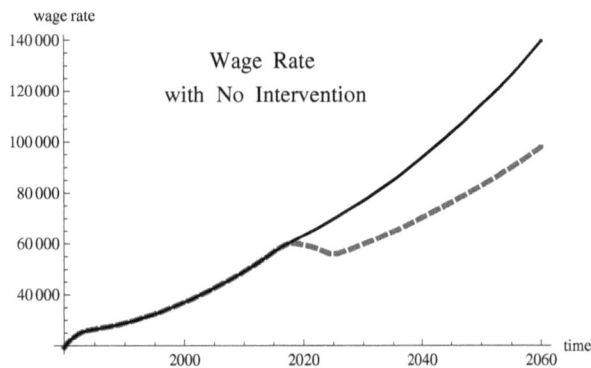

Figure 5.7: The wage rate was reduced during the rate hikes, and its subsequent rate of growth, after the rate hikes stopped, was reduced somewhat.

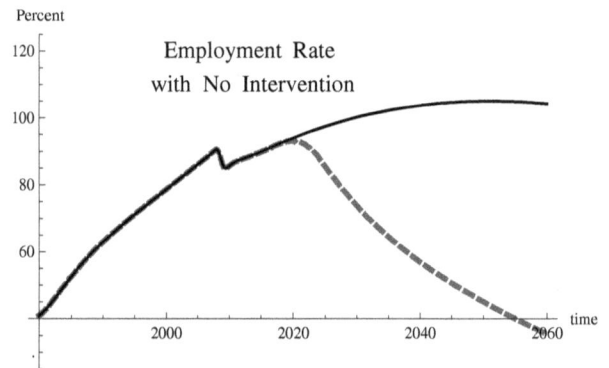

Figure 5.8: The employment rate reached a peak about 2020 and would have been crashing at a moderate rate after that.

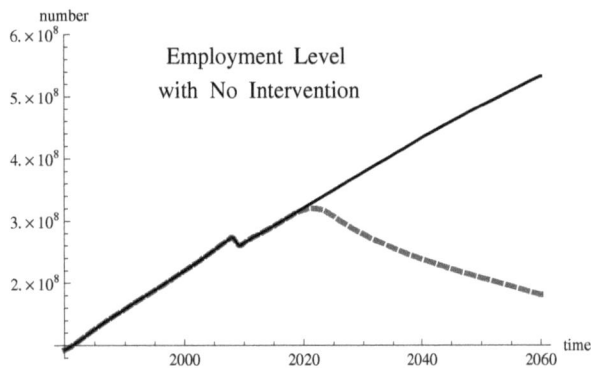

Figure 5.9: Without intervention, the employment level crests in about 2020 and then would slowly decline all the way to 2060.

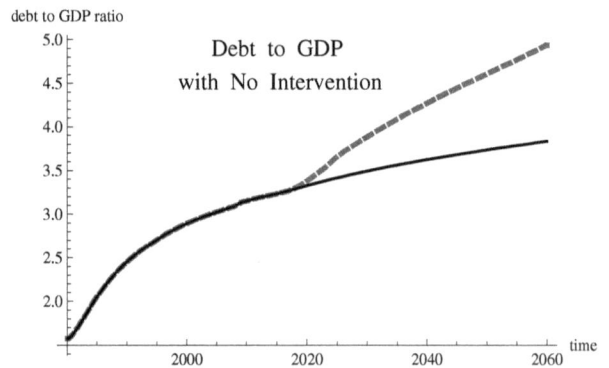

Figure 5.10: The debt-to-GDP ratio in the economy, after seven years of Fed rate hikes, climbs steadily without Government intervention.

hikes would reduce the rate of debt growth. These two results by themselves are mixed and do not tell us whether the economy as a whole would have become healthier or not.

In Figure 5.5, we see that investment would begin to crash during the interest rate hikes but stop when the interest rate hikes stop. The investment would start to grow again but at a noticeably decreased rate. In Figure 5.6, we see a similar thing concerning the total profit in the economy. Here we see that profit would have crashed during the rate hikes and like investment would have begun to recover as soon as the rate hikes stopped. However, the recovery would not be complete because the profit would continue its growth at a very much reduced rate. Taken all together, this seems to indicate that the Federal Reserve interest rate hikes would noticeably weaken the economy.

In Figure 5.7, we see that the average wage rate fell somewhat before the end of the interest rate hikes. The average wage rate then recovered to begin growing again at a very slow rate. The wage rate rise after the Fed interest rate hike is slower than it would have been, had the economy not experienced the rate hike. However, more ominous than that is the fact that the macroeconomic employment rate, seen in Figure 5.8, would have been declining at a moderate rate since about 2020. This decline, in the face of a declining GDP growth rate, seems very disturbing. When we look at the macroeconomic employment level in Figure 5.9, we see that its level is declining while the population is increasing. Finally, we see, in Figure 5.10, that the debt-to-GDP ratio has risen to 4.9 in 2060, from a debt-to-GDP ratio of 3.3 before the start of interest rate rises.

All of this indicates that we would have been living in a sick and dying economy, which would have crashed long before 2060 unless the Government would have stepped in to mitigate the effects of the Federal Reserve's raising of interest rates.

5.2   A Debt-Free Government Intervention that Mitigates the Damaging Effects Caused by the Fed's Interest Rate Hikes

Because the people of the United States have not caused the economic problems of the United States, the people of the United States should not have to pay for the solution of these problems. Accordingly, in this section, we will see what would happen if the government of the United States were to add money to the debt payments, which were created by investments that added to the output of the United States, but not add monies to the debt payments of investments made for speculative purposes. The payments added to debt payment would include consumer debt payments because consumer borrowing adds to the output of the United States, just not as efficiently as borrowing made for direct investment. Note, too, that these monies that are added to debt payments would include the debt payments of governments—local, State, and Federal—because governments also contribute to the output of the United States.

We note here that banks create the overwhelming majority of the money in every modern economy, from ninety-five to ninety-eight percent of the money. Moreover, they create it out of nothing. See the International Monetary Fund article "The Truth about Banks" (Kumhof and Jakab, 2016). In addition, the banks charge interest. This means that there is more money owed than there was created into the economy. Credit creation of money is an inherently unstable system because the economy has to keep pace in order to pay for the money in the economy that keeps it running.

It matters not who creates the money out of nothing in our economy. The banks presently do it, but there is no inherent reason why the Government can not also do it. The Government can do it by printing cash. This is essentially a free process where the only cost is the cost of printing the money. The banks do it differently, and there is a slight cost connected with the way they do it, also.

The Government would spend the cash they print into the economy as a partial payment for each investing entity within the economy. That is, the Government would add to the debt payments made by each of the various entities within the economy, making sure that the small and medium-size businesses would receive an appropriate part of the added debt payments because they employ the great majority of workers.

The amount of debt-free debt payments that the Government will add to the economy will be stated as a fraction of an approximation of GDP, $c_{Deflate} * \widehat{Y}$. This means the debt equation becomes

$$\frac{dD}{dt} = I - \Pi - c_{Deflate} * \widehat{Y}, \tag{5.1}$$

where $\widehat{Y}$ is an approximation to the GDP. The approximation used in the calculations for this example was calculated from $\widehat{Y} = Y[1980] * e^{0.05 * floor(t-1980)}$, where $floor(x)$ equals the greatest integer in x. For example, $floor(2.9) = 2$. This would make for the easy practical implementation of the policy, while at the same time, it would be an easy calculation in Mathematica.

If started in 1980, this formula would have produced a GDP in 2015 of $\$16.47 \times 10^{12}$ compared to the actual value of $\$18.04 \times 10^{12}$—a slightly slower GDP growth rate than when the economy was healthier. However, the GDP growth of the formula is greater than the present GDP growth rate of about 3.7 percent, from 2010 to 2017.

We will start the Government debt-free, debt deflation at the beginning of 2019 because it is all but impossible that it could start before then, given the reality of our political system. This will give the Federal Reserve's interest rate hikes a two-year head start. We will run the debt-free Government debt deflator policy for forty-one years. Running the calculations for this scenario should give us a good idea of what this kind of intervention can do. We show the deflator coefficient $c_{Deflate}$ used in the calculations in Figure 5.11. Then, as in the previous section, we will present the results en masse and follow with a discussion.

We see that the debt-free debt reduction policy of the United States Government would have improved the output of the United States Economy in the more realistic Fed rate hike scenario because, as shown by comparing Figure 5.12 with Figure 5.3, the economy's GDP would have fallen only about half as much as in the United States Economy without intervention. However, as we also see, the economy would still fall well behind a United States

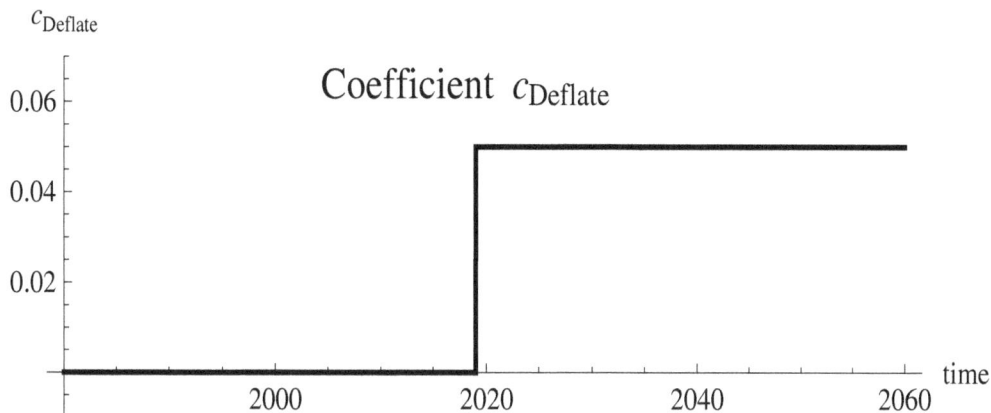

Figure 5.11: Here, we see the value of the coefficient $c_{Deflate}$ used in the calculations in this section. The value of $c_{Deflate}$ during the Federal Government's deflator policy is 0.05.

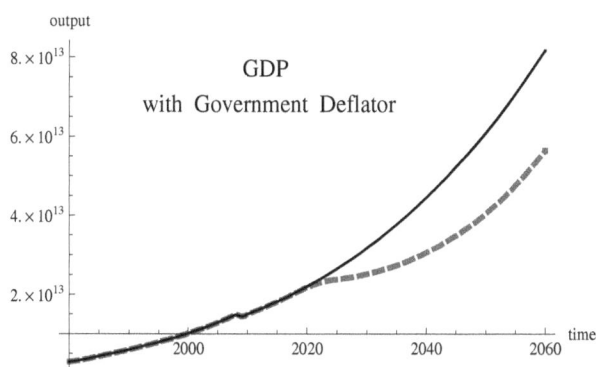

Figure 5.12: Under the Government's debt deflation policy, US output has almost doubled, but it does not keep pace with the no rate hike GDP.

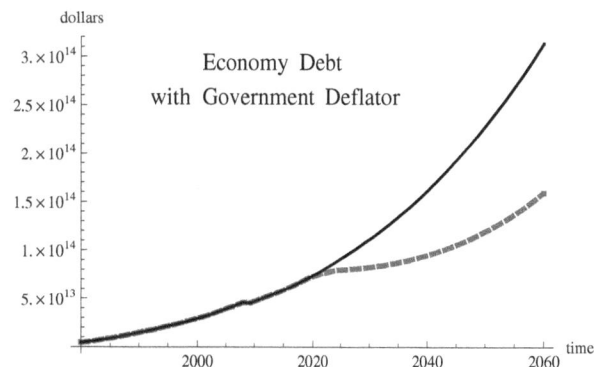

Figure 5.13: The growth of total debt is much less than it would be under the Fed no rate hike scenario but slightly more than with no intervention.

Economy that would exist had it been left alone and not been subjected to any interest rate hikes.

From Figure 5.13, we observe that the total debt in the economy would have increased under a policy of debt-free Government debt aid. However, we note that the rate of growth of the debt within the economy would have slowed noticeably relative to its rate of growth in the no rate hike scenario.

By comparing Figure 5.14 with Figure 5.5, we can discern that the United States Economy with debt deflator intervention would be receiving about four times as much total investment in 2060 as the economy would receive without intervention. However, total investment driving the economy in 2060 would still be well short of the investment driving the economy if there had been no interest rate increases.

We see in Figure 5.15 that the total profit in the economy would have improved signif-

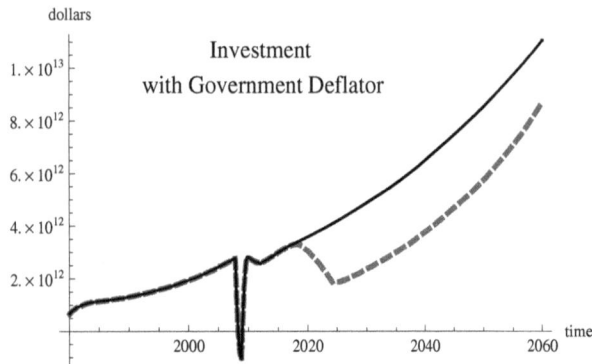

Figure 5.14: The deflator policy stops the crash in investment and then rapidly increases it. However, the investment does not catch up with investment in the no rate hike scenario.

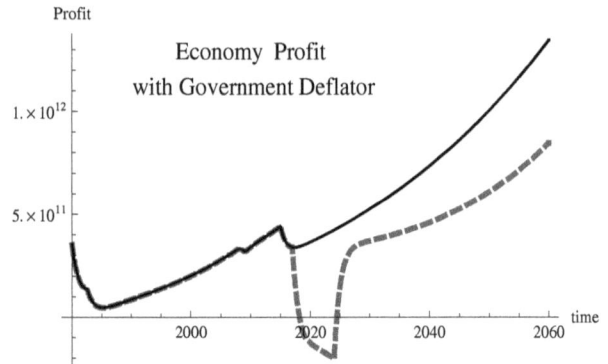

Figure 5.15: The total economy profit has been reduced, and its rate of growth has been slowed relative to the no rate hike scenario, but it has been improved relative to no intervention.

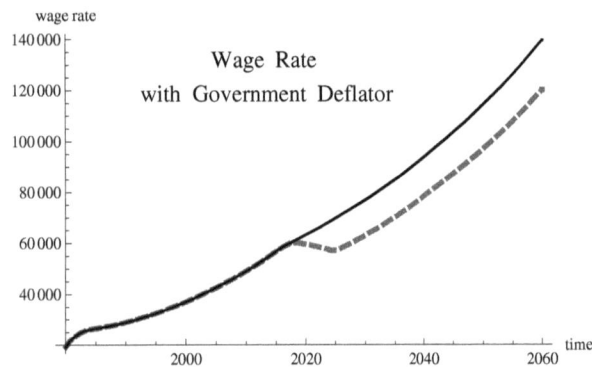

Figure 5.16: As occurred without intervention, the wage rate is initially reduced, but its subsequent rate of growth returns to about what it would be without the Fed rate hikes.

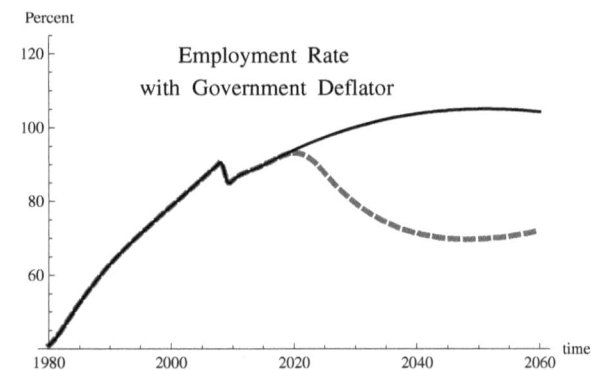

Figure 5.17: The crash in the employment rate is stopped and then ever so slowly reversed by the Government's intervention.

icantly over the economy without intervention, as shown in Figure 5.6. However, the total economy profit would still not be as high as it would have been if there had been no interest rate increases. While not all of what we might like, Government debt deflator intervention would still provide an improvement.

In Figure 5.16, we see that the average wage rate would have fallen somewhat during the interest rate hikes, and then, once the rate hikes stopped, wages would have started to rise again, at roughly the same pace as the wage rate in the no interest rate hike scenario. Moreover, when we look at the employment rate and the employment level, in Figures 5.17 and 5.18, we see that the employment rate would have stopped crashing and started to climb slowly. While we see, at the same time, that the employment level under the debt-free debt deflation aid policy would have stopped its decline and would again have started rising, roughly in line with population growth.

In Figure 5.19, we see that the economy debt-to-GDP ratio would have decreased from 3.3 at the beginning of 2017, when the Federal Reserve interest rate hikes began, to roughly

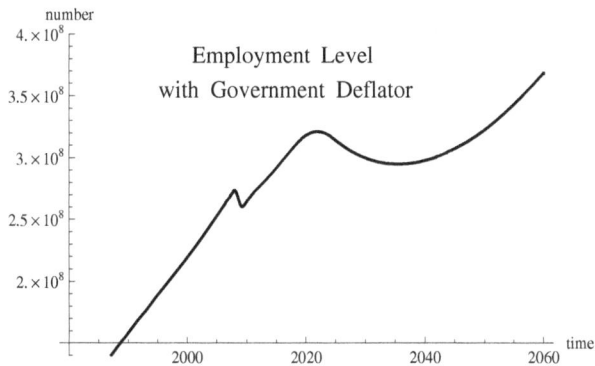

Figure 5.18: The Government intervention has stopped a moderate crash in the macroeconomic employment level and restored its growth rate to roughly consistent with the projected population growth.

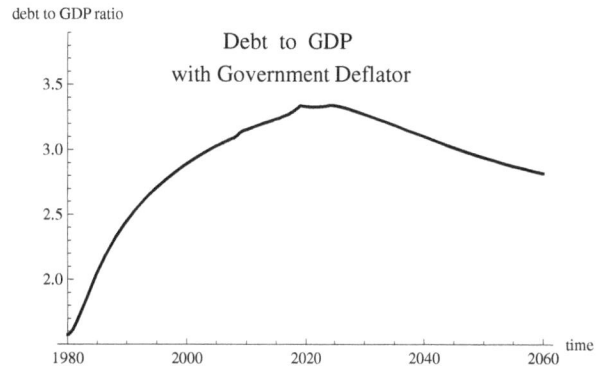

Figure 5.19: The Government's policy of adding debt-free money to debt payments within the economy has stopped the relentless growth of the debt-to-GDP ratio in the economy and started a slow decline in the ratio.

2.8 in 2060. This decrease means that the economy would have gotten fundamentally stronger under the Government's debt deflator policy when compared to the no interest rate hike scenario. However, the graphs of the other economic variables indicate that the people would be suffering a great deal more than they would be if there had been no interest rate hikes.

We see that there has been a definite improvement in the economy under the Government's intervention relative to what it would have been without it. Nevertheless, this improvement in the fundamental strength of the economy has come at a cost—the people are suffering. Moreover, we have not fixed the economy.

Maybe the Government, in our scenario, has not employed a massive enough debt deflation policy? If we increase the debt deflator by a factor of two and one-half, the output of the economy grows to be 1.4 times the GDP of the no rate hike scenario by 2060, and the debt-to-GDP ratio shrinks to 1.8. Both are very good results. Nevertheless, the macroeconomic average wage rate would be more than four thousand dollars a year below the macroeconomic average wage rate of the no interest rate hike scenario in 2060. Moreover, the macroeconomic employment rate would have ballooned to 150 percent, an all but impossible level. Thus, we see that different economic variables within the economy are changed (here improved) at different rates. Therefore, we can not fix the debt problem by more of the same. Accordingly, we must find a Government policy that alters at least one other macroeconomic variable in a manner that coordinates with the debt deflator policy to improve all macroeconomic economic variables in a synchronized and beneficial way.

5.3 Fixing the Debt Problem

We know that the enormous size of the debt is a major underlying cause of the problems with our economy. We see from Equation 1.6, $dD/dt = I - \Pi$, that debt increases as investment from borrowing increases. These are macroeconomic variables, so that debt is the total debt in the real economy. We also know that in a present-day modern economy, 95 to 98 percent of the money within the economy is created from "borrowing". Thus, the macroeconomic investment variable, I, essentially represents the money existing at any time within the economy. This means that in our GDP equation, $dY/dt = I/v - \gamma * Y$, the investment I represents the total amount of money in the economy.

In addition to having the Government add debt-free money to help pay off the economy debt, we propose to have the Government add debt-free money to investment within the economy. To see how this works, we write the total investment as I_{total}. Then we have

$$
\begin{aligned}
I_{total} &= I_{borrow} + I_{Gov} \\
&\equiv I + I_{Gov}
\end{aligned}
\tag{5.2}
$$

That is, we have defined I to be strictly investment created by borrowing. This means our modified debt equation, Equation 5.1, remains

$$
\frac{d}{dt}D = I - \Pi - c_{Deflate} * \widehat{Y}.
$$

However, our output equation becomes

$$
\frac{d}{dt}Y = \frac{I + I_{Gov}}{v} - \gamma * Y,
\tag{5.3}
$$

instead of Equation 1.5.

We will want and need to be able to calculate the total Government investment. Because the Government investment is created free of debt, it will never need to be paid back. Thus, it will stay in the economy forever. This means money contributed to investment in the first year of the policy remains in the economy during the second year of the policy. Moreover, it and the second-year Government contribution to total economy investment remains in the economy during the third year, et cetera. Thus, the quantity of money in the economy contributed by the Government can be an easily calculable and known quantity.

Earlier, we created the quantity $\widehat{Y}$, which is equal to $e^{0.05*floor(t-1980)}$ times the GDP in 1980. This function, $\widehat{Y}$, produces values that will be, in rough order of magnitude, the GDP of the economy it is being used to change; and also it will be, in rough order of magnitude, the GDP of an economy we would like to move toward. We show $\widehat{Y}$ in Figure 5.20. Note that throughout any year, it produces a constant value, and at the beginning of a new year, it steps to a new value.

The amount of debt-free investment that the Government would add to the real economy each year would be $c_{Inflate} * \widehat{Y}$. Because this money is debt-free, it remains in the economy forever. Thus, the amount of money in the economy that is debt-free, which has been contributed by Government money printing, for the smooth running of the economy, is the

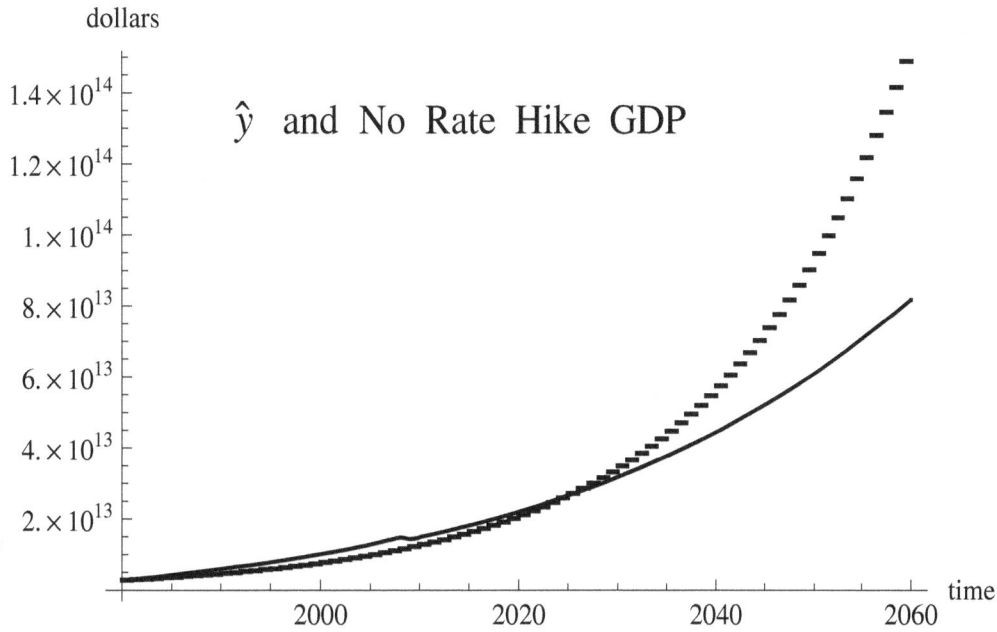

Figure 5.20: Here, we see how the inflator deflator amount $\widehat{Y}$, which grows at five percent per year, compares to the value of GDP calculated for the Fed no interest rate hike scenario.

running sum of the Government's yearly debt-free investment. That is, for our work

$$I_{Gov} = \int_{1980}^{t} c_{Inflate}(t') * \widehat{Y}(t')\, dt', \tag{5.4}$$

where $c_{Inflate}$ is identically zero until the Government policy begins. The coefficient $c_{Inflate}$, which we have used in the Government's debt-free investment money creation policy, is displayed in Figure 5.21.

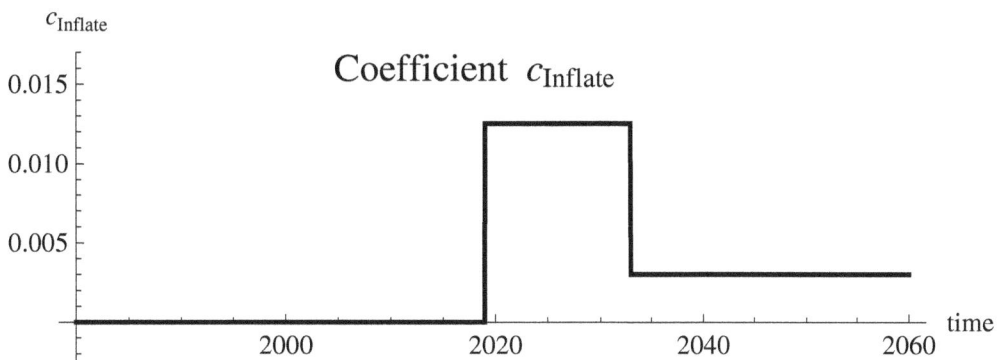

Figure 5.21: Here, we display the value of the coefficient $c_{Inflate}$, which helps determine the Government's debt-free investment aid policy.

We have seen that the Government debt-free investment that the Government contributes to the economy directly enters the output equation $dY/dt = (I + I_{Gov})/v - \gamma * Y$ via the total amount of money, $(I + I_{Gov})$, present in the economy. Taken just by itself, we see that this would have the possibility of inflating the output too quickly. When we look at the investment equation, Equation 1.1, which we repeat here,

$$\frac{d}{dt}I = \Pi + c_1 * \Pi * \left(\frac{\Pi}{Y}\right) - c_2 * \Pi * \left(\frac{D}{v * Y}\right),$$

we see that the Government's policy of reducing the debt will increase the debt by borrowing because as debt in the investment equation is decreased more borrowing occurs, worsening the debt problem we are trying to cure. Thus, we need to modify the investment equation to prevent this effect.

We also want to stop here to consider what type of economy we want to reset the economy to, once we fix the debt problem, if, in fact, we can. Do we want an economy in which the banks create all the money in the economy as debt-laden money? Do we want to have the Government create all the money in the economy as debt-free money? Or, do we want a hybrid economy in which the Government creates some fraction of the money, as debt-free money, and the banks create the remaining fraction of the money as debt-laden money? These are real questions. For example, some people might like to take out a thirty-year mortgage to buy a house to live in, rather than pay somewhat less rent for thirty years. People might prefer this because at the end of thirty years they would have a home that is theirs, while if they had paid rent for thirty years they would have nothing. We will include these options within the structure of our investment equation.

A modified investment equation, which speaks to our concerns, is:

$$\frac{d}{dt}I = \left[\Pi + c_1 * \Pi * \left(\frac{\Pi}{Y}\right) - c_2 * \Pi * \left(\frac{D}{v * Y}\right) - c_{RI} * \widehat{Y}\right] * \left[\frac{I}{I + I_{Gov}}\right], \quad (5.5)$$

where $c_{RI} = c_{Inflate}/cz$. In the first bracket of Equation 5.5, $c_{RI} * \widehat{Y}$ is the amount that businesses would be required to reduce their investment borrowing. This requirement would be made in order to prevent borrowing from defeating the policy of reducing the debt within the economy. The second bracket in Equation 5.5 would tend to stabilize the debt-laden investment toward the fraction of money created by debt. Banks would likely tend to resist their shrinking share of the total investment pie by pushing loans. This would tend to overheat the economy. Accordingly, bank regulation would require banks to keep their lending to the real economy reasonable, as defined by the second bracket of Equation 5.5.

All the quantities in the equations presented are well defined and knowable. Thus, it is clear that the Government could cause the policy to be implemented if they chose to do so because the amount of debt-free money given for debt repayment aid and investment aid are known quantities. Also, the banking investment quantities would be known, so that banking investment limits could be set up to keep bank loans to the real economy reasonable, no matter the details of the policy. Therefore, in order not to get bogged down with abstractions or specific policies concerning the way we might implement Government policy, we will present the results of the debt-free Government debt deflator and investment aid policy on the economy. The specific quantities used, or the way the Government might intervene, are not the only ways that the following general result can be obtained. This method of fixing the debt problem is only meant to be a proof of concept. I think it is important that people become aware that there are ways to fix the debt problem without the economy having to crash in order to reset itself.

In order to solve the debt problem and get the economy back to a healthy state, we will have the Government run the debt-free Government investment aid policy with the same debt deflator policy presented in the previous section. Therefore $c_{Deflate}$ will have precisely the same values, as shown in Figure 5.11. This choice will allow us to obtain a much clearer understanding of the effect of each policy.

In the fixing the debt problem scenario that we present below, we have set $c_z = 2/3$, so that all borrowers receiving Government aid are required to reduce their investment by their share of $1.5 * c_{Inflate} * \widehat{Y}$.

In Figure 5.22, we show that the combined Government policy has "fixed" the output in the economy, while Figure 5.23 shows that the Government debt-free debt deflation and investment aid policy has gotten rid of the total debt within the economy.

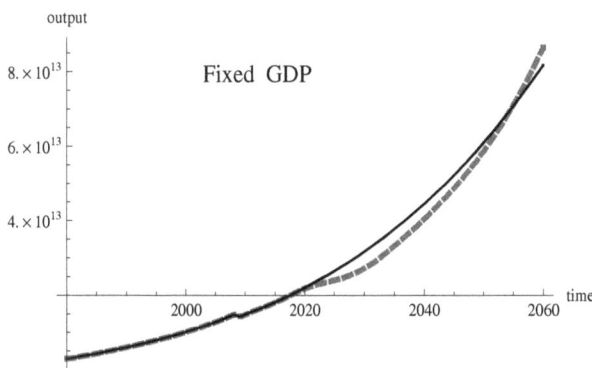

Figure 5.22: Here, we see that the output of the economy would at first be reduced by the Fed's interest rate hikes, but that the Government's intervention would keep the GDP close to the no interest rate scenario. Then, about 2050, the GDP would pass the no interest rate hike GDP and continue to pull away.

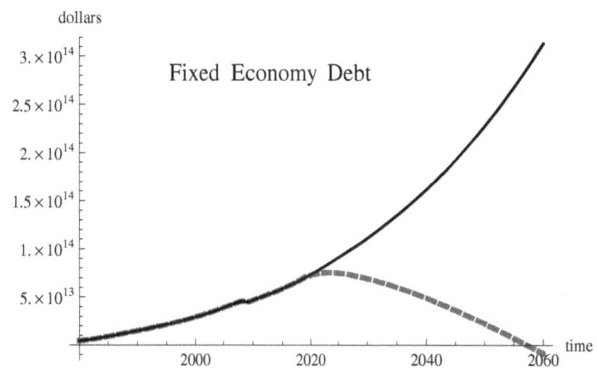

Figure 5.23: In this graph, we see that the economy's total debt would reach a peak and start to decline by 2020. Moreover, by 2060, we see that all the total debt in the economy would have vanished and that there would be a total net savings of a bit more than ten percent of GDP.

We see from Figure 5.22 that the Government's debt-free debt deflator and investment aid policy has brought the output of the economy back up to and beyond what it would have been if the Federal Reserve had not raised interest rates. In this sense, the GDP of the economy would have been fixed.

However, there is a more basic sense in which we can say that the GDP has been fixed or more correctly, almost fixed. In 2024, when the Fed in our scenario stopped raising interest rates, the GDP was 23.6322 trillion dollars. The 2060 value of the GDP that is obtained by fixing the debt problem is, by calculation, 86.5897 trillion dollars. Assuming the output is an exponential-like increasing function of time, we find that the average value of the exponential time constant for the rate of GDP increase from 2024 to 2060 to be 3.6 percent per year.[1] If we do this for other times between 2024 and 2060, we find that the average exponential time constant for the growth of GDP is, in general, a slowly increasing function of time, with the GDP growth rate in 2060 being well estimated to be just over four percent per year. This means the economy, while running well in comparison to the scenario in which the Fed did not raise interest rates, is still not running like the healthy economy we had in the past.

From 1980 to 2015, the United States had a much higher debt-to-GDP ratio than it would have had in the latter years of the debt-free Government aid policy. In those earlier times, the United States Economy's GDP was increasing at better than five percent per year. See Figure 5.20.

We see from Figure 5.23 that the total debt in the economy would have become negative in 2060 under the Federal Government's debt-free intervention—meaning that the United States Economy would have net savings. This result would be a better, healthier state of affairs for economy debt than at any time in the past. If this is so, then what is the reason why the United States' GDP growth rate did not become better than just over four percent per year by 2060? Is the reason for this that total investment was not high enough?

Next, for completeness, in Figure 5.24, we present the economy debt-to-GDP ratio as a function of time in our scenario, attempting to fix the debt problem. We also present the total investment to GDP in Figure 5.25.

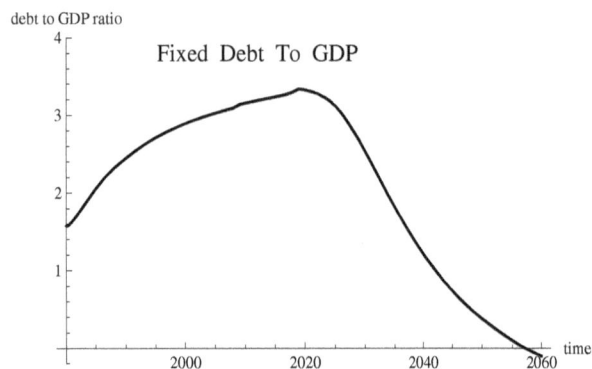

Figure 5.24: This graph indicates that if the United States Government implemented the economic plan that we suggested above, then the debt problem in the United States would be fixed.

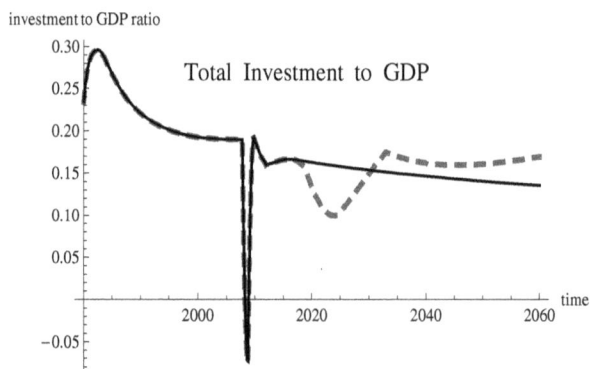

Figure 5.25: Here, we see that the total investment-to-GDP ratio in the United States would stabilize in the period from 2033 to 2060 at a value that is higher than would exist in the no rate hike scenario.

Figure 5.24 confirms that the debt-to-GDP ratio in the United States could be fixed under a debt-free spending policy of the United States Government. We see under the policy that we implemented in our scenario, in the space of forty years, the total debt in the United States would go from something well above three times GDP to a state in which there would be no net debt, but instead to one in which there is a small net savings.

---

[1]If $f(t)$ is an approximately exponential function between t_0 and t, with $y = f(t)$ and $y_0 = f(t_0)$, then $y = y_0 e^{\gamma(t-t_0)}$ is an exponential function that is an approximate fit to the function f(t) between t_0 and t. Because $y = y_0 e^{\gamma(t-t_0)}$, $\ln(y/y_0) = \gamma(t - t_0)$, and the average growth rate, $\gamma = [\ln(y/y_0)]/(t - t_0)$.

Figure 5.25 indicates that our scenario would have fixed the investment problem that would eventually occur if the Fed continues with its interest rate hikes as in our more realistic scenario. See Figure 5.5 for the total investment in the US economy for the scenario when there is no Government intervention. We see from Figure 5.25 that total investment would have popped back up to be two to four percent of GDP higher than total investment would have been in the no rate hike scenario during the period from 2033 to 2060. In this sense, we can certainly say that Government policy would fix the investment problem that would be created by the Fed interest rate hikes in our more realistic scenario.

We also see that the total investment under the Government's debt-free aid policy during the period from 2033 to 2060 is about two to five percent of GDP less than investment during the period from 1985 through 2005, a time when the economy was running at an average GDP growth rate of better than five percent. This lack of investment should at least partially explain why the GDP growth rate was only about four percent in 2060 under our Government debt-free aid program.

We present a graph of the total investment in the economy and a graph of the fraction of debt-laden investment, by borrowing, in Figures 5.26 and 5.27, respectively.

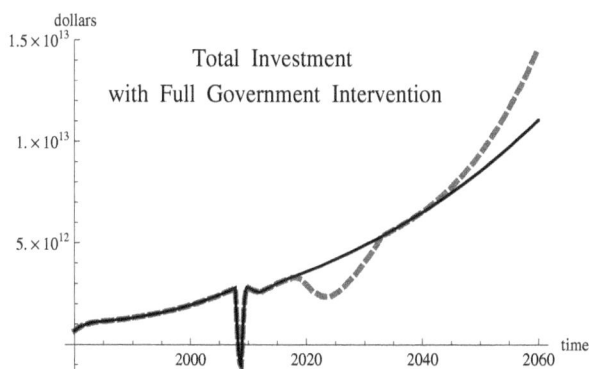

Figure 5.26: This plot shows that full Government intervention would significantly slow the drop in total investment during Fed rate hikes and cause it to be about one third greater than it would have been in 2060 under the no rate hike scenario.

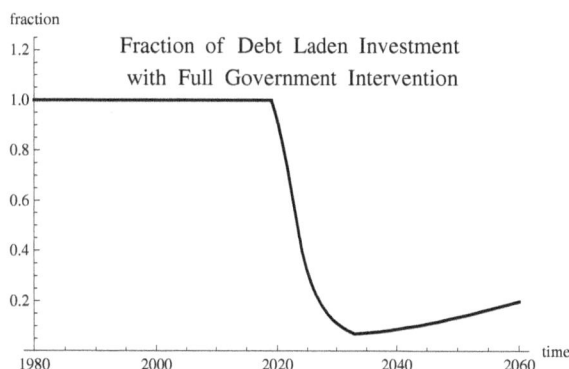

Figure 5.27: This plot shows the fraction of investment money created by borrowing from banks in the economy. In other words, the plot shows the fraction of the money within the economy that is laden with debt.

Figure 5.26 indicates that we have fixed total investment within the economy in comparison to the no interest rate hike scenario. A by-eye estimate, using a clear ruler, indicates that the Government aid scenario's total investment is about one third greater than the no rate hike scenario in 2060. What do our equations suggest it should be? Looking at the output equation,

$$\frac{dY}{dt} = \frac{I_{Total}}{v} - \gamma * Y \approx \frac{I_{Total}}{v},$$

indicates that the output growth rate, dY/dt, is approximately proportional to I_{Total} because v is a constant. By direct calculation from the output values in the no interest rate scenario, we find that the exponential growth rate of GDP in 2060 would be a little under three percent per year. Our previously calculated estimate for the growth rate of GDP under the debt-free Government aid scenario was four percent per year in 2060, confirming that the GDP growth rate is approximately proportional to I_{Total}.

Therefore, we can say that the absolute minimum value of the total investment we would have needed in order to obtain a GDP growth rate of better than five percent per year in 2060 would have been at least one quarter more than the investment that occurred in the debt-free Government aid scenario and at least fifty percent more to obtain a better than six percent GDP growth rate. This result confirms our earlier hypothesis that the total investment in the economy under the Government's debt-free aid policy was insufficient to create a GDP growth of five percent or more.

The fraction of the money in the economy that has arisen from bank credit creation is shown in Figure 5.27. In the particular scenario chosen, the banks were reduced to creating something less than ten percent of the money in the economy before the Government, in 2033, reduced its rate of debt-free investment. This change allowed banks to increase the fraction of the money that they created into the economy. However, the increase in bank-created money that entered the economy seems to have occurred at a relatively slow and linear rate. This gives us an indication that it would be possible for the Government to control the fraction of debt-laden money in the economy by controlling the amount of debt-free money it, itself, invests or spends into the economy.

Finally, we present the average wage rate, in Figure 5.28, and the employment rate, in Figure 5.29, that would result if the Government were to follow the debt-free debt deflator and investment aid policy we have presented.

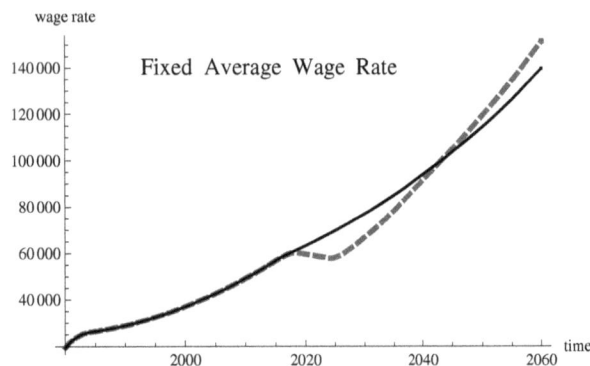

Figure 5.28: In this plot, we see that the macroeconomic average wage rate has been fixed relative to what it would have been in the scenario in which the Federal Reserve did not raise interest rates. The fixed wage rate is some 8 percent greater than what it would have been in 2060 under the no rate hike scenario.

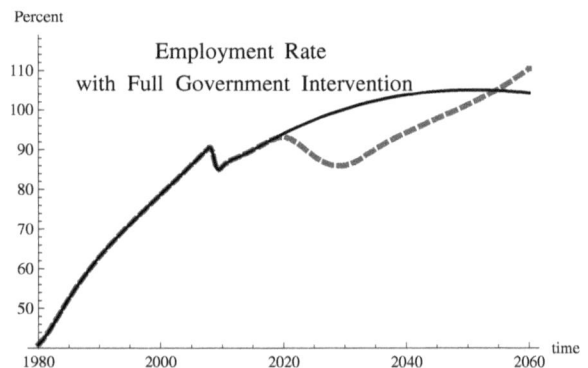

Figure 5.29: In this plot of the macroeconomic employment rate, we see that we raised the employment rate to something just over 110 percent in fixing the economy relative to the scenario in which the interest rates were left unchanged. In fact, we should notice that even the no rate hike scenario required the employment rate to crest at just over 105 percent.

Figure 5.28 tells us that the Government's debt-free deflator and investment aid policy would have fixed the average wage rate relative to the no interest rate hike scenario. However, because we do not have a good independent analysis of the macroeconomic average wage rate, the result is somewhat fuzzy.

In Figure 5.29, we show the macroeconomic employment rate during the Federal Government's debt-free debt deflation and investment aid policy scenario in comparison to the macroeconomic employment rate during the no interest rate hike scenario. We see from the figure that the macroeconomic employment rate, in the no rate hike scenario, appears to crest at something just over 105 percent, a 105.06 percent by the numbers, at the beginning of 2051 and that in our debt-free Government intervention scenario the macroeconomic employment rate reaches about 110 percent, 110.477 percent by the numbers, in 2060.[2]

These high macroeconomic employment rates might seem barely believable if we realize how many people might be counted or partially counted. Besides the people we mentioned earlier in our previous discussion on the same issue, we would include the employees working in offshore jobs. Such workers would include people in India who help you with your Internet difficulties when you call, or possibly employees of US automobile companies who work in Canada or Mexico in plants that produce cars for direct shipment into the United States.

Furthermore, there seems to have been a fundamental change to the nature of our economy in the early 1970s. Between 1948 and 1973, wages and productivity growth moved in tandem (Bivens and Mishel, 2015, p. 4). However, Bivens and Mishel noticed that the growth of wages and the growth in net productivity began to separate beginning in about 1973. Between 1973 and 2014, the productivity rose 72.2 percent while the wage rate of the median worker rose only 8.7 percent. That is, productivity rose eight times faster. Furthermore, from 2000 through 2014, productivity rose 21.6 percent while the wage rate of the median worker rose only 1.8 percent, indicating that productivity grew twelve times faster during this period (Bivens and Mishel, 2015, pages 3–5). Taken together, this means that the discrepancy between productivity and the wage rate was is getting worse with time.

The Economic Policy Institute article also shows that the wage rate discrepancy was not uniformly discrepant. During the period from 1973 through 2014, in which the productivity rose 72.2 percent, the average wage rate rose 42.5 percent, and the median wage rate rose 8.7 percent (Bivens and Mishel, 2015, p. 5). Bivens and Mishel give an even more fine-grained analysis between 1979 and 2013. During this time period productivity went up 61.9 percent while the wage rate of the top one percent increased 137.7 percent, the top 95 to 99 percent of wage earner's salaries rose 59.5 percent, and the bottom 90 percent of wage earner's salaries went up by just 15.2 percent (Bivens and Mishel, 2015, p. 19).

Does the growing disparity between the income of people within our society cause fundamental problems for our economy, or does it just infringe upon many people's sense of fairness? Will we be able to see any fundamental problems caused by the loss of the wage

---

[2]There is an enigma associated with the employment level, the wage rate, and the correctness of our results. It will turn out that the economic output, debt, investment, and profit results will be correct for any consistent set of employment levels and average wage rate initial conditions that are chosen. This strange result will be shown in the part of the book dealing with fits that begin in 1964.

rate's association or causal connection with the productivity in the United States Economy? Because we have not fitted the United States Economy for any time period between 1948 and 1973, during which time the wage rate and productivity moved in tandem within the US economy, it may require a nuanced indirect approach to see any fundamental problems caused by the growing wage disparity or loss of contact of wage rates with productivity. However, it probably is possible, just as it is possible to see that one is traveling along a curved surface whose surface is so large that it is all but impossible to observe the curvature directly.

Our equations are macro, and as such, they reflect the full macroeconomic reality of our economy. This means that the present underlying social structure of the United States is hidden within these equations. For instance, the United States Economy could not run with the same number of low-wage, macroeconomic native-born workers while still keeping the same underlying social structure of the United States. Directly indicated above is that we imported such workers, which increased the population.

The particular debt-free Government aid policy presented above was chosen with just enough stimulus to be strong enough to fix the economy relative to the no interest rate hike scenario while at the same time not being so strong as to overwhelm credulity concerning the employment rate. Something seems to be hidden here, which we would like to bring out if we can.

However, we must finish the job of fixing the economy. We are not yet finished. We need to have the Government stop its aid policy and release the economy to follow its own course.

5.4   Releasing the Fixed Economy

Now we must return to the question: How do we want the money in the economy to be created? Do we want banks to create the money via credit with the consequence that the money created is burdened with debt? Do we want a mixed economy, in which a certain fraction of the money is created by banks "lending" money into the economy for investment, and the remainder of the money is created debt-free by the Government spending money into the economy? Or, do we want the Government to create all the money by spending debt-free cash into the economy? There are strengths and weaknesses in each case.

To implement either of the first two cases of money creation requires that banks should be divided into two groups, those that choose to do speculative lending and those that choose to do only lending into the real economy. In the third case in which the Government creates all the money, only speculative banks would be allowed. In either of the first two cases, only those banks that loaned into the real economy would be allowed the privilege of credit creation of money, while those banks that choose to deal in speculative lending should not be allowed to create money from credit. They would have to lend their own dime or the dime of others whom they could induce to invest with them, for example, by depositing money with them.

To try to get a handle on how we need to regulate the banks after we fix the economy, we present a plot of the debt-to-GDP level, from 1952 to 2007, in Figure 5.30. In Figure 5.31, we present an expanded view of the debt-to-GDP level when the economy was running better.

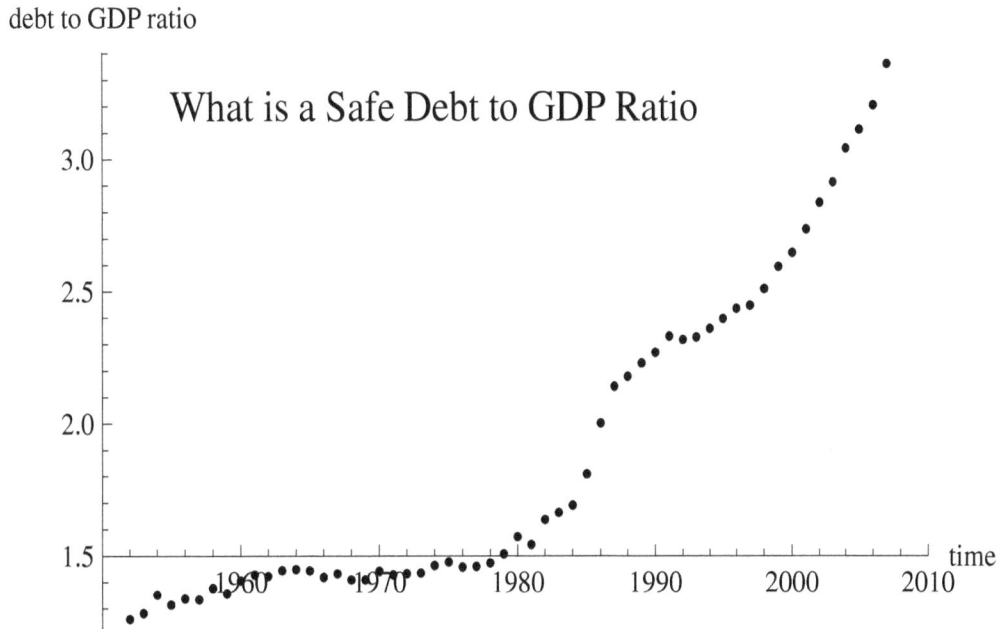

debt to GDP ratio

What is a Safe Debt to GDP Ratio

Figure 5.30: Here, we see the economy debt-to-GDP ratio during the period 1952 to 1973, when our economy's wages were keeping up with productivity, along with the following period through to 2007. The average rate of GDP growth during the period from 1952 to 1973 was 6.46 percent per year.

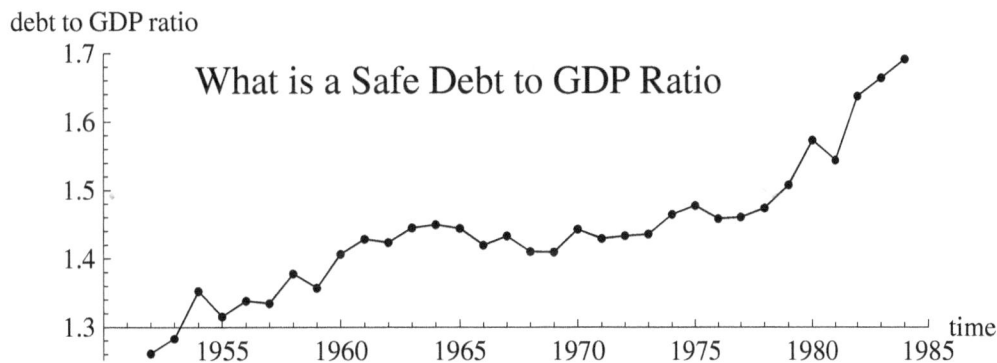

debt to GDP ratio

What is a Safe Debt to GDP Ratio

Figure 5.31: Here, we see that the economy debt-to-GDP ratio bounces up and down when the ratio is relatively low.

In Figure 5.30, we see that when the debt-to-GDP ratio became greater than 1.5 in 1979, for the first time, the ratio never again returned to being 1.5 or less. In fact, once the debt-to-GDP ratio crossed 1.45, in 1974, for the first time, it never returned to 1.45 again!

Some of the relatively sharp or long upward changes in the debt-to-GDP ratio correspond to the beginning of the relatively mild recessions during the period from 1952 to 1973. The following decline in the debt-to-GDP ratio is associated with coming out of recession. We also see that once the economy debt-to-GDP ratio reaches 1.5, the amount of the ratio bouncing about seems much diminished. Instead, the ratio seems to have a much stronger tendency to rise. Thus, for safety's sake, we would suggest that the limit should be less than 1.45.

As we see in Figure 5.31, the debt-to-GDP ratio was continuously bouncing up and down, while the debt-to-GDP ratio was less than 1.45. This likely means that the banks with the guidance of the Federal Reserve would be able to control their lending and interest rates such that they would be able to keep the debt-to-GDP ratio lower than 1.45 without shocking the economy too much.

Letting the banks create money, with little real regulation, has, in part, led to the problems we are facing today. Not only is the economy very weak, but because of their own greed, so is the banking system. The banks have not been given proper direction as to what they must do in order to be granted the privilege of creating the money within the economy, nor have they been given proper oversight. With proper directions, they can keep an economy from tying up because of too much debt. Along with other requirements, they can be required, for instance, to keep the total debt-to-GDP ratio below say 1.4. If they do not do it, they lose the privilege of creating money or some other very harsh penalty. Once they become aware that we know how the economy works, they will likely be chastened. They will know that we know how the economy works if we fix the debt problem.

If the Government set the debt-to-GDP ratio upper bound at 1.4, we know that the banks would prefer to operate as close to that limit as they can without going over because the more debt there is in the economy, the more money they make. Consequently, there would only be mild ups and downs in the economy debt-to-GDP ratio, likely indicating there would be at worst only a relatively few mild recessions occurring from time to time. Thus, if the banks were well regulated and overseen, it might be that the people would prefer to have the bankers, with their expertise, create the money within the economy, rather than having the Government and the politicians directly controlling the money creation.

Another possibility would be a mixed economy in which banks would create money from credit for mortgages and other business investments, while the Government would get to create some money by printing cash and directly spending it into the economy. In an economy of our present size, this would likely amount to eighty to one hundred and fifty billion dollars per year of extra spending. The amount would depend on the amount of money also being created by the banks. This debt-free spending would be a real benefit to the Government because this money would not come from taxes or borrowing. It would come from the Government's sovereign power to create money.

Even though the debt-free money stays within the economy, adding more and more money to the economy will not necessarily cause inflation. The economy is always growing because the population and productivity are always growing. Thus, there is always a need to expand the money supply because it will take more and more money to run the economy. However, just like with the money the banks create, the Government spending too much money into the economy would cause inflation, and spending too little money into the economy would cause a recession.

Some people would rather pay a bit more per month for a mortgage to buy a house than they would have to pay for rent, because, at the end of thirty years, they would own the house. However, if they had rented, after thirty years, they would have nothing, except next month's rent. Consequently, many people are likely to want banks for such purposes. Similarly, some businesses might want them for similar reasons. Thus, people might prefer a mixed economy in which the banks and the Government create money because of the convenience and benefit that "borrowing" offers and because debt would be much less of a factor within the economy.

How should we regulate the banks in a hybrid economy? In order to try to get an idea as to how we should regulate the banks, we present a plot of the ratio of the difference between the total economy debt and Federal debt all divided by the GDP, $(D - National\,Debt)/GDP$, in Figure 5.32.

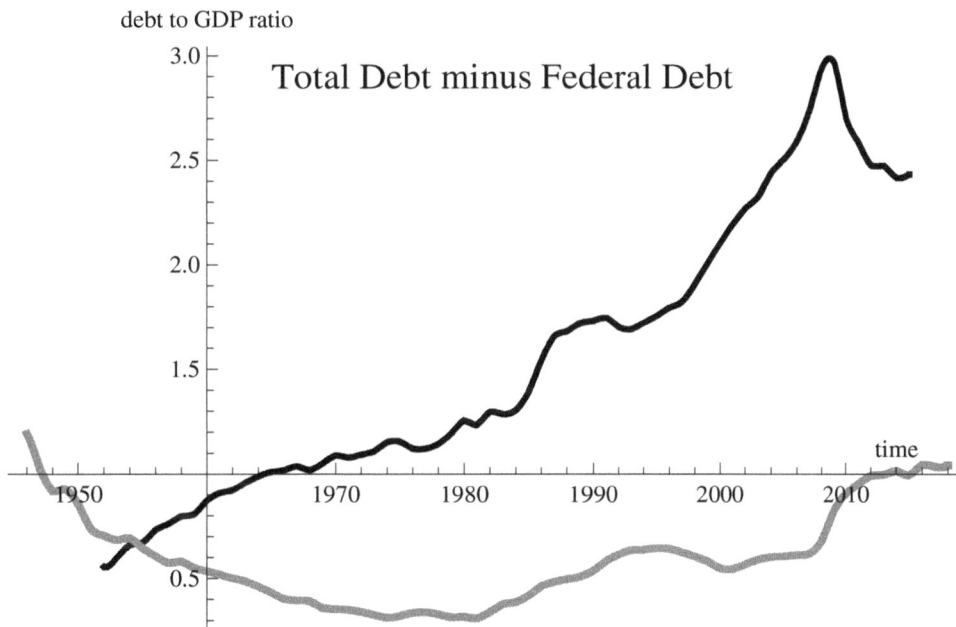

Figure 5.32: In this figure, we display the total debt-to-GDP ratio less the Federal debt-to-GDP ratio—black line—and the Federal debt-to-GDP ratio— thick gray line.

In Figure 5.32, we see that the non-Federal-Government sectors of the real economy have been steadily piling up debt since the end of World War II. We see that the build-up of debt in the non-Governmental sectors of the economy has been continuous and relentlessly upward.

The National debt, on the other hand, has gone from a high debt-to-GDP ratio of something over 1.2 at the end of the War to a low between 0.3 and 0.4 in the 1970s through the early 1980s. Then the National Debt slowly rose through the 1980s into the early 1990s to a bit over sixty percent of GDP. The Government debt to GDP ratio held there for a few years, and then under President Clinton and the Republican "Contract with America," the debt was reduced to about one half the GDP.

This discussion has shown us is that the Federal Government has a much greater ability to handle debt created from the credit creation of money than the non-Federal-Government sectors of the economy. When we look at the debt-to-GDP ratio for the non-Federal-Government sectors between 1950 and 1963, we see that it was always below 0.9. This debt-to-GDP ratio only rose past 1 in 1965. So it seems that requiring the banks to keep the non-Federal-Government sector of the real economy debt-to-GDP ratio at or below 0.9 would be safe. Although a non-Federal-Government debt-to-GDP ratio limit of 1 might be okay.

However, we can see more in Figure 5.32. Figure 5.32 also shows us that the Federal Government increased its debt by about 0.5 GDP in its efforts to stop the crash of the financial system in the crisis of 2008–9. We see that this helped the non-Federal-Government sectors of the economy because their debt-to-GDP ratio was reduced by about 0.6 percent of GDP. However, when we compare our present national debt-to-GDP ratio with the national debt-to-GDP ratio that we had at the height of our efforts in World War II, it seems unlikely that we will be able to fix our debt problem with more of the same. This feeling is strengthened when we note that the total economy debt-to-GDP ratio is relentlessly rising in the Federal Reserve no rate hike scenario, as shown in Figure 5.10 on page 56.

We will run two scenarios, one in which we release the economy back into a state in which the banks continue to be the ones who create the money supply, and a second scenario in which the economy is a hybrid, in which both the banks and the Government create the money supply.

5.4.1 The Release Setup

To return the economy to the state in which the banks create the money within the economy, we need to return to the meaning of our original macroeconomic differential equations. To do this, we set $c_{Inflate} = 0$ from beyond 2060 in our modified investment equation, Equation 5.5. We repeat it here for convenience:

$$\frac{d}{dt}I = \left[\Pi + c_1 * \Pi * \left(\frac{\Pi}{Y}\right) - c_2 * \Pi * \left(\frac{D}{v * Y}\right) - c_{RI} * \widehat{Y}\right] * \left[\frac{I}{I + I_{Gov}}\right],$$

where

$$I_{Gov} = \int_{1980}^{t} c_{Inflate}(t') * \widehat{Y}(t') \, dt',$$

and where $c_{RI} = c_{Inflate}/cz$. We see that c_{RI} equals zero when $C_{Inflate}$ does and that I_{Gov} will stop growing and remain constant when $c_{Inflate}$ is reset to zero in 2060. Therefore, the investment equation that holds when the banks again create all the new money in the economy through credit is

$$\frac{d}{dt}I = \left[\Pi + c_1 * \Pi * \left(\frac{\Pi}{Y}\right) - c_2 * \Pi * \left(\frac{D}{v * Y}\right)\right] * \left[\frac{I}{I + I_{Gov}}\right].$$

Note that the bracket $I/(I + I_{Gov})$ multiplies the original right-hand side of the investment equation. This term is necessary because it represents the fact that people will not need to borrow all the money necessary for businesses to pay employees and for consumers to make purchases. The total amount of money, I_{Gov}, that the Government spent into the economy during their investment aid policy will remain and continue to circulate in the economy. Slowly, $I/(I + I_{Gov})$ approaches one as I grows large relative to I_{Gov} over time.

In addition, in 2060, we need to reset $c_{Deflate} = 0$ in our modified debt equation, Equation 5.1. We repeat it here:

$$\frac{dD}{dt} = I - \Pi - c_{Deflate} * \widehat{Y}.$$

This returns us to the original debt equation.

The original, hidden meaning of I in the output equation, Equation 1.5, turns out to be that I represents the total money flowing within the real economy. When we wrote down the output equation, we were considering the present day, in which essentially all the money within the economy is investment money. I, at least, thought of this as investment and did not realize until much later, when we were considering debt-free Government money, that the investment symbol I must really mean the total money which is flowing within the economy. Therefore, because the money that the Government has put into the real economy remains in the economy, the correct output equation when we release the economy, is our modified output equation, Equation 5.3,

$$\frac{dY}{dt} = \frac{I + I_{Gov}}{v} - \gamma * Y.$$

The values of $c_{Inflate}$ and $c_{Deflate}$ for the release scenario, in which banks again create the money in the economy, are shown in Figure 5.33 and Figure 5.34.

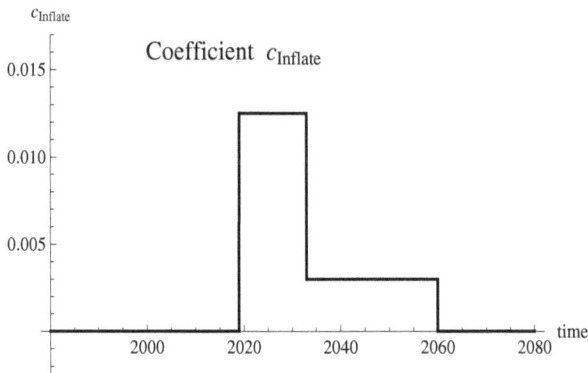

Figure 5.33: This figure shows the values of the coefficient $c_{Inflate}$ from 1980 to 2060 plus the release period from 2060 to 2080 for the scenario, in which the banks again create the money through credit.

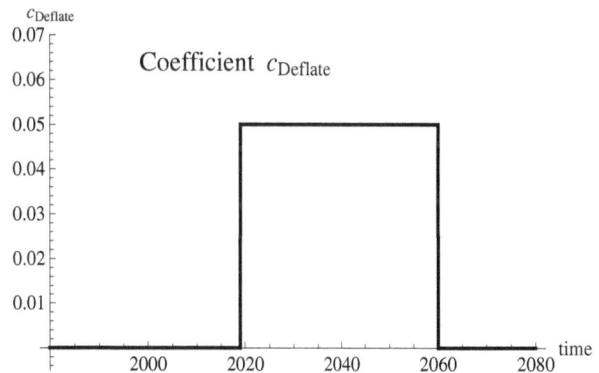

Figure 5.34: Here, we see the value of $c_{Deflate}$ from 1980 to 2060 plus the release period from 2060 to 2080 for both the bank and the mixed economy scenarios.

To release the economy into the mixed state in which the banks create a certain fraction of the money in the economy from credit while the Government creates the remaining fraction of the money in the economy by spending it debt-free into the economy, we need to remove the debt deflation term from the modified debt equation, $dD/dt = I - \Pi - c_{Deflate} * \widehat{Y}$. We do this by setting $c_{Deflate}$ equal to zero. We did this for the scenario in which the banks returned to creating all the money in the economy. This returns us to the original debt equation, $dD/dt = I - \Pi$. The value of $c_{Deflate}$ that we have used in our calculations was shown in Figure 5.34.

To terminate the investment aid policy and release the economy into a hybrid economy, we mathematically need to eliminate the term $-c_{RI} * \widehat{Y}$ from our modified investment equation. However, because $c_{Inflate}$ will be used to calculate the yearly Government debt-free spending, we can not set $c_{Inflate} = 0$ to do this. However, because $c_{RI} = c_{Inflate}/cz$, we can make c_{RI} equal to zero, if we make cz huge. We have made cz equal to 10^{32} in our release calculations. We show the value of $c_{Inflate}$ that we have used for the mixed economy in our calculations in Figure 5.35.

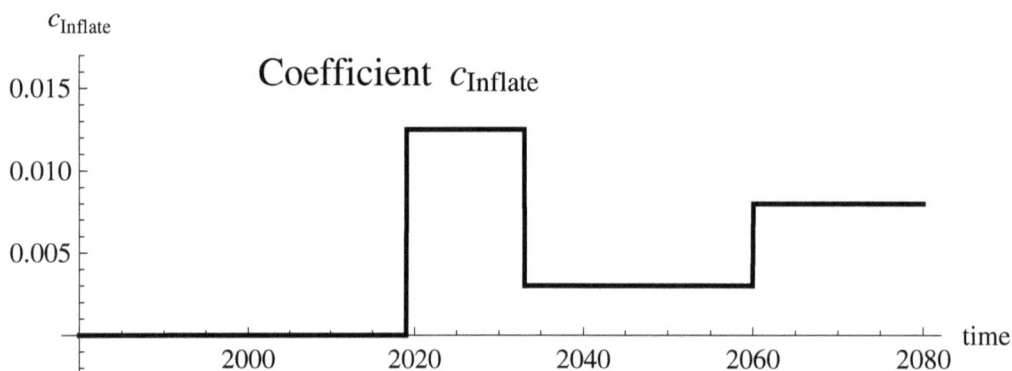

Figure 5.35: Here, we see the value of $c_{Inflate}$ from 1980 to 2060 plus the release period from 2060 to 2080 for the mixed economy scenario.

Next, we present the amount of debt-free money circulating throughout the economy as a function of time. Figure 5.36 shows this in the scenario in which the banks again create all new money in the economy, while we show this in the hybrid economy scenario in Figure 5.37.

Finally, in Figure 5.38, we show the amount of money added to the banking system as debt-free cash.

This debt-aid money remains in the banking system, acting as an asset that helps to stabilize the banking system against the derivative mess they have gotten themselves into. As long as the Government does not allow this money to "leak" into the real economy, it will not cause inflation. The total Government debt repayment aid was 132.75 trillion dollars.

We have described the setup of two different scenarios into which we could release the United States Economy after we have fixed its debt problem. In the following subsection, we will present how the renewed United States Economy might be expected to act under these two specific scenarios. We will examine and comment upon the calculated results as we present them.

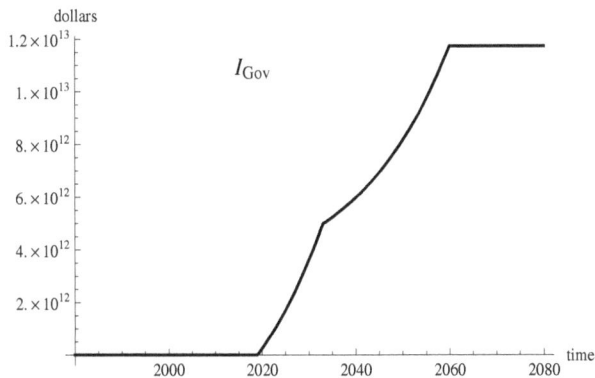

Figure 5.36: This figure shows the amount of money in the economy that was created debt-free by the Government in the banks create the money scenario.

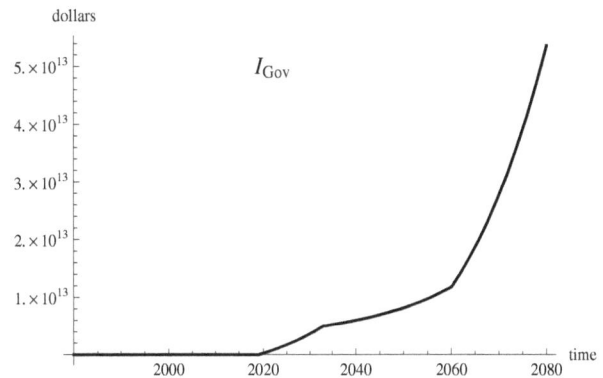

Figure 5.37: This figure shows the total amount of debt-free money spent into the economy by the Government in the mixed economy scenario.

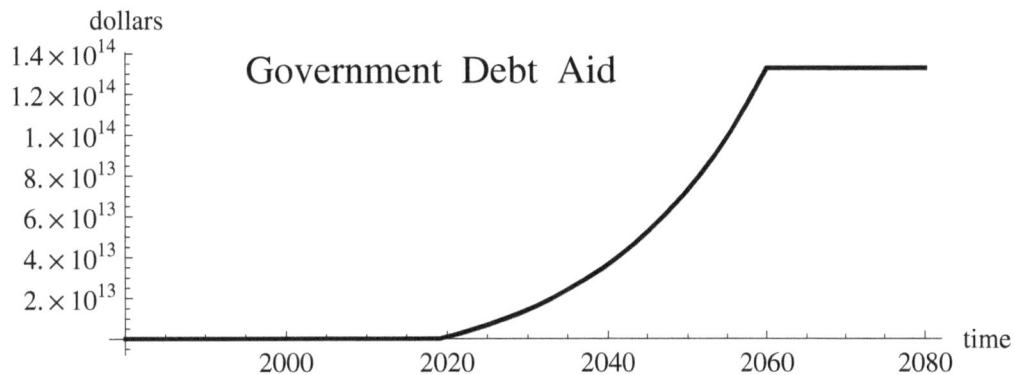

Figure 5.38: Here, we show the amount of Government debt aid that was contributed to debt repayment. The amount is the same in both scenarios: in the banks again become the sole creator of money within the economy, and in the mixed money creation economy.

5.4.2 The Renewed Economy

We will present our results as a series of comparison graphs. Each graph will plot the projected values for a particular economic quantity. Each graph will contain the no rate hike scenario in which the economy was left as it was at the end of 2016. The no rate hike scenario will be represented by the solid black line. Each figure will also contain the values for the scenario in which the bankers regain the position of being the sole creators of the new money that enters the economy. The bankers' money creation scenario will be represented by a thin dashed black line.

Also, the mixed money creation scenario values will be represented in each figure. The mixed money creation scenario will be represented by a thick, dashed gray line. The presence of the no rate hike scenario will act as a kind of standard that may allow us to make conclusions that could be difficult to see clearly if this scenario is not present.

We display the GDP versus time comparisons in Figure 5.39 and the Debt versus time comparisons in Figure 5.40. Then after a preliminary discussion of the GDP and economy debt comparisons, we present the economy debt-to-GDP comparisons in Figure 5.41 and the total investment-to-GDP comparisons in Figure 5.42.

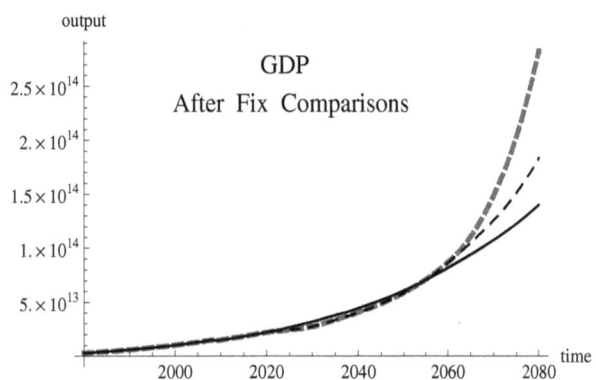

Figure 5.39: This figure shows that both release scenarios show a faster GDP rate of growth than the no rate hike scenario, with the mixed money creation scenario showing the fastest rate of GDP growth.

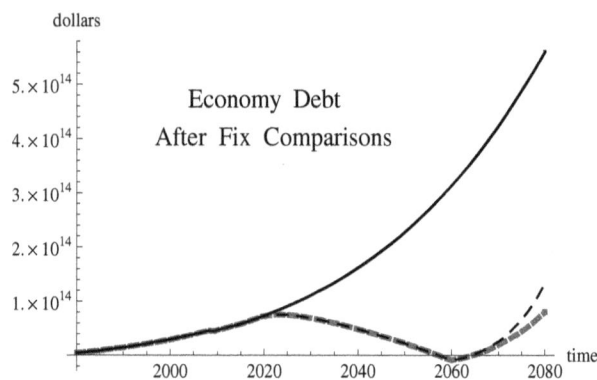

Figure 5.40: This figure shows that total economy debt twenty years after the release of the United States Economy is highest in the no rate hike scenario, and lowest in the mixed money creation scenario.

We see from Figure 5.39 that the rate of GDP growth in both the mixed economy scenario and the bankers' money creation scenario grows at a faster rate than the GDP in the no rate hike scenario. When we look at numbers in the mixed economy scenario, we find the GDP would have a growth rate of over 5.9 percent per year. This growth rate is not quite as good as when the US economy was running well, but it is still very good. Also, when one looks at the average growth rate in the mixed money creation economy over the ten-year period between 2070 and 2080, one calculates an average exponential growth rate of 6.42 percent per year.

However, when one looks at the numbers in the bankers' money creation release scenario, one sees that the growth rate in the output of the economy is noticeably less than it was when the United States Economy was running well. Between 1952 and 1973, the United States had an average rate of growth in output of 6.46 percent per year, while the average growth rate between 2060 and 2080 would only be 3.86 percent per year in the bankers' money creation scenario.

We do not have any experience with a hybrid economy. However, we have a great deal of experience with the bankers' money creation economy. When we released the economy, there was no net economy debt. In fact, the real economy had a slight net savings. This net savings compares to a significant economy debt when the economy was running well in the years between 1950 and 1973. This recognition makes the GDP growth rate of 3.86 percent per year seem even more anemic. This anemic growth rate may indicate that there is some unidentified problem that is harming our economy.

In Figure 5.41, one sees the debt-to-GDP ratio of both release scenarios is well below the

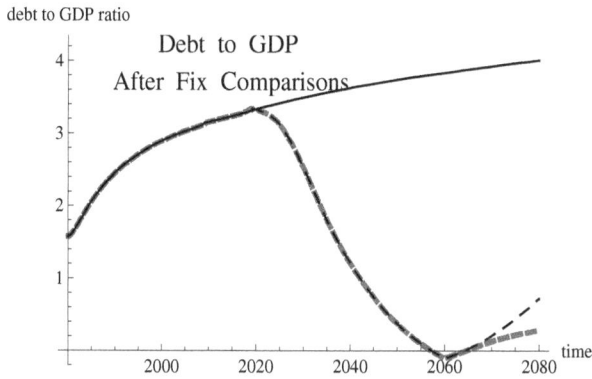

Figure 5.41: This figure shows that the economy debt-to-GDP ratio for all release scenarios is increasing, with the debt-to-GDP ratios of the no rate hike scenario and the hybrid scenario flattening out.

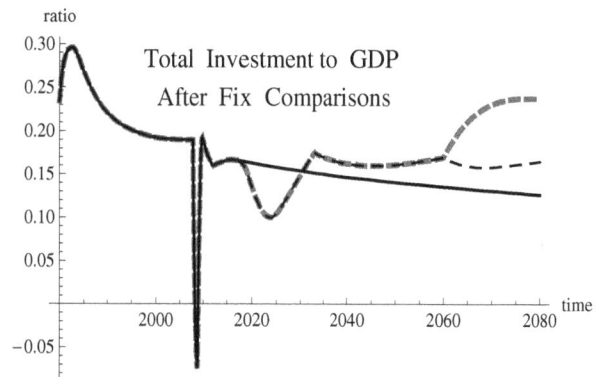

Figure 5.42: This figure shows the total investment-to-GDP ratios of the three scenarios, with the mixed money creation scenario having the highest ratio and the no rate hike scenario having the lowest.

1.2 to 1.45 that held between 1952 and 1973. This fact should, by itself, give the advantage to the release scenarios. However, when one looks at the total investment-to-GDP curves in Figure 5.42, one sees that in the bankers create the money scenario, the total investment-to-GDP ratio was just shy of 0.17. This ratio is noticeably below the usual 0.22 to 0.24 range for the investment-to-GDP ratio when the economy was doing well. This disparity would mean that investment needs to be about one third greater in the bankers create the money scenario if the economy were to run well.

Again we need to ask: "Why is investment in our economy so low?" in the bankers' money creation release scenario, and: "What problem in our present economy might be hindering the investment within our economy?" In order to help explore a possible hidden problem in our economy, we display a plot of the Federal Funds rate in Figure 5.43.

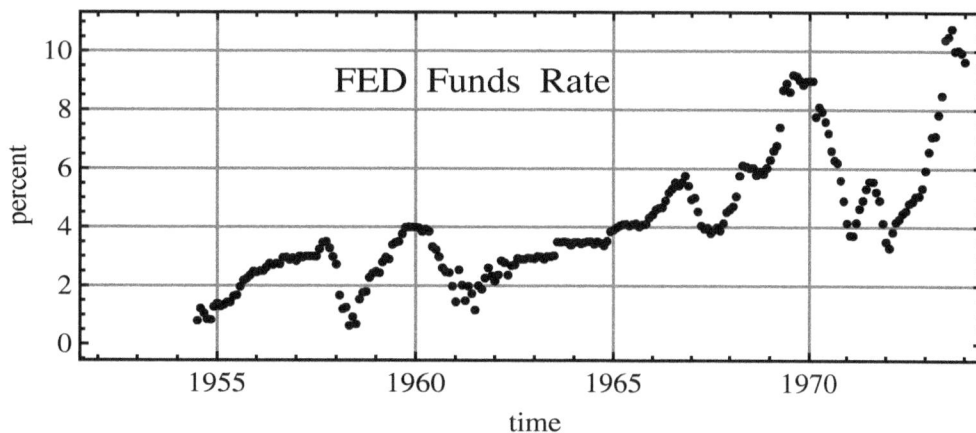

Figure 5.43: In this plot of the data retrieved from the Federal Reserve's St. Louis website, we see that the Federal Funds Rate does not top four percent until early 1965. After that, there is a general increase in the Federal Funds interest rates associated with the Vietnam War, the ramp-up of which began in 1965.

We can see in Figure 5.43, the Federal Funds Rate between 1953 and 1973 is, on average, well less than the value for the Federal Funds Rate in our banker and mixed economy release scenarios. The average Federal Funds Rate between 1954 and 1973 is about 3.8 percent, while in our banker and mixed money creation scenarios, the average interest rate was 7.4 percent, as shown in Figure 5.2 on page 55.

To investigate further, we consider the debt repayment term in the economy profit equation $-r * D$ with the average interest rate from our work being "pegged" roughly 1.75 percent above the Federal Funds Rate. This means that in the well-running economy of earlier times, we would expect the debt repayment term to be roughly given by $r * D = 0.0555 * (1.4 * GDP) = 0.0777 * GDP$,[3] while we would expect the debt repayment term in the bankers create the money scenario to be roughly $r * D = 0.0740 * (0.722 * GDP) = 0.0534 * GDP$ in 2080. That is, $r * D$ is a somewhat smaller fraction of the GDP in the release scenario that it was in earlier times when the economy was running well.

Note that the investment equation, Equation 1.1, is a function of economy profit and is essentially proportional to it times a slowly varying function of time. Here we have rewritten the investment equation to show the approximate proportionality that we just mentioned,

$$\frac{d}{dt}I = \Pi * \left[1 + c_1 * \left(\frac{\Pi}{Y}\right) - c_2 * \left(\frac{D}{v * Y}\right)\right]. \tag{5.6}$$

Thus, because $r * D$ is somewhat smaller in the release scenario, we would expect the investment to be noticeably stronger in the bankers again create the money scenario unless the wage term, $-w * L$, in the economy profit equation,

$$\Pi = Y - w * L - r * D,$$

represents a problem in the real economy.

We can apply similar reasoning to the results of the mixed economy scenario. In this case, the debt repayment term of the economy profit equation produces a value of $r * D = 0.0740 * (0.286 * GDP) = 0.0212 * GDP$ in 2080. As we calculated in a previous paragraph, this would only be about one quarter the size of the debt repayment term in an economy that is equivalent to the economy that was running well in earlier times. Therefore, we would expect that the macroeconomic economy profit to GDP ratio would be noticeably larger in the mixed money creation economy than in the well-running economy of the past, unless the wage term in the mixed economy, $-w * L$, is associated with a problem in the economy. This result would also extend to investment. The investment equation makes clear that the bigger the profit and the smaller the debt, the faster investment increases.

We do not have any independent macroeconomic economy profit-to-GDP ratio data. However, we do have investment-to-GDP data. Unfortunately, the Quandl investment-to-GDP data that we have been using only extends down to 1980. The World Bank's investment-to-GDP data extends down to 1960. Moreover, the values of the investment-to-GDP ratio

---

[3]Appropriate debt levels can be approximated from Figure 5.31 on page 71 and Figure 5.41 on page 79.

from 1980 to 2015 for the World Bank data is similar to the Quandl data. It only differs from the Quandl data average by 0.6 percent, unlike the Federal Reserve average that differs by some 18.1 percent.

Using the World Bank data as a stand-in for the Quandl data, we calculate the average investment-to-GDP ratio over the period from 1960 to 1973 to be 0.230. This ratio compares to the total investment-to-GDP ratio in the mixed money creation economy of 0.237 in 2080. While the ratio is a bit higher than the average for the earlier well-running economy, it is nowhere near as high as might be expected. The right-hand side of the investment equation is equal to the economy profit times, a term that increases as the debt-to-GDP ratio decreases, and the profit increases. Because of the greatly reduced debt-to-GDP ratio (1.4 to 0.29), the economy profit-to-GDP ratio would be expected to increase noticeably over the earlier time when the economy was running well unless the wage term in the profit equation has become pernicious over time.

Furthermore, the very substantial decrease in the debt-to-GDP ratio in the subtracted Banker's Term, $-(c_2/v)*(D/Y)$, in the factored investment equation, Equation 5.6, would be expected to cause an increase in investment. The expected increase in profit and the known decrease in debt-to-GDP ratio, taken together, would lead us to believe that a very noticeable increase in investment should have been present in the mixed money creation economy unless there is a problem within the economy associated with the wage part of the profit equation, $-w*L$.

We will return to this issue when we present the figures that depict the wage rate and the employment rate as functions of time. However, first, we will present the total investment comparisons in Figure 5.44, and the fraction of banker created money in circulation in the various scenarios in Figure 5.45.

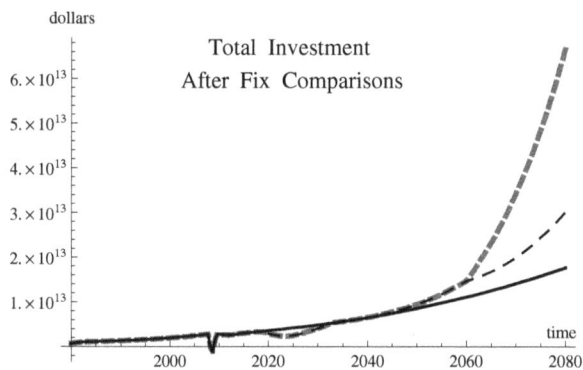

Figure 5.44: This graph shows the total investment within the United States Economy in the no rate hike scenario and in the two release scenarios which were presented.

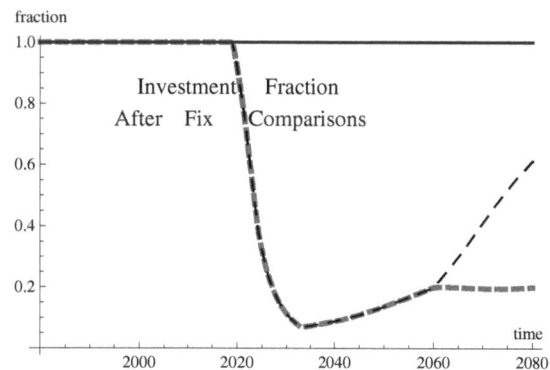

Figure 5.45: This figure displays the fraction of money in circulation within the United States Economy, which was created by the banks, in the no rate hike scenario, and in the two release scenarios.

In Figure 5.44, we see that total investment in both release scenarios is significantly more than the investment would be in the no rate hike scenario. We see that the release into a scenario in which the banks again create the money within the economy has resulted in the investment within the United States in 2080 being nearly twice what the investment would be under the no rate hike scenario. We also see that investment in the mixed money creation scenario is more than two times the investment that would be created in the release scenario in which the banks create all the new money in the economy. This seems to be an astounding difference. When we look at Figure 5.39, this vast difference in investment appears to be reflected, to a large extent, by the output of the economy. What about wages?

In Figure 5.45, we see that the banks, in the banks, again, create all the new money in the economy scenario, are rapidly increasing their fraction of the money within the economy. The debt-to-GDP ratio in 2080 would only be equal to about half of the suggested regulation upper limit of 1.4. In the release scenario, there would be a chance of a significant shock to the economy if the banks were to crash right into the 1.4 limit, and then stop increasing the debt-to-GDP ratio. So, another suggested regulation that they, the banks, might be required to undergo is that they keep the debt-to-GDP ratio under the 1.4 limit in such a way that the GDP growth over any year is greater than or equal to zero, or to some other value that keeps the shock on the economy from being too harsh. If they fail, then they pay a fine equal to some stated fraction of their failure. However, a better solution would be to release the fixed economy closer to a debt-to-GDP ratio of 1.4 than it was in our sample scenario.

In Figure 5.45, we also see that the fraction of the investment money created by banks in the mixed economy stays relatively constant. In our particular scenario, it stays roughly at twenty percent. However, we could have made it stay at whatever level we wanted to keep it at. We could have released the economy earlier, but our purpose was to show that debt could be brought all the way down to zero. No attempt was made to find some optimal ideal fixed and released state. Instead, we are attempting to show the facets of fixing an economy clearly, in separate pieces. Once people know that it can be done and in general, how it is done, people can design a scenario to fit their idea of policy priorities given our situation.

Finally, we come to the figures displaying the wage rate and the employment rate. In past discussions, we have reasoned that these macroeconomic variables may be associated with a possible problem within our economy. We present the wage rate in Figure 5.46 and the employment rate in Figure 5.47.

We see, in Figure 5.46, in both the banks create all the new money scenario and the mixed money creation scenario, that the average wage rate does not pull away from the reference no rate hike scenario. In fact, if we look closely, both release scenarios turn ever so slightly toward the no rate hike scenario when those economies are released in 2060. This truly is an astounding result given that the GDP output of the economy and the total investment in the economy accelerated away from the GDP and the total investment in the reference economy. This result shows that there genuinely is something amiss in our economy if the macroeconomic average wage rate is left behind as the rest of the economy recovers.

In Figure 5.47, we see by 2080, twenty years after the economies were released, the macroeconomic employment rate would be well above one hundred percent in both the hybrid economy and the banks again create the money economy. In the mixed money creation

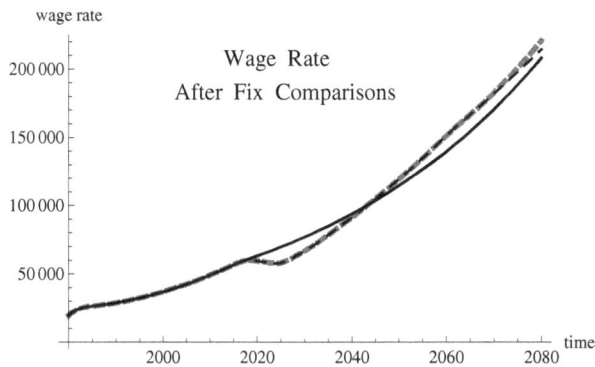

Figure 5.46: Here, we see that the average wage rates of the release scenarios have not accelerated away from the average wage rate of the reference, no rate hike scenario.

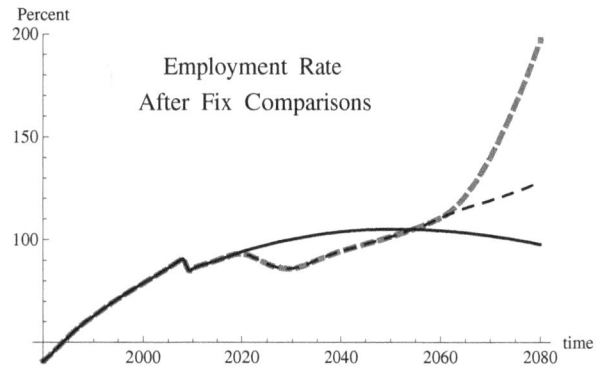

Figure 5.47: Here, we see the employment rates of both release scenarios reach well above one hundred percent, while the reference, no rate hike, scenario employment rate has started to slowly crash.

economy, the macroeconomic employment rate would be higher than 197 percent, while in the banks create the money scenario, the employment rate would be higher than 128 percent.

These high macroeconomic employment rates are not with respect to the present population of the United States but are with respect to the total population of the United States that would naturally come to exist because of population growth. There is no conceivable way that the macroeconomic employment rate is going to double in just sixty years and end up being twice the population that the United States would be projected to have in 2080. Nevertheless, these employment rates would have to be true if my interpretation of the employment level results given by our macroeconomic equations is correct. *However, my interpretation of the employment level has been in error all this time!* See footnote 2, on page 69.

When we were discussing the investment-to-GDP ratio, shown in Figure 5.42, we concluded that the economy profit-to-GDP ratio, in both release scenarios, should be higher than it was when the economy was running well in the past. Furthermore, we concluded that if it was not, then the average wage rate, employment level term, $-w * L$, in the economy profit equation must be associated with a problem in the economy. Accordingly, we present the economy profit-to-GDP graph in Figure 5.48 and the graph displaying $w * L$ in Figure 5.49.

After the debt problem in the economy was fixed, we see from Figure 5.48 that not only is the economy profit-to-GDP ratio not higher than the economy profit-to-GDP ratio when the economy was running well, but it is below the average for the times when the economy was doing well. In fact, in the bankers' money creation scenario, the economy profit-to-GDP ratio curve falls below that of the no rate hike scenario during the release period. Moreover, the mixed economy scenario's economy profit-to-GDP ratio is just barely above the weak no rate hike scenario's economy profit-to-GDP ratio. Therefore, we must conclude that there is still something wrong with the United States Economy that fixing the debt problem did not cure at all.

When we examine Figure 5.49, we see that the problem term, $w * L$, of the economy profit equation, is very large. When we compare its value in 2080 for each curve with the

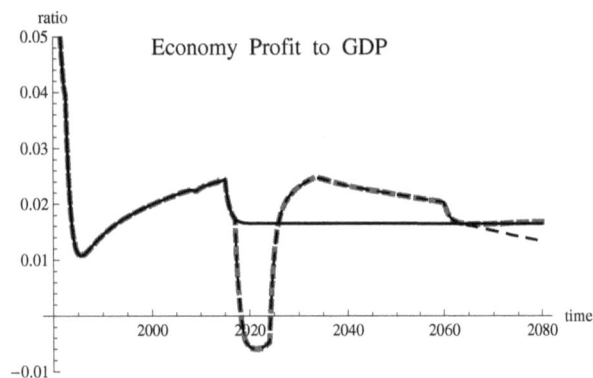

Figure 5.48: In this plot, we see that the economy profit-to-GDP graphs for the no rate hike scenario and the two, after the economy is fixed, money creation scenarios.

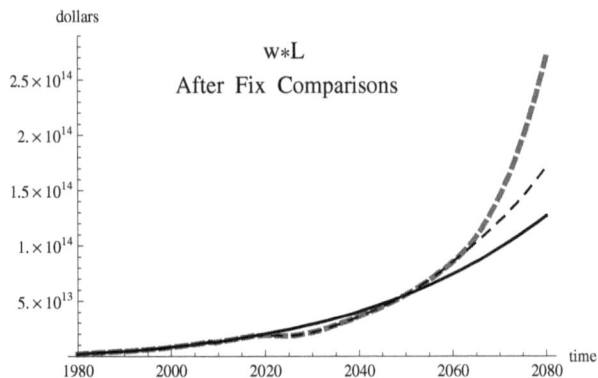

Figure 5.49: Here, we display the average wage rate times the employment level term that appears in the economy profit equation, discussed on page 80, for our after the fix comparisons.

corresponding GDP value in the GDP curves of Figure 5.39, we see that $w * L$ values are very close to the GDP values themselves. Thus, for some reason within the economy, the $w * L$ term is too large.

Consequently, we are forced to conclude that there is something fundamental in the working of the United States Economy, which has come into existence and is causing this problem. That is, there is something fundamental that is causing a problem with the product of the average wage rate times the macroeconomic employment level becoming too large. Furthermore, we know that this fundamental change is present in the United States Economy today. We know this because we have not input any change into the economy. We have reset the economy by getting rid of the debt, but in the banks create the money release scenario, we have not changed the equations or their coefficients. Thus, the fundamentals of the economy today have been transported into the future. This means that the fundamental changes that affected the economy in our projections are with us today.

Chapter 6

A Hidden Macroeconomic Problem

In an earlier discussion on page 69, we noted that Bivens and Mishel stated the fact that wages had started to lose contact with productivity increases in about 1973, with the divergence getting wider and wider with time. Moreover, their analysis found that the higher the percentile the worker's wage, the less it lost contact with productivity increases. In fact, the wages of the top one percentile of workers had the growth of their salaries significantly outpace the rate of productivity growth (Bivens and Mishel, 2015).

This divergence of the wage rate between people in the economy would not in itself result in a change in the average wage rate because, if nothing else were to change, then one would just have the same number of workers and the same total wage paid. Thus, producing the same average. One would have to change more than the distribution of wage rates in order to change the average wage rate.

We have really been watching the deterioration in the growth of the average wage rate of the ordinary worker occur for a long time, without recognizing it for what it is macroeconomically. When workers pay taxes so that others can perform essential services, or so that others can be paid for their past contributions to our society, it really results in a reduction in the wages workers receive. A similar result occurs when companies pay taxes in that the tax monies go to pay others. In addition, taxes reduce the company's profit, and this directly affects the company's ability to compensate its workers, decreasing the total wages that will be paid. This we have recognized before. It also effectively increases the number of people being paid for work that directly creates the GDP output, increasing the macroeconomic employment rate.

However, this is not all that we have seen. We have seen a slow increase in the numbers of migrant workers, both documented and undocumented. The need for these workers is justified by employers and their supporters, stating that: "We can not get Americans to do the work." But the sentence is never completed. The sentence really is: "We can not get Americans to do the work at the price we want to pay." Why do employers want these low-wage workers? The answer is simple. So they, the employer, can make more money.

Large corporations often offshore their work to low-wage workers in other countries. The auto companies employ some low-wage workers by building automobile factories just over the border in Canada and Mexico, from which they ship the cars that they manufacture there directly back to the United States. Apple makes its expensive iPhones in low-wage China. Other companies out-source their customer service telephone calls to workers overseas. One might call for help with their Internet connection, and the person is connected with someone in India. However, it is not just large corporations that employ low-wage foreign workers. It is well known that migrants are used to pick crops. They are also employed by small to very small construction companies to erect houses, to renovate buildings, and to paint houses. Landscape company business owners sometimes use migrants in their jobs. H1B visas are sometimes used to hire low-wage immigrants, who will be trained by people that will be let go after they train their replacements. On an even smaller scale, H1B visas are used to hire foreigners who speak English to work on Cape Cod in the summer at or just above minimum wage. They are often provided with low-priced accommodations that are sometimes created by dividing rooms up by hanging sheets between beds. When I was young, these types of jobs provided highly-prized jobs as summer work for young people.

These people, too, are macroeconomic United States workers. We can easily see from this that the number of macroeconomic workers is not limited as one would expect by the population of the United States. Now we can begin to see how the profit equation's wage term, $-w * L$ may have become a problem in which the ordinary worker's average wage is too low, yet the average wage is too high, while the number of ordinary workers appears too high. The average wage is high because, as Bivens and Mishel discovered, the economic elites are taking more and more of the economy profit for themselves. The results from our equations have shown that this has become a real problem in the United States Economy.

6.1 An Opinion: A Fix to the Employment Level–Wage Rate Problem

If there truly is an employment level and wage rate problem, why did it not develop earlier, and why has it been getting worse? What was it about the nature of the United States Economy that inhibited the problem in the past? And, what has come to allow the continued and increasing nature of the problem, now?

To answer these questions, we first need to recognize that if there is a macroeconomic problem associated with the hiring of low-wage workers, the problem stems from employers seeking to make more money for themselves through this hiring practice. So the answer to the above questions might be resolved simply by asking and answering the question: In the past, what inhibited employers from making much more money?

When I was a young boy in the early 1950s, a neighbor two doors down was the Vice-President of New England AT&T. AT&T at the time was the supplier of telephone service for the whole Country. There was no Verizon, Sprint, and Western Bell, et cetera. So this was quite an elite position. My father, at the time, was making about 2500 dollars per year.

From what my parents said, our neighbor was making about 25,000 dollars. We played with and were friends with his kids. There was a spirit of togetherness among people at the time—that spirit of togetherness is nowhere near as great today. In part, I am sure this was due to the fact that we all pulled together during the War. But partly, I am sure this was true because we were all in the same economic boat.

About sixty-six percent of the people earned more than my father, and only about half of one percent of the people earned more than our neighbor (U.S. Department of Commerce and Bureau of Census, 1954). A very wide percentile difference between our families, yet he earned only about ten times what we did. While their after-tax income dropped to only about five times what our family's income was after taxes (Chamberlain, 2013).

In 1952, the median family income in the United States was about 3900 dollars. If somebody earned thirty times the median income back then, they would have reached a marginal tax bracket of ninety percent or better. Back in 1952, the marginal tax brackets were close together, and the tax rates in those brackets built up to a top tax bracket of a little over ninety percent. This tax structure made it all but impossible to take home a huge amount of money and therefore was probably the primary reason that incomes back then did not have the vast spread that they do today.

The ninety percent marginal tax brackets and the closeness of the brackets explain the lack of hiring to lower wages back in the 1950s. However, does the history of the income tax qualitatively fit the history of the divergence of incomes in the United States?

6.1.1 Income Inequality and Tax Structure Evolution

In 1963, before he was assassinated, President Kennedy got Congress to pass a bill reducing taxes. It reduced the top marginal tax rate to seventy-seven percent.

When one looks at the marginal tax brackets in 1963 before the tax took effect, one sees that the top rate in 1963 was ninety-one percent. However, one also sees that the top rate also kicked in at the same monetary value that it did in 1952 (Chamberlain, 2013)! Moreover, the median family income in 1963 had risen to 6249 dollars (U.S. Department of Commerce and Bureau of Census, 1966). This means the wages of the people at the bottom were getting closer to the wages that would trigger higher tax rates. This could mean there was a slight lessening in the divergence of the after-tax incomes among people during this time, though I have never seen a discussion on this possibility.

A year later, the top marginal tax rate for 1965 was lowered to seventy percent. Also, however, the income at which the highest marginal tax rate would kick in was cut by about a factor of two.

When we check the results of these changes in 1968, after having given the changes several years to adjust, we find: the 34th percentile income is about 5500 dollars, the 99.6th percentile income is slightly less than 50,000 dollars, and the median income is 7743 dollars, while the mean income is 8760 dollars (U.S. Department of Commerce and Bureau of Census, 1969). My father's 34th percentile income and my neighbor's 99.6th percentile income in 1952 had both almost exactly doubled in value by 1968, indicating that the spread in incomes stayed relatively constant over those sixteen years. We also see that the median income, too, had almost precisely doubled, indicating that the whole distribution of incomes had moved upward as a group as if everyone were in the same economic boat.

However, there has been one very limited area where this is not quite true. The incomes and the after-tax incomes of the very, very high percentile incomes had likely increased to a very slight extent relative to those at lower levels. The reason for this is because the seventy percent marginal tax bracket had more than doubled before the seventy percent rate kicked in. Moreover, for those who previously had part of their income taxed at the ninety percent rate, they then, would no longer have had any of their income taxed at this rate, so they would have kept more of the high income and would thus have had a slightly increased incentive to raise their incomes.

As we noted earlier, Bivens and Mishel stated that 1973 was the last year that the wage rate growth kept pace with the growth in productivity. In 1973, the tax brackets were essentially what they were in 1968. We found in 1968 that the distribution of incomes had not diverged from their earlier relations. If we try to compare my father's approximate income percentile with our neighbor's income percentile in 1973, we find that the yearly Census Bureau publications no longer go to a high enough income in order to be able to find a 99.6th percentile to compare with a 34th percentile.

From what we observed before, we expect that the distributions will remain relatively the same, except possibly at the very highest end of the distributions. The people at the top often have the ability to raise their own salaries and because they fall into somewhat lower brackets than they did when the ninety percent top brackets held sway, and because the spread in the tax brackets has increased, we may find that the very top incomes have been raised to skew the distribution of incomes slightly to the upside.

While we are not able to directly compare the very highest income levels, we can do so indirectly. We find that the United States Census Bureau provides us with the fact that the mean income in the United States for 1973 was 12,157 dollars, and the median income was 10,512 dollars. This data means that there was a fractional discrepancy between the mean and the median of 0.156, while in 1968 the fractional discrepancy was 0.131.[1] This change in the fractional discrepancy indicates that there had been a very slight skewing of the income distribution in favor of the very highest incomes relative to the bulk of incomes that moved more or less together.

The United States Census Bureau put out a publication that contains the mean quintile incomes along with the mean of the top five percent of incomes for the years from 1967 to 2016, which can be found at

```
https://www.census.gov/data/tables/time-series/demo/
    income-poverty/historical-income-households.html.
```

This data was used to calculate the ratio of the mean income of the top five percent of

---

[1]The fractional discrepancy between two values, V and V_0, is calculated as $(V - V_0)/V_0$.

incomes to the mean income of the second quintile of incomes, for every year from 1967 to 2016. After doing this, the fractional discrepancy between these ratios and the ratio for 1967 was found. The change in the calculated fractional discrepancy data is plotted in Figure 6.1 along with a plot of the top income tax bracket for the mean income of the top five percent of incomes as a function of time (Chamberlain, 2013). The gray line connecting the points represents the change in fractional discrepancy relative to 1967, while the black line represents the maximum tax bracket on the income value for the mean of the top five percent of incomes as a function of time.

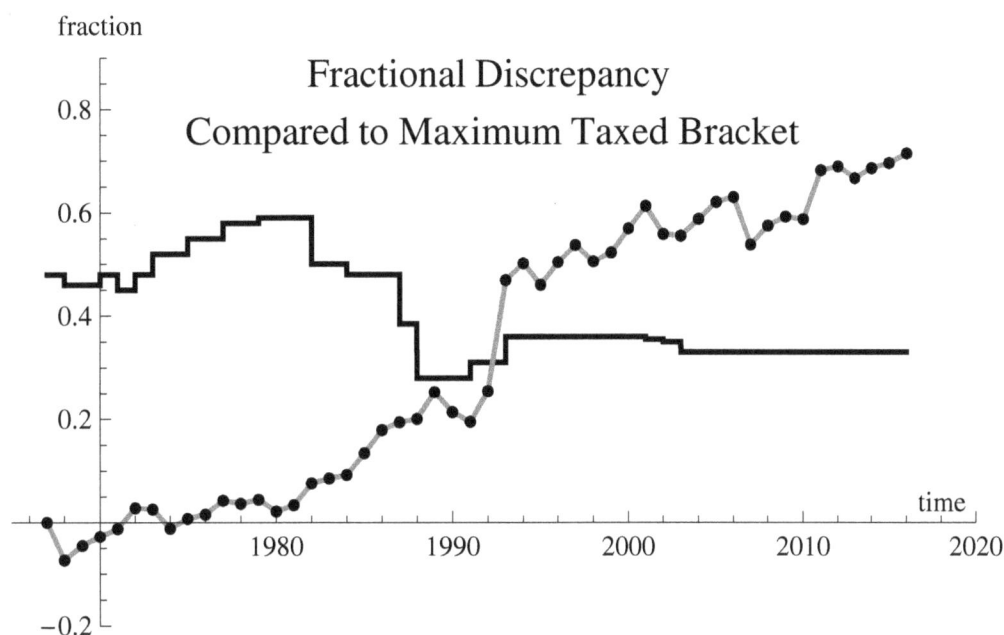

Figure 6.1: The solid black line indicates that the trend of the maximum tax bracket for the mean income of the top five percent of incomes declined over time, while during the same time period the incomes of these very high wage earners had increased by some seventy percent in a real sense over the income gains of more moderate wage earners.

The maximum tax rate was lowered to 77 percent under President Kennedy in 1963 and took effect in 1964. It was further reduced to 70 percent the following year. This maximum tax rate, which held at 70 percent through 1981, was changed to fifty percent under President Reagan. We can see from Figure 6.1 that the mean income of the top five percent of wage earners was not enough to trigger the top bracket at any time between 1964 and 1981. However, we can see that the maximum rate at which they were taxed slowly increased during this period. Note that this period between 1964 and 1981 corresponds with the slowest rate of growth in the discrepancy between the incomes of the high wage earners, at the mean income of the top five percent of wage earners, and the lower wage earners, at the mean income of the second quintile of wage earners.

Furthermore, note that during the period from 1982 to the present, these higher wage earners have been taxed at a markedly lower maximum marginal tax rate, while at the same time these higher wage earners' incomes have increased much more rapidly relative to the rate of growth in the incomes of the lower wage earners.

When the maximum tax rate dropped to fifty percent in 1982, the maximum tax bracket of these higher wage workers dropped from the previous year's fifty-nine percent to the new maximum tax rate of fifty percent. Two years later, their wages dropped out of the maximum tax rate into a slightly lower rate of forty-eight percent. After three more years, the maximum rate dropped again, this time to 38.5 percent. This was followed by a further drop to twenty-eight percent for three years, which was followed by a rise in the maximum tax rate to thirty-one percent. Each time, the maximum rate paid by these higher-income earners was the new maximum rate. This meant that people who earned even higher incomes paid the same maximum tax rate.

In 1993, the tax bracket situation changed slightly; these higher wage earners fell into the penultimate tax bracket, which was typically two to four percentage points lower than the maximum tax bracket. The top tax bracket for these higher wage earners moved up to 36 percent in 1993, while the top marginal tax bracket moved up to 39.6 percent. These low maximum tax rates for very high wage earners encouraged speculation.

Finally, with the repeal of Glass-Steagall in 1999, financial institutions were all but unconstrained. The uncorking of personal greed, which the lowering of the top income tax brackets allowed, resulted in the housing bubble and financial instruments, such as derivatives, that were the direct cause of the crisis of 2008–9. The highest income tax bracket in 2008 was just thirty-five percent.

In this regard, we might take note that the top income tax rate in 1918 after World War I was seventy-seven percent. It was reduced the following year to seventy-three percent. Then, in 1922, it went to fifty-eight percent, followed by a drop to forty-six percent in 1924. Finally, in 1925, the top marginal income tax rate dropped to twenty-five percent. Rampant speculation arose and had four years to grow and ripen before the stock market bubble that was created burst and took down the banking system, causing the crash of the economy and subsequent great depression.[2]

We see from all this that relatively low maximum tax brackets releases a constraint on greed and speculation, which creates an economy that becomes one made for personal gain of a few, and not one that tries to benefit all. Contrariwise, high maximum tax brackets appear to be influential in hindering the outbreak of rampant speculation. In addition, high maximum tax brackets help to foster an economy in which all of the people are in the same economic boat. This is influential toward creating an economy in which the people pull together for the benefit of all. That is, when most people find themselves thrown into a common situation, they seem to know, instinctively, that it is in their own best interest to work together.

---

[2]We should probably note here that the Government can stop the crash of the real economy if the financial system starts to crash. The Government can do this if they are *prepared* to step in with cash, replacing, dollar for dollar, the money in the real economy as it dries up from the crash of the financial system. It matters not who creates the money or how, as long as the money is there. If the money is there, the economy will run.

6.2 A Solution

We have seen that a low top marginal tax rate tends to encourage greed in the top income earners. Because these top income earners are often involved in setting company policy and salaries, greed may cause them to try to substitute low-wage workers for higher wage workers. If and when a way to do so becomes open to them, they may jump at the chance because they perceive that lowering the wages paid for their company's workers will allow them to make more money without effecting the company's profit. They do not see the whole macroeconomic picture. They are unlikely to consider that this substitution of a low-wage worker for a higher wage worker is going to cost them anything. And, even if such a thought were to cross their mind, they would think the effect would amount to peanuts. They will not consider that they and everyone else will be paying for this person who has dropped out of the workforce. Nor will they consider that anything much will result when others do precisely the same thing as they have done. They may think the Government will take care of it. However, the Government can only take care of it by draining more and more money out of the real economy. Thus, this whole process raises the macroeconomic employment rate—the new low-wage worker and the person who has been dropped from the workforce, while at the same time lowering the average wage paid to the ordinary macroeconomic worker. Furthermore, the employers, who do this, have no idea what this increased macroeconomic employment level and reduced macroeconomic average wage does to the ability of the economy to run properly.

To solve this macroeconomic problem, which is a global system problem, one should find a global solution, not a micro or meso solution. Micro solutions to a global problem almost always result in a system that has unseen holes in the fix. This happens in physics, and I am sure it happens in economics, too. Fortunately, high enough tax rates can constrain pathological greed within the economy. However, to be hole-proof, there must be no loopholes.

The United States Constitution allows the Federal Government just two direct taxes, a uniform tax based on the census (i.e., on the population) or a uniform tax based on enumeration and a tax on income, all income, from whatever the source. The government of the United States does not have the Constitutional power to tax based on how someone earns their income, on how somebody spends their money, on what group a person may belong to, nor on what lifestyle one may choose. We are all to be equal under the law. Not that we follow the Constitution, but if we did, we could create a leakproof fix to the problem of greed and speculation within the economy.

The principal real problem for taxation for the present wage structure of the United States is how to handle the case of low-wage workers with children. Presently, the lowest wage workers do not make enough money to provide for their children, even if they pay no tax.

Utilizing the present taxing scheme and the Constitution, the Government can make a uniform per capita tax, which is negative. That is, each person "pays" a negative tax that provides each person with say, three thousand dollars per year. The income tax would then be in the form of graduated tax brackets just as is presently done. For example, let us say, a low-wage worker who makes twenty thousand dollars per year has an income tax that takes one thousand dollars. Then, under the example, the person would receive back three thousand dollars for each person in the family. Accordingly, a single person would have a net income of twenty-two thousand dollars for the year minus the 1240 dollar Social Security tax, while a person supporting a family of four would have a net income of thirty-one thousand dollars per year minus the 1240 dollar Social Security tax.

The first power granted to Congress in Article I, Section 8, of the United States Constitution is to be able to spend the monies of the United States to provide for the general welfare, so Congress has the power to spend for food stamps for low-wage people and to send them supplemental income, if they so choose. However, it is a sad state of affairs that the government of the United States, which was instituted to secure the rights of the people, has allowed economic predators to so distort our economy such that a person who works hard all year can not support his or her family. Such a government has not done its job. We will see that there is an easy global fix to the problem.

We would like to set up the outline of an income tax structure that solves the two fundamental macroeconomic problems that we have identified, namely the average wage rate, employment level problem, and the livable low-wage problem. If we consider the quantity, *GDP per capita*, we might consider it the country's output per person. If we consider it as some kind of average income, we might look at how this income value has been represented in the United States' distribution of incomes and in the income tax rates.

In the 1950s and early 1960s, when there was a top marginal tax rate of at least ninety percent, how did the GDP per capita, person fare? In 1952, the GDP per capita was $2333.86, which is found using a GDP equal to 347.7 billion dollars and a population equal to 157.55 million people. A person earning such a wage would have been somewhere *between the twenty-third and twenty-fourth percentile* of wage earners (U.S. Department of Commerce and Bureau of Census, 1954). Such a person would have paid a top marginal tax rate of either 23.4 or 24.6 percent, depending upon which family-related group he or she fell into (Chamberlain, 2013).

In 1962, the GDP per capita wage earner would have earned $3243.81 and fallen into *the 22nd percentile* of wage earners (U.S. Department of Commerce and Bureau of Census, 1963) and paid a highest marginal tax rate of 20, 21, or 22 percent, depending upon what family group he or she happened to fall into (Chamberlain, 2013).

People were able to live at the GDP per capita wage and even half of this wage back in the 1950s and early 1960s. Note also that the lot of the lower-wage worker actually improved very slightly relative to the higher-wage workers because the percentile standing of the mythical GDP-per-capita worker sank from about the 23.5 percentile to the 22nd percentile.

From 1965 through 1981, the top marginal tax rate was seventy percent, what if anything did this change in the tax structure do to the position of the GDP per capita income within the household income distribution? What if anything did this change in the tax structure do to the top marginal income tax bracket of a person who happened to earn an income equal to the GDP per capita?

In 1968, the GDP per capita was $4695.83, and a person earning an amount equal to this would have fallen into about the twenty-eight and a half percentile of wage earners (U.S. Department of Commerce and Bureau of Census, 1984). Such a person would have paid a top marginal tax rate of 19, 20, or 22 percent depending upon which family group the person fell into (Chamberlain, 2013). In 1978, a GDP per capita wage earner would have earned $10,587.65, fallen into the thirty-fifth percentile of wage earners, and paid a top marginal tax rate of 19, 23, 25, or 28 percent depending upon which family group the person would have belonged to (Chamberlain, 2013). We see that during this period, there has been a steady decline in the low-wage earner's share in the output of the economy. This decline has been allowed to occur because of structural changes in the income tax. We should also note that the mythical GDP per capita wage earner would have been paying taxes throughout at approximately the same top marginal tax rate.

There was a lull in the percentile climb of the GDP per capita during the period of the 1980s and early 1990s. The highest marginal tax bracket for the GDP per capita wage earner during this period was found to have various values. However, these values resided within the same band of tax rates as in the previous period. Then, in the mid-1990s, the GDP per capita income value started to climb higher into the household income percentile distribution. In 1993 the GDP per capita income value was at about 35.5 percentile. In 1998, it was at the 41.9 percentile, followed by 43.9 percentile in 2001 and the 49.5 percentile in 2013. However, during the period between 1987 and 2000, the highest marginal tax rate was either 15 or 28 percent depending on the family group that the taxpayer fell into, while between 2003 and 2013, it was either 15 percent or 25 percent.

One of the reasons for running through all these figures was to show that the GDP per capita income can be used as a reference point in setting up an income tax schedule. What one would like is to make a tax structure that can be understood and thus used as an economic tool by the Government rather than as a political tool to garner votes. We know from what we have discussed that we could set the tax rate for the GDP per capita income at twenty or twenty-two percent, and it would not cause hardship.

The other reason we went through all these numbers is to show that it will allow the Government to set a minimum wage that is a livable wage. We know from the *Prelude* that back in the 1950s, people were able to raise a family of four when one wage earner was earning an income of about 65 to 70 percent of the GDP per capita. It was not in any way an extravagant existence, but it was independent and doable. We also know that low-wage earners earning this amount of money did not damage the economy because that wage was too high.

Would a worker today earning an income of sixty-six percent of the GDP per capita be able to support a family of four? The Bureau of Economic Analysis states that the GDP for

2017 was 19.387 trillion dollars. The webpage

`www.multpl.com/united-states-population/table`

gives the value for the United States population on July 1, 2017, as 325,719,178. Considering a work year to be fifty, forty-hour work weeks, this means that a livable wage equal to sixty-six percent of the GDP per capita would be $39,283.59 per year or $19.64 per hour. A frugal family of four probably could have lived on this wage in 2018. This livable wage would have been more than sufficient for a single person. However, a young family of eight, with one income earner making this livable wage, would probably have had to find another source of income.

We have seen in the *Prelude* that setting the minimum wage equal to one half the GDP per capita would be a livable wage for a single person. The *Prelude* tells us that a family of four needs at least another sixteen percent of the GDP per capita in order to have a livable wage. So if, in addition, to this single person minimum wage, the Government created a negative capitation tax that is about five percent of the GDP per capita, then all family sizes would have a livable income. This would secure the right of the people to a livable income. Moreover, it treats everybody exactly the same under the law as required by the Constitution.

So in the discussion that follows, we will be assuming that the livable wage consists of a minimum wage of one half the GDP per capita plus a negative per capita tax equal to five percent of the GDP per capita. This would put the minimum wage in 2018 equal to $29,760.30 per year or $14.88 per hour. While the negative per capita tax would provide each person with $2980 when rounded up to the nearest ten dollars.

Before we continue to the income tax itself, we should discuss two other taxes because they bear on how one should implement an income tax. First, everyone should pay the Social Security tax on all their income. In earlier times, people often worked on a family farm or worked together at a family business. Elders had a status earned through many years of contribution, and they were valued for their knowledge or advice. They did not have to worry about their old age. Now there is rarely a lifetime extended family. Today, the whole society is a person's extended family. A retired person has often contributed to society for their whole life. Today, they rarely have a respected status as an elder. Today, if there were no Social Security retirement insurance income, many elderly citizens would end up homeless and starving or freezing to death. While they may not have the status that their lifetime of work for our society deserves, they presently receive a very modest retirement income from Social Security. However, the Social Security system is threatened because when the present funding of the system is projected into the future, it is seen to be severely insufficient. Low-wage workers have contributed to the wealth of the Country way more than the wealth they have received. While correspondingly, the highest wage earners have contributed less than the wealth that they have received. There is no person on this Earth that has contributed more through a lifetime of work to the wealth of the Nation than ten thousand ordinary workers have done through their lifetime of work.

Therefore, to solve the long-term problem of Social Security and to have a just society, everyone should pay the 6.2 percent payroll tax on all their income. It is really no different than medical or automobile insurance. The people with healthy lifestyles help to pay for insurance for those who do not have healthy lifestyles, and good drivers help to pay the insurance costs of those who are not good drivers. In addition, businesses should have to pay their 6.2 percent share on all of the income that they pay out to their employees.

However, a business should not have to pay any income tax on their before-tax profits greater than their share of the infrastructure and security created for everyone. As our investment equation, $\frac{d}{dt}I = \Pi + c_1 * \Pi * (\Pi/Y) - c_2 * \Pi * D/(v * Y)$, shows, the amount of investment is intimately connected to the amount of profit. Reduce the amount of profit, and you reduce the amount of investment. Reduce the amount of investment, and you reduce the output of the economy. Therefore, because an income tax on business reduces the profit that allows a company to invest, it is really a self-defeating tax for society. It is like driving a car with the brakes on.

In the sample income tax table, Table 6.1 below, in order to solve our macroeconomic problems, we are assuming the income tax is taxing gross income from whatever the source as required by the Sixteenth Amendment to the Constitution. In particular, the income tax is not to be based on adjusted gross income. That is, all income from whatever the source is to be taxed and taxed in the same way. Thus, a different tax rate for *Capital Gains* is not allowed under the Constitution. If two people make exactly the same income, then they are to pay exactly the same income tax. This taxation would be consistent with the principle that we are all to be equal under the law.

Also, we are assuming that both employer and employee are paying the 6.2 percent Social Security tax on all employee income. If one does not attempt to solve the Social Security problem, then one could always take the top marginal bracket up to 102 percent to create a hard stop in the maximum amount of income allowed to be earned. Moreover, in this case, if one wanted the same cutoff income, one could just adjust the spacing of the bracketing.

In this discussion, we are assuming a person is paying a Social Security tax of 6.2 percent on all their income in addition to an income tax on their total *gross income* at the marginal rates given in the tax table on page 96. What does Table 6.1 tell us? First, note that if a person has an income of more than fifty million dollars a year, the person will actually take home less money than a person who earns precisely $50,000,000 a year. Thus, the table tells us that there will not be people in the nation, making hundreds of millions or billions of dollars a year. It tells us that a maximum income has been hardwired into the tax structure. In fact, it would be easy to hardwire into Federal Law a tax code that would self adjust so that the top marginal tax bracket is equal to a value of 1680 times the suggested minimum wage, as it happened by chance to be equal to here, or to any other value that is deemed appropriate. If the suggested livable minimum wage were in place, then we would know that every full-time worker in the economy would earn a livable wage. When we calculate the net income of the suggested minimum wage worker making $29,760.30, assuming the negative $2980 capitation tax is in place, we find that a single person would have an after-tax

Marginal Tax Rate	Tax Bracket >	Tax Bracket ≤	Marginal Tax Rate	Tax Bracket >	Tax Bracket ≤	Marginal Tax Rate	Tax Bracket >	Tax Bracket ≤
0	0	2000	34	155700	188700	68	4100000	4970000
2	2000	4000	36	188700	228800	70	4970000	6000000
4	4000	6000	38	228800	277300	72	6000000	7300000
6	6000	8000	40	277300	336100	74	7300000	8850000
8	8000	11000	42	336100	407500	76	8850000	10730000
10	11000	14500	44	407500	493900	78	10730000	13000000
12	14500	19000	46	493900	598700	80	13000000	15800000
14	19000	24000	48	598700	725700	82	15800000	19100000
16	24000	30000	50	725700	879600	84	19100000	23200000
18	30000	38000	52	879600	1066000	86	23200000	28100000
20	38000	48000	54	1066000	1292000	88	28100000	34000000
22	48000	59500	56	1292000	1570000	90	34000000	41250000
24	59500	72120	58	1570000	1900000	92	41250000	50000000
26	72120	87420	60	1900000	2300000	96	50000000	
28	87420	106000	62	2300000	2790000			
30	106000	128500	64	2790000	3380000			
32	128500	155700	66	3380000	4100000			

Table 6.1: This sample income tax table utilizes the GDP per capita income to set the twenty-two percent marginal tax rate and makes a hard stop on the amount of money that can be earned at $50,000,000 under the assumption that people and employer pay the 6.2 percent Social Security tax on all employee income.

net income of $27,843.99 and that a family of four, with one wage earner, would have an after-tax net income of $36,783.99.

If we look carefully at Figure 1 on page 4, we see that the single person livable wage is several cents per hour lower than the minimum wage from 1950 to the middle 1960s. However, if we include a negative per capita tax of say one-twentieth of the GDP per capita, a family of four people would have done about as well a family of the same size making the minimum wage from 1950 through the middle of the 1960s. While a family of five or more would have done better with our livable wage consisting of the single person minimum wage and a negative capitation tax equal to one-twentieth of the GDP per capita than a similar family did with the minimum wage. A single person would have done slightly worse during those times with this suggested livable wage structure, but better than the single person livable wage.

If we extend this livable wage scheme forward to 2018, for which we found a minimum wage equal to $29,760.30 per year, each person would be paid a negative per capita tax of $2980, when rounded up to the nearest ten dollars. We see, from our example, that such a livable wage scheme system would not get out of whack and thus would not have to be reset. We also see from this tax scheme that every person who earns a particular income pays the same income tax, and each person of the United States receives the same tax based on population. That is, we are all treated in exactly the same way under the Constitution.

When we look at the spread of incomes allowed in this sample tax plan, we see that they are much tighter than the present spread of incomes in our nation. However, if we compare the spread with the spread of incomes that were "allowed" by the taxes back in the 1950s and early 1960s, we find that sample spread would be much wider than the spread in incomes back then. In fact, the spread would be more than ten times wider.

There is one thing we have not mentioned in our discussion about setting up the income tax brackets that is very important. In order to make sure that everybody resides in the same economic boat, we must make sure that the effective range between the minimum wage and the maximum wage is not too wide.

In 1982, if Congress had added a top tax bracket of 95 percent that kicked in at 10 billion dollars and that top tax bracket remained until today, then nothing would have changed. We would still have the same income inequality problem we have today.

It is also essential to have many tax brackets between the lowest and the highest tax bracket. What if, in addition to our present top tax bracket of 37 percent for all income beyond $518,400, we added fifty-eight multiplicatively evenly spaced brackets to the 95 percent tax bracket at 10 billion dollars? In this case, each one percent rise in the tax rate would occur when the income increased by approximately 18.55 percent. Then a 68 percent tax bracket would start at approximately 100 million dollars, and a 72 percent tax bracket would start at approximately 200 million dollars. One can see that it is likely that this tax structure would shrink the wage inequality to some extent because a 70 percent top tax rate has been shown to be somewhat inhibiting to high wage rates. Moreover, no matter what, the after-tax income disparity would be shrunken significantly.

Regarding having many tax brackets, it should be noted that there were about two dozen tax brackets during the 1950s and 1960s. This number had shrunken to about 16 tax brackets when the top tax rate of fifty percent took effect in 1982. It shrank to just two brackets in 1988 and held to just two brackets for four years. Then Congress added a third bracket for two years before slowly increasing the number of tax brackets to 5 in 1993, to 6 in 2002, and 7 in 2014.

It is probable, the relatively large number of tax brackets relative to the income spread was influential in keeping everyone in the same economic boat. The number of tax brackets helping to keep everyone in the same economic boat is likely to have been more influential during the period after the top tax bracket was lowered to seventy percent.

6.2.1 Increased Government Revenues

If we look at how much of the elite fifty million dollar income a person would actually take home, we find that such a worker would be taxed $41,168,179.20 via the income tax and another $3,100,000 from the Social Security tax. This means that the Government would take in $44,268,179.20 from this elite individual, neglecting the negative per capita tax. In 2012, the top 0.001 percent of income earners paid total federal income taxes of $38,563,000,000 (Dungan, 2015). There were 1361 taxpayers in this group so that the

Government would have received an average tax payment from the top 0.001 percent of taxpayers of $28,341,139, including a *normal* year's Social Security tax. Under the sample tax scheme, the Government would receive $44,268,179.20 from such an elite individual. Comparing the two quantities, we can see that the Government would not lose tax revenue from these elite individuals who would be forced to cut their income by the sample tax scheme. Instead, the Government would take in much more money from these high-income people even though their wages would be cut drastically under the sample tax scheme.

We will make the same comparison with the top five percent of wage earners in an effort to determine whether or not the Government will take in more or less money under the sample tax scheme. Because all of the top 0.001 percent of wage earners would have their income reduced to fifty million dollars, the first calculation is exact. However, for the lower-income elite earners, we do not have gross income statistics that would allow us to calculate the tax paid by the top five percent of wage earners. However, we do have the threshold adjusted gross incomes for the top 0.001, 0.01, 0.1, 1, 2, 3, 4, and 5 percent of incomes. This is cumulative overlapping data. From this data, we can calculate an approximation of the total tax paid by each of these income groups. These approximations will be too low, but it is the best we can do. To find the best approximation given the data we have available to us, we have to proceed in steps.

To find the approximation for the income tax that would be received from the top 0.01 percentile, we first calculate the tax for a person with a gross income equal to the threshold adjusted gross income for the 0.01 percentile using the sample tax table. Then we multiply this tax by the number of tax returns between the top 0.001 percentile and the top 0.01 percentile. This gives us an approximation to the tax paid by all the workers between the top 0.001 percentile and the top 0.01 percentile. Adding this tax payment to the tax payment, we found for the top 0.001 percent of taxpayers, will give us an approximation for the amount of tax paid by the top 0.01 percent of wage earners. We then proceed in the same way for the top 0.1 percentile.

We proceed downward in income until we have calculated the tax for the top five percent of all incomes. All the relevant data needed is found in an IRS, Statistics of Income Bulletin (Dungan, 2015). When we finish the calculation, we find that the approximation to the income tax money taken in by the Government in 2012 for the top 5 percent of taxpayers under the sample tax scheme would have been 839.388 billion dollars. Comparing this value with the 698.543 billion dollars actually taken in, we see that our approximation significantly beat the actual amount of money taken in, even though the approximation is several hundred billion dollars lower than the amount that would have been taken in by the sample tax scheme.

Moreover, the Government would have collected more than 200 billion dollars in Social Security income from the top five percent of wage earners. Thus, even though the top wages in the economy would be cut drastically under the sample tax scheme, the Government would take in much more tax money with the income tax and Social Security tax than they do now.

6.2.2 Increased Economy Profits

However, when we look at the tax scheme from the point of view of business, we find something else. We see that much less money would be paid out by a business for their elite high salaried individuals. Finally, after a long search, I came across the average *adjusted* gross income of the top 0.001 percent of individual taxpayers. This data is not the correct data to use. It is too low. However, we have no choice. In 2012, the top 0.001 percent of individual taxpayers numbered 1361, and the average *adjusted* gross income of these taxpayers was 161 million dollars (Dungan, 2015). This means that at least $1361 * (\$161,000,000 - \$50,000,000)$ or a 151.071 billion dollars more money would have been retained by businesses as profit in 2012 if the sample tax had been put into effect then. If we normalize this change in profit by dividing by the GDP in 2012, we should have a good estimate of the effect of the sample tax scheme if it were to be implemented in the near future. The GDP in 2012 was 16.1553 trillion dollars. Therefore, the increase in the economy profit to GDP ratio would have been 0.9351 percent. This estimate is too low because we were forced to use the average adjusted gross income rather than the average gross income.

This group of income earners paid a lower average tax rate than the top 0.01 percent, the top 0.1 percent, the top 1 percent, the top 2 percent, the top 3 percent, the top 4 percent, the top 5 percent, and the top 10 percent of wage earners (Dungan, 2015, pages 6 and 8). Thus, we can conclude that the reduction in their average gross income has been so massive that the change in the economy's profit-to-GDP ratio would have been at least one percent. The top marginal tax bracket in 2012 was thirty-five percent. Because the top 0.001 percent of wage earners make so much money, we know that almost all of their income would be taxed at the top marginal tax rate. However, because they only paid an average tax rate of 17.6 percent, we know, one way or another, almost half of their total income must have been eliminated from taxation. Therefore, the amount of money that businesses would save in salaries of these elite wage earners should be almost doubled.

In addition, there is a further underestimation. Because the lower limit on the average adjusted gross income of the top 0.001 percent is sixty-two million dollars, this means that many of the top 0.01 percent of wage earners would have had their pay reduced to fifty million dollars. This would further reduce the amount that businesses paid in wages.

Furthermore, some small business owners might lower their own pay in the face of higher taxes in order to keep "their" money within their business rather than passing it along to the Government. Therefore, the increase in the economy's profit-to-GDP ratio would be well north of one percent.

One, of course, has to worry about how much a business would have to spend to raise the wages of those who would be making less than the new livable minimum wage. However, because of the vast wage disparity between the income of elites at the top and the low-wage workers at the bottom, the total wages of people at the bottom, even though they are many, are small in comparison to the total wages of the elite. The Institute for Policy Studies released a study of bonuses paid out by Wall Street in 2015. This study showed that less than half the money contained in just these bonuses was enough to raise the pay of all the full-time minimum wage workers in the country to fifteen dollars an hour (Anderson, 2016). Yes, there would be many people making more than the minimum wage and less than the new minimum wage whose pay would have to be raised, too. So, increasing the pay of all these workers would take the amount of profit increase back toward one percent. One can very crudely estimate that business would have to add income to these low-wage workers of about sixty to two hundred billion dollars.

6.2.2.1   Details of the Low-Wage Worker Cost Estimate

The bottom fifty percent of wage earners earned an adjusted gross income of 1.004 trillion dollars in 2012 (Dungan, 2015). Estimating the average deduction for these workers, in going from gross to adjusted gross income at a generous fifteen percent, would put the gross income of the bottom fifty percentile at about 1.2 trillion dollars. By calculation, the livable minimum wage in 2012 was $25,694.15. The Social Security Administration provides us with a data table that allows us to conclude that all the taxpayers earning less than or equal to the suggested minimum wage, equal to one half of the GDP per capita, would earn slightly less than one-third of the total income earned by the bottom fifty percent of workers (Social Security Administration, 2018). Thus, we estimate that this bottom group of wage earners would have earned a gross income of something a little less than 400 billion dollars. To be conservative, we will say it is 400 billion dollars.

However, we do not know the distribution of hours worked or the hourly pay distribution of these workers. We will assume that all of the workers were making at least the minimum wage of $7.25 per hour. We will assume that a uniform distribution of hourly wages from the minimum wage up to the livable minimum wage of $12.85 hour will be a reasonable approximation to the actual distribution. We know this does not have to be so. For instance, everyone could be making precisely the minimum wage. We know this was not the case. The Institute for Policy Studies' report about Wall Street bonuses mentioned that there were less than a million full-time minimum wage workers in 2015 (Anderson, 2016). We also know that it was not the case that everyone was making the suggested livable minimum wage with the hours just being adjusted to make up the correct total in each income bracket. It was something in between. Thus, just so we can get a rough handle on the total amount of money that businesses would need to add to their low-wage workers, we will assume a linear distribution of wage rates rising from the 2012 minimum wage to the suggested livable minimum wage. A sketch of this distribution is shown in Figure 6.2.

This distribution looks like a trapezoid. The base of the trapezoid is the number of low-wage workers we are considering times their average number of hours worked in the year. The vertical left-hand side would be the minimum wage of $7.25 per hour, and the vertical right-hand side is the livable minimum wage of $12.85 per hour in 2012. The diagonal line from $7.25 to $12.85 would represent the uniform distribution of wages rates. The figure created by these four sides is a trapezoid whose area would be equal to the gross income

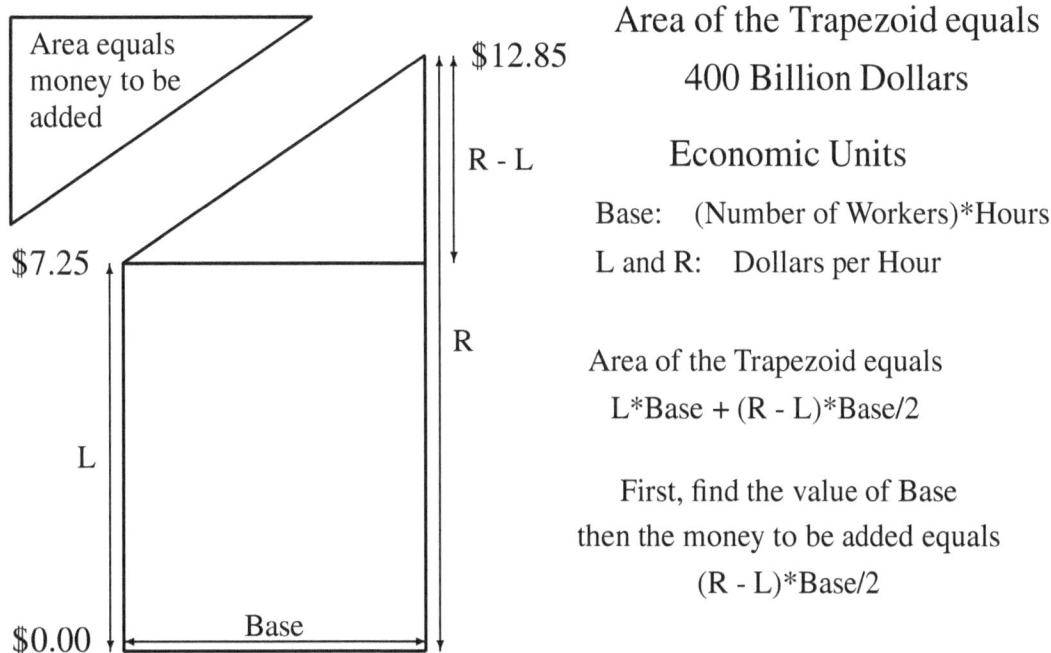

Area equals money to be added

$12.85

R - L

$7.25

R

L

$0.00

Base

Area of the Trapezoid equals

400 Billion Dollars

Economic Units

Base: (Number of Workers)*Hours

L and R: Dollars per Hour

Area of the Trapezoid equals

L*Base + (R - L)*Base/2

First, find the value of Base
then the money to be added equals

(R - L)*Base/2

Figure 6.2: This figure presents a sketch of a linear distribution of wage rates; the vertical axis runs along the left-hand side of the trapezoid. The horizontal axis runs along the base of the trapezoid. Its value at the right-hand edge of the trapezoid is Base. The value of Base is unknown.

of 400 billion dollars earned by these low-wage taxpayers. If we then extended the left-hand side of the trapezoid up to the livable minimum wage of $12.85, then the rectangle so formed would represent a distribution in which everyone was making the livable minimum wage. This means that the area of the top left-hand corner right triangle that is added to the trapezoid to make the rectangle would represent the amount of money needed to be added to these low-wage workers in order for all of them to be making the livable minimum wage. Therefore, the amount needed to be added to the income of these low-wage workers by calculation of the area of the triangle would be 111.4 billion dollars.

We know that many people have jobs that give them an income that is mainly made up of tips. Waitresses, waiters, and cabbies fall into this class. The change in the minimum wage should have very little effect on the pay they would receive directly from the restaurants or cab companies for whom they work. There are also many workers that are self-employed and set their own wage. For instance, a handyman who paints a room or fixes a fence sets the price for the job, which is accepted or not by the customer. They are not covered at all by a minimum wage law. However, all of these workers pay taxes, and there are millions of them. If there were only four million or so such workers, they would lower our estimate to about 90 billion dollars. Furthermore, if the distribution is more heavily weighted toward the $7.25 side, then the amount needed to be added to the pay of low-wage workers would go up.

Now that we have an estimate of the amount of money that business would have had to add to the pay of low-wage workers in 2012, if the livable minimum wage discussed had been implemented, we would like to find reasonable boundaries for this estimate. If we knew the average wage rate paid for all the hours worked by all the low-wage workers that received pay at a rate less than the suggested livable minimum wage, then we could calculate directly the amount needed. Let L_W be the suggested livable wage rate in 2012 of \$12.85 per hour and let $\overline{w}$ the average wage rate. Then, with Base equal to the number of hours worked by all the low-wage workers earning less than the suggested minimum wage in 2012, we have Base $* \overline{w} = 400x10^9$ dollars, so that

$$\text{the amount needed to be added} = (L_W - \overline{w}) * \text{Base}$$
$$= \frac{L_W - \overline{w}}{\overline{w}} * 400x10^9 \text{ in dollars.}$$

If we let $\overline{w}$ equal \$10.05, the midpoint between the 2012 minimum wage and the suggested livable minimum wage in 2012, we find the amount of money that businesses need to add to low-wage workers' pay is 111.4 billion dollars, which is consistent with our previous estimate. It is hard for me to conceive that the average wage rate that we are seeking would be greater than eleven dollars per hour. When we assume that the average wage rate is eleven dollars per hour, we find that the money businesses would have to add to the low-wage earners would be 67.3 billion dollars. On the other hand, it would be hard to imagine that the average wage rate for this group of low-wage workers would be less than nine dollars per hour given that the minimum wage rate that was legal to pay this group workers was \$7.25 per hour. When we assume the average wage rate is \$9.00 per hour, we find that businesses would have had to add 171.1 billion dollars to their low-wage employees in order to be in compliance with the suggested livable minimum wage in 2012. Note in this regard, if the average wage rate, $\overline{w}$, were only twenty-five percent of the way from the old minimum wage toward the new livable minimum wage, the average wage rate would be \$8.65 per hour, and the money businesses would need to add to the pay of their low-wage workers would be 194.2 billion dollars. Therefore, to be safe, we will assume that the amount of money businesses would have had to add to the wages of their low-wage workers is somewhere between 60 and 200 billion dollars.

All of this amount and a little more would likely be covered by the missing amount between the adjusted gross income and the gross income of the top 0.001 percent of wage earners in our previous estimate.[3] The main difficulty that would be likely to arise in setting a livable minimum wage is that small business owners might feel severe hardships if this policy were implemented so quickly that prices and wages were not given enough time to stay in sync. Thus, such a livable minimum wage policy should probably be implemented

---

[3]See discussion on page 99, 1361*(2*\$161,000,000 - \$50,000,000) minus 151.071 billion dollars equals 219.121 billion dollars, or more conservatively, 1361*(\$310,000,000 - \$50,000,000) minus 151.071 billion dollars equals 202.789 billion dollars.

over a three or four year period.

6.3   The Significance of an Increased Economy Profit for the Average Wage Rate

To see whether a one percent increase (or decrease) in the economy profit-to-GDP ratio would be likely to have a significant effect on our economy, we present Figure 6.3. This figure presents a graph of the economy profit-to-GDP ratio as a function of time for the no rate hike scenario, our reference scenario.

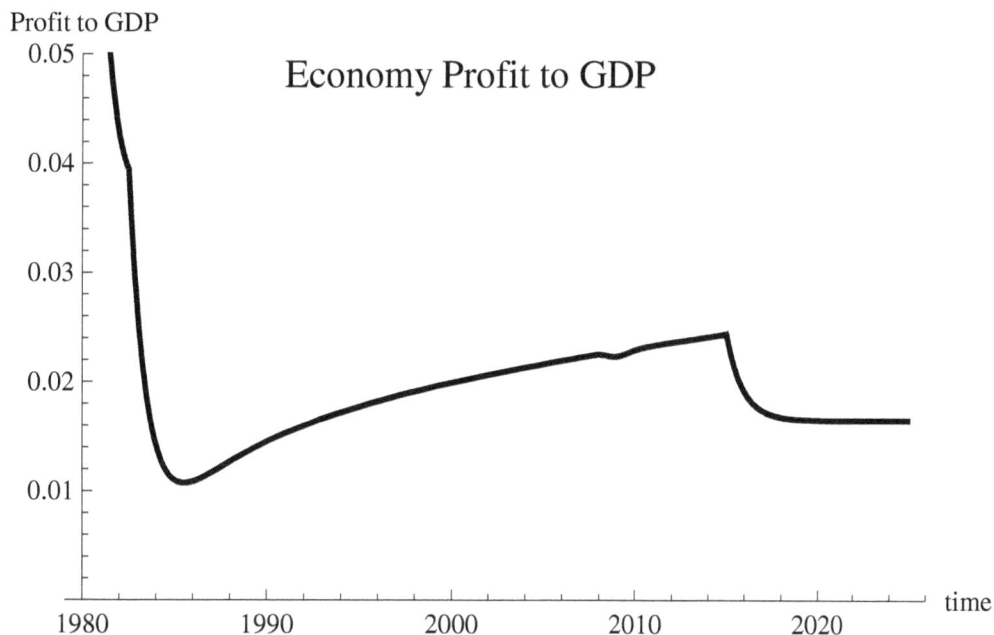

Figure 6.3: This figure shows that in 2015, there was a sudden drop in the ratio of economy profit to GDP from 2.44 percent down to a relatively constant, but very slowly decreasing value, of about 1.65 percent. The ratio's sharp decline in 2015 was caused when the decline in average interest rates came to an abrupt halt.

We see from looking at Figure 6.3 that a one percent rise in the economy profit-to-GDP ratio would be a relatively big change, visually. Such a change would be noticeably larger than the attention grabbing steep decrease of 0.79 percent in the economy profit-to-GDP ratio displayed in Figure 6.3. If we use the steep decline that occurred in the economy profit-to-GDP ratio, which happened in 2015, as a guide, we can get an idea of what an increase of about one percent in the economy profit-to-GDP ratio might have on the economy.

When we look at Figure 2.12 on page 28 or Figure 3.12 on page 40, we can see what a drop in the economy profit-to-GDP ratio of the size that occurred in 2015 makes in the average wage rate in the no rate hike, reference scenario. The change that occurs in the reference scenario appears subtly. One can see before 2015, the exponential-like rise of the wage rate was faster than it was after 2015. In addition, the wage rate curve got rotated slightly more horizontal at the time of the change.

However, these changes in the reference scenario's average wage rate may seem insignificant. So in order to convince the reader that such changes are significant, we present the result of running a scenario in a manner that allows the average interest rate to decline all the way to zero, instead of letting the average interest rate stop declining at 1.9 percent as it did in 2015. This change will allow the scenario to follow its path for another 6.86 years until the average interest rate hits zero.

We display the average interest rates for the average interest rate decays-to-zero scenario and the no rate hike reference scenario in Figure 6.4. In Figure 6.5, we follow this by displaying the change in the average wage rate that this drop in the profit-to-GDP causes.

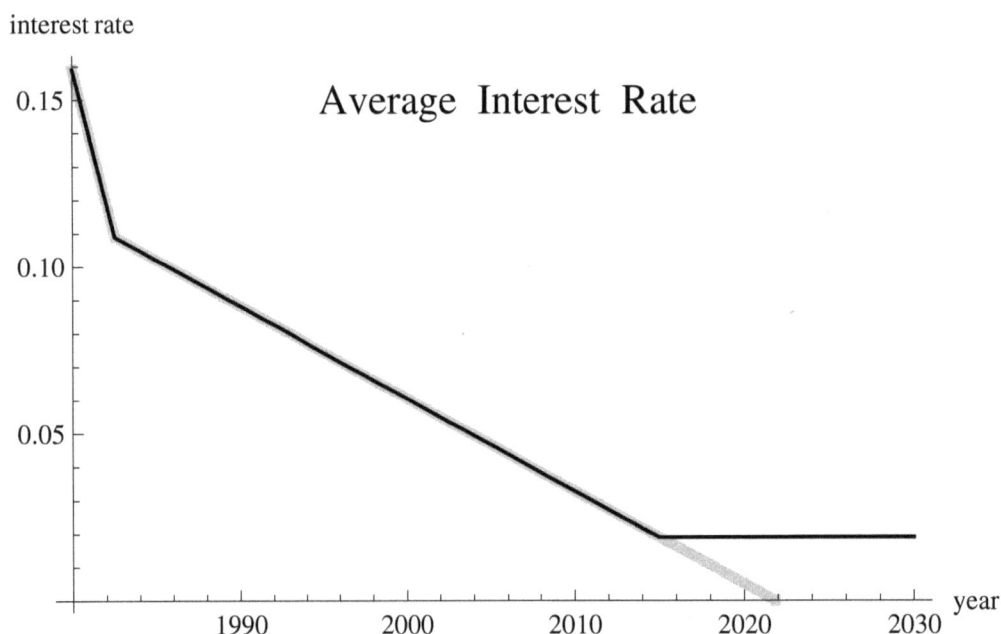

Figure 6.4: In this figure, we show the average interest rate for the no rate hike scenario—black line—and the average interest rate decays-to-zero scenario—thick gray line.

We see from Figure 6.5 that a one percent increase in the economy profit-to-GDP ratio would make a significant change in the macroeconomic average wage rate because a lesser change would have done so.

6.4 Summary

So what has all the discussion about the sample tax scheme and the raising of the minimum wage to the livable wage equal to one-half the GDP per capita shown us? First of all, it has shown us that the Government would take in more money, thus raising the macroeco-

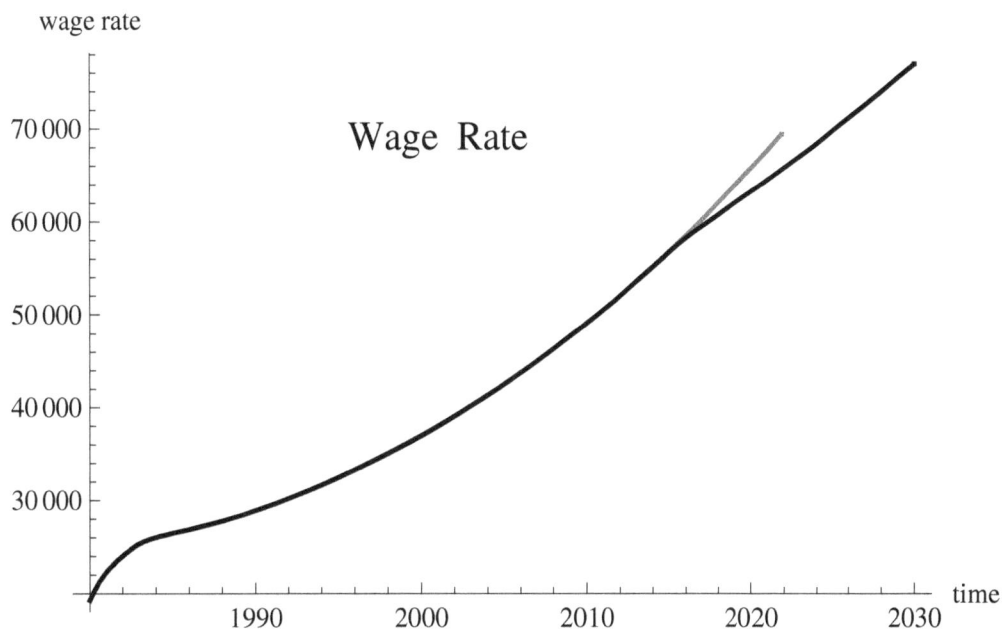

Figure 6.5: Here, we see a very real difference in the average wage rate has occurred when we run the linearized average interest rate to zero rather than having its decline stop in 2015 at 1.9 percent. The zero average interest rate would be reached in 2021.86, and thus the gray line indicating that scenario ends there. The linearized average interest rate, shown in Figure 1.1 on page 15, was used in all the fits of Chapters Two, Three, and Five.

nomic wages of the people it supports, directly or indirectly. Second, businesses would have to pay their lower-wage workers more money and slowly increase the pay of other workers because their profits will increase under this policy. Moreover, the increased profits will increase investment, directly causing an increase in the economy's output. Therefore, we see that the sample income tax, including a top bracket that hardwires a maximum income into the economy, along with the floating livable wage based on the GDP per capita, will raise the average wage rate of the United States. The maximum income should also float like the livable wage so that everybody moves up and down together.

One other thing that we have not mentioned is that low-wage earners consume a much larger percentage of their income than high wage earners do. Thus, by increasing the wages of the people at the bottom, the Government would stimulate the economy because the people of the nation will consume more. Therefore, we see that the Government would increase the GDP of the country if they were to increase the minimum wage significantly so that it would equal to one-half of the GDP per capita and if they were to institute a negative uniform capitation tax.

Moreover, because the very top income earners' incomes would be limited so that they can not make as much as they would wish, their incentive to hire low-wage workers would be severely weakened. Thus, they would tend to reduce or stop the practice of hiring such workers, here and offshore, because there would be no loophole around their limited income.

Furthermore, because of the noticeably higher minimum wage, which will cause other wages to rise, some people, who have become discouraged and have stopped seeking work, will find the incentive to seek work again. Also, if the highest income wage earners come to understand the rationale for the policy, they might see that it would be in their self-interest to raise the macroeconomic wage, which as a result, would increase their own income. While it is likely to take some time for the wage rate, employment level problem to resolve fully, a large part of the problem would resolve fairly quickly.

A rational tax structure also would allow the Government to have some control over macroeconomic results. For instance, much of the infrastructure of the United States, both public and private, needs to be modernized and rebuilt. To do this, the Government could spend debt-free money directly into the economy. They could offer to pay for the sweat hogs at a wage rate equal to one and a half times the suggested livable minimum wage. This policy would pull back into the economy many discouraged workers and pull into the economy many unemployed people who have never been employed before. Thus, this policy would do much to rebuild the self-esteem of many people, while the country rebuilds the roads, bridges, water and sewer works, and creates a modern high-speed train system in the public sphere. At the same time, the Government could help to pay for the rebuilding of private infrastructure and the modernization of manufacturing facilities within the country. Spending several hundred billion dollars a year directly into the economy, without "borrowing," in this rebuilding effort might start to become inflationary. However, the Government can take some of the money used in these endeavors out of the back end of the funding process by tightening the income tax rates should it become necessary to slow or stop inflation. Taxation does not have to be only a funding tool.

One thing that we have not mentioned at all is that, under this tax structure, no single individual or group of individuals would earn enough money to be able to corrupt the whole Government, whether with direct payouts of money, or indirectly with campaign contributions. This would mean that the ordinary person's interests would regain some consideration in the eyes of the politician.

To this end, one should not allow the wage range between minimum wage workers and the top wage earners to be too large. Expressed in terms of GDP per capita, the range between the minimum wage worker and the top tax bracket in the 1950s and early 1960s varied in the rough range between 65 and 85 times the GDP per capita. As someone who lived through those times as a boy and a young man in a family on the low end of the wage scale, even I felt the wage range was a *hair* narrow. In addition, because the population has more than doubled, I suspect that a range of incomes between two hundred and three hundred times the GDP per capita would be safe. I think it likely that a range four hundred times the GDP per capita would likely be safe, but I would have real trepidation about a range of 840 times the GDP per capita as the sample tax table and livable wage would setup. I prefer to be conservative here, as I would hate to lose the connection between people that the economic boat of the 1950s and early 1960s fostered for some intangible benefit that might be brought forth from a somewhat broader wage range.

6.5 The Relation to the Financial System

Lastly, we need to mention the financial system because the financial system and the real economy are intertwined to a high degree. In Subsection 5.4.1 on page 76, we stated that the banks were paid 132.75 trillion dollars, in cash, during the Government's debt repayment aid. There is nothing magic about this quantity of cash. It might have been 40 or 50 trillion dollars instead of 132.75 trillion dollars if the Government had increased the amount of its yearly debt-free debt repayment aid by a factor of three or more and ended its debt repayment aid after eight or ten years. Then, by adjusting its debt-free investment aid policy, it could have released the economy when the total economy debt was eighty percent of GDP. However, no matter how it would be done, in order to fix the debt problem, the Government would need to add at least several tens of trillions of dollars to the financial system's assets.

This amount of cash is an asset that could be used to help balance a bank's liabilities. At the present time, many big banks have gotten themselves into a real financial mess with derivatives, reportedly amounting to seven or eight hundred trillion dollars or more. Clearly, one hundred and thirty trillion dollars is a large amount, and even forty trillion dollars is a significant amount given the way financial institutions weigh their assets and liabilities with respect to their solvency.

Moreover, this cash is a real asset for the banks. It can be exchanged between banks, it can be loaned to customers, and it can be held as a financial asset that stabilizes the bank against bankruptcy. As long as this money, no matter the amount, remains within the financial system and only enters the real economy in a normal manner, it will cause no inflation. Therefore, the Government needs to make sure that there are proper regulations and procedures in place in order to be certain that this money does not "leak" into the real economy.

In my opinion, the cash should be distinct from Federal Reserve Notes and should be something like President Kennedy's United States Notes. The money should be for use only within the United States because the United States can only control well the manipulations of this money within the United States. It should be absolutely worthless outside the United States. Federal Reserve Note dollars would still have their regular use outside of the country. In the "leak" sense, bankers or elite corporate executives giving themselves multi-million or multi-billion dollar bonuses would be prevented by the suggested income tax structure, which limits the maximum amount that someone can earn.

6.6 Afterward and Conclusions

In setting up the presentation of the fix to the economy's debt problem, no attempt was made to indicate the best or most efficient way to fix the problem. Instead, we tried to present the solution in pieces so that people could see how the two distinct parts, debt payments, and investment payments, affect the nature of the solution. The solution to the debt problem can be made to take less time and can be made more efficient with respect to "money" spent.

The real point was to show proof of concept.

Preliminarily, we conclude from our results that it is likely that:

1. The coupled macroeconomic equations we presented can competently model the United States Economy.

    a. The equations can be used to create a rough but smooth fit of the economy.

    b. The equations can be used to create a fine-grained, refined fit.

2. Both the refined fit and the cruder smooth fit can be used to project the United States Economy forward under assumed hypothetical economic conditions with the projections producing essentially the same qualitative and quantitative results.

These results give us confidence that we can develop solutions to the present economic problems of the United States based on these macroeconomic equations and that these solutions will work if put into practice.

However, more work needs to be done in order to confirm that our set of coupled differential equations are accurately representing the reality of the United States Economy.

Chapter 7

Construction of an Average Interest Rate Function

As we discussed earlier, the Federal Reserve could require banks to provide them with the information necessary for the calculation of a relatively accurate average interest rate function. However, they have not calculated such a function and made it available to economists. We are not at a total loss here because we do have continuous long-term data of the base interest rate in the United States, the Federal Funds Rate. This will allow us to create an average Federal Funds Rate and then "peg" the economy's average interest rate to an average Federal Funds Rate that is a function of time.

When one goes to the Federal Reserve's website in St Louis, one can get the monthly data for the Federal Funds Rate all the way back to the first of July in 1954. This data is displayed in Figure 7.1.

7.1 Fitting the Federal Funds Rate

We have extended the data to 1950 in order to be able to use the Federal Funds Rate to create an average interest rate function from 1980 that includes thirty-year mortgage investment data. We have set the missing or non-existent Federal Funds Rate from January 1, 1950, through June 30, 1954, to a constant one percent. We can see from the plot that the extrapolated data does not look out of place. Although this extended data is unlikely to be correct, it is also unlikely to cause much of a problem with the average interest rate function from 1980 because essentially only thirty-year mortgages would be involved in the average interest rate from back in the early 1950s investment borrowing.

When one looks at the monthly Federal Funds Rate data, one sees that it is difficult to perceive exactly how the interest rate data is trending during the period from about mid-1979 to 1983 because the data is so sparse and chaotic. A search of the web found daily Federal Funds Rate data at www.macrotrends.net. A plot of this data between 1979 and 1984 is shown in Figure 7.2.

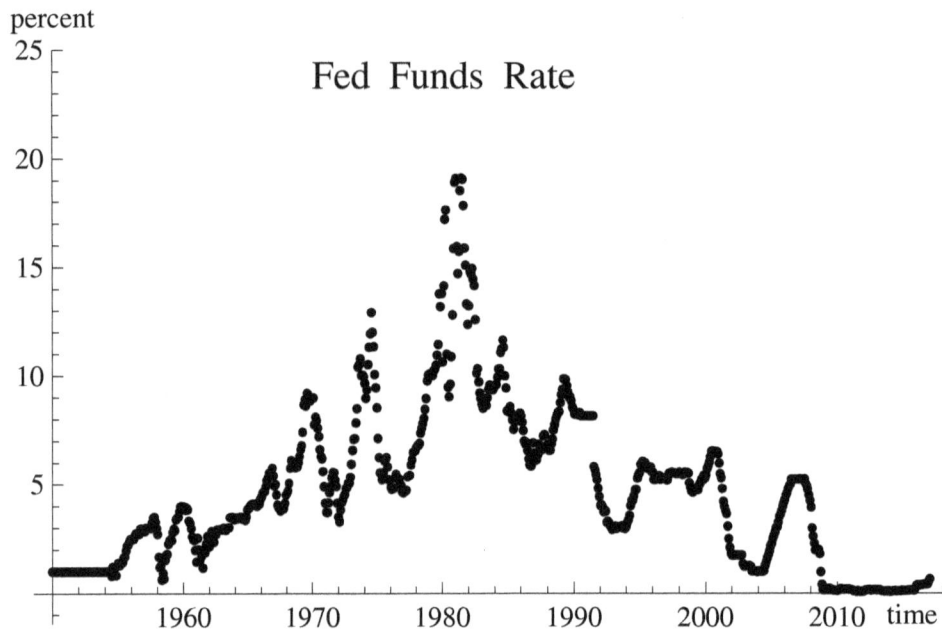

Figure 7.1: This plot shows the monthly Federal Funds Rate data along with the extension we added from January 1, 1950, to June 30, 1954.

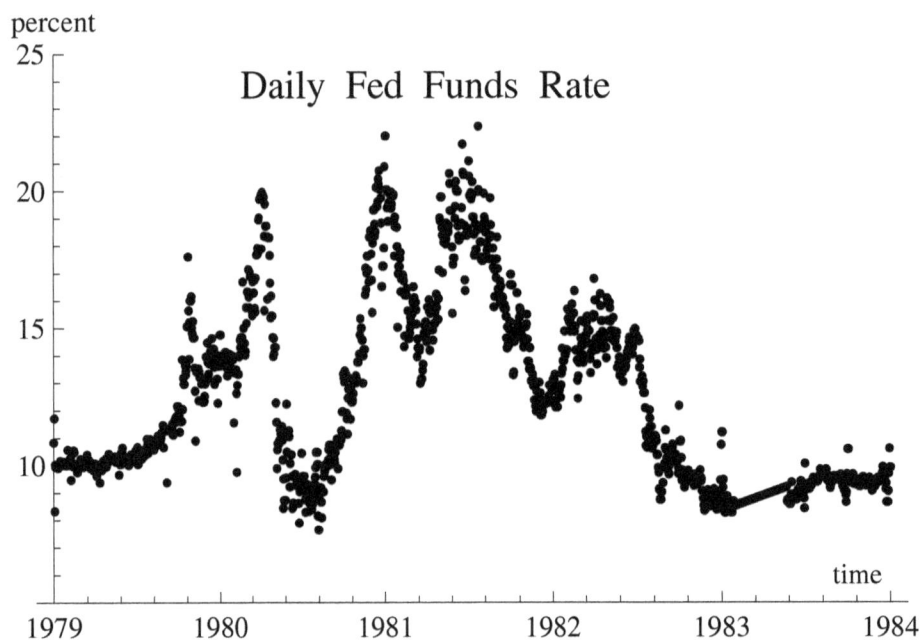

Figure 7.2: This plot shows the portion of the daily Federal Funds Rate from 1979 to 1984 obtained from www.macrotrends.net. The data is thick enough to show the underlying trend of the data throughout this period. Note that much of the peak data is missing in the monthly data plot of Figure 7.1.

The daily Federal Funds Rate data shows the trend of the data through the sparse and seemingly chaotic data shown in the monthly Federal Funds Rate. The daily Federal Funds

Rate data also reveals daily outliers from the general trend of the data. These outliers can cause problems when trying to get a fit to the Federal Funds Rate data by automatic means. Instead, a total of eighty-eight fit-by-eye linear equations were linked together in finding a fit to the general trend to the Federal Funds Rate from January 1, 1950, to January 1, 2017. This fit is shown in Figure 7.3.

Figure 7.3 shows that the straight lines in the eighty-eight linear equation fit to the Federal Funds Rate connect continuously one to the other. The figure also shows that the daily data has allowed the fit lines to fill in the sparse and seemingly chaotic region from 1979 to 1984.

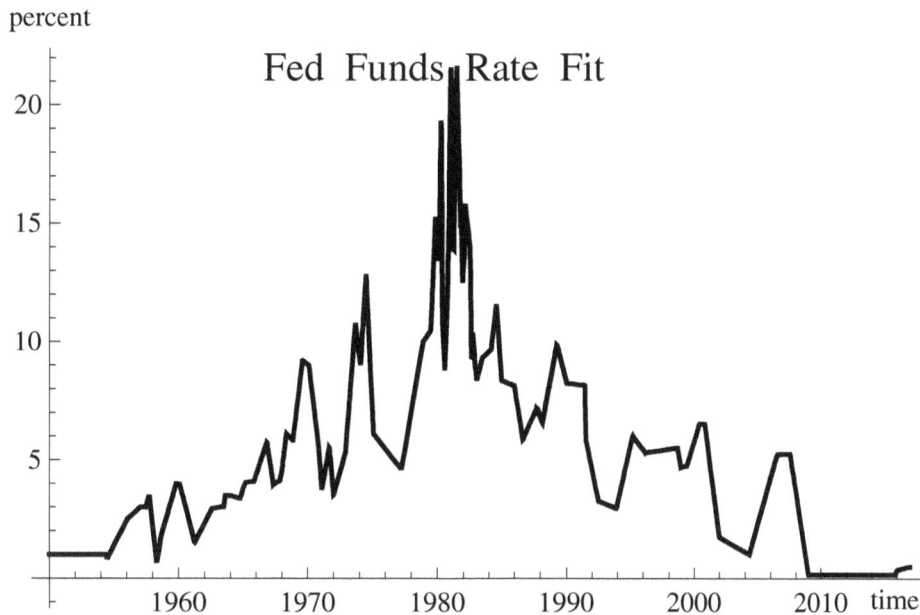

Figure 7.3: This figure shows our eighty-eight equation fit to the Federal Funds Rate made with the aid of the daily Federal funds rate.

We show the extended monthly Federal Funds Rate data superimposed over the eighty-eight fit lines in Figure 7.4.

Figure 7.4 shows that the fit matches the monthly data and fills in the gaps of the missing daily data. While the fit does not extend to match the outliers of the daily data, it fits well the general trend of the Federal Funds Rate interest rate data as a function of time. This fit will allow us to create an approximate average interest rate function.

7.2 Construction of the Average Interest Rate

In the real average interest rate, at any particular time, ten-year loans will count in the average, whether they are two days old, 93 days old, 3.1 years old, or 9.99 years old. The same will hold for a loan of any other length. With all the appropriate data, an average interest rate could be calculated. Our average will be different. It will be front-loaded, as is

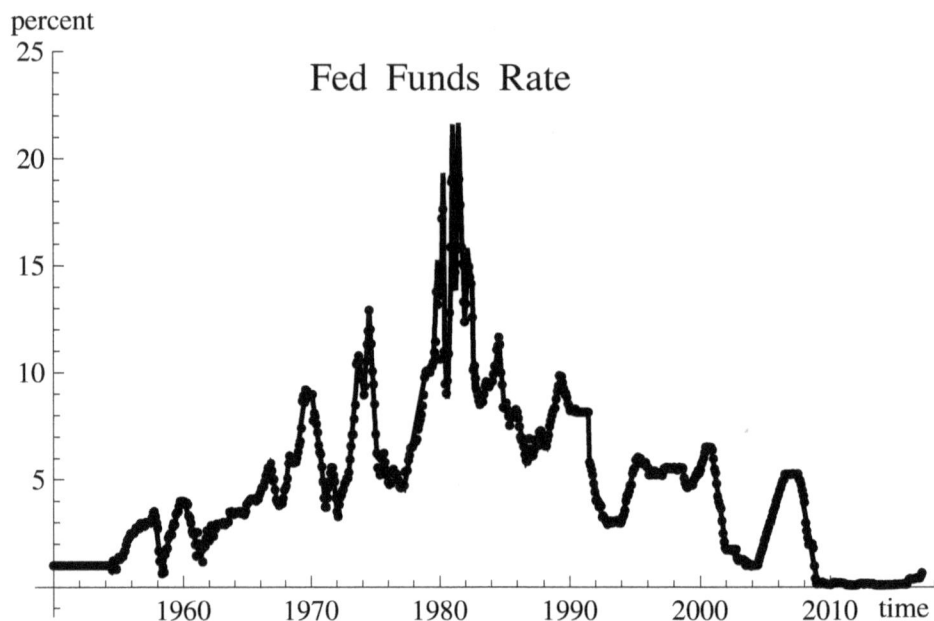

Figure 7.4: In this figure, we display the eighty-eight equation fit, which we created, plotted over the Federal Funds Rate monthly data.

the real average interest rate. To make an average interest rate function, we need to use the interest rate at the time a loan was made, not the average interest rate at the time a loan was made. Thus, we will use the Federal Funds Rate fit at the instant of the average interest rate we are creating.

At the instant under consideration, all loans made at that time are in the mix. However, loans of a duration of a year or more, made one year before, are also in the mix of outstanding loans. Similarly, loans of two years or more duration, made two years before, are also in the mix of outstanding loans, et cetera. This will cause a decrease in the weighting of the "pegged" Federal Funds Rate the further back in time we are adding loans into the mix of the average. We will do the average creation with discrete steps back in time. This is the same procedure we followed earlier when we created an average interest rate to see its affect on our predictions concerning the results caused by the Federal Reserve's interest rate hikes. The average interest rate at any instant will be pegged 1.75 percent above the average we create from the Federal Funds Rate.

The simple sample weighted average, whose distribution is front-loaded, is created from our Federal Funds Rate fit by:

1. Choosing the first sample at the instantaneous present time, weighted at (100 percent)/355.
2. Choosing the second sample one year earlier, weighted at (70 percent)/355.
3. Choosing the third sample two years earlier, weighted at (50 percent)/355.
4. Choosing the fourth sample three years earlier, weighted at (36 percent)/355.
5. Choosing the fifth sample four years earlier, weighted at (26 percent)/355.
6. Choosing the sixth sample five years earlier, weighted at (22 percent)/355.

7. Choosing the seventh sample six years earlier, weighted at (15 percent)/355.
8. Choosing the eighth sample eight years earlier, weighted at (12 percent)/355.
9. Choosing the ninth sample ten years earlier, weighted at (10 percent)/355.
10. Choosing the tenth sample twelve years earlier, weighted at (8 percent)/355.
11. Choosing the eleventh sample fifteen years earlier, weighted at (4 percent)/355.
12. Choosing the twelfth sample thirty years earlier, weighted at (2 percent)/355.

The percents have been written so that one can think of 100 percent of the present loans are in play at year zero, and 70 percent of the loans one year earlier are in play, et cetera, in making the average at a particular instant of time. The division by 355 normalizes the sample distribution.

To implement this average interest rate function, we will create a table of values for the various scenarios we wish to run. Then, from each table, we will create a first-order interpolating function. This allows for a comparison of our piecewise linear, guesstimate, average interest rate approximations with the piecewise linear approximation to the average interest rate function we have created from our fit to the Federal Funds Rate. In Figure 7.5, we present a comparison plot to the average interest rate that we have used throughout our calculations. In Figure 7.6, we also present a comparison plot to the modified average interest rate we put forth in the Addendum.

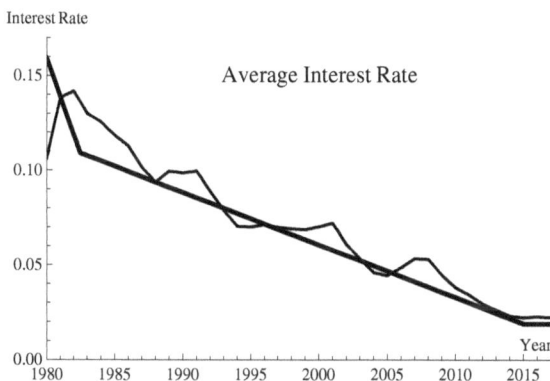

Figure 7.5: This figure displays a comparison of the average interest rate function created from the Federal Funds Rate—thin black line—with the average interest rate function used in most of our calculations—thick black line.

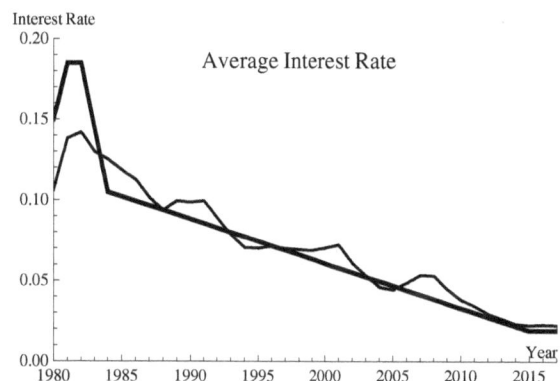

Figure 7.6: This figure displays a comparison of the average interest rate function created from the Federal Funds Rate—thin black line—with the average interest rate function introduced in Section 4.2 of the Addendum—thick black line.

We see from the comparisons in Figures 7.5 and 7.6 that the average interest rate introduced in the Addendum and shown in Figure 4.4 and compared in Figure 7.6 is qualitatively a better fit during the early 1980s, when the interest rates were very high, than is the average interest rate function we have used throughout most of the calculations.

We also see from the comparison plots that the average rate of decrease of the average interest rate, from the mid-1980s to 2015, of all three average interest rate functions was essentially the same. The average rate of decline of the average interest rate during this period was well shy of one half of one percent per year. In fact, the rate of decline in the average interest rate was only about 0.3 percent per year.

One can see from Figure 5.1, on page 54, that during this time frame, the lower the average interest rate, the slower the rate of growth in the economy's debt-to-GDP ratio. However, even a much more rapid decline in interest rates would have only resulted in two or three-tenths of a percent decrease in our debt-to-GDP ratio by 2005. The die to our present predicament had already been cast. There was no way once the debt-to-GDP ratio had reached two, in 1984, that the Federal Reserve and the banks, by themselves, would be able to return it to a manageable 1.4 without severely damaging the economy and or themselves.

7.3   Exploring the Nature of the Constructed Average Interest Rate

Now let's see how the much bumpier average interest rate function that we created from the Federal Funds Rate influences the economy's macroeconomic variables. We will do a simple fit of the economy using a smooth fit that does not try to match the ups and downs in the GDP data through 2008. We show the coefficients c_1 and c_2 that produce this fit in Figures 7.7 and 7.8.

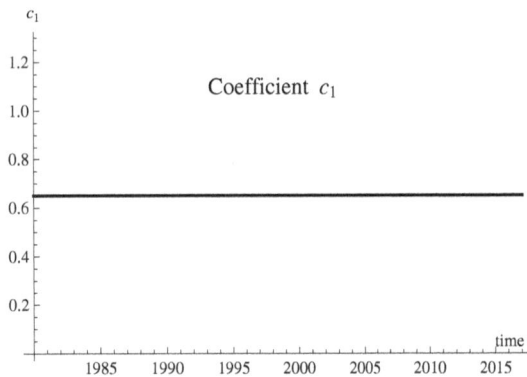

Figure 7.7: Displayed here is the coefficient c_1 that, along with coefficient c_2, allow a smooth fit to the United States' GDP through 2008.

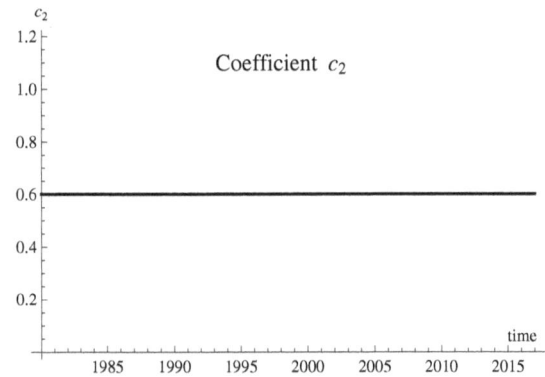

Figure 7.8: This graph displays the constant coefficient c_2 that, along with the constant coefficient c_1, allow a smooth fit to the United States GDP.

In Figure 7.9, we show the fit to the United States GDP produced by these very simple coefficients in the investment equation. The fact that these coefficients are constants means the propensity to borrow and propensity to loan did not change throughout the fit.

We see from Figure 7.9 that the smooth fit to the GDP of the United States is quite good until 2008. One can perceive ever so slight undulations in the general smoothness of the output curve from 1980 to 2008 introduced by variations of the average interest rate derived from the Federal Funds Rate as compared with the previous straight line monotonically

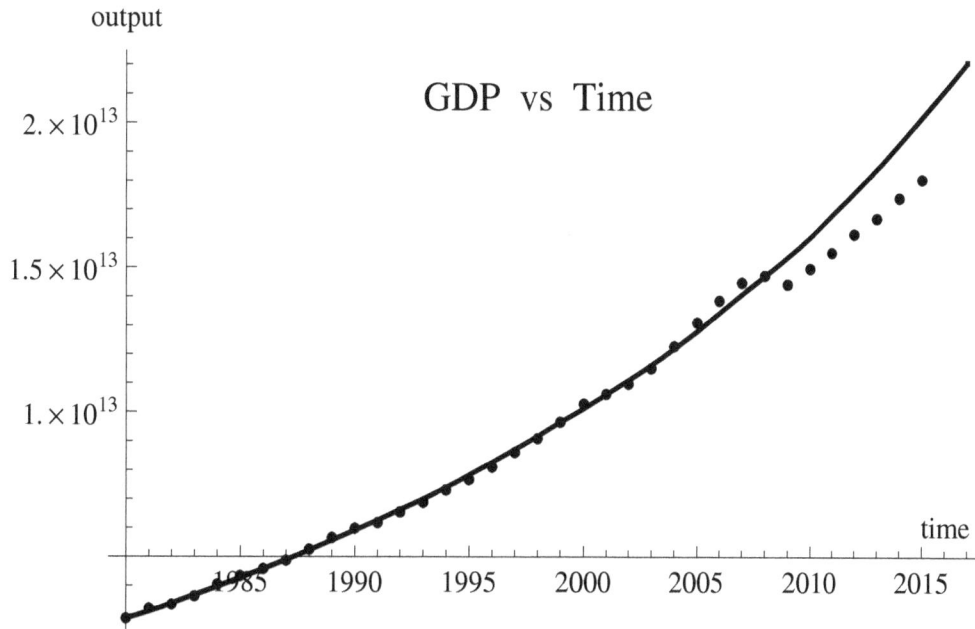

Figure 7.9: This plot shows the fit to the United States output produced by the constant coefficients c_1 and c_2 from 1980 to 2017 along with GDP data from 1980 to 2015.

declining average interest rate fits. The lack of any noticeable response of the output curve to the relatively large variations in interest rates undeniably demonstrates that interest rates are an ineffectual control of the output of the economy.

However, we note that the crisis of 2008–9 is not fit at all. Even the subsequent data after the crisis is not matched in slope and curvature. This demonstrates, without ambiguity, that the faltering of the real economy in 2008 did not occur as a natural occurrence within the real economy itself because, during this period, the interest rates were rapidly decreasing, which, if anything, would have caused an increasing output rate.

Instead, we must conclude that the financial system sharply and significantly reduced their propensity to loan, causing a credit crunch. We know, after the fact, that this was caused by the collapse of asset speculation within the real economy (housing) that was funded by credit, and by the unstable highly leveraged derivative bets within the financial system itself.

The financial system needed a government bailout in order to survive. Once they were assured of that bailout, they pushed loans at very low interest rates in order to stop the collapse of the real economy, and to get it started growing again. This action is shown by the stoppage of the very sharp decline in output between 2008 and 2009 and by the very abrupt return to growth between 2009 and 2010.

In Figure 7.9, the data points included in the plot make it almost impossible to see the small undulations introduced into the output caused by the relatively large variations of the average interest with time. In Figure 7.10, to show more clearly the variation in GDP caused by changes in the average interest rate, we show an expanded output curve from 1980 to 1997 without distracting data.

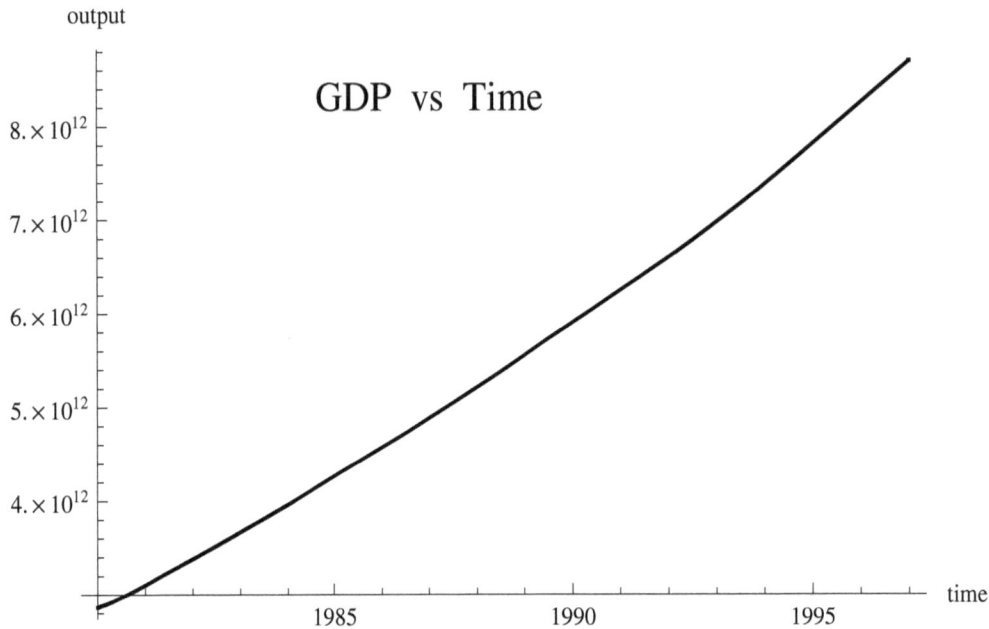

Figure 7.10: Here, we see what tiny undulations in the GDP are caused by relatively large variations in the average interest rate.

Even without distracting data, we more sense the undulations in the GDP output curve than see them cleanly. This weak effect shows us what a feeble control raising and lowering interest rates are as a tool to control the output of the real economy. Their real benefit is to the bankers because the banks make more money with higher interest rates and less money with lower interest rates. This is, of course, what interests bankers because this is how they receive their pay for the service that they perform for the country. The service they perform for the country is creating money through credit, the money upon which the economy runs. The more the banks profit, the higher the bankers' pay.

7.4   A Smooth Fit Using the Constructed Average Interest Rate

The average interest rate functions used in the calculations in this section are shown in Figure 7.11. The average interest rate functions for both the Federal Reserve does not increase interest rates scenario, and the Fed increases interest rates at three-quarters of a percent per year scenario are shown in this figure. These average interest rate functions were calculated using the weighted average interest rate function we constructed.

Now we will explore how the constructed average interest rate affects the nature of the various macroeconomic variables. To create the fit, we tried to get a very good smooth fit to the output of the United States Economy without trying to fit all the slight undulations in the GDP. In the fit, the coefficients c_1 and c_2 were made constant from 1980 to 1997, then adjusted simply from 1998 to 2008 and adjusted again from 2008 to 2015, leaving them at their original constant values beyond 2012. The coefficients c_1 and c_2 used are shown in

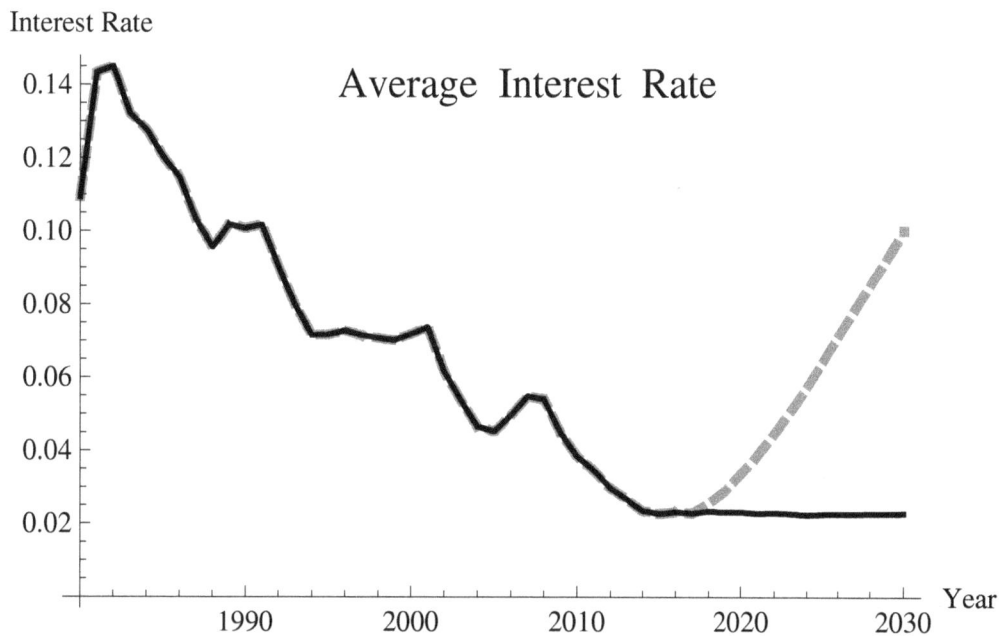

Figure 7.11: Here, we see the average interest rate function for the no rate scenario, black line, and for the Federal Reserve increases interest rates at three quarters of a percent per year, thick dashed gray line.

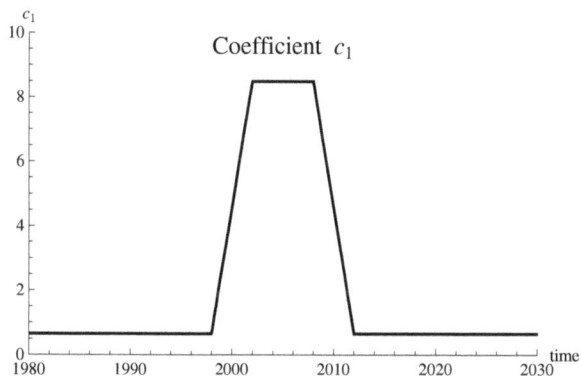

Figure 7.12: This figure shows the coefficient c_1 used in the smooth fit.

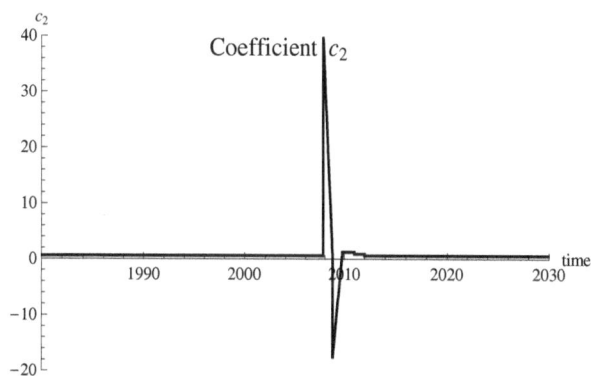

Figure 7.13: This figure shows the coefficient c_2 used in the smooth fit.

Figures 7.12 and 7.13. The output that resulted from these coefficients and the no rate hike average interest rate function, which was shown in Figure 7.11, is pictured in Figure 7.14.

Here we see that the coefficients, which were used to make the smooth fit with the constructed average interest rate, have the same general form as the coefficients used in the smooth fit created using the much smoother guesstimated average interest rate function shown in Figure 1.1 on page 15.

When we compare the output curve in Figure 7.14, created by the coefficients c_1 and c_2 shown in figures 7.12 and 7.13 and our more realistic constructed average interest rate function, with the smooth fit output curve of Figure 2.3, shown on page 21, we see that the

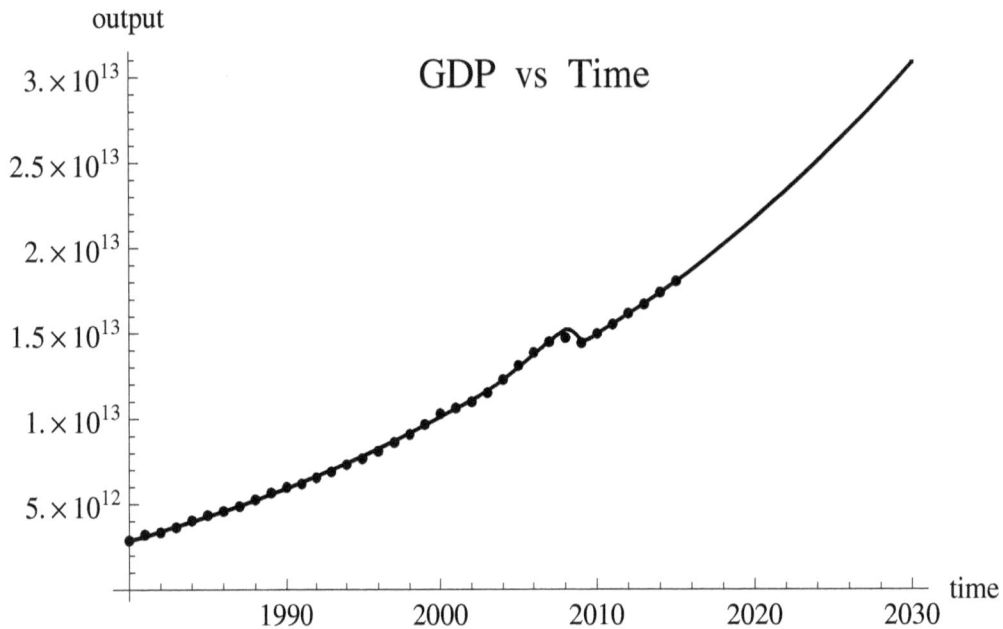

Figure 7.14: Here, we display the smooth fit to the GDP data that was calculated using our constructed average interest rate function.

output using the constructed average interest rate follows the undulations of the GDP more closely. Thus, we can see that the average interest rate does influence the GDP output, but probably not as much as we expected.

Also, when we compare the smooth fits of Figure 2.3 and Figure 7.14, we see that the curve of the output created from the more realistic average interest rate overshoots the GDP data in 2008 by more than the smooth fit in Figure 2.3, but is closer to the GDP in 2007. This mistiming results from a lack of economic awareness. My understanding at the time I had found a set of equations that allowed a fit to the United States Economy was insufficient to correctly set the time frame for setting the coefficients c_1 and c_2 of the investment equation, particularly in the smooth fit.

At the time, I was aware of the Congressional panic introduced during the Presidential Election of 2008 and dimly aware of the failure of sub-prime mortgage lenders earlier in the Spring of that year. This deficiency resulted in the creation of a function for the Banker's Coefficient, c_2, within the investment equation that did not allow for the correct timing of the impulses in a smooth fit. This caused me to put a late start in the changes allowed in the bankers' c_2 coefficient for the smooth fit. I have since learned that banks sharply put the brakes on lending starting toward the end of winter in 2007. And that J.P. Morgan and Goldman-Sachs had in the Fall of 2006 moved to decrease their exposure to sub-prime mortgages.

The fix is, of course, simple. One only needs to introduce the ability to add another impulse into the coefficient c_2 starting in early 2007. I have done this, and it allows one to drive the output through the GDP data points of 2007, 2008, and 2009. However, by doing this, a new element would be added into the mix that was not present in any of the earlier presentations. This would muddy the waters. One could, instead, rerun the various plots with a better c_2 function and produce noticeably better smooth fits during the crisis of 2008–9. However, this would hide the fact that discovery and learning are not a smooth process. More importantly, this result highlights the fact that people with a background in economics can make better and more efficient use of these equations than can I, a physicist, with a limited economics background.

Next, in Figure 7.15, we present the investment-to-GDP curve, and in Figure 7.16, we present the total economy debt. Both curves were calculated from the smooth fit and plotted over the corresponding data compiled for the United States.

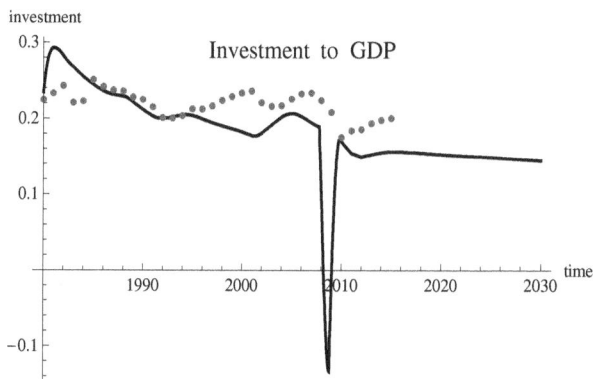

Figure 7.15: This plot shows the investment-to-GDP data along with the investment-to-GDP curve, which was calculated from the smooth fit using the average interest rate function that we constructed.

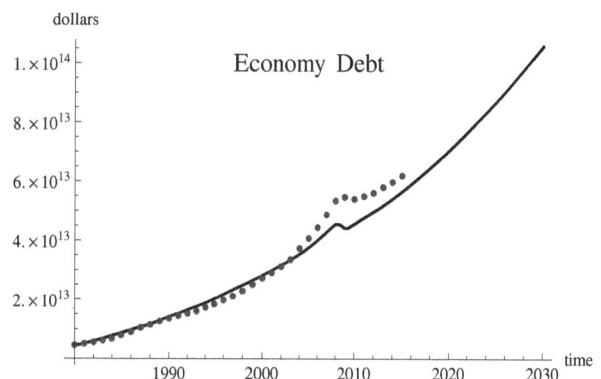

Figure 7.16: This figure shows the total economy debt, calculated from our constructed average interest rate function using a smooth fit. It is plotted over the data.

First, we notice that both these fits are very little different from the corresponding fits in Figure 2.5 and Figure 2.4, both shown on page 23, that were created using our more primitive average interest rate function. This is a second indication that the relatively large variations in interest rates along their general trend have a more subtle affect on macroeconomic variables than we might have expected.

Second, we see that the later in time data in both Figures 7.15 and 7.16 are noticeably above the fit curves. This is also true in Figures 2.4 and 2.5, as well as these same curves created in all the other fits.

If one looks carefully at Figure 7.15, we see that the data points for the investment-to-GDP ratio from 1995 and 1996, while above the fit curve, are tracking parallel to the fit curve. However, the direction of the data points from 1996 to 1997 turn upward and away from the direction along the fit curve. After that, they move further away from the fit curve and remain so on average. If one looks at the economy debt curve, one sees a similar thing. The direction of the 1995, 1996, and 1997 data points, while below the fit curve, parallel the fit curve's direction. However, the direction from the 1997 data point to the 1998 data point turns upward from the direction of the fit curve. The data points soon pass upward of the economy debt fit curve and remain noticeably above the fit curve throughout the rest of the total debt data collection.

In December of 1996, the Federal Reserve further weakened Glass-Steagall's restrictions on the commercial banking system's ability to deal in securities. They did this by allowing bank holding companies to own investment banks as long as less than twenty-five percent of their total revenue came from their securities business. Later in the summer of 1997, the Federal Reserve further weakened Glass-Steagall by allowing commercial banks to own securities companies. This weakening of Glass-Steagall allowed more and more of a commercial bank's loans to be to people or companies for speculative purposes. This speculative "investment" is really gambling. It does not add to the production of the real economy. When the investment data is tabulated from commercial banks' records, it is likely that speculative investment credit creation is included. However, when the fit equations are run, they produce their estimate of the real economy's GDP and the real economy's investment. This means that the investment data would tend to be larger than the modeled real economy investment because the investment data includes the real economy investment and part of the speculative investment. The same would be true for the modeled economy debt because the debt data in the real economy of the United States will include both the real economy debt and part of the speculative debt. This discrepancy would be expected to grow until the full effects of the repeal of Glass-Steagall, which occurred at the end of 1999, had come to pass. I expect that this change in the nature of our economy is being mirrored by Figure 7.15 and Figure 7.16.

7.4.1 Understanding the Investment Equation

To understand the investment equation, we rewrite the investment equation as

$$\frac{d}{dt}I = \Pi * \left[1 + c_1 * \left(\frac{\Pi}{Y}\right) - c_2 * \text{Sign}(\Pi) * \left(\frac{D}{v * Y}\right)\right],$$

where $\text{Sign}(\Pi)$ is $+1$ when the economy profit, Π, is positive and -1 when it is negative. As we can see from this equation, both the economy profit-to-GDP ratio, Π/Y, and the debt-to-GDP ratio, D/Y, are important elements of the investment equation. Because we have not presented an economy profit-to-GDP plot, we do so here in Figure 7.17. Also, in order to have everything in front of us, we present the debt-to-GDP plot in Figure 7.18, both calculated from the more realistic average interest rate function shown in Figure 7.11.

When we look at the debt-to-GDP ratio in Figure 7.18, we see that the economy debt-to-GDP ratio was below 1.6 in 1980 and that it increased to about 3.1 by 2017, according to our calculations. Because the capital stock to output ratio, v, has been assumed constant in every calculation setup that we have done and has had a value in these calculations of 2.682, this means that the term $D/(v * Y)$ has gone from about $1.57/2.682 = 0.59$ in 1980 to about $3.17/2.682 = 1.18$ in 2017. Similarly, when we look at the profit-to-GDP curve in Figure 7.17, we see the economy profit-to-GDP ratio, Π/Y, in our calculations has been less than 0.05 except during 1980, here and in all our other calculations. Thus, the

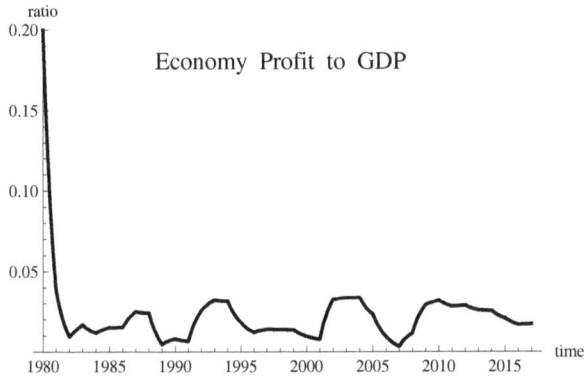

Figure 7.17: This plot shows the economy profit-to-GDP ratio calculated using the more realistic average interest rate function we constructed.

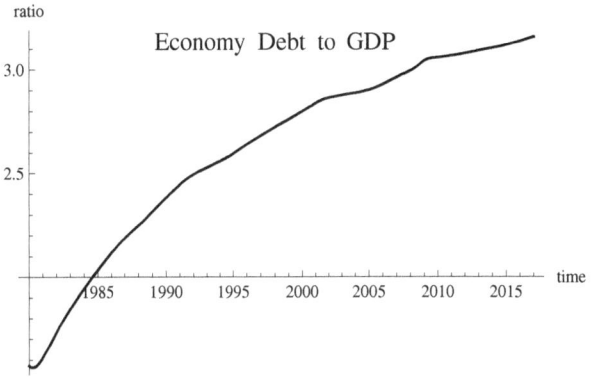

Figure 7.18: This figure shows the economy debt-to-GDP ratio calculated using the average interest rate function shown in Figures 7.5 and 7.6.

economy profit-to-GDP ratio in the United States has always been significantly smaller than the debt-to-GDP ratio throughout the period we have covered in our fits.

From the investment equation, shown above, we note that the investment will decrease (that is, the slope will become negative) only if the economy profit, Π, becomes negative, or the bracket becomes negative, but not both. We recall in the present calculations, with this average interest rate function, that in ordinary times, the coefficient of the Banker's Term is $c_2 = 0.6$ and the coefficient of the Businessman's Term, $c_1 = 0.65$. Thus, in ordinary times, the bracket can become negative only when $0.6 * [D/(v * Y)]$ is a little greater than one. This will occur if the debt-to-GDP ratio becomes greater than about five, since $0.6 * [5/2.682] = 1.12$. However, this will not occur in the present situation because the banks will collapse first because they cannot continue to be solvent for that long on zero or near-zero percent interest rates.

However, the bracket can become negative in a credit crunch as occurred in the crisis of 2008–9. This crisis in the real economy occurred because the banks decreased sharply their propensity to loan. This is represented in the investment equation by sharply increasing the value of the coefficient c_2, making the bracket negative. It is also possible to make the economy profit negative. The banks can do this easily in the present situation by raising interest rates. Looking at the economy profit equation,

$$\Pi = Y - w * L - r * D,$$

we see that increasing the average interest rate will decrease the economy profit. Therefore, if the banks raise the interest rate high enough, the economy profit will become negative. In Figure 7.19, we show that the economy profit for the smooth fit using the average interest rate function we created, in the Federal Reserve's scenario of increasing interest rates by three-quarters of a percent per year, will eventually produce a negative economy profit. In Figure 7.20, we show the corresponding total economy investment versus time graph.

In Figure 7.19, we see that the profit within the United States economy appears to become negative sometime during the first half of 2021, under the scenario in which the Federal

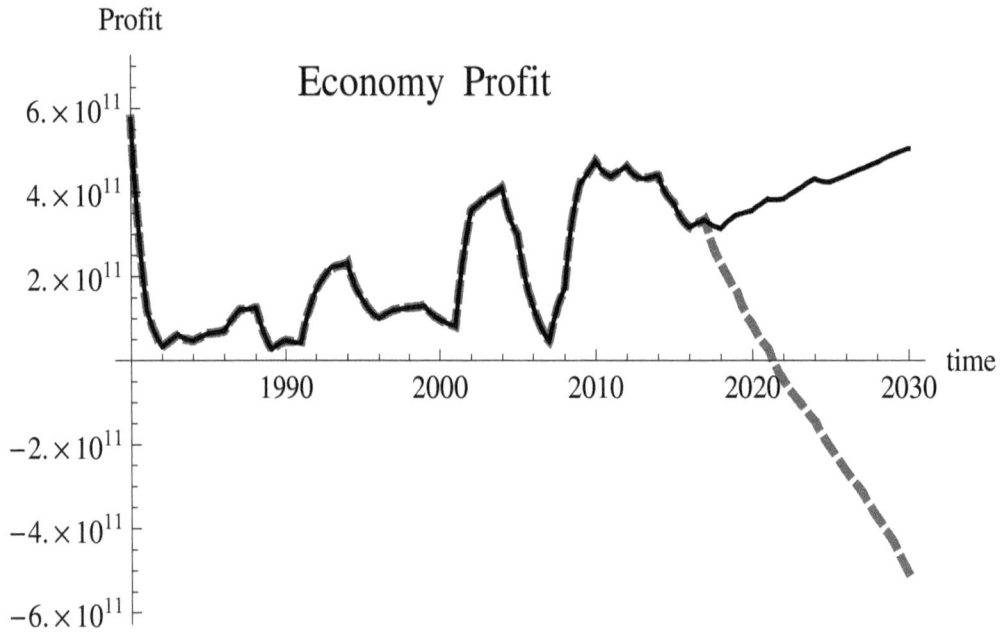

Figure 7.19: This plot shows economy profit within the economy for the Federal Reserve no rate hike scenario, solid line, and the three-quarters of a percent per year rate hike scenario, dashed line.

Reserve raises interest rates at a pace of three-quarters of a percent per year. If we solve for the time the economy profit becomes zero using the interpolating functions created by the fit, the solution predicts the economy profit becomes zero at 2021.28. This is a delay of about three years when compared to the results predicted by just attaching the Fed rate hikes onto the estimated average interest rate at the beginning of 2017. This result is slightly more than the 2.4-year delay that our toy average interest rate function for the Fed rate hikes produced in Section 4.3.

In Figure 7.20, we also see that the slope of the calculated investment curve, in the Fed increases interest rates at three-quarters of a percent per year scenario, appears to turn negative sometime in the first half of 2021. If we use the interpolating functions created by the fit to solve for when the slope of the investment curve equals zero, that is when $dI/dt = 0$, we get 2021.28 to within the precision provided by the solution. However, when we check the numbers, the time the slope of the investment curve peaks turns out to be predicted to be on the evening of April 13'th in 2021. This is about two-thirds of a day later than when we use the numbers to find when the economy profit equals zero. That is, the precision of the numbers we are using seems to produce results that are good to within plus or minus something somewhat less than a day. Whereas, our previous work suggested that our fitting and predicting procedure, itself, produced results that were good to within plus or minus something somewhat less than two months.

Here in Figure 7.20, we also see that the credit crunch caused by the banks' response to the financial system's cascading system failures suddenly produced a steep negative slope in the investment curve. In the crisis, we see that investment crashed, even becoming negative

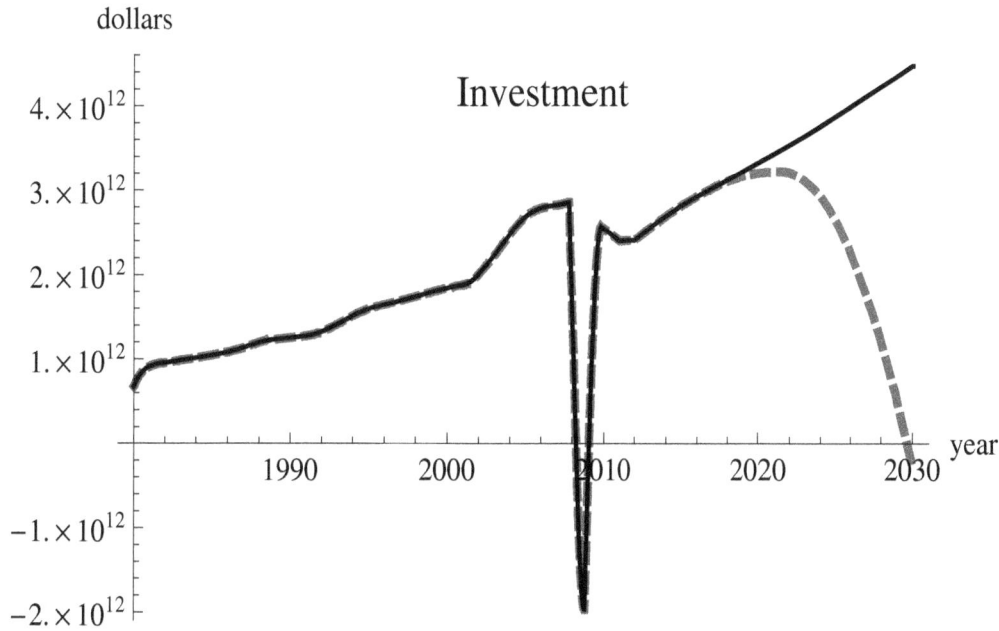

Figure 7.20: This plot shows investment within the economy for the Federal Reserve no rate hike scenario, solid line, and the Fed's three-quarters of a percent per year rate hike scenario, dashed line.

for a short period. Then, the banking system responded, almost as strongly, by pushing credit once their system bailout had been assured. That is, the sharp and rapid crash in investment is represented in the investment equation by a very sharp and large, positive change in the Banker's Term coefficient c_2. While, the corresponding almost as sharp and powerful rebound in investment is represented in the investment equation by a sharp and strong, negative impulse in the coefficient c_2. See Figure 7.13.

7.4.2 Other Fits

In order to allow a complete comparison with our previous fits, we present comparison plots between the no rate hike scenario and the Federal Reserve increases interest rates at three-quarters of a percent per year scenario, for fits created using our constructed average interest ratio functions for these scenarios shown in Figure 7.11. We show the comparisons grouped together in pairs. In Figure 7.21, we show the GDP versus time comparison, and in Figure 7.22, we present the economy debt versus time comparison. Then, we present the employment rate versus time and the wage rate versus time comparisons, in Figures 7.23 and 7.24, respectively.

When we look at the GDP versus time curve and the total economy debt versus time curve for the United States in Figure 7.21 and Figure 7.22, we see that both the output of the United States and the total economy debt for the United States would peak and then begin to crash as the Federal Reserve continues to raise interest rates at three-quarters of a percent per year. When we compare the timing of the output and economy debt peaks with

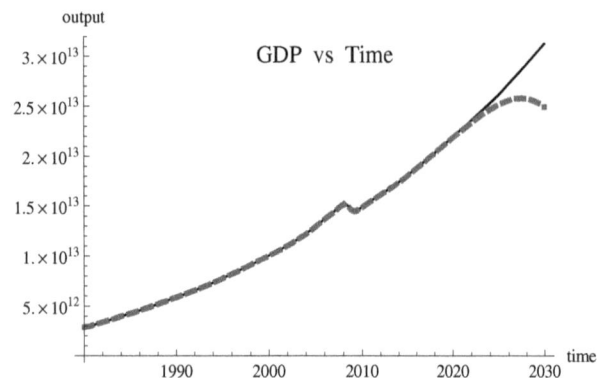

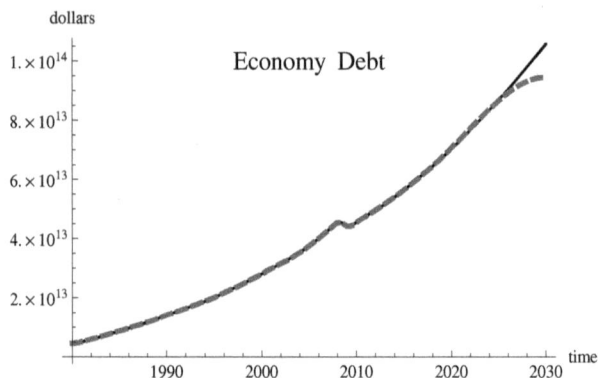

Figure 7.21: This plot shows the GDP versus time in the no rate hike scenario—solid black line—and in the Federal Reserve increases interest rates at three-quarters of a percent per year scenario—thick gray dashed line.

Figure 7.22: Displayed in this plot is the economy debt versus time for the no rate hike scenario—solid black line—and the Fed increases interest rates at three-quarters of a percent per year scenario—thick gray dashed line.

the corresponding curves for the smooth fit in Figures 2.8 and 2.9 on pages 25 and 26, we see that the peaks of both of these curves are retarded by about three years. This result occurred because we used our constructed average interest rate function instead of our earlier, more primitive method of just tacking the Federal Reserve's rate hikes onto the average interest rate when the Federal Reserve began its policy. We see the same retardation occurs when we compare the timing of the output and economy debt peaks in Figures 7.21 and 7.22 with the corresponding figures for the refined fit on pages 36 and 37.

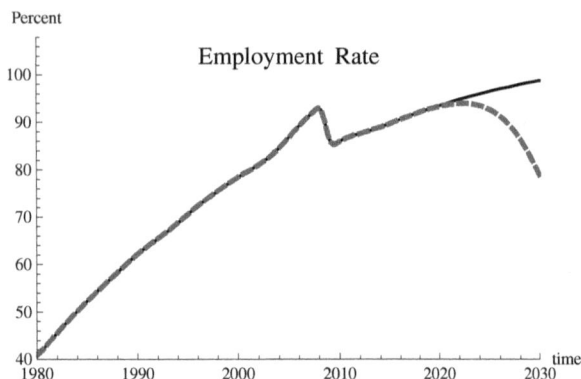

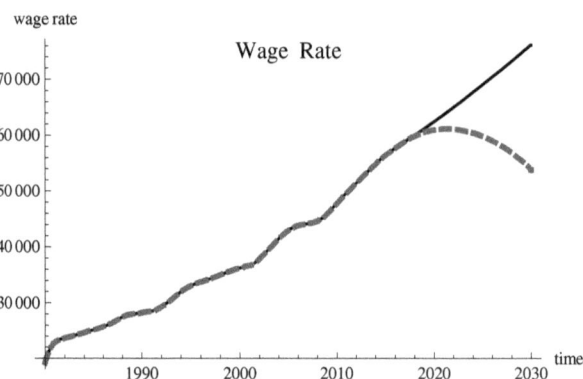

Figure 7.23: This plot shows the employment rate versus time in the no rate hike scenario—solid black line—and in the Federal Reserve increases interest rates at three-quarters of a percent per year scenario—thick gray dashed line.

Figure 7.24: Displayed in this plot is the average wage rate versus time for the no rate hike scenario—solid black line—and the Fed increases interest rates at three-quarters of a percent per year scenario—thick dashed gray line.

When we look at the employment rate and the average wage rate, displayed in Figures 7.23 and 7.24, we see that some four to five years after the interest rates hikes begin, both rates reach a peak. Then, they begin to crash, with the average wage rate crashing more slowly. We see that the timing is about three years later than it was for our previous smooth fit employment rate projection in Figure 2.11 and the average wage rate projection in Figure 2.12. Both figures are shown on page 28. Precisely the same comparisons hold in the refined fit, as shown in Figure 3.11 on page 39 and Figure 3.12 on page 40, respectively.

Unfortunately, we do not know how well our constructed average interest rate function represents the average interest rate at any given instant in time. Thus, we do not know how well the timing of events is predicted by our set of macroeconomic differential equations. If the Federal Reserve created average interest rate data, then economists could create an average interest rate function, from the Federal Funds Rate, that would accurately construct the actual average interest rate for future Federal Reserve interest rate policies. Such a function would allow economists and the Federal Reserve to make accurate predictions of the outcome of a particular interest rate policy.

Chapter 8

What is Really Going On with the Dynamics of the Real Economy

We are going to discuss the dynamics of the real economy by analogy with the dynamics in physics. In physics, we know that dynamics is governed by the simple Law of Newton that says that the sum of the forces on a particle is equal to the mass of the particle times its acceleration. If we know a particle's trajectory, then we know its acceleration.

If a particle is moving in a straight line, then it has acceleration if it is speeding up or slowing down. If a particle is following a curved path, even if it is not speeding up or slowing down, it has acceleration because its direction is changing. The quicker a particle is changing direction, the greater the acceleration, which is associated with its change in direction. Thus, a particle that is speeding up or slowing down while at the same time it is curving in space has both a tangential acceleration—an acceleration in the same direction of its motion if it is speeding up or in the opposite direction of its motion if it is slowing down—and a so-called normal acceleration, which is perpendicular to the particle's direction of travel with the normal acceleration's direction toward the inner sense of the curve.

We, physicists, are taught that the force necessary to change a particle's acceleration is caused as a natural consequence of changing a particle's momentum. However, Einstein and Newton thought otherwise. Newton called the resistance to change in the velocity of a particle, its inertia. He said it had a magnitude equal to the mass of the particle times the magnitude of its acceleration and a direction opposite to its acceleration. Einstein added to this that inertia was a consequence of the matter make up of Our Universe and that a correct model of Our Universe must explain inertia. That is, there was a real physical reason for Newton's Law. However, we can work out the dynamics of a situation without knowing the nature of the physical cause.

One can see from our equations that the Law governing the dynamics of a real economy is much more complex than the Law governing the dynamics of a particle in physics. However, by analogy with physics, knowing the trajectory of an economy will tell us a lot about what will be needed to change an economy from one trajectory into another, different economic trajectory.

In Figure 8.1, we consider a slightly modified version of the smooth fit trajectory of Figure 7.9, in the neighborhood of 2007. It is plotted over the yearly GDP data. The smooth fit trajectory of Figure 8.1 was created by keeping $c_2 = 0.6$, the same value it had in creating the smooth fit trajectory of Figure 7.9 shown on page 115. However, coefficient c_1 is no longer equal to the constant value 0.65. We have added the large impulse to c_1 between 1998 and 2012 that we used in creating the smooth fit shown in Figure 7.14. We plotted c_1 in Figure 7.12 on page 117. Comparing Figure 7.9 with Figure 8.1 shows us that the relatively large impulse added to the Businessman's Coefficient c_1 has only made a very modest change in the GDP trajectory.

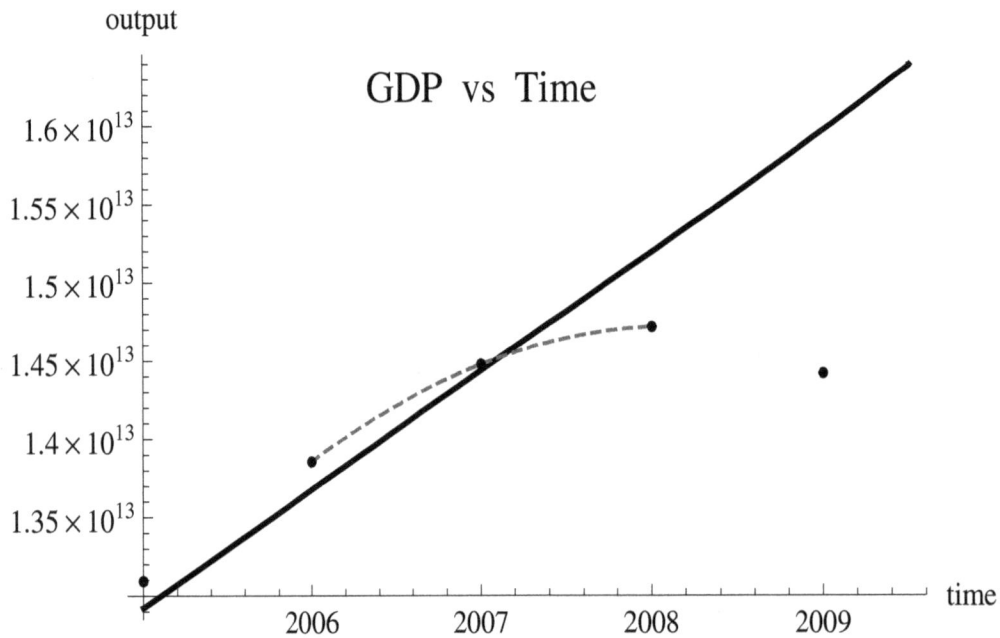

Figure 8.1: Here, we present the calculated smooth fit trajectory—solid black line—along with GDP data points. We cover only the smooth fit range from 2005 to 2010 in order to have an expanded view that will show the angular difference between the trajectories of the real economy and the smooth fit economy.

In Figure 8.1, the solid black line represents the smooth fit trajectory. The GDP data itself should give us a good idea of the actual GDP trajectory taken by the United States Economy. The thin gray dashed line was created by fitting the 2006, 2007, and 2008 GDP data points with a parabola. This should provide the reader with a good idea as to the direction of the United States' GDP trajectory at the beginning of 2007.

If one places a thin, very-bendable clear plastic ruler, such as a C-Thru 12Y or a number 36 Westcott bendable plastic ruler, edgewise along neighboring pairs of GDP data points, one can see that the growth in the real economy's GDP trajectory from 2006 to 2007 has weakened—that is, the trajectory is curved more tightly, downward—relative to the trajectory between 2005 to 2006.

We see the trajectory from 2007 to 2008 has a greater curvature relative to the trajectory from 2006 to 2007, and the GDP trajectory from 2008 to 2009 has a greater curvature relative to the trajectory from 2007 to 2008. Therefore, to fit the real economy's GDP trajectory, the impulse between 2006 and 2007 should be stronger than the impulse between 2005 and 2006; the impulse between 2007 and 2008 should stronger than the impulse between 2006 and 2007; and, the impulse between 2008 and 2009 should be stronger than the impulse between 2007 and 2008. If one checks the refined fit impulses in coefficient c_2 in Figure 3.2 on page 32, which were found by trial and error, this is precisely the size relationship between the impulses that one will find.

In Figure 8.1, when one compares the angle through which the trajectory of the smooth fit turns in going from its value for the GDP in 2007 through the value of the GDP in 2008 with the turning angle of the trajectory of the GDP in the real economy, one sees that the smooth fit turns through a much larger angle. This means the impulse from 2007 to 2008 must be much larger in the smooth fit than the impulse that was given by the bankers to the coefficient c_2 when they restricted lending leading up to the crisis of 2008–2009. The estimate of the bankers' impulse can be better made in the refined fit of Figure 3.2 because the refined fit was made to closely follow the real economy's GDP trajectory throughout the period leading up to the crisis of 2008–9.

Moreover, when one lines up a thin, bendable ruler edgewise along the smooth fit's trajectory and bends the ruler at 2007 such that ruler goes through the GDP data point at 2008, one finds that if one keeps roughly the same curvature in the ruler, then it goes through or comes very close to going through the GDP data point in 2009, as well. Does this mean that there would be very little to no impulse needed between 2008 and 2009 because the smooth fit trajectory will come very close to gliding through the GDP data point in 2009? What will happen to the trajectory of the GDP if the coefficient c_2 returns to its normal value of $c_2 = 0.6$ after the impulse? So far, our explorations have not touched upon these questions.

8.1 Applying the Impulse

Let's say that bankers had found themselves in an economy that was following the trajectory of the smooth fit in 2007 and wanted to see, for some reason, if they could drive the GDP of that economy through the GDP data values that our economy had in 2008 and 2009. Perhaps they were experimenting to see if their theory was correct and whether they could do it. So they withheld loans to the extent predicted by their theory and then went back to lending as usual just as shown in Figure 8.2.

In Figure 8.2, we show two Banker's Term c_2 impulses that would drive the smooth fit economy GDP trajectory through the real economy's GDP data values in 2008 and 2009. While in Figure 8.3, we show the result of these two impulses on the GDP of such an economy.

Figure 8.2 shows the first large-amplitude impulse from 2007.25 to 2008, which includes a small piece of the tiny triangular impulse that runs from 2007.8 to 2008.8. The second impulse, from 2008 to 2008.8, is needed to complete the driving of the trajectory through

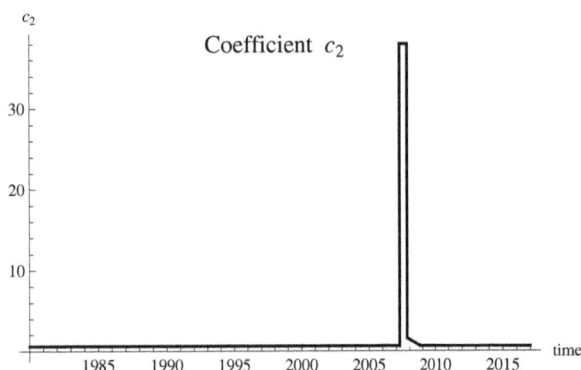

Figure 8.2: Here, we display the coefficient c_2 that will drive the output fit trajectory through the data points for the real economy's GDP in 2008 and 2009 and then return the lending practices to their normal state.

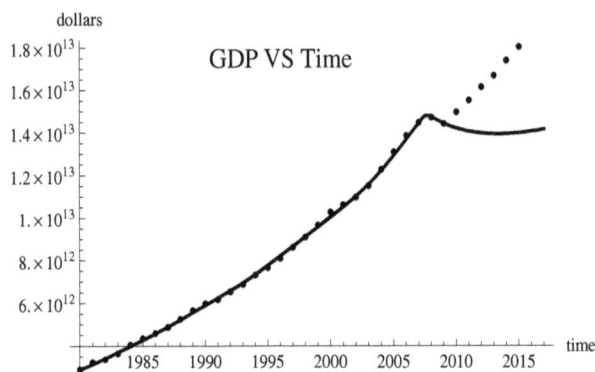

Figure 8.3: Here, we see the result of driving an economy following the smooth fit through the real economy's GDP values in 2008 and 2009 and then returning to normal credit practices after the credit crunch impulse.

2009. Both impulses are consistent with what we qualitatively questioned might be needed to drive the smooth fit economy from its GDP in 2007 through the GDP of the real economy in 2008 and 2009 using our bendable ruler.

We see from Figure 8.3 that the impulse pictured in Figure 8.2 did cause the output of an economy following the smooth fit trajectory to go through the real economy's GDP values in 2008 and 2009. However, we see that even though the financial system returned to normal credit practices, after their credit crunch inducing impulse, the economy did not recover. The GDP continued to decrease slowly for a while, and even by 2017, the GDP of this hypothetical economy would not have quite returned to the GDP value it continued its collapse from in 2009. It looks worse than the result Roosevelt achieved after fighting hard against the Great Depression, for eight years, during his first two terms.

However, would these impulses have induced a depression? To consider this question, we display the employment level during this scenario in Figure 8.4.

We see from the macroeconomic employment level in Figure 8.4 that this scenario would have caused a depression. This would have been so because the employment level continued to fall after lending practices returned to normal, and there would have been some 57.5 million fewer macroeconomic workers at the beginning of 2017 than there were at the peak employment level in July 2007.

Thus, in this scenario, to avoid the depression, the financial system would not only have to stop the credit crunch, but it would have to push credit in order to re-invigorate the real economy. In order to do this, the banks might need to reduce the restrictions needed to be met in order to borrow and possibly moderate penalties and other inhibiting conditions. Furthermore, they would want to reduce the cost of credit in order to induce businesses and consumers to borrow, so they could invest and consume in the real economy. They could do this by reducing interest rates.

In Figure 8.5, we display the c_2 impulse representing the banks' effort to re-invigorate

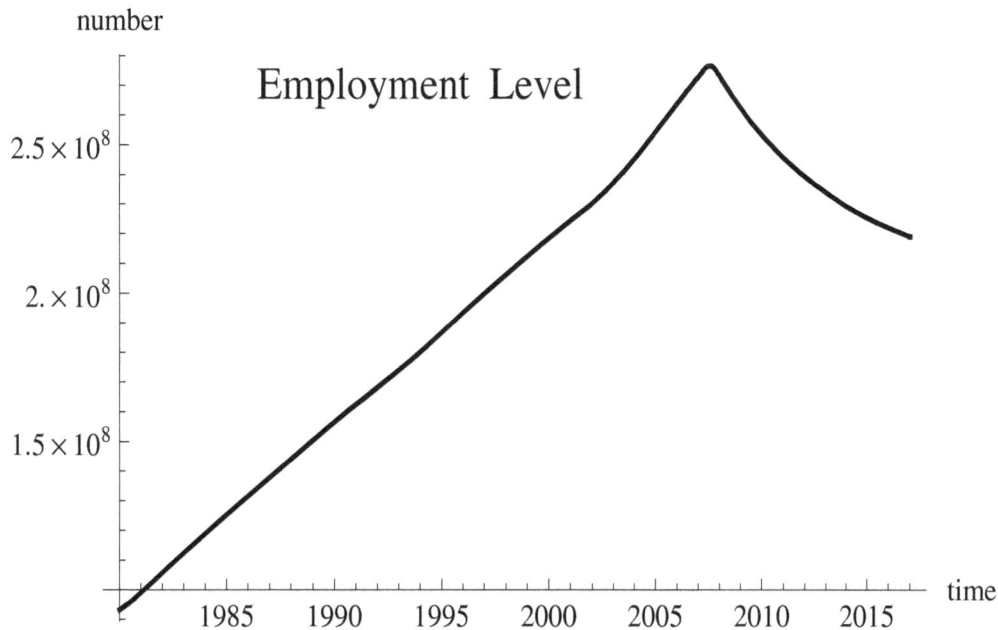

Figure 8.4: Here we see that this scenario would have caused a rapid and steep rate of job loss. The job losses would still be continuing eight years after the financial institutions returned to their normal credit practices.

the economy by pushing loans after the credit crunch. In Figure 8.6, we present the Federal Funds Rate and the Prime Interest Rate that were set up to entice investment and consumption within the real economy. These rates were set up so that very low rates would be ready when they would be needed, at the beginning of 2009, when the banks would push credit. These interest rates are appropriate for the present scenario and our original smooth fit scenario because the Banker's Term impulse to induce borrowing begins at the same time in both scenarios; moreover, this pushing of credit begins at the time in the real economy when the banks started to push credit after the credit crunch.

In order to contemporaneously discuss the affect of the Banker's Term impulses with the output of our macroeconomic equations, we present the calculated GDP output for the present scenario in Figure 8.7.

Looking at the form of c_2 in the plot shown in Figure 8.5, we see that it has a slightly different feel than the other smooth fit Banker's Coefficients that we have used during the crisis. The primary upward impulse that retards credit lending is separated in time from the main downward impulse that pushes credit. We know that the timing for when bank lending really tied up borrowing and caused a credit crunch is not correct. According to all reports, the main credit crunch occurred in 2008, not 2007. However, that is not the point of a smooth fit. The purpose of a smooth fit is to keep the fit close enough to the trajectory of the real economy so that, over the space of a few years, one can align the fit with the trajectory of the real economy. Doing so then makes it possible to make accurate predictions and policies using the fit.

We see from Figure 8.7 that the extra impulse allows the smooth fit to go nicely through

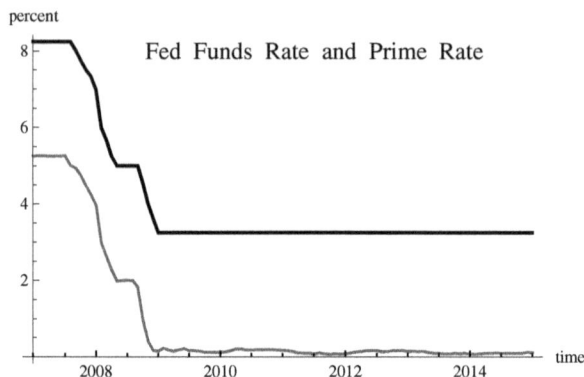

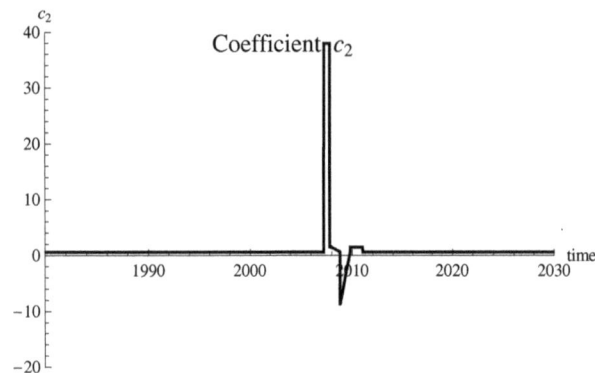

Figure 8.5: This figure shows a graph of the coefficient c_2 with its extra impulse that allows a smooth fit to be driven through the data points for the GDP in 2008, and 2009. The negative impulse in c_2 encourages investment, which allows the output to go through the GDP in 2010.

Figure 8.6: He we display the Prime Interest Rate, black line, and the Federal Funds Rate, gray line, that were in effect during both the original smooth fit in Section 7.4 and the present scenario, which creates an extra impulse that causes the output to pass through the GDP of 2008 and 2009.

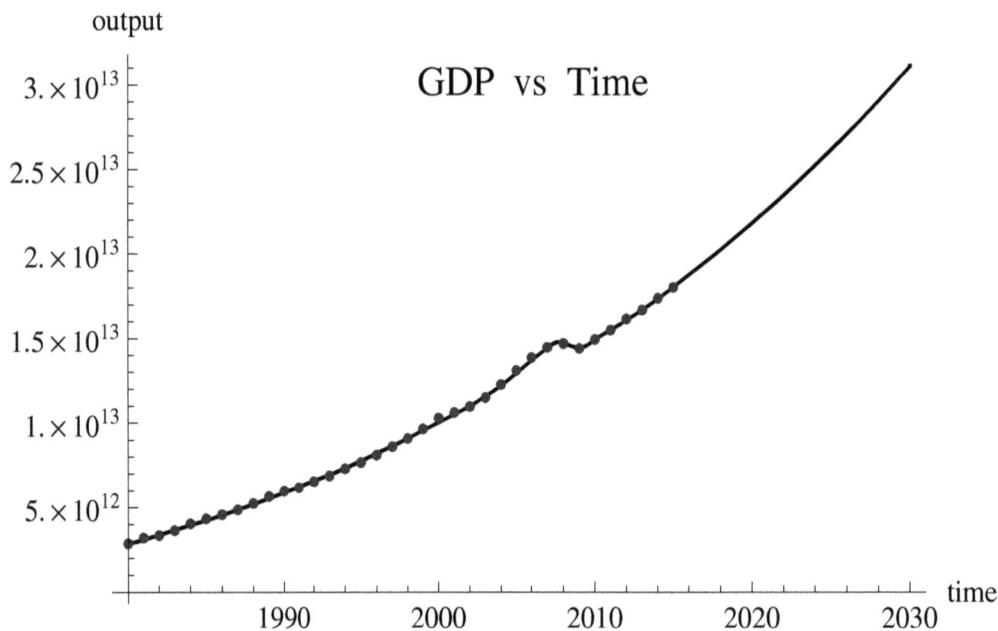

Figure 8.7: This plot shows the fit to the output using the extra impulse that allows a smooth fit to drive the output through the GDP data points in 2008 and 2009.

the 2008 and 2009 data points for the GDP in the crisis of 2008–9. Furthermore, as we saw in the output plot in Figure 8.3, we needed a Banker's Term impulse that would push credit in order to cause the output fit to rebound through the GDP data point in 2010. As we see in Figures 8.5 and 8.7, the downward impulse that started in very late 2008 caused the output curve to rebound through the GDP data point in 2010. In addition, we see that the very weak positive impulse between 2010 and 2011 has tempered the response of the output fit such that the trajectory of the output curve glides along the trajectory of the real economy from 2012 to 2015 while using the natural fit parameters that allowed a good smooth fit to the GDP over the period from 1980 to 1997. This indicates the multidimensional trajectory of the smooth fit is now synchronized with the trajectory of the real economy.

The reason why we can say that the trajectory of the whole model is synchronized with the trajectory of the real economy once the trajectory of a single macroeconomic variable of the model is synchronized with the corresponding macroeconomic variable of the real economy for a significant period is the following. We all know and expect that if the rest of the macroeconomic variables were substantially discordant, then where the macroeconomic variable of the fit and the trajectory of the real economy become equal, what we would have is a crossing of the model trajectory for that variable and the real economy trajectory for that variable. Also, we would expect that the less discordant the other variables, the more shallow the crossing. Moreover, if the discordance were small enough, then it would take some time to perceive the crossing of the variable's trajectories. Because we are unable to see the trajectories cross in three years, this likely means the discrepancy from synchronization between the model and the real economy is all but insignificant.

If we compare the c_2 impulse in Figure 7.13 on page 117 of the original smooth fit model in Section 7.4 with extra impulse model in Figure 8.5, we find that major impulses of the original smooth fit, which drove the credit crunch and the rebound of the economy, occurred very close in time to where they are said to have occurred, whereas the impulses of our second model did not. However, the original smooth fit missed the 2008 GDP, with the crash in the GDP starting a few months late. That is, both smooth fit models missed aspects— different aspects—in the dynamics of the crisis of 2008–9.

Moreover, it took a few years to synchronize the trajectories of both models to the trajectory of the real economy. If one looks carefully, one sees that the manipulation of the c_2 impulses causing the synchronization of the smooth fit "economy" trajectory with the real economy trajectory took place over a period of about four years, in both manipulations.

In order to get a quick rebound, financial institutions had to push loans. However, even more was required, one needed to have borrowers who would be eager to take out a loan given the financial burden it entails. The lower the interest rate on a loan, the lighter the financial burden a loan entails. This is particularly important for small businesses because they often pay an interest rate at or somewhat above the Prime Interest Rate when they take out a loan. It is also essential that the real economy does not experience a prolonged steep decline because then a discouraged attitude can develop. The more such an attitude develops in a person, the harder it is for the person to act. So, it was important for low-interest rates to be there when they were needed. When we look at the Prime Interest Rate and the Federal Funds Rate in Figure 8.5, we can see that rates reached bottom at or just before the beginning of 2009. Thus, we see that the low rates were there at precisely the time they were needed.

In Figure 8.8, we present the investment versus time curves for the present smooth fit. We do this so we can compare the results between our two smooth fit scenarios, both of which use the average interest rate functions shown in Figure 7.11.

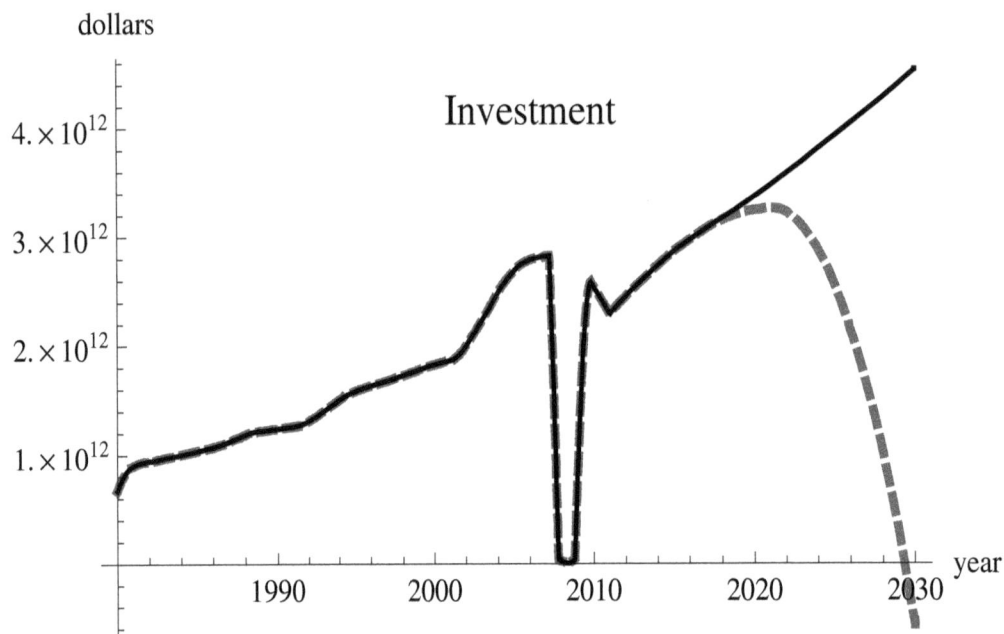

Figure 8.8: Here, we see the investment versus time graph for the smooth fit created using the coefficient c_2 pictured in Figure 8.5.

In the investment versus time plot of Figure 8.8, one sees that the crash in investment during the crisis of 2008–9 stops just above zero. This is not a general result. In the present scenario created with the c_2 shown in Figure 8.5, a fit to the two data points for the GDP of 2008 and 2009 was found by first adjusting the additional c_2 impulse over the interval $2007.25 \leq t < 2007.8$ so that the fit glided into GDP value in 2008. Then, a minimal amount of c_2 impulse was added over the interval $2007.8 \leq t < 2008.8$ in order to adjust the output curve so it would just glide into the GDP of 2009. Then a following needed negative impulse, which would push loans, was added over the interval $2008.8 \leq t < 2009.8$ so it would drive the output fit through the GDP for 2010. However, this impulse, because it started before 2009, actually pushed the output slightly above the GDP in 2009. Finally, a small tempering c_2 impulse, over the interval $2009.8 \leq t < 2011$ was added so that the output was caused to go through the GDP of 2011 and then glide through values for the United States GDP from 2012 through 2015. A last interval of $2011 \leq t < 2012$ was available for use, in case it was needed, in order to allow the output to glide through the GDP values for 2013, 2014, and 2015.

However, if in the second interval, $2007.8 \leq t < 2008.8$, the impulse for c_2 is increased slightly—with appropriate changes made to the later impulses so that the output glides through the GDP values of 2013, 2014, and 2015—then investment during the crisis of 2008–9 can be made to become negative. However, because this smooth fit, as we have seen above, does not get the dynamics right just before and during the time period of the crisis, it is not an appropriate method for determining whether or not the investment actually turned negative for a short period during the crisis of 2008–9. A refined fit that goes through the GDP data of 2005, 2006, 2007, 2008, 2009, and 2010 is much more appropriate if one has the desire to answer this question.

We have claimed that the present scenario, which added an extra impulse to the smooth fit that caused the output to go through the GDP of the United States in 2008, was made synchronous with the trajectory of the real economy of the United States. We can also make the same claim for the original fit we created in Section 7.4. We can make this claim because the original scenario in Section 7.4 was made to *glide* through the values for the United States GDP in 2013, 2014, and 2015. This can be seen by examining the Banker's Term coefficient for the original scenario shown in Figure 7.13 in conjunction with an examination of the GDP versus time graph for that scenario shown in Figure 7.14. Therefore, because both scenarios have been synchronized with the real economy through 2015, we conclude that their trajectories will be synchronized with each other beyond 2015. If so, then both smooth fits should give the same predictions in the Federal Reserve scenario that raised interest rates by three-quarters of a percent per year.

When we look at the investment comparisons plots of the two Federal Reserve Scenarios created by two very different sets of impulses, shown in Figure 7.13 on page 117 and Figure 8.5, we see that the comparison plots, shown in Figure 7.20 on page 123 and Figure 8.8, look very similar beyond 2015.

When we calculate the peak of the investment versus time graph in the Federal Reserve increases interest rates at three-quarters of a percent per year scenario, we find that Mathematica's FindRoot function returns a value of 2021.28 for both smooth fit scenarios. While the corresponding value for the time when the economy profit equals zero is also found to be 2021.28 in both scenarios. (The exactness of these results to within the accuracy of the calculations can be nothing but luck.) While the values obtained for the time when the crashing investment becomes zero were found by FindRoot to be 2029.37 for the original scenario in Figure 7.4, and 2029.36 for the present scenario created using c_2 shown Figure 8.5. Again, the closeness of these results indicates a very fortuitous coincidence between the two scenarios in the trial and error, by-eye lineups of the *gliding* output with the GDP values for 2012, 2013, 2014, and 2015.

8.1.1 Summing Up

In this chapter and in Section 7.4 of the previous chapter, we have shown that a more realistic form for the average interest rate function does not change the fundamental results we found with a much smoother average interest rate function. In this section, we have used the curvature of the GDP trajectory of the real economy to indicate qualitatively and semi-quantitatively how the output trajectory can be changed using the Banker's Term in order to line up the trajectory of a smooth fit with the trajectory of the real economy. That we were able to use trajectories in the manner that we were, likely indicates that there is a complex Law of Economics governing modern economies for which we have stumbled upon a workable mathematical approximation—after a couple centuries of thought and hard work.

8.2   A Comment

We have seen in the example associated with Figure 8.2 and Figure 8.3 that a credit crunch of an effective length of about seven or eight months, followed by a return to normal credit practices, would cause a long but shallow depression. To have this kind of depression, the financial system would have to be in a healthy state in order to return to normal business practices and to be able to do so for more than nine years.

The crisis of 2008–9 did not occur under a healthy financial system. In fact, the credit crunch occurred because the financial system had become unstable due to the high level of credit that they had advanced for speculation and due to the enormous amount of their derivative bets. When the speculative bubble started to burst, the financial system responded by withholding credit in an effort to curtail future losses. This loss of credit started to shrink the money in the real economy, and the economy started to falter. This set up a positive feedback loop so that the financial system and hence, the real economy started to cascade downward.

The financial system could not handle the problem. They had to go to Congress. Once they had gotten their bailout, they were able to push credit and reduce their interest rates for loans to rock bottom. They did this in order to entice businesses and consumers to borrow. This quickly halted the crash in the real economy and got it growing again, but at a noticeably reduced rate of growth.

This result shows that we have learned since the Great Depression of the 1930s. In the Great Depression, the output dropped like a rock for the first three years. The GDP was dropping yearly by double-digit percentages, and it was accelerating. The GDP dropped almost 12 percent the first year, 16 percent the second year, and then 23 percent the third year. Finally, in the fourth year after the crash, the drop in the GDP was only 3.4 percent. It was followed, at last, by a 16.8 percent increase in the GDP in 1934—five years after the crash. The Roosevelt Administration had gotten a handle on the situation. However, it was still not until 1941 that the GDP of the United States exceeded the GDP in 1929.

During World War II, we accelerated out of the Depression. The rest of the World was not so lucky, because the War was fought on their lands. We escaped that destruction because we did not have armies marching over our lands, and bombs destroying our cities and people. It was a long, deep, and damaging depression that did not end for the World until a few years after World War II ended.

Some economic pundits have said that we should not have bailed out the financial system in the crisis of 2008–9. Instead, they say, we should have let the system crash in order to reset the system. They say we have not fixed the problems and that we have only kicked the can down the road. Furthermore, they say: we can not prevent the eventual crash; moreover, the longer we put off the crash, the worse it will be.

They may be correct if we accept the inevitable crash as a Law of Nature. However, we see that we were able to learn how to stop a financial and economic system collapse. In the crisis of 2008–9, we reacted quickly; we pushed credit and dropped interest rates to the floor.

We stopped the crash. We did not know how to do that in 1929!

It is true that we did not fix our problems. We still have a huge debt problem. We have a speculation problem in which people are gambling with the wealth of the Nation for their own personal gain. In addition, we have an income inequality problem that has become so severe that it is beginning to rip our Nation apart.

However, we learned back in the 1930s how to fix the speculation problem. The solution we came up with was Glass-Steagall. Glass-Steagall separated banks into two classes, commercial banks that could "loan" money for investment into the real economy but could not loan for speculative purposes, and investment banks that could lend for speculative purposes but could not lend into the real economy. It worked quite well for more than sixty years until it was repealed in 1999.

We have seen that with taxation, we can keep income inequality from becoming wildly disparate. In fact, we can keep the income gap within any bounds we see as appropriate. A side benefit of such taxation is that it could prevent people from obtaining enough income to be able to corrupt the whole system for their private benefit, as is possible now.

Lastly, we have seen how we can resolve the debt problem. We can do so at almost no cost, while at the same time providing cash to the banking system that would stabilize it against collapse. We have also seen how we could regulate the financial system by requiring the banks to keep the *debt-to-GDP* ratio below 1.4 in order to help stabilize the economy and to prevent it from getting into an economic situation like the one we now face.

We could also adopt a hybrid economy. This would allow the Federal Government to spend a limited amount of debt-free money into the economy each year. Also, because this money would remain within the economy, it would eliminate much of the need for money creation by credit. Then people and businesses would only need to resort to credit for the less usual and more significant expenses, such as buying a home or car and starting or expanding a business. Debt-free money would dramatically mitigate the effects of a credit crunch on the real economy because only a fraction of the money within the economy would be affected by the credit crunch.

Thus, if we act upon what we have learned, we will not have kicked the can down the road, as the pundits have said. Instead, we will have made use of the time given to us by the Federal Reserve and the Government who stepped in, stopping the crash in the crisis of 2008–9. Our job, now, is to communicate to people how we can fix our problems so that we can salvage the situation. Our fate is not inevitable.

Part II

FITS THAT BEGIN IN 1964

Chapter 9

An Economy Fit that Starts in 1964

9.1   Introduction

So far, we have begun all our fits from the year 1980. We have also used a productivity with a fixed constant average growth rate in all our fits. I lived through the time from 1964 to 1980, and I was aware during this period that there was very high and disrupting inflation in the 1970s. The output, investment, and debt, in our fits, are all expressed in current dollars so that inflation, at least, would be implicitly represented in their macroeconomic equations. However, what about a productivity with a constant growth rate?

In macroeconomics, it seems productivity is often considered to be an exponential function that has an approximately constant growth rate such that output divided by productivity equals the employment level used to create that output. This has seemed intuitively somewhat unsettling to me. In addition, I have heard from various pundits, economic and otherwise, that productivity is not rising or even decreasing at the present time.[1] This seems like an erroneous view of productivity to me. To me, productivity is equal to the number of worker hours that it would take to produce a given output of product, measured in terms of the quantity of the product output, rather than in the dollar monetary price of the goods output. Thus, productivity growth is the "growth" in the decrease in the number of worker hours that it would take to produce a given output of product, and therefore, to me, productivity would tend to be always growing, except possibly in some extraordinary times during which knowledge is being lost.

In the following chapters, we will fit the United States Economy in four distinct ways. The first two methods will use two distinct productivities with fixed growth rates starting in the year 1964. The second two methods will use productivities whose growth rates are not fixed. These latter two methods will use different productivities, which will be designed in such a way that they will also allow projecting the United States Economy forward under various assumed economic conditions.

---

[1]This supposed slow increase or possibly decrease in productivity often seems to be used as a justification as to why wages are rising so slowly for the average worker.

During the period from 1964 to the early 1980s, significant changes occurred in the nature of the United States Economy. Except for a couple of years during this period, in which it was a few percent higher, the maximum tax bracket was seventy percent. In the period which followed, starting in 1982, the maximum tax bracket was fifty percent or less.

The gold standard for our money supply changed over the years from 1964 through 1971. First, as a prelude to the ramp of the Vietnam War, the gold cover for the Federal Reserve was decreased from twenty-five percent to zero, This allowed for the creation of money through credit, which meant the war and social programs could be financed without the need for tax increases to pay for them. This increased spending caused a slow but steady increase in inflation as the war ramped up from 1965. In response to this problem, the Government under President Nixon closed the gold window, which had allowed foreign governments to redeem United States Dollars for gold. The current price for gold when this policy was instituted in 1971 was $120 per ounce. However, the United States Government sold the gold to the foreign governments at the legally mandated price of $35 per ounce, which caused a gold drain that needed to be stopped. The closing of the gold window resulted in a change in the way international trade was paid for.

Also, during this time, the Mid-East Oil Embargo occurred, causing a sharp decrease in the availability of gasoline and a concurrent relatively large increase in its price. These price increases added significantly to inflation within the economy. The inflation and resulting Federal Reserve interest rate hikes attempting to fight inflation lasted into the early 1980s.

Because the economy during the added period from 1964 to 1980 is so different from the periods following, there is a real question as to whether or not the macroeconomic equations which we have used for our earlier fits will work well for the new period. Moreover, even if they do work, will they give us consistent results when it comes to predicting the United States Economy? We investigate these questions along with the nature and generality of our macroeconomic equations in the following chapters.

9.2   A Fit with an Initial Productivity Defined Relative to a 1980 Fit

The second starting date of 1964 was eventually picked in order to provide a relatively smooth start that would allow the fit to the first five or six data points to be made without adjusting any of the parameters of the macroeconomic differential equations during the period from 1964 through 1969. This approach was chosen in the hopes that the parameters that were found, which would allow this, would create a reasonable representation of the United States Economy during *stable economic conditions*, such as those that occurred from 2010 through 2015.[2] This should then allow the fit equations to be synchronized with the economy during the 2010 to 2015 time period. This synchronization would allow various

---

[2]Note that "stable economic conditions" means that the economic conditions under which the economy is running are held relatively fixed and not that the economy or even the economic conditions themselves are inherently stable.

economic policies to be assumed, which the macroeconomic differential equations could project forward in order to predict the results of those policies.

The initial productivity in the 1980 fits was chosen so that the output of the economy divided by the productivity equaled the employment level in 1980. Specifically, the productivity a(t) in 1980 was defined as $a(1980) = 2.796 * 10^{12}/90,994,000 = 30,727.3$. After messing with a great deal of data, back at the beginning of my research, the productivity growth rate I settled on was a growth rate of $\alpha = 0.0201$ per year.

In this fit, the productivity has been chosen to be consistent with the productivity used in all the 1980 fits. That is, the initial productivity in this 1964 fit is given by:

$$a(1964) = a(1980) * e^{\alpha*(1964-1980)} = 30727.3 * e^{0.0201(-16)}$$
$$= 22,276.93.$$

In this fit, the initial value of the wage rate was adjusted in order to get the fit to travel along the first five or six GDP data points. Other than this change, all the other initial fit parameters remain the same as in the 1980 fits created using our constructed average interest rate function of Chapter 7. The purpose of this procedure was to have coefficients c_1 and c_2 that would allow the economy to be synchronized and projected forward in time.

Our chief objective in creating the fits starting in 1964 is to determine the validity of our macroeconomic differential equations. Our main way of doing this will be to compare the predictions made by the 1964 fits with those made by the fits starting in 1980.

The coefficients c_1 and c_2 used in the fit are shown below.

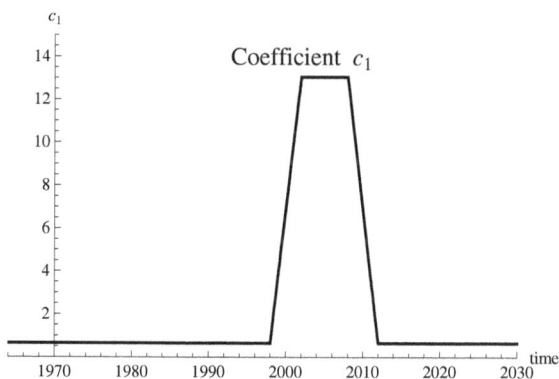

Figure 9.1: This figure displays the Businessman's Coefficient c_1 used in the fit.

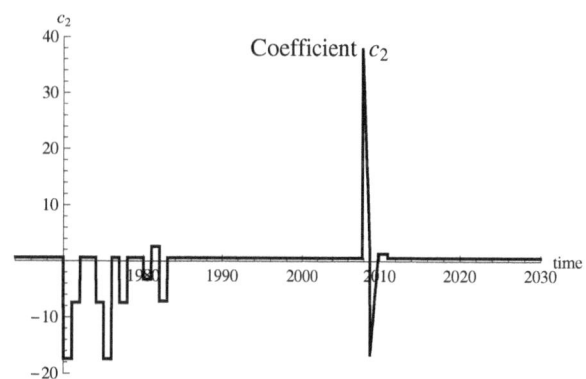

Figure 9.2: This figure shows the Banker's Coefficient c_2 used in the fit.

Note in Figure 9.1 that the coefficient c_1 has the same beginning values and projection values beyond 2013 as it did for the 1980 fit, which used our constructed average interest rate function. From Figure 9.2, we see that the same thing is true for coefficient c_2. Also, we note from Figure 9.2 that a smooth fit to the output was created between 1998 and 2008.

The average interest rate functions used in the first two fits that start in 1964 are shown in Figure 9.3. We constructed the average interest rate function in Chapter 7 and used it with that chapter's 1980 fit. The dashed curve shows the interest rate for the Federal Reserve's rate hike scenario, and the solid black curve shows the interest rate for the no rate hike scenario. The output curve's fit to the GDP data is shown in Figure 9.4.

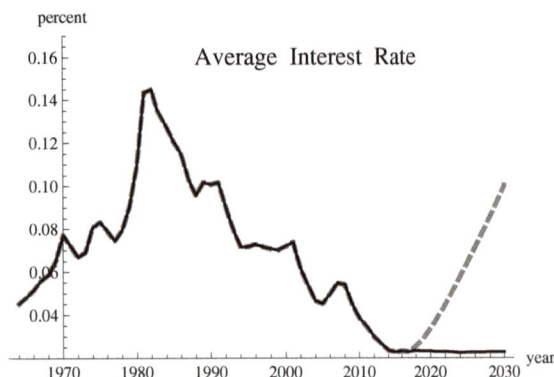

Figure 9.3: This figure shows our constructed average interest rates used in fitting and projecting forward the Federal Reserve interest rate scenarios.

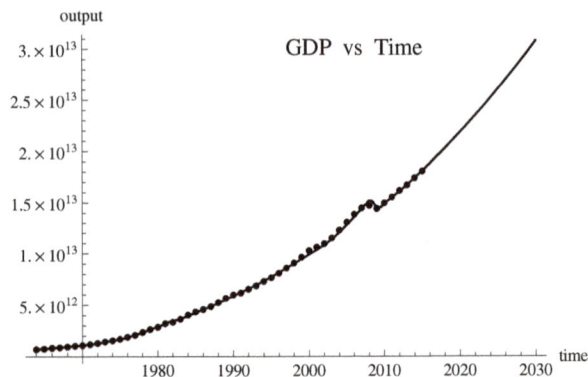

Figure 9.4: This figure displays the smooth fit of the output curve plotted over GDP data in the no rate hike scenario.

The average interest rate curves in Figure 9.3 look exactly the same as the average interest rate curves shown in Figure 7.11, on page 117, from 1980 onward. The output curve starting in 1964 is seen to make a good fit to the GDP data. Because the output curve tracks smoothly through the GDP data points of 2013, 2014, and 2015, it appears likely that our model will allow us the project the United States Economy forward in time.

Next, we show the fit curves to the economy debt in Figure 9.5 and investment to GDP in Figure 9.6, with each curve overlaying the data for the economy.

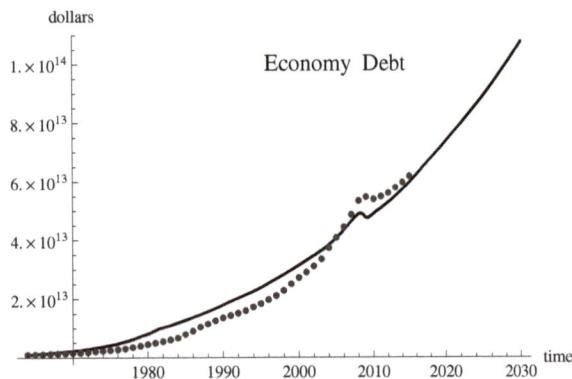

Figure 9.5: Here, we see the economy debt data for the United States overlaying the economy debt curve created by the fit.

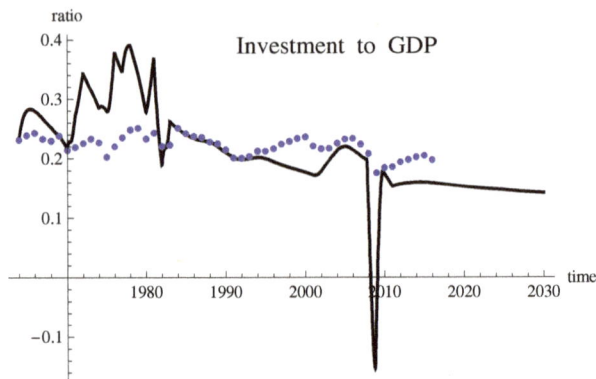

Figure 9.6: This figure displays the investment-to-GDP data overlaying the investment-to-GDP curve created from the present fit starting in 1964.

We see from Figures 9.5 and 9.6 that the total economy debt curve and the investment-to-GDP curve fit the economy debt data and the investment-to-GDP data about as well as the curves for the fits, which began in 1980. However, we note the economy debt curve in Figure 9.5 is a bit higher above the data from 1980 to 2000, but somewhat nearer to the debt data beyond 2000 in comparison to the 1980 fit, which was pictured in Figure 7.16 on page 119. While when we look carefully at the investment-to-GDP curve in Figure 9.6 and compare it with the investment-to-GDP curve in Figure 7.15 on page 119, we see that it is ever so slightly a better fit beyond 1980. However, the present investment-to-GDP curve appears to be systematically too high from 1964 to 1980.

9.2.1   Federal Reserve Scenario Projections

Next, we want to examine whether or not starting our macroeconomic equations from a different time materially affects the predicted results we obtain from projecting the economy forward. We will start with the GDP and economy debt, forward projection curve comparisons, for the two Federal Reserve interest rate hike scenarios in Figures 9.7 and 9.8, respectively. Just as before, the thin solid black line will represent the Federal Reserve no rate hike scenario, while the thicker dashed gray line will represent the Federal Reserve three-quarters of a percent per year, interest rate hike scenario.

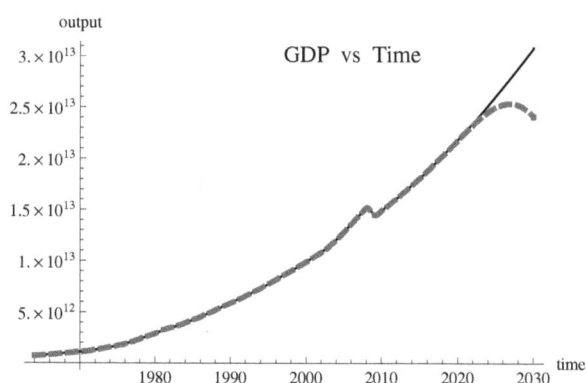

Figure 9.7: Displayed in this figure is the United States output projected forward under the Fed no rate hike scenario–black line—and the Federal Reserve interest rate hike scenario.

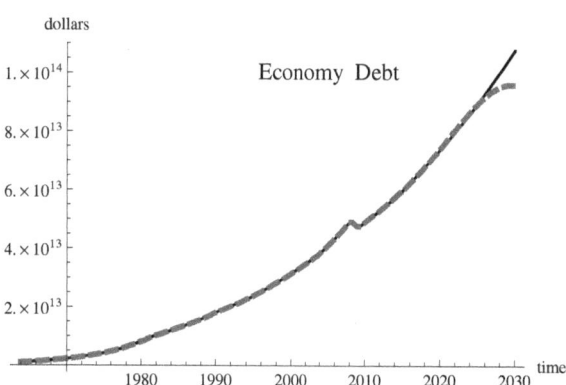

Figure 9.8: This figure shows total economy debt for the United States projected forward under the Federal Reserve no rate hike policy, and the Fed interest rate hike policy—dashed line.

When these figures are compared directly with their counterparts, in Figures 7.21 and 7.22 on page 124, one sees that the plots are visually very similar. However, when we look at the numbers, we see that the peaks of the output and the debt projections for the fits starting in 1964, in the Fed interest rate hike scenario, would occur about six months earlier than they do in the projections for the fit starting in 1980—2026.92 to 2027.41 for the GDP and 2029.38 to 2029.95 for the economy debt.

Next, we present the economy profit comparisons in Figure 9.9 and the investment comparisons in Figure 9.10.

When one compares the economy profit projection curves in Figure 9.9 with the economy profit curves in Figure 7.19, on page 122, for the fit starting in 1980 that uses the same average interest rate function, we again see that the total economy profit forward projections look very similar. When we compare the numbers for when the economy profit in the Fed's three-quarters of a percent per year, interest rate hike scenario crashes to zero, again, we find

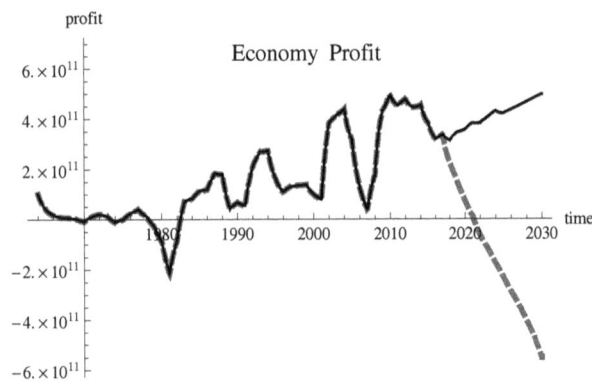

Figure 9.9: This figure shows the economy profit for the no rate hike scenario—thin black line—and for the three-quarters of a percent per year, interest rate hike scenario—gray dashed line.

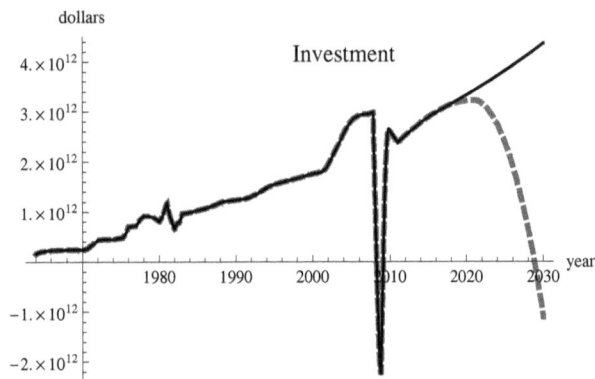

Figure 9.10: This figure shows the total investment within the economy under the Federal Reserve no interest rate hike scenario and the three-quarters of a percent per year rate hike scenario.

that the fit starting in 1964 is earlier, but this time by only about two months—2021.12 to 2021.28.

Comparing the total investment in the United States Economy projected forward in Figure 9.10 with the investment fit that was projected forward in Figure 7.20, on page 123, we see that the investment curves are very similar. Examining the numbers shows that the fit that started in 1964 projects that the investment will crash to zero about six months earlier than the projected fit that started in 1980—2028.82 to 2029.37.

Lastly, we present the employment rate comparison plot in Figure 9.11 and the wage rate comparison plot in Figure 9.12.

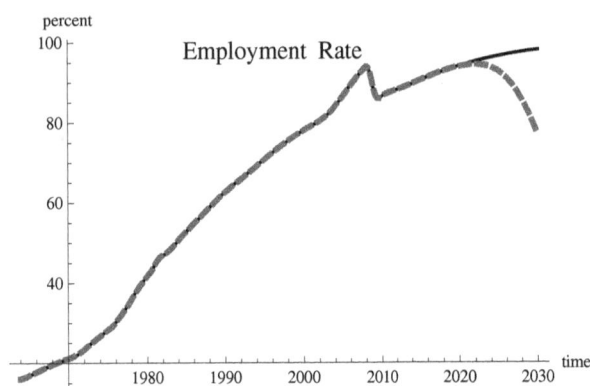

Figure 9.11: Displayed here is the employment rate under the assumption of no interest rate hikes—black line—and under the assumption of Federal Reserve rate hikes of three-quarters of one percent per year—dashed line.

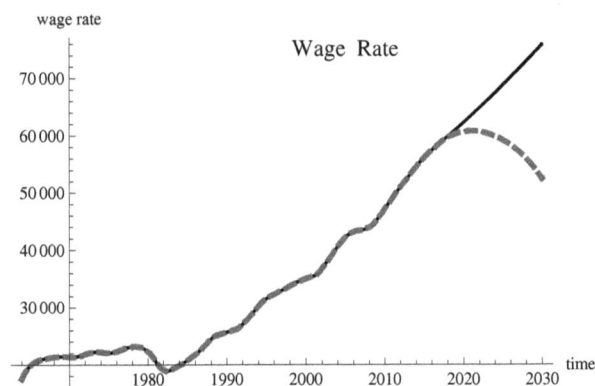

Figure 9.12: This figure shows the average wage rate projected forward, assuming the no interest rate hike scenario and under the assumption that the Federal Reserve raises interest rates by three-quarters of a percent per year.

Again when we compare the employment rate and the wage rate comparison graphs shown in Figures 9.11 and 9.12, above, with the employment rate and wage rate graphs shown in Figure 7.23 and Figure 7.24 on page 124, we see that they are again remarkably similar. When we consult the numbers, we find that the peak of the employment rate, for the Fed increases interest rates scenario, in the fit that starts in 1964 occurs about four months earlier than the peak of the employment rate that occurs in the fit that starts in 1980—2022.05 to 2022.39. Similarly, the numbers tell us that the wage rate peak, before wages crash in the Federal Reserve increases interest rates at three-quarters of a percent per year scenario, occurs about two months earlier in the fit that starts in 1964 than it does in the fit that starts in 1980—2021.12 to 2021.28.

We should note something else. The values for the employment rate and the wage rate for the fit starting in 1964 are very close to the corresponding employment rate and wage rate for the fit starting in 1980.

We might expect this should be the case because the productivities, which define the employment level within the economy for each fit, have been tied to each other so that they reproduce the same productivity in 1980. Because our productivity equation is

$$\frac{da(t)}{dt} = a(t) * \alpha,$$

its solution is the exponential function,

$$a(t) = a(t_0) * e^{\alpha * (t - t_0)}.$$

Then if we define a productivity function for a different initial value but with the same growth rate so that it lies on the curve of the original exponential function $a(t)$, we might expect this new function will reproduce precisely the same productivity as the original function.

Specifically, in our fits we define the productivity in the fit starting in 1980 as

$$a(t) = a(1980)e^{\alpha(t-1980)},$$

while we define the productivity in the fit starting in 1964 as

$$\tilde{a}(t) = \tilde{a}(1964)e^{\alpha(t-1964)},$$

where $\tilde{a}(1964) = a(1980)e^{\alpha(1964-1980)}$. Therefore, we have:

$$
\begin{aligned}
\tilde{a}(t) &= \tilde{a}(1964)e^{\alpha(t-1964)} \\
&= \left[a(1980)e^{\alpha(1964-1980)}\right] * \left[e^{\alpha(t-1964)}\right] \\
&= a(1980)e^{\alpha(1964-1980)+\alpha(t-1964)} \quad (\text{because } e^c e^d = e^{c+d}) \\
&= a(1980)e^{\alpha(t-1980)} \\
&= a(t).
\end{aligned}
$$

Thus, the productivity function of each fit produces the same values for the productivity as a function of time. This means that each fit would produce precisely the same employment level if their calculated values for the output were the same for a particular time. Even though this would rarely be the case, the values for any time will likely be close to one another because the fits are created by trying to match the United States GDP data.

Note further that the productivity is independently calculated from the GDP, the debt, the investment, the profit, and the average wage rate. That is, the number of workers will be calculated from the output of the economy, no matter how it comes about, divided by the independently calculated productivity. Therefore, the employment level, which is calculated as the output divided by the productivity, will only tell us how many workers would be needed to produce the output of the economy being described by the macroeconomic differential equations, independent of the economic conditions that obtain during the production of that output. This shows the error of my original interpretation of the meaning of the high employment rates.

For example, we started out this fit in 1964 with $a(1964) = 22,276.93$ and our productivity growth rate $\alpha = 0.0201$, and thus over the next 53 years the value of the productivity in 2017 would become

$$a(2017) = 22276.93\, e^{0.0201*53}$$
$$= 64641.147,$$

no matter what the economic conditions. In 2017, the GDP was 19.3906 trillion dollars and thus the employment level, according to our theory, would be

$$\frac{19.3906 \times 10^{12}}{64641.176},$$

or 299.97 million workers. This means that no matter what the inflation, the interest rates, or the economic policy, there would be 300 million workers when the United States Economy gets to 19.4 trillion dollars. What sense does this make? How can this be?

Yet, our coupled differential equation model, which uses this productivity, gives reasonable results for the output, the economy debt, and the investment in the real economy, so there must be something hidden here that we need to uncover.

In our next fit, we will define the initial value of the productivity to be independent of the productivity in our 1980 fit. This fit, too, will use the average interest rate function we created in Chapter 7.

Chapter 10

An Economy Fit that Starts in 1964, with an Initial Productivity not defined by a 1980 Fit

In this fit, we will calculate the initial productivity so that it equals the GDP data value for 1964 divided by the employment level value that we are accepting for 1964. For this fit, we will use an output expressed in dollars per year of $Y(1964) = 0.6858 \times 10^{12}$ and an employment level of $L = 57,775,000$ workers. This means the initial productivity used in our coupled differential equations is $a(1964) = 11870.2$. Note, the initial productivity for this fit will be created without reference to the productivity of any fit that began in 1980.

Just as in our previous fit that began in 1964, the initial value of the wage rate will be adjusted in order to get the fit to travel through the first five or six GDP data points. Other than this change, all the other initial fit parameters remain the same as those in the 1980 fit, which we created using our constructed average interest rate function of Chapter 7. The constructed average interest rate functions used in the fit and their projection forward were shown in Figure 9.3 on page 144.

The coefficients c_1 and c_2 used in the present fit are shown below. Note, the initial value of c_1 was 0.65 and the initial value c_2 was 0.6. These initial values are the same as those used for c_1 and c_2 in the first fit that started in 1964.

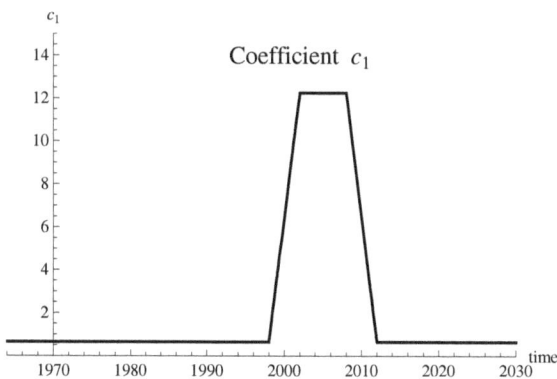

Figure 10.1: This figure shows the Businessman's Coefficient c_1 used to make this fit.

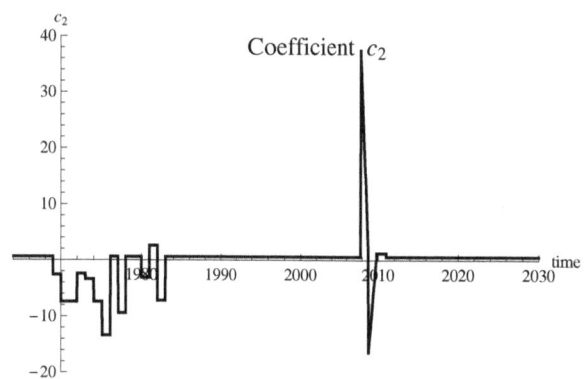

Figure 10.2: This figure shows the Banker's Coefficient c_2 used in the fit.

10.1   Fit Results

Next, we show the fit of the output curve to the GDP data, in Figure 10.3, and the fit of to economy debt curve to the debt data, in Figure 10.4.

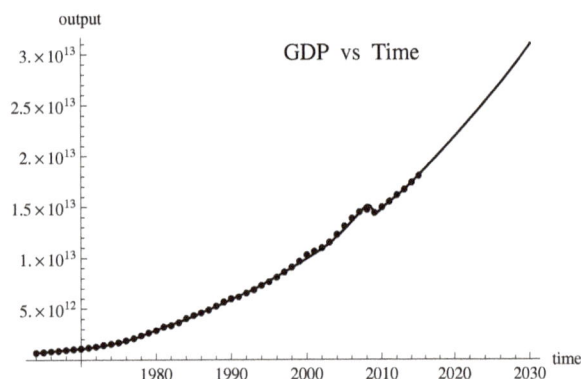

Figure 10.3: This plot shows how well the output function created by the present fit overlays the GDP data.

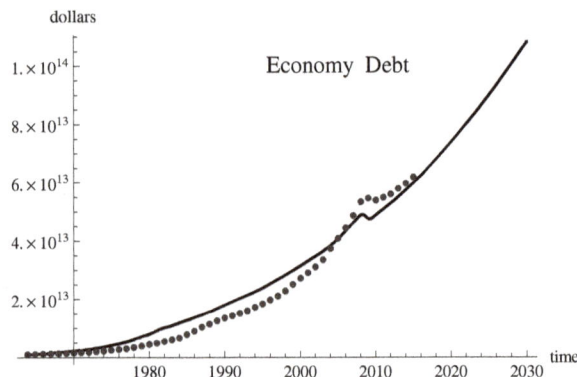

Figure 10.4: This figure shows the fit of the present model to the data for the total debt within the economy.

Here, in Figure 10.3, we see that visually, the output curve fits the crisis of 2008–9 as well as any of the smooth fits that started in 1980. The economy debt plot in Figure 10.4 looks virtually the same as all the other economy debt plots.

In Figure 10.5, we show the fit of the investment-to-GDP ratio plotted over the investment-to-GDP data gathered for the United States Economy. In Figure 10.6, we plot the consumer price index using data that was retrieved from the Federal Reserve in Minneapolis.[1]

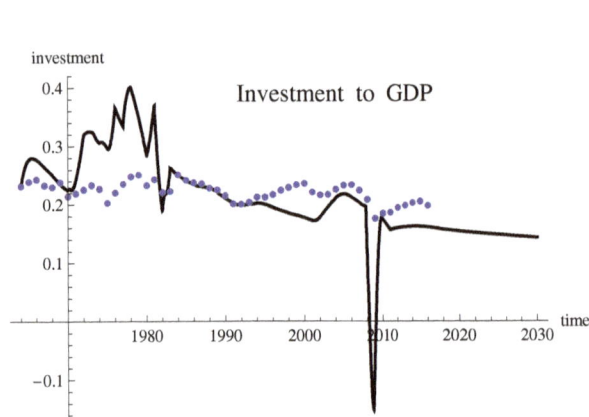

Figure 10.5: This plot displays the fit of the present model to the investment-to-GDP data for the United States Economy.

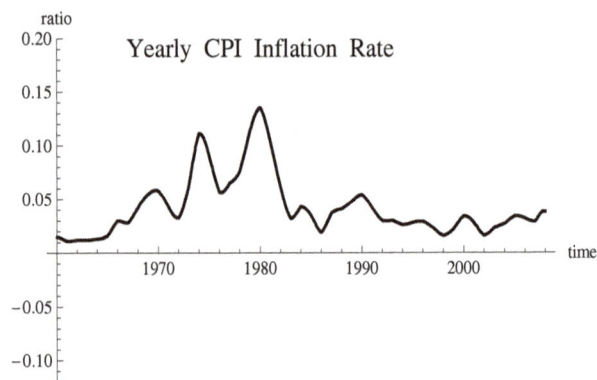

Figure 10.6: Here, we plot the consumer price index. We see from the plot that during the 1970s, there was high and sharply changing inflation, while during the rest of the fit period, inflation was relatively mild in comparison.

---

[1] Link to CPI data: `https://www.minneapolisfed.org/community/financial-and-economic-education/cpi-calculator-information/consumer-price-index-and-inflation-rates-1913`

We see that the investment-to-GDP plot, shown in Figure 10.5, looks essentially the same as the investment-to-GDP curve, shown in Figure 9.6 on page 144, which was produced by our first fit that started in 1964. Like our first fit that started in 1964, this model fits the investment-to-GDP data from 1980 to 2015, as well as the smooth fits that started in 1980. Moreover, like the first model that began in 1964, this model produces investment values that are noticeably too large from 1964 to 1980. At least part of the cause of this discrepancy is likely due to the high inflation of that period, for which our coupled differential equation macroeconomic model has given no explicit attention.

Our model uses current dollars, which reflect inflation and deflation, so to some extent, at least, inflation is included in our model. However, in the 1970s, there were two periods of very sharp peaks of rapidly changing inflation. See Figure 10.6. When prices change, businesses get the first bite at the apple. They set the price, and the consumer, that is, the worker must pay the price.

When an external event such as the Mid-East Oil Embargo occurs, business executives are more aware of the extent of the likely monetary impact on their business than are the workers on their welfare. Moreover, they can do something about it. They can raise prices to the changing situation in anticipation of the changing situation. The worker can not, he or she can only react to the changes as the prices rise. If the prices change quickly and steeply, the worker has to face them at first with no pay increase. It is typically only after a year or two that workers are able to get a pay raise to mitigate the damage of inflation to their well-being. Because of their superior knowledge and ability to act, the business-person can build into the price of their product a cushion that acts as investment borrowing over a short period. Thus, this will mean that our model will probably produce an estimate of investment that is somewhat too large in periods of relatively high and rapidly changing inflation. Note the possibility of this effect might be what we are viewing in the investment-to-GDP plot of Figure 10.5 and also in the corresponding plot in Figure 9.6, on page 144, of our first model starting in 1964.

Next, we present the GDP comparison plot in Figure 10.7 and the economy debt comparison plot in Figure 10.8. These figures will be followed by the economy profit comparison curves in Figure 10.9 and the investment comparison curves in Figure 10.10.

The output comparison curves and the economy debt comparison curves look virtually the same as the corresponding plots for the first 1964 model, shown in Figures 9.7 and 9.8 on page 145, whose productivity was directly related to the productivity for the plots beginning in 1980. The 1980 comparisons are shown in Figures 7.21 and 7.22 on page 124. All fits were created using the average interest rate we constructed. The peaks occur about two and one-half weeks later than the peaks for the first 1964 model and a little more than five months before the 1980 model.

Comparing the economy profit curves and the investment curves for the two models that start in 1964, we see that they look almost exactly the same. The economy profit for the latest model with its productivity not directly related to the 1980 fit occurs about three days later than the earlier model starting in 1964—2021.13 to 2021.12. The investment curve

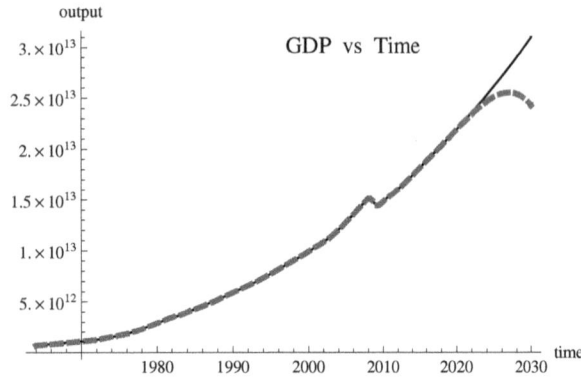

Figure 10.7: Displayed in this figure is the comparison of the output curve in the no interest rate hike scenario—black line—and the output curve in the Fed raises interest rates at three-quarters of a percent per year scenario—dashed gray line.

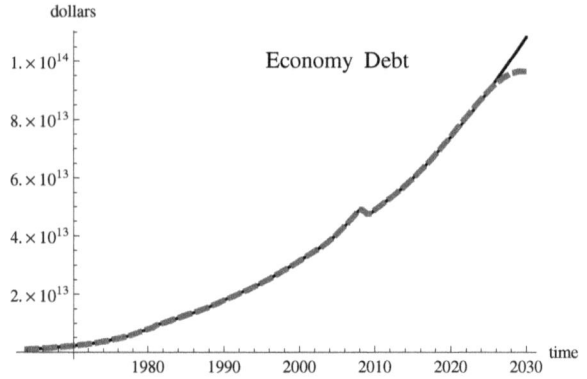

Figure 10.8: Shown here is the comparison of the economy debt in the Federal Reserve no interest rate hike scenario, and the total economy debt in the Federal Reserve raises interest rates at a pace of three-quarters of a percent per year.

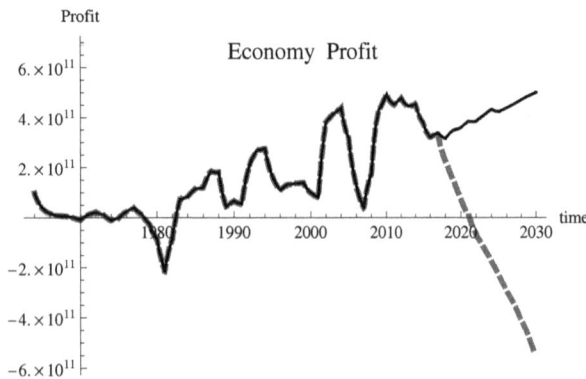

Figure 10.9: This figure shows the total profit in the US economy in the Fed no rate hike scenario—thin black line—and the three-quarters of a percent per year Fed rate hike scenario.

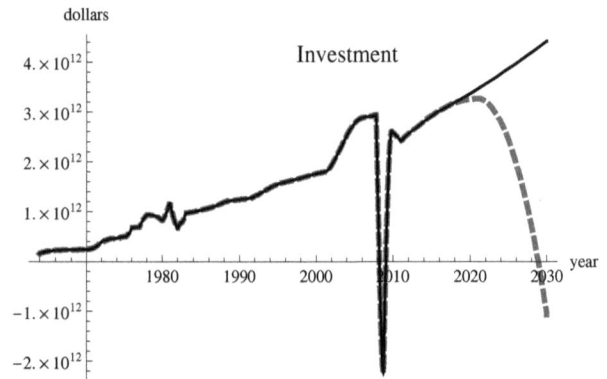

Figure 10.10: This plot shows the total investment in the United States Economy in the Federal Reserve, no interest rate hike scenario, and in the Fed's three-quarters of a percent per year rate hike scenario.

crashes to zero about two weeks later than the first model that started in 1964—2028.86 to 2028.82.

Finally, we display the employment rate and wage rate comparison plots in Figures 10.11 and 10.12.

Again, we see that the economy employment rate and wage rate comparison plots are very similar to the corresponding plots created from the first model starting in 1964. The peak for the employment rate in the Fed rate hike scenario is reached about one month later in the present scenario than in the first model starting in 1964—2022.16 compared to 2022.05.

In the first model starting in 1964, we reasoned that the model really was not adding macroeconomic workers into the economy, but was instead just calculating how many work-

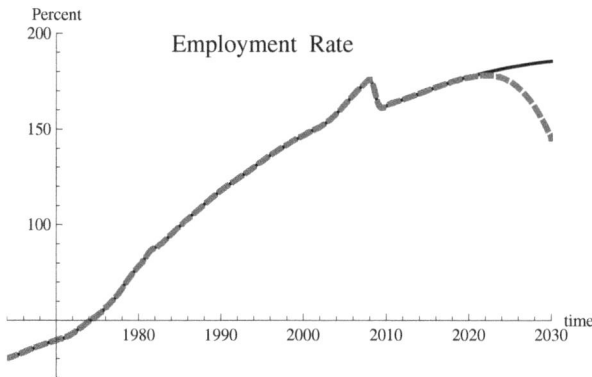

Figure 10.11: Here, we display the comparison between the employment rate in the Fed no rate hike scenario and the three-quarters of a percent per year, interest rate hike scenario.

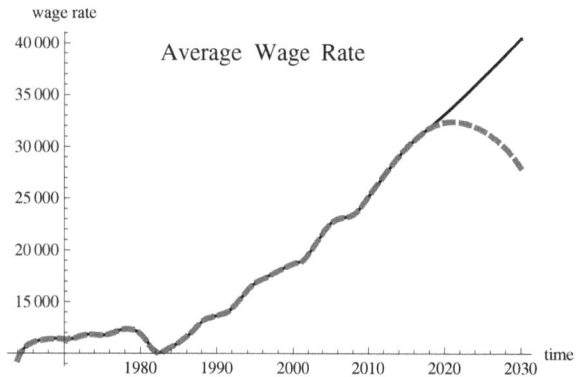

Figure 10.12: Shown in this figure is the average wage rate for the no rate hike scenario—thin black line—and the average wage rate for the Fed increases interest rates by three-quarters of a percent per year scenario.

ers would be working if the nature of the productivity we were using, happened by chance, to be correct. Under our assumption that the nature of the two productivities is given by $a_i(t) = a_{0i} e^{\alpha(t-1964)}$, then the ratio of the initial values should always produce the ratio between the productivities of the two models.

Therefore, since the employment level, L, is calculated as $Y(t)/a(t)$ and because we fit the output $Y(t)$ of both models to the GDP of the economy, then the ratio of the employment levels calculated should always be very close to the inverse ratio of the initial values of the productivities.

The initial value of the first model was $a_{01}(1964) = 22276.93$ and the initial productivity of the present model is $a_{02}(1964) = 11870.2$. This means that the employment level calculated by the present model should be about 1.9 times larger than the employment level of the first model. Because the populations of both models are identical, the employment rate of the present model should be about 1.9 times higher than the first model's. Putting a ruler across the graph in Figure 10.11, we find that the peak employment rate in the present method is about 180 percent. Dividing this by 1.9 predicts that the employment rate obtained by the first method, which was shown in Figure 9.7, should be about 95 percent. This is exactly what we find when placing a ruler across the plot in Figure 9.7.

What about the average wage rate? First, the peak of the average wage rate occurs at 2021.13, which is about three days after the first method that starts in 1964. The wage rate equation

$$\frac{dw}{dt} = m\frac{\Pi}{Y/a} = m\frac{\Pi}{Y} * a$$

would suggest that the average wage rate calculated by the present method would be about 1.9 times smaller than the wage rate calculated by the first method that starts in 1964. This inference assumes that the numerical projection of the coupled differential equations comes close to preserving the relatively direct relation that the first derivative of the wage rate has to the productivity. When one places a ruler across the wage rate graph in Figure 10.12, one reads that the peak value of the wage rate is about \$32,000. This measurement gives the prediction that the wage rate in the first method should be about 1.9 times \$32,000 or \$60,800. Placing a ruler across the plot in Figure 9.8 gives a peak wage rate of about \$61,000.

We have seen explicitly in the example of these two fits that the value of the growth rate for productivity expressed in monetary terms must have inflated. That is, we have seen that the productivity expressed in the monetary terms of current dollars inflates (and deflates). Therefore, because the growth rate of the productivity expressed in monetary terms changes, using an exponential productivity function with a fixed growth rate does not give one the correct employment level.[2]

However, we have also seen in our results that the output, the debt, and the investment are relatively consistent with their counterparts in all models using a productivity with the same constant exponential growth rate. This fact seems to indicate that our set of coupled macroeconomic differential equations may model an economy consistently using a "non-inflating" productivity, even when the reality in the economy is that the monetary expression of the productivity has a growth rate that is increasing or decreasing.

We will investigate productivity further in the next chapter with an eye to learning how to set up an inflating productivity function that will allow our model to produce consistent employment level results, while at the same time continuing to produce consistent results for the output, debt, profit, and investment. Moreover, we will try to develop such a productivity function in a manner that will not be limited to just fitting the economy but will allow us to project the economy forward in time.

---

[2]The employment level, $L = Y/a$, so in order to calculate the correct employment level, the productivity must be expressed in monetary terms of current dollars because the output is.

Chapter 11

Productivity and Inflation Explorations

In order to explore productivity, we need to come to what seems a reasonable idea of how we think it should be defined. Productivity is supposed to represent how productive, on average, a worker is. The natural way to do this would be to consider how much a worker, on average, produces per unit of time worked. For a particular worker, this could be widgets per day, per hour, or per year. The time unit is not that important other than it should be convenient.

Adding monetary value, either price or cost, to the definition seems to be a complicating factor. For instance, increasing the price of the output widget is typically not up to the worker. It is usually up to the employer or the market environment. Price or cost may be important, but it is almost always better to deal with simple pieces of the puzzle and fit those pieces together to make a more complicated whole. So our first assault on productivity will not be directed toward the productivity of the worker. Instead, we will look at the growth of the number of ordinary workers in the economy.

11.1   Employment Level Growth

One of the simplest growth relationships we have is the case in which something grows at a rate proportional to the quantity of the thing growing. The function that describes this type of growth is the exponential function. Bacteria population does this, at least for a while. So does the human population, at least for a while, until something interferes to stop or hinder the growth. Thus, we might look for the number of workers in an economy to grow exponentially in times when their growth is not hindered by some factor. To check for this possibility, we make a plot of the number of ordinary workers in a given year in the United States as a function of time. We start in 1950 to avoid the influx of soldiers returning after the War and continue through to 2017. The plot is shown below in Figure 11.1.

The plot of the number of workers in the United States Economy, shown in Figure 11.1, indicates that an exponential fit might be possible for the number of workers in the United States Economy between 1950 and 2000. Accordingly, we create the exponential fit shown

number of workers

Number of Workers in
the US Economy

1.4×10^8

1.2×10^8

$1. \times 10^8$

$8. \times 10^7$

time

1960   1970   1980   1990   2000   2010

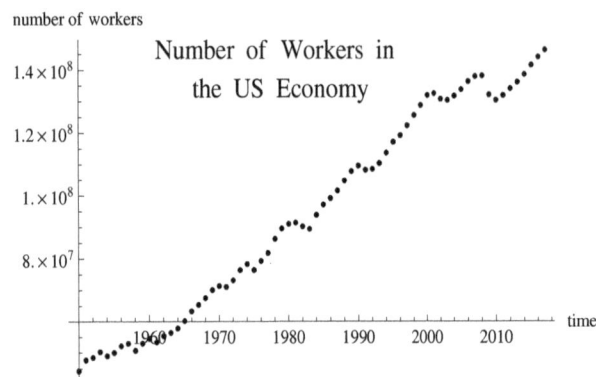

Figure 11.1: Shown here is the number of ordinary workers in the economy from 1950 to 2017.

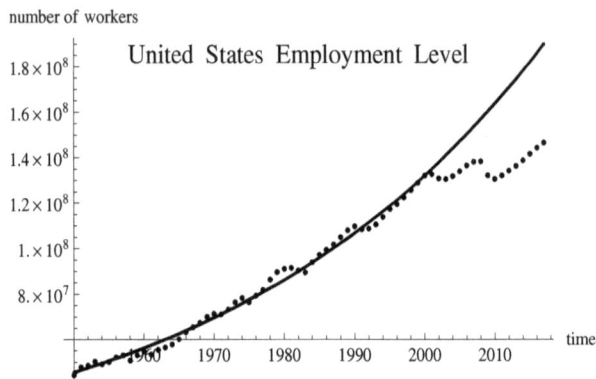

number of workers

United States Employment Level

1.8×10^8

1.6×10^8

1.4×10^8

1.2×10^8

$1. \times 10^8$

$8. \times 10^7$

time

1960   1970   1980   1990   2000   2010

Figure 11.2: This figure shows an exponential fit to the number of ordinary workers in the United States Economy overlying the data.

in Figure 11.2. This plot shows that a very nice exponential fit can be made to the number of workers in the United States Economy from 1950 to 2000.

In this plot, one sees the more euphoric times when the economy is growing at a faster growth rate than the fit curve. During these euphoric times, the data values proceed from a little below the fit curve to a bit above the fit curve. Then, we see the start of recessive times in which the data points reach a peak distance above the fit curve and start to fall back down toward the fit curve. When the data is falling and dips below the fit curve, the economy is in recession.

One sees the periodic nature of the business cycle as the data peaks in roughly ten-year intervals. The data peaks, relative to the fit curve, in 1970, 1980, 1990, and 2000 as the data winds around and around the fit curve. One also sees that the business cycle is not perfectly cyclic because one sees a peak between 1970 and 1980, along with a more messy looking, complex cyclic period between 1950 and 1970.

However, the plot also jolts us. Starting abruptly in 2000, the number of workers in the United States no longer follows the fit curve. In fact, the data appears to be running away from the fit curve. The plot in Figure 11.2 indicates that some kind of fundamental change to the United States Economy must have happened, starting approximately in the year 2000. The figure indicates that the difference in the number of ordinary workers in the United States in 2017 is about ***forty million workers less*** than the number of ordinary workers that there would have been if the nature of the economy had not changed.

When we search to find out what caused this massive loss of jobs within the economy, we find that outsourcing of jobs began in earnest with the collapse of the dot-com bubble in 2000 (Mother Jones, 2005). During the period from 2001 to 2009, the United States lost 42,400 factories, and the manufacturing employment level dropped to 11.7 million workers. The last time the United States had such a small number of workers in manufacturing was in 1941 (Huffington Post, 2012). According to the president of an outsourcing consulting firm, by the year 2004, large companies were outsourcing approximately half of their IT work (Corbett, 2004).

The question is, why would companies in the United States do this? It is a fact that because the workers in the United States are paid much more than the workers in the countries to which the work was outsourced, the companies would make more money and be more profitable. It might seem reasonable that this is the answer. However, this is not the answer. We need another piece of the puzzle before the answer, why, can become clear.

11.2 Productivity with Inflation

We have seen in our previous work that the output of the economy usually has exponential-like growth. In addition, we have just seen that the employment level has exponential-like growth periods. Therefore, we should expect that the ratio of the output of the economy divided by the employment level of the economy would be an exponential-like function during periods of exponential growth because

$$\widehat{a}(t) \equiv \frac{Y(t)}{L(t)} = \frac{Y_0 \, e^{\eta*(t-t_0)}}{L_0 \, e^{\lambda*(t-t_0)}}$$

$$= \frac{Y_0}{L_0} \, e^{[(\eta-\lambda)*(t-t_0)]},$$

during periods of exponential growth. We will call the function $\widehat{a}(t)$ the macroeconomic productivity because, by definition, when it multiplies the employment level, that product is always equal to the output of the economy. [1]

The Bureau of Labor Statistics (BLS) has a short video on their website in which they define productivity in terms of the amount of product produced per hour of work. However, this is probably not what they do when they measure productivity and the growth of productivity within the economy. The nature of the products produced is very varied at any given time, and this variety changes over time. In addition, there is no tally, I am aware of, for the number of products produced along with the number of hours taken to produce each. And even if there were, some products may take only minutes to produce and others hours or days of work. How would these productivities for each individual product be meaningfully added into the calculation for the economy productivity, if not by price? Thus, the BLS almost certainly must measure the output of the economy in constant dollars and then use it as a measure of the output from year to year. While this is not easy, it is doable and would allow them to come up with an estimate of the productivity when they divide it by the total number of hours worked in producing the economy's output.

We do not want to work in constant dollars because constant dollars need to be continually calculated from economic data. If we did so, this would mean that no accurate projections could be made into the future because the constant dollars for the projection time

---

[1]There is a conceptual problem here that would be all but impossible to resolve at this point. So, we will push on as if it does not exist. Sometimes one has to do that, because it is not until after one makes other discoveries that one comes to understand. Discoveries that one would not have made if one had not pushed on.

period would be unknown. We will instead work in current dollars and try to find an accurate method of calculating the macroeconomic productivity and projecting it forward.

We will make a table of values of the macroeconomic productivity using the yearly GDP data and the yearly value for the number of ordinary workers in the economy. This table will give a macroeconomic productivity value for each year from 1950 to 2017 in current dollars. We will not try to convert these macroeconomic productivities into productivities measured in terms of constant dollars. We show a plot of the resulting macroeconomic productivity data and an interpolating function fit to that data in Figure 11.3. Also, in Figure 11.4, we show the plot of the best fit exponential function to the macroeconomic productivity data from 1950 to 2017, along with the productivity data.

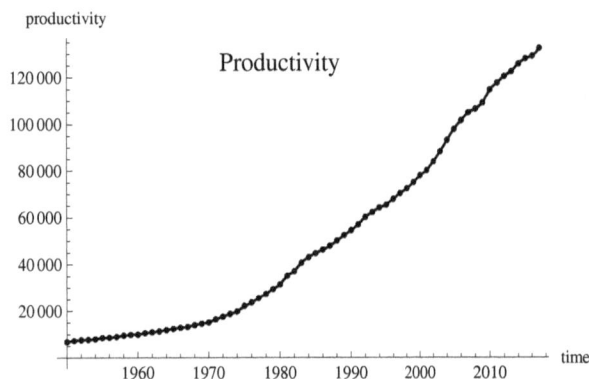

Figure 11.3: Shown here is the macroeconomic productivity data calculated for the years 1950 through 2017. Plotted over this data is an interpolating function fit to that data.

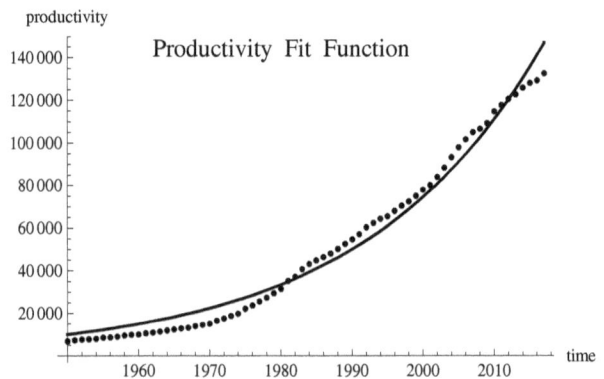

Figure 11.4: Here, we see the graph of the best fit exponential function, which we calculated using the macroeconomic productivity data from 1950 to 2017. The graph is plotted over all the productivity data from 1950 to 2017.

First, we see that from the plot, shown in Figure 11.3, that all data points used in the calculation of an interpolating function lie on the plot of an interpolating function. This property is fundamental to the nature of the interpolating function. That is, all data points used in the calculation of an interpolating function lie on the curve of the interpolating function. This characteristic is contrary to the nature of the best fit line, for which not a single point needs to lie on the best fit line.

Second, we see, in Figure 11.3, that the macroeconomic productivity in the United States Economy from 1950 to 2017 is a very bumpy upward climbing function of time. Third, we see, in Figure 11.4, that the productivity data winds around the curve of the best fit exponential function that was calculated using productivity data from 1950 to 2017. However, there are many places along the curve that look quite discrepant from the data. Thus, it is not clear that such a macroeconomic productivity function would be useful.

Because, in Figure 11.2, the employment level data between 1950 and 2000 was shown to nicely fit an exponential function, we will try fitting the macroeconomic productivity between 1950 and 2000 to an exponential function in the hopes that it might turn out to be a more useful productivity function to use in our work. The plot of this best fit exponential function, along with all the macroeconomic productivity data, is shown in Figure 11.5.

The productivity is really a tangential economic entity to our results. It is the employment level that appears in the natural expression of our macroeconomic equations, such as the economy profit equation,

$$\Pi = Y - w * L - r * D. \tag{11.1}$$

Productivity is important to us because it facilitates our calculations. We use it to calculate the employment level in our macroeconomic equations through the relation that the employment level equals the output divided by the macroeconomic productivity, $L = Y/\hat{a}$. In our earlier work, we used the productivity, a, rather than the more correct macroeconomic productivity, $\hat{a}$.

In order to test how well our two best-fit productivity functions work, we use the best-fit exponential function shown in Figure 11.4 to calculate the employment level in the economy. We also calculate the employment level for the best-fit exponential function calculated from the macroeconomic productivity data from 1950 to 2000. Then we calculate the fractional discrepancy between our calculated employment level data for both best-fit productivity functions and the known employment level. Also, we note for completeness that the fractional discrepancy for any quantity is given by:

$$fractional\ discrepancy = \frac{calculated\ value - known\ value}{known\ value}.$$

In Figure 11.6, we show how well these productivity functions fared in calculating the employment level in the United States using known values of the yearly GDP.

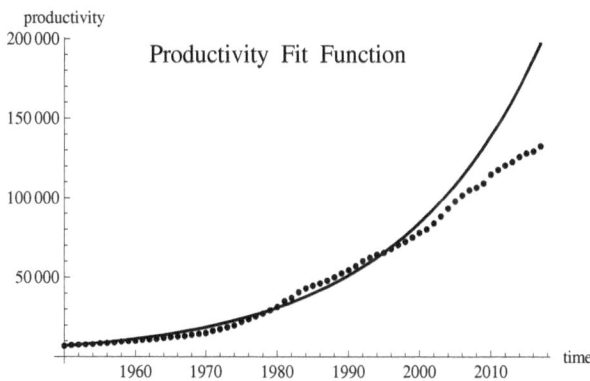

Figure 11.5: This figure shows the best fit productivity curve, which is calculated using an exponential function to fit the macroeconomic productivity data from 1950 to 2000. All the data from 1950 to 2017 overlays the best fit productivity curve.

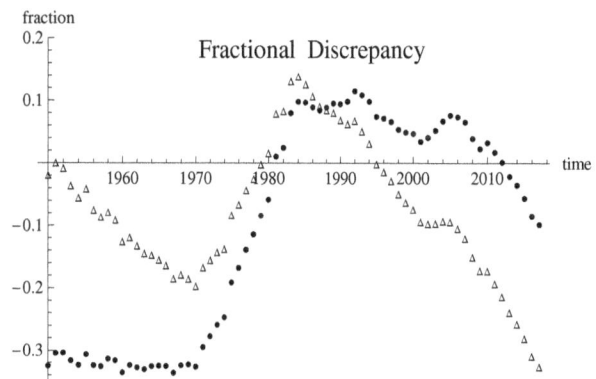

Figure 11.6: Here, we display graphs of the fractional discrepancy for the employment level as calculated from the function displayed in Figure 11.4—black filled circles—and for the employment level calculated from the productivity function displayed in Figure 11.5—open triangles.

In Figure 11.5, we see that the best-fit productivity function fits the productivity data from 1950 to 2000 better than the productivity fit curve in Figure 11.4, which was created using all the macroeconomic productivity data from 1950 to 2017. However, beyond 2000, the productivity fit function shown in Figure 11.5 is a noticeably poorer fit to the macroeconomic productivity than the productivity fit function shown in Figure 11.4.

We see from Figure 11.6 that both productivity fit functions produce values of the employment level that are quite far away from the known values. In fact, many of the values are better than 30 percent from the accepted values. In addition, both productivity fit functions look to be producing values that would cause employment levels to run further and further away from their likely values if the economy were to be projected forward. Thus, we can conclude with good justification that neither productivity fit function would be likely to give satisfying results when used to project the economy forward.

11.3   Macroeconomic Basis of the Bivens and Mishel Wage Separation

In all our earlier fits, we used a productivity growth rate, α, equal to 0.0201. This growth rate increased the productivity by a factor of 1.75558 over the twenty-eight years between 1980 and 2008. The Bureau of Labor Statistics, back when I started, gave productivity values of 55.1 in 1980 and 99.0 in 2008, which means productivity increased by a factor of 1.7963 between 1980 and 2008. The slightly revised present figures, from the BLS, produce a ratio of 1.7940. If instead, we use the worker growth rate of 0.0213205, which produced the employment level fit in Figure 11.2, for the productivity growth rate, we would find that the productivity would grow by a factor of 1.8166 between 1980 and 2008. While we should not expect these growth rates to be equal, we should expect them to be similar during ordinary times.

Let us examine the ratio of growth in the economy's output and the ratio of growth in the macroeconomic productivity in the economy. To do so, we consider their ratio, where macroeconomic productivity is defined to be the economy's output divided the employment level. Thus, we have:

$$
\frac{\left(\dfrac{Y}{Y_0}\right)}{\left(\dfrac{\hat{a}}{\hat{a}_0}\right)} = \frac{\left(\dfrac{Y}{Y_0}\right)}{\left(\dfrac{\left(\dfrac{Y}{L}\right)}{\left(\dfrac{Y_0}{L_0}\right)}\right)}
$$

$$
= \frac{L}{L_0}.
$$

(11.2)

We saw in Figure 11.2 that the employment level was well fit by an exponential function between 1950 and 2000. Therefore, we see from Equation 11.2 that the ratio of the output of the economy to the macroeconomic productivity must be well fit by an exponential function during the period from 1950 to 2000 because the employment level was.

Moreover, as we have seen during the period from 1980 to 2008, the rate of growth of the employment level was about equal to productivity growth determined by the Bureau of Labor Statistics. Therefore, in order to explore the macroeconomic productivity further, we create a test productivity function that increases at the worker growth rate $\alpha = 0.0213205$, which we found in our best exponential fit to the employment level between 1950 and 2000. We show a plot of this function plotted over the yearly macroeconomic productivity values in Figure 11.7.

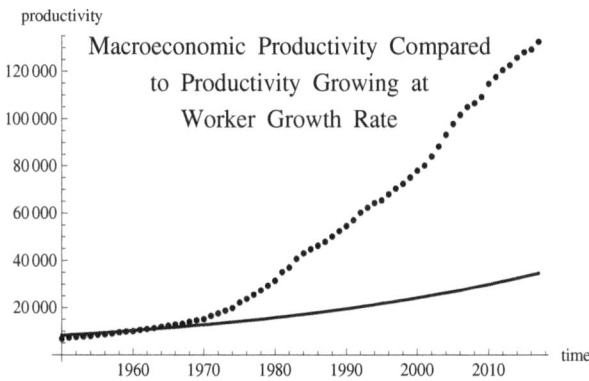

Figure 11.7: In this figure, we compare the data for the macroeconomic productivity with our test productivity function for which the productivity grows at a rate equal to the worker growth rate.

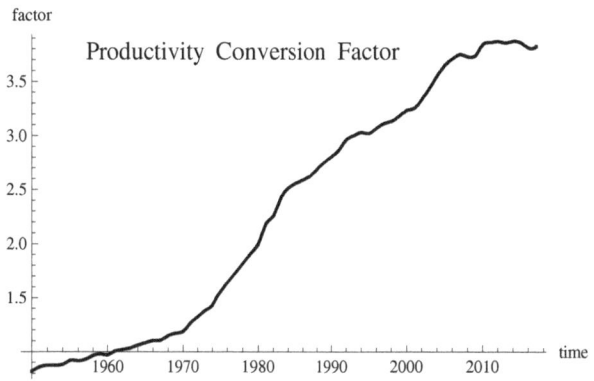

Figure 11.8: In this figure, we display a plot of the multiplicative factor interpolating function that changes the productivity that is growing at a rate of 0.0213205 per year into the macroeconomic productivity.

The main thing that stands out in Figure 11.7 is that there is a large and ever-widening gap in the values between the macroeconomic productivity and the real productivity that we have modeled as growing at a rate, which is consistent with Bureau of Labor Statistics' productivity values. However, we also notice that between 1950 and the early to mid-1960s, the macroeconomic productivity and our worker model of the productivity appear to be staying relatively the same.

We can easily find a conversion factor between the two productivities. We take the ratio of the macroeconomic productivity value and the real productivity value for a particular year as given by our slowly growing real productivity function. This ratio times the real productivity function value must give back the macroeconomic productivity. So, we construct a table of these ratio values for each year from 1950 to 2017. Then, we construct an interpolating function from this table of ratios. Remembering that the values that are used to create an interpolating function lie along the curve of the interpolating function, then, we know that the conversion factor function times our slowly growing real productivity function will reproduce the exact values of the macroeconomic productivity for each year. In between the yearly values, there will be extremely accurate interpolated values for the macroeconomic productivity and the directly related productivity conversion factor. A plot of the productivity conversion factor interpolating function is shown in Figure 11.8.

What do we see in the graph of the productivity conversion factor in Figure 11.8? We see that it rises in a bumpy episodic fashion and that the conversion factor flattens out beyond 2010, after the crisis of 2008–9. We also note that the shape of the conversion factor curve does not resemble either curve in Figure 11.7. However, it does resemble the shape of many of the productivity and wage graphs within Bivens and Mishel's article on the divergence of a worker's pay from the productivity within the economy (Bivens and Mishel, 2015). See, for example, Figures A, B, or C from their article. Figures A and B are reprinted with permission from the Economic Policy Institute on pages 169 and 170.

So what does our productivity conversion factor curve represent? It essentially represents the amount by which the productivity inflates such that this inflated productivity will give the number of workers in the economy when one divides it into the economy's output. In effect, it monetizes the productivity into current dollars in a manner such that productivity is directly related to employment level, i.e., productivity becomes the macroeconomic productivity.

Bivens and Mishel work in "real" dollars, not current dollars. They noted that productivity and wage rates had been tied together in real dollars terms from 1948 up until 1973. That is, they were tied together in un-inflated dollars. Here, "tied together" means that as productivity increases or decreases by some factor, the wage rate goes up or down by roughly the same factor. Their graphs then show that the wage rate of the typical worker started to fall well below the productivity in the economy after 1973. Note well here, that because both Bivens and Mishel's productivity and wage rates are expressed in terms of uninflated dollars, then the ratio between these two quantities will be the same when both are expressed in terms of inflated dollars.

In Equation 11.1, we wrote the economy profit equation, Equation 1.8*, in its more natural form, $\Pi = Y - w * L - r * D$. We saw in Figure 7.17 on page 121 that economy profit-to-GDP curve calculated from our macroeconomic equations was roughly constant once the initially calculated values settled down. Because the economy profit is small in comparison to the output of the economy, there is a delicate balance within the economy. The Federal Reserve private bankers know that they make more money when they raise interest rates. However, they also know that if they raise interest rates when the debt is high relative to the output of the economy, then they raise the possibility of killing the golden goose that lays their golden egg. Thus, because of this delicate balance, it is likely that the bankers try to keep the interest payments relative to the difference between the output of the economy and the total wages paid, $\frac{r*D}{GDP-w*L}$, roughly constant in order to preserve the delicate balance. If they were to do this, then they would raise interest rates when the economy heats up and lower interest rates when the economy cools down. They may do this by taking into account inflation, but because wages are sticky, their actions would be late. And, this is exactly what we observe.

Because the three terms Y, $R * D$, and Π are roughly proportional to the output, Y, this means that the term $w * L$ must be roughly proportional to the output. Using $\widetilde{\propto}$ to signify "roughly proportional to", we have

$$Y \;\widetilde{\propto}\; w * L = \frac{w * Y}{\hat{a}},$$

which means that the average wage rate, w, is roughly proportional to macroeconomic productivity, $\widehat{a}$. In other words, we know that the average wage rate will inflate in the same way that macroeconomic productivity will. Thus, we can say that $w(t) \approx k * \widehat{a}(t)$ and $w(t_0) \approx k * \widehat{a}(t_0)$. Accordingly,

$$\frac{w(t)}{w(t_0)} \approx \frac{\widehat{a}(t)}{\widehat{a}(t_0)}.$$

This means that the average wage rate inflates by approximately the same factor, between the time t_0 and the time t, as the macroeconomic productivity does.

Now we can examine how the average wage inflates as the money in the economy inflates. We can do this by directly comparing how the macroeconomic productivity inflates in the economy relative to the inflation rate. This will tell us how the average wage rate inflates in the economy relative to the inflation rate because the average wage and the macroeconomic productivity inflate in the same way.

To proceed, we construct a graph of the average yearly CPI inflation data, which can be found at the Minneapolis branch of the Federal Reserve at the link:

```
https://www.minneapolisfed.org/community/
financial-and-economic-education/cpi-calculator-information/
consumer-price-index-and-inflation-rates-1913
```

This graph is shown in Figure 11.9.

Next, we construct a table of the cumulative CPI data obtained from the Minneapolis Federal Reserve, which we normalize so that the CPI value "1" is positioned in 1964. We also normalize the macroeconomic productivity data to be one in 1964. We show the cumulative CPI interpolating function graph and the macroeconomic productivity graph both normalized to one in 1964 in Figure 11.10.

We normalized the data to the year 1964 rather than the year 1973 that Bivens and Mishel use as their discussion reference year in their productivity wage separation article. We chose 1964 as our reference year because that was the year that the maximum tax bracket changed from a very high 91 percent to a less inhibiting 77 percent. This was followed the very next year by a further drop to 70 percent in the maximum tax bracket. We noted in our earlier discussions that the ninety-plus percent maximum tax bracket seemed to result in an "economic boat" in which everyone moved up and down together.

In Figure 11.9, we see that there are three relatively large spikes in inflation between 1950 and 2017. The first spike between 1950 and 1952 does not seem to effect the separation between the two curves shown in Figure 11.10. However, that does not seem to be true about the second and third spikes in inflation. The second two somewhat larger spikes in inflation seem to facilitate the rate of separation between the two curves.

If we look at the productivity versus wage, separation plots, in Figure A, Figure B, and, Figure D, in Bivens and Mishel's article on productivity and wage separation (Bivens and Mishel, 2015), we see that the shape and size relationships seem very similar between their

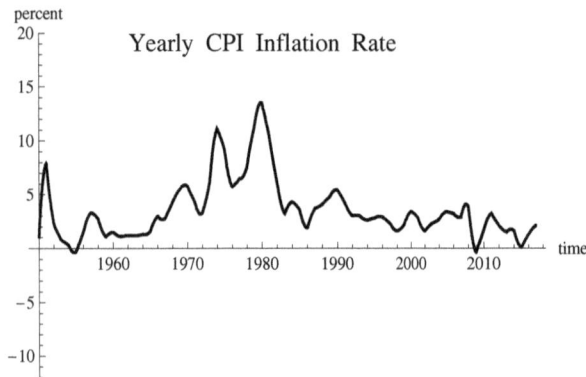

Figure 11.9: Here in this figure, we display the annual consumer price index data from the Minneapolis Federal Reserve, graphed from 1950 to 2017, using an interpolating function.

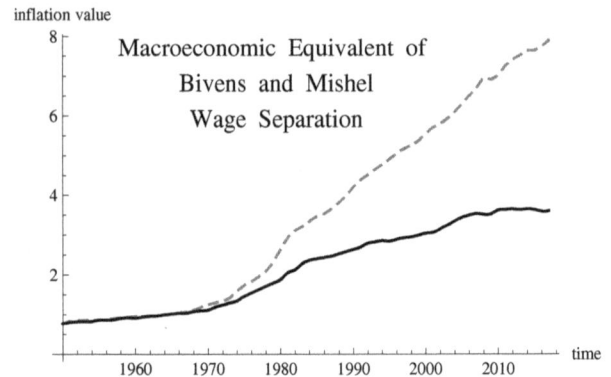

Figure 11.10: Here, we see the interpolating function fit of the normalized cumulative CPI inflation data—gray dashed line— and the normalized macroeconomic productivity data—black line.

plots and our plot in Figure 11.10. As we have discussed, we expect that the average wage rate will grow roughly the same way as our macroeconomic productivity. Consistent with this expectation, we see their real average wage rate in their Figure B looks similar to our macroeconomic productivity shown in Figure 11.10.

However, only Figure A runs through our "economic boat" data. However, if one looks backward in their Figure D, one sees that all their wage groups converge toward the point in 1973 from which the typical worker's wage diverged from productivity. This means that all wage groups moved together from 1948 to 1973.

Bivens and Mishel normalize the start of their data to zero, in 1948. Their scale is additive so when the net productivity reaches 100%, it means that the net productivity is twice what it was in 1948. In their Figure A, the productivity and the typical worker's hourly compensation graphs run right on top of each other all the way from 1948 to 1973, just as the cumulative CPI and macroeconomic productivity run right on top of each other from 1950 to 1973 in Figure 11.10. Bivens and Mishel's Figure A, Figure B, and Figure D may be found on pages 169 and 170.

The meaning of their overlapping curves and ours is similar. In our graph, the overlapping of the macroeconomic productivity and cumulative CPI curves means that the average wage rate in the United States Economy is keeping pace with inflation growth in the economy. In Bivens and Mishel's Figure A, the overlapping the hourly compensation of the "typical worker" is keeping pace with productivity and thus, the average wage rate. Their typical worker is defined to be non-supervisory private-sector production workers. They found through their analysis that typical worker compensation changes almost exactly like that of the median worker compensation. To see this, compare their Figure A and Figure B.

If one looks carefully at their Figure A, one sees that the hourly compensation of the typical worker rides just above the productivity from 1950 to the early 1960s and then rides just below the productivity from mid-1960 to 1973. This shows that the wage of the typical or median worker was losing ground very very slowly to productivity increases. If one looks closely at our comparison graph between cumulative inflation and the macroeconomic productivity in Figure 11.10, one sees that from the mid-1960s to 1973, the macroeconomic productivity and thus, the average wage rate are ever so slowly losing ground to inflation.

Thus, Bivens and Michel's work and our own work indicates that there was a period from 1950 to the mid-1960s in which everybody was in the same economic boat. Although, they did not state this in terms of everybody being in the same economic boat. Nor did they make the connection between the highest top tax brackets and the livable minimum wage with everybody being in the same economic boat.

Our cumulative inflation versus macroeconomic productivity graph, which we display in Figure 11.10, shows that after 1973, cumulative inflation started growing much faster than the average wage rate. This indicates that the United States Economy as a whole was getting less well off. Bivens and Mishel's work is more fine-grained than ours regarding wage separation. Their work from beyond 1973 shows that most of the people in the economy had wages that grew less fast than the net productivity. Only the elite top one percent of wage earners were shown to have had their real wages grow faster than net productivity. Their wages grew 137.7 percent between 1979 and 2013, while net productivity grew 61.9 percent during the same period (Bivens and Mishel, 2015, Figure D, p. 19). From Bivens and Mishel's Figure D, we see that the real wages of the top 95 to 99 percent of wage earners just about kept even with the growth in net productivity. Their wages grew 59.5 percent between 1979 and 2013, compared to 61.9 percent for net productivity. The growth in the wages of all other wage earners lost significant ground to the growth in net productivity.

Thus, taken together, our work and the complementary work of Bivens and Mishel have shown that this long slow evolutionary process has done significant damage to the United States Economy.

Note that our macroeconomic plots show inflation separating from macroeconomic productivity, which we associated with the average wage rate. Comparing Figure 11.9 and Figure 11.10, we see that the separation started to appear with the ramp-up of the Vietnam War, in 1965, and that the separation picked up speed when the high inflation of the 1970s and the early 1980s hit. It would seem likely that inflation would have helped facilitate, to some extent at least, the separation of the growth of the average wage rate from the growth in productivity. Note, however, from our graphs and theirs that wage *separation* picked up significant speed after the top tax rate became 50 percent in 1982.

However, for some reason, the high inflation in the very early 1950s did not produce the same result. In order to explore why we carry our calculations back to the beginning of 1944. The War still had almost two years to go, so the times were very different, but the maximum tax bracket in 1944 and 1945 was a very high 94 percent. So let us see what happens to our macroeconomic "Bivens and Mishel" relationship through the high inflation of the late 1940s. To aid in our comprehension, we show the tax rate in the maximum tax bracket and the annual inflation rate in Figure 11.11. In Figure 11.12, we show a plot of the cumulative consumer price inflation and the macroeconomic productivity from 1944 to 2017. We redid the exponential best fit to the employment level data from 1948 to 2000 to establish the macroeconomic productivity growth rate in the years after the War. Starting the fit in 1948 gave the economy time to adjust to the return of the soldiers into the workforce. An exponential best fit for the employment level data was found to have an exponential growth rate of 0.0213127.

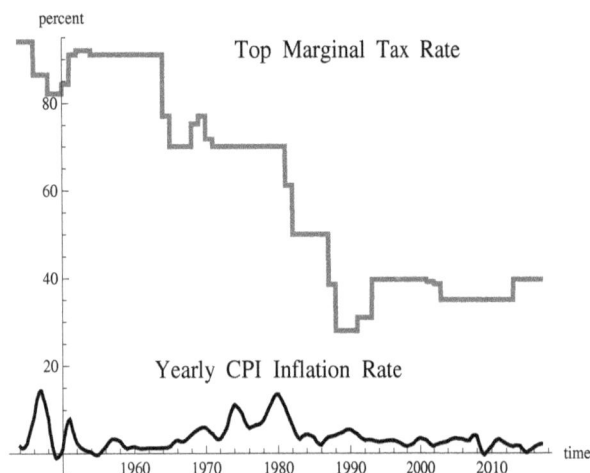

Figure 11.11: In this figure, we have plotted the maximum tax rate in the top tax bracket from 1944 to 2017—thicker gray line—along with the annual consumer price inflation for those years—black line.

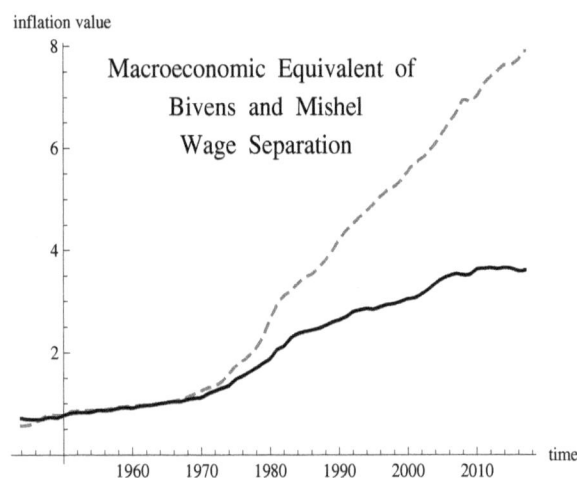

Figure 11.12: Here, we present a plot of the macroeconomic equivalent of the Bivens and Mishel productivity wage separation extended until 1944, so it includes the last year of World War II.

As we can from Figure 11.11, there was high inflation during the late 1940s and the early 1950s. In fact, the peak in inflation that occurred in 1947 was just a bit higher than the peak that occurred in 1980. Yet, even during that inflation period, there was no obvious separation in the macroeconomic equivalent of the Bivens and Mishel wage separation shown in Figure 11.12. However, if one looks more closely, one sees that there is a separation between macroeconomic productivity and cumulative inflation. At the end of World War II, we can see that macroeconomic productivity (average wage rate) was actually higher than cumulative inflation. This was due to the price controls instigated at the end of 1942 after we had entered the War.

Then we see that just before the end of 1945, after the War was over, the inflation curve in Figure 11.12 begins to rise. It rises until it becomes entangled with the macroeconomic productivity curve at the beginning of 1948. Looking back at Figure 11.11, we see that this time period corresponds precisely with the huge spike in inflation, which peaked in 1947.

Consulting the literature, we find that the female employment level peaked in February 1945 and fell to a minimum at the end of May in 1946. After this time, the female employment level slowly increased (Evans, 1982, Figure 4). In Figure 3 of Evans's article, we find that the male civilian employment level reaches a minimum in August 1945, followed by a peak in December 1947. Afterward, the male civilian employment level levels off.

When one consults the numbers in Figure 3 and Figure 4 of Evans's article, one finds that during the period of high inflation between the very end of 1945 and the very end of 1947 that civilian employment level of women dropped by a little over one and a half million women and male employment level increased by a little over eight and a half million people. This net increase in the employment level by about seven million people required money to pay the salaries of the newly employed people. In order to do this, prices were raised, causing a spike in inflation. So, the people had to continue their sacrifice by facing the inflation without a pay raise. The high top tax bracket all but guaranteed that the sacrifice was shared by all.

This result allowed the United States Economy to be released smoothly back into a peace-time economy. Because the top tax brackets were not reduced during the release, after the release, macroeconomic productivity kept pace with inflation. Consequently, all the people in the economy were in the same economic boat, so they rose and fell together.

As we reasoned earlier, a very high top marginal tax rate strongly inhibits a wage separation between the ordinary worker and the elites in society. In fact, a high enough maximum tax rate on *gross income* along with a reasonable range of allowed incomes would actually prevent a wage separation. Such a range should be based on the output of society. For example, a range allowing a top income of, say, two to four hundred times the GDP per capita, a livable minimum wage of one half the GDP per capita, plus a negative per capita tax of five percent of the GDP per capita, would keep everyone in the same economic boat. Moreover, such a wage tax structure would not need to be continually fiddled with because it could be written in macroeconomic terms so it would self-adjust each year. Therefore, such a tax structure would keep everybody in the same economic boat. In addition, a second benefit of such a tax structure would be that it would prevent a few elites from amassing enough wealth such that they could easily corrupt the Federal Governance for their own benefit.

11.4 An Incompleteness in Our Macroeconomic Equations

In our plots of investment to GDP in Figure 9.6 and Figure 10.5, shown on page 144 and page 150, we noted that when our macroeconomic differential equation model fits the GDP in the economy between 1964 and 1980, it required more investment in the economy than was observed to have occurred. We argued that this might be because businesses would be able to raise their prices to obtain excess capital before the consumer/worker could recoup their "investment" in the businesses by getting a wage increase.

Another discrepancy between our macroeconomic differential equation model occurs when we create a fit of the output curve to the GDP data to set the fit parameters. There is a discrepancy in the resulting fit of the economy debt-to-GDP curves to the data in the graphs created by all fits, but it is particularly and most notably displayed in the fits starting in 1964. We show this discrepancy in a fit starting in 1964 in Figure 11.13 and for a fit starting 1980 in Figure 11.14.

In the fit that begins in 1964, shown in Figure 11.13, we see a jarring misfit of the

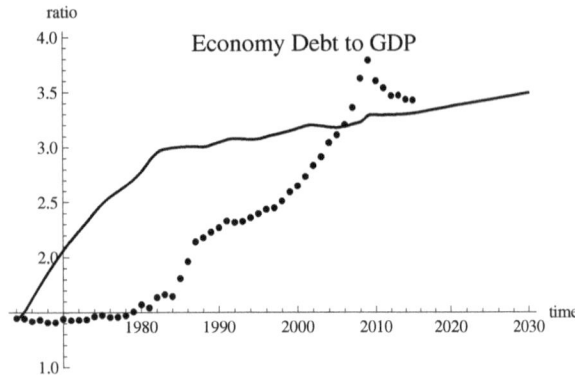

Figure 11.13: In this figure, we have plotted the debt-to-GDP curve of Chapter 10, which begins in 1964, over the debt-to-GDP data from 1964 to 2017.

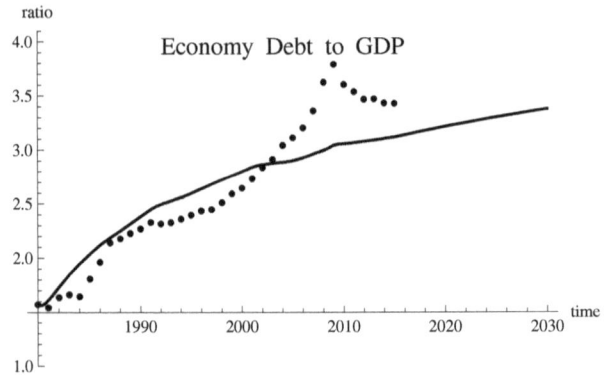

Figure 11.14: Here, we have plotted the debt-to-GDP curve of Chapter 7. We have plotted it over the debt-to-GDP data from 1980 to 2017.

debt-to-GDP curve with the data. The debt-to-GDP data begins its steep rise about fifteen years after the debt-to-GDP fit curve begins its steep rise. The two curves make an almost parallelogram-like formation. This malalignment is in stark contrast to the fit that begins in 1980. In that fit, the debt-to-GDP curve begins its steep rise, at most, only a couple of years earlier than the debt-to-GDP data begins its steep rise.

When we look at Figure 11.9 or, even better, Figure 10.6 on page 150, we see that the periods of the rising and falling of high annual inflation rates occurred from about 1966 to 1982. Note that this is the same time period, which occurs between the beginning of the fast rise of the debt-to-GDP curve (~1966) and the beginning of the fast rise of the debt-to-GDP data (~1982), as seen in Figure 11.13. We also saw in the investment-to-GDP curves of Figures 9.6 and 10.5 that investment to GDP was predicted to be noticeably too high during that same period of high inflation for these two fits of the United States Economy that began in 1964.

We argued that the reason the fits, which began in 1964, caused the investment within the economy to appear too high was that our macroeconomic coupled differential equation model did not explicitly take inflation into account. Specifically, we argued that when a business raised prices during an inflation spike, they would gain more income relative to the amount of money they would have to pay out in wages because it would take some time for their employees to bargain successfully for a wage increase. Thus, the new-found cash would act as investment money that they would not have to obtain by borrowing money from a bank. This would mean that the economy would reach a particular value of output, with businesses borrowing less money than our incomplete macroeconomic differential equation model would calculate.

In the real economy, this would mean that profits would be higher than calculated, and the amount of investment money borrowed would be less than calculated. However, because our economy debt equation is

$$\frac{dD}{dt} = I - \Pi$$

and because the investment, I, is lower than the model calculates while the economy profit, Π, is higher than the model calculates, we see that the economy debt grows at a significantly slower rate than our macroeconomic model predicts throughout the period of high inflation— explaining the departure from reality, which is observed in the fit curves.

11.5   Figures from Bivens and Mishel's Article

Shown here is Bivens and Mishel's Figure A. We display their Figure B and Figure D on the next page. They are reproduced with permission from the Economic Policy Institute.

FIGURE A

Disconnect between productivity and a typical worker's compensation, 1948–2014

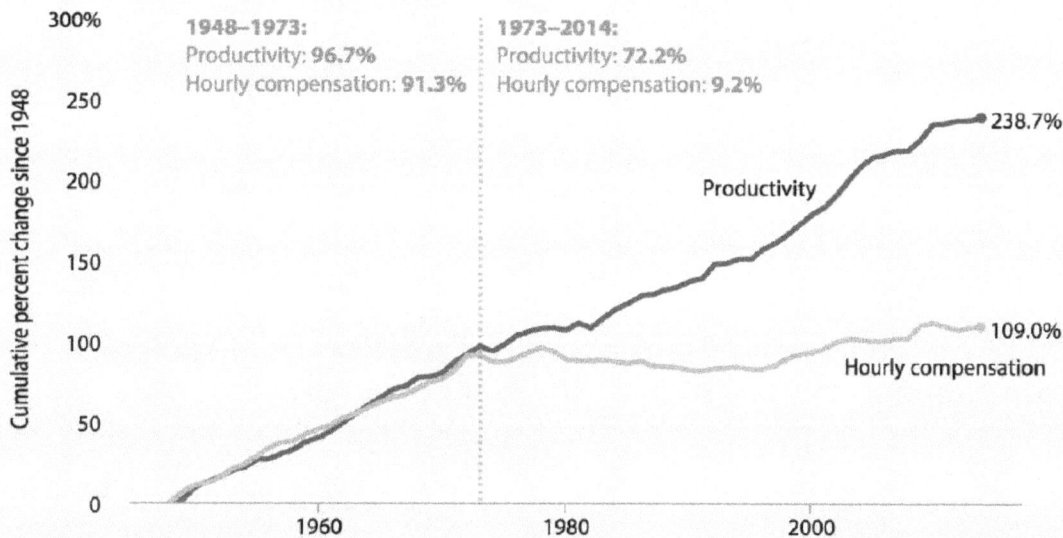

Note: Data are for average hourly compensation of production/nonsupervisory workers in the private sector and net productivity of the total economy. "Net productivity" is the growth of output of goods and services minus depreciation per hour worked.

Source: EPI analysis of data from the BEA and BLS (see technical appendix for more detailed information)   **Economic Policy Institute**

If you let your eye follow the curves of Figure D, you will notice that all curves funnel back toward a single point. This means that the growth rate of all incomes in 1979 was close to the same. When we look at the expanded scale of Figure B, we see that growth rates were not quite the same in 1979. However, they appear to converge to a point in 1973.

When we examine the even more expanded scale of Figure A, we find that the growth rate of all income levels and productivity did converge to a point in time when they all grew with the same growth rate. From Figure A, we see that all incomes and productivity grew at the same rate between 1948 and 1965, but when we examine Figure 11.12 on page 166, we also see that inflation did, too. This was a unique time and place in economic history. A flicker in time not seen before or since. A time when we were all in the same economic boat.

FIGURE B

Growth of productivity, real average compensation, and real median compensation, 1973–2014

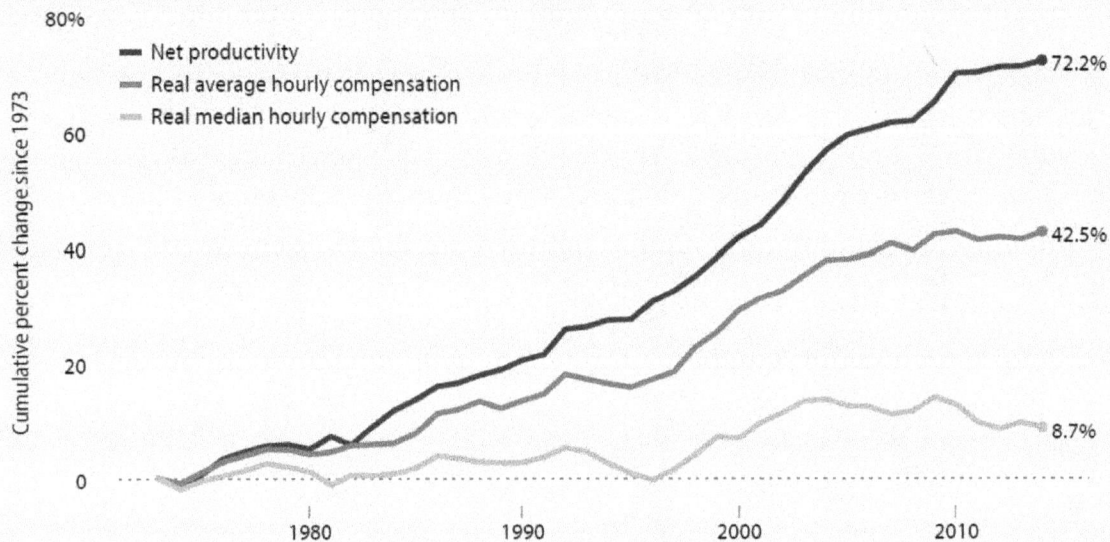

Note: Data are for all workers. Net productivity is the growth of output of goods and services minus depreciation, per hour worked.

Source: EPI analysis of data from the BEA, BLS, and CPS ORG (see technical appendix for more detailed information)   **Economic Policy Institute**

FIGURE D

Growth in productivity and wages of workers at different earning levels, 1979–2013

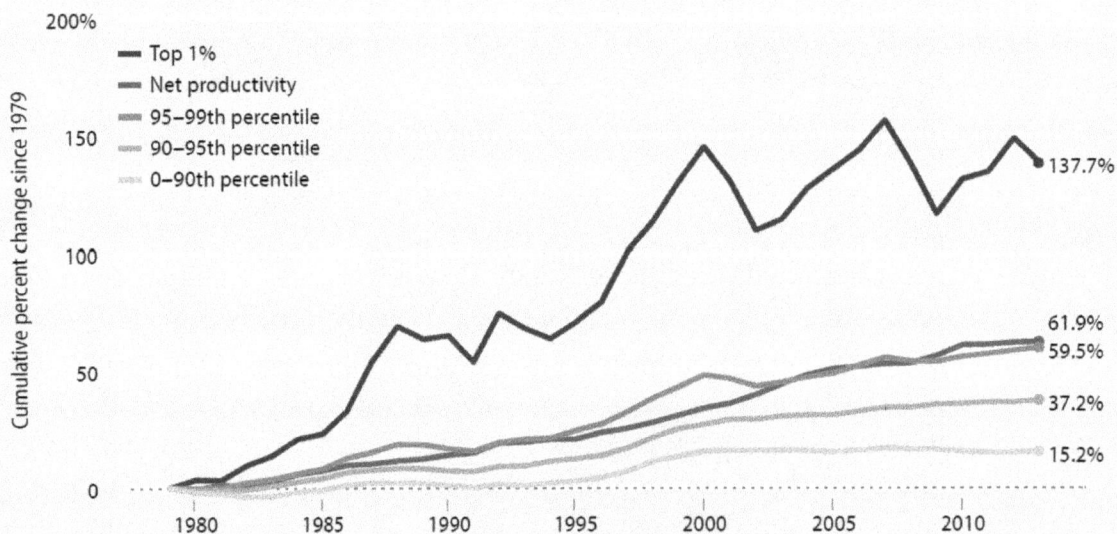

Note: Data are for all workers. Net productivity is the growth of output of goods and services minus depreciation, per hour worked.

Source: EPI analysis of Kopczuk, Saez, and Song (2010, Table A3), and data from the BLS and SSA (see technical appendix for more detailed information)   **Economic Policy Institute**

Chapter 12

Piecewise Continuous Macroeconomic Productivity: Ordinary Worker Model

In our productivity explorations in the last chapter, we saw that productivity seemed to grow in a natural way. On page 156, we saw an example supporting this when we fit the employment level to an exponential function in Figure 11.2. However, we also saw in Figure 11.2 that something within the economy must have changed because after the year 2000 the exponential employment level fit we created, and which worked very well from 1950 to 2000, suddenly, no longer worked at all.

Similarly, we saw in our explorations concerning the Bivens and Mishel wage separation phenomenon, that wages and productivity slowly started to transition away from a period in which wages and productivity moved together, into a period in which productivity grew faster than average wage growth. We saw this also applied to the equivalent macroeconomic properties of consumer price index inflation and macroeconomic productivity. There was a period of time in which they moved together, and then, around 1964, the cumulative CPI inflation rate slowly started to grow, a tiny bit faster than the macroeconomic productivity rate grew.

12.1 Separating Macroeconomic Productivity into Periods

We intend to try to fit the macroeconomic productivity into separate economic periods for which an exponential fit of the macroeconomic productivity will give a good value of the employment level when divided into the output of the economy expressed in current dollars. To that end, we create a table of the macroeconomic productivity for ordinary workers and farmers such that when we divide that productivity into the GDP, we get back the number of those workers. We show a plot of that data, which runs from 1950 to 2017 in Figure 12.1. In Figure 12.2, we show the macroeconomic productivity divided into four distinct fits plotted over the macroeconomic data. In order to make our fits, we divided that data into periods from 1950 to 1970, 1972 to 1982, 1984 to 2000, and 2005 to 2017.

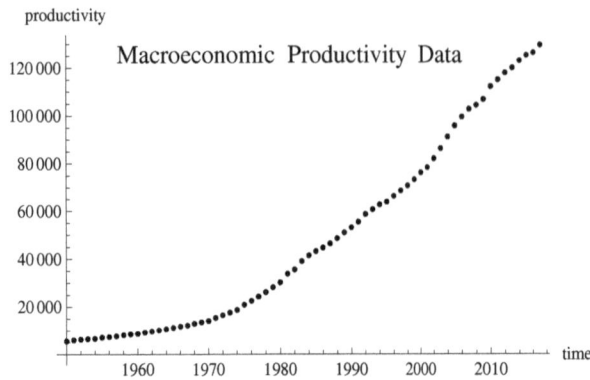

Figure 12.1: Here, we display the macroeconomic productivity data for each year. This data was created by dividing the number of ordinary workers plus farmers in a year into the GDP for that year.

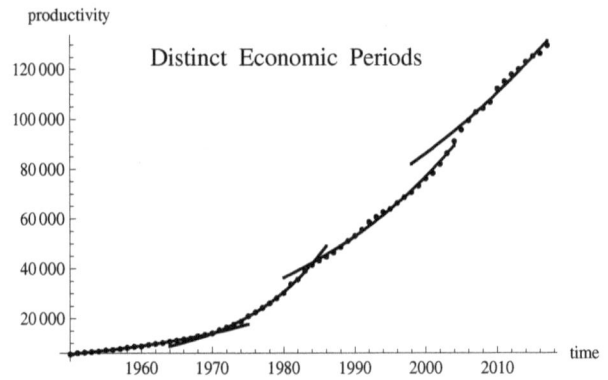

Figure 12.2: Here, we show the four best fits for the periods of macroeconomic productivity described above. We plot these fits over the data in order to get an idea as to where we might create functions that will connect the fits.

After looking carefully at the data and the exponential fits, we decide to make a polynomial connective fit, between the first fit and second fit between 1970 and 1972, between the second fit and third fit between 1982 and 1984, and between the third fit and fourth fit between 2003 and 2005. In order to make the connection fit function, we will match the value and the first derivative of the connective fit polynomial function with the appropriate period's exponential fit function value and its first derivative value. The value of the data point between the two times connecting two exponential productivity fit curves is not used in making the connection. That is, the data point in 1971 is not used at all in making the connection between the first fit and the second productivity fit. The fully connected four-period macroeconomic productivity function is shown plotted over the macroeconomic productivity data in Figure 12.3.

We should mention here that we can use the four-period macroeconomic productivity function and our macroeconomic coupled differential equations to project the United States Economy forward because the macroeconomic productivity function's fourth-period function will extend forward as a known function of time. The macroeconomic productivity function's fourth, best-fit function produced appropriate values of the ordinary worker employment level that matched well with the economic data from 2005 through 2017.

Therefore, the fourth best fit function would be expected to continue to generate appropriate macroeconomic productivity values unless economic conditions changed. For example, if the outsourcing and the offshoring were to stop or slow down drastically, then the economic conditions would change back toward conditions that produced a different macroeconomic productivity function. Also, if the maximum tax rate in the top tax bracket returned to some value above seventy percent, then we would return back toward the earlier macroeconomic productivity growth rates modulo our higher debt-to-GDP ratio. However, as long as we are able to input expected changes into our model equations, and no other large economic changes occur, our equations would be expected to predict the economy forward if these equations truly represent the macroeconomic dynamics of the United States Economy.

We also tested how well our macroeconomic productivity function reproduced the worker data when it was divided into the GDP. In Figure 12.4, we present the results of that test in the form of a percent discrepancy plot. This plot shows the percent discrepancy of the calculated worker employment level from the Bureau of Labor Statistics' value for each year from 1950 to 2017.

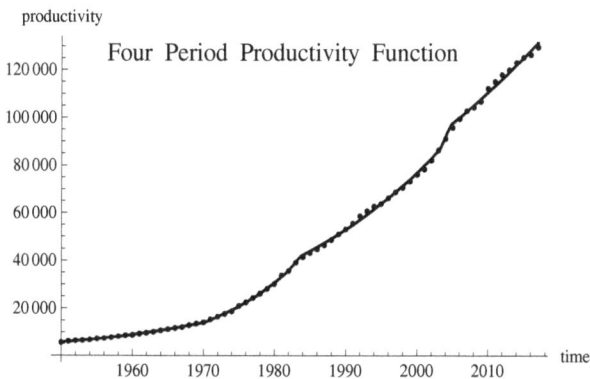

Figure 12.3: Here, in this figure, we have plotted our connected macroeconomic productivity function plotted over all the macroeconomic productivity data from 1950 through 2017.

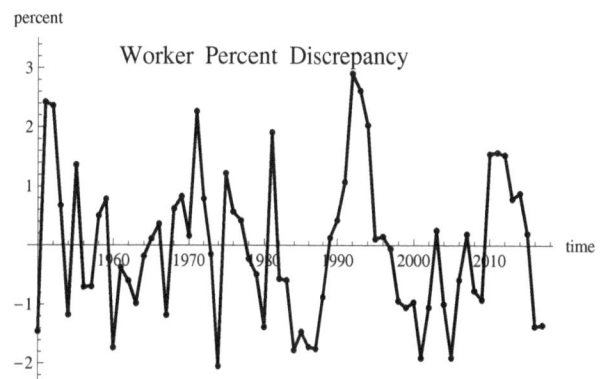

Figure 12.4: In this figure, we display a plot of the percent discrepancy between the calculated number of ordinary workers, including farmers, compared to BLS employment level values.

We see from Figure 12.3 that the four-period productivity function that we created fits the macroeconomic productivity data quite well. We see, from Figure 12.4 that the employment level, calculated by dividing our four-period macroeconomic productivity function into the GDP expressed in current dollars, reproduces the real employment level of the ordinary worker well. This is so because, as we see, from the percent discrepancy plotted in Figure 12.4, the calculated value is always less than three percent from the accepted value.

12.2 Creating a Fit

We have changed the average interest rate interpolating function used in our calculations slightly. We have used the same average interest rate function we created in Chapter 7. However, we have changed the time interval between values given by the average interest rate function used in finding the average interest rate interpolating function from one year to 0.63 years. This change has caused the new interpolating function to match more closely the full average interest rate function. We show the average interest rate function that will be used in the present calculations in Figure 12.5. We chose not to use the average interest rate function itself because it noticeably slows down the calculations. Moreover, we choose not to use the average interest rate interest interpolating function we used in the fits we created in Chapter 9 and Chapter 10 because it is somewhat discrepant from the average interest rate function during the inflationary period of the late 1960s through the early 1980s.

We will compare the present average interest rate function with the average interest rate function shown in Figure 9.3, on page 144, which we used in the previous fits starting in 1964. The previous interpolation function was based on a one-year sampling of the average interest rate function we created in Chapter 7. The average interest rate function that we will use was created from a 0.63-year sampling of the average interest rate function we created in Chapter 7. The only reason that the average interest rate function, itself, was not used is that using it would add days to the time it would take to make a single fit. Thus, because time is of the essence, we did not take that route. However, in order to show the reader that using this new present version has made a difference in the average interest function during the period of high inflation, we show the previous version of the average interest rate interpolating function plotted over the present version in Figure 12.6.

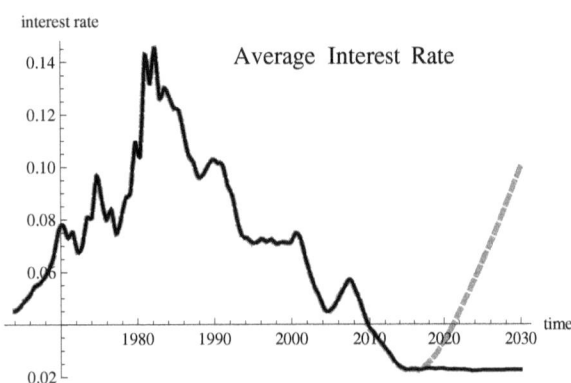

Figure 12.5: In this figure, we display a plot of the average interest rate functions that will be used in our calculations. The solid black curve will apply during the no rate hike scenario, and the dashed gray line will apply during the Fed rate hike scenario.

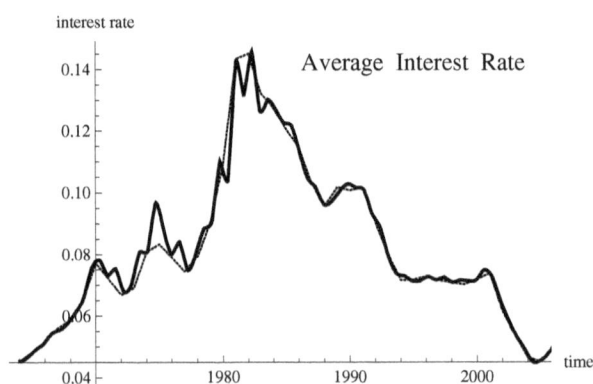

Figure 12.6: In this figure, we have plotted the older one-year step based interpolating function of the average interest rate—thin gray line—against the 0.63-year step based interpolating function—black line.

In Figure 12.5, we see that the present version of the average interest rate looks very similar to the previous version, shown in Figure 9.3, except that it appears a bit more bumpy. However, when one examines Figure 12.6, one sees that there are a few spots during the period of high inflation, in which the two average interest rate functions are discrepant by more than one percent. For instance, the double peak between 1980 and 1982 is such a region. Also, the period of time around 1975 is a second such region. More subtly, we can see that around 1980, the present interpolating function version of the average interest rate takes a short sharp turn downward while the previous version continues its fast upward rise in the average interest rate. This creates a discrepancy between the versions of over one percent for a short period of time.

There are still discrepancies between the present interpolating function version and the average interest rate function we created. However, they are smaller and more on the size that we see in the plot from 1982 to 1986.

Once past the period of high inflation from 1982 onward, the discrepancies become less. At first, the discrepancies are visible on the scale of the plot, but slowly as the influence of the high and chaotically changing interest rates on the calculated average interest rate lessens, the discrepancies, on the scale of the plot, disappear.

Next, we present the parameters that allowed us to fit the economy's GDP. In essence, we make the fit in the same manner that we used in the previous fits that started in 1964. Here we used the four-period macroeconomic productivity function that we created. Because the productivity function is already created, we do not need to integrate it along with the rest of the macroeconomic variables. The values of the macroeconomic productivity function, which is a function of time, are made available to Mathematica's numerical integrating function, NDSolve. The initial value for the curious is $\hat{a}(1964) = 10,672.2$.

From this point, we adjust the initial value of the average wage rate until it allows a fit to the first five or six GDP data points. However, we also note whether or not the output during the period from 2012 to 2017 seems to have roughly the same curvature as the data points out there. The output, of course, does not lie along these GDP data points. Our purpose in doing this is to get parameter values for c_1 and c_2 that will be base values of the parameters, which will work when the economy is running smoothly.

After we achieve the fit to the first five or six GDP data points as described above, we then adjust the investment equation parameters c_1 and c_2 as needed in order to make the output curve fit the rest of the GDP data in a satisfactory manner. We show the values of c_1 and c_2 in Figures 12.7 and 12.8 that allowed us to make our fit.

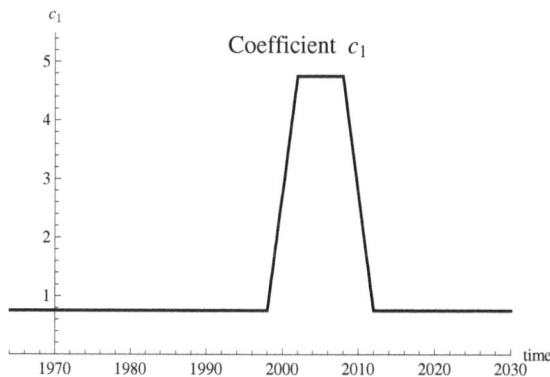

Figure 12.7: Here, we display the values of the Businessman's Coefficient, c_1, that helped to make the output fit.

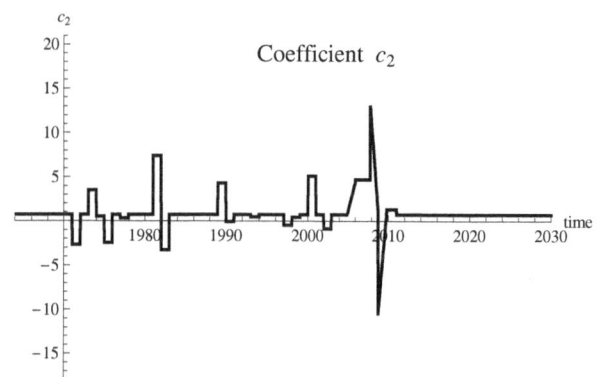

Figure 12.8: In this figure, we show the Banker's Coefficient, c_2, that helped us make the present output fit.

Now we present the output fit, in Figure 12.9, and the employment level fit, in Figure 12.10, from 1964 through 2030.

In Figure 12.9, we see that we can fit the output of the economy well, as we have been able to do with all our fits. However, one can see that we did need a good deal of help in making the fit during the high inflationary times from about 1970 through the early 1980s. As one can see from Figures 12.7 and 12.8, we used the Banker's Term in our investment equation exclusively to wind the output of our fit through the GDP trail of the United States Economy. This was done strictly because of the ease and efficiency of the fitting effort and

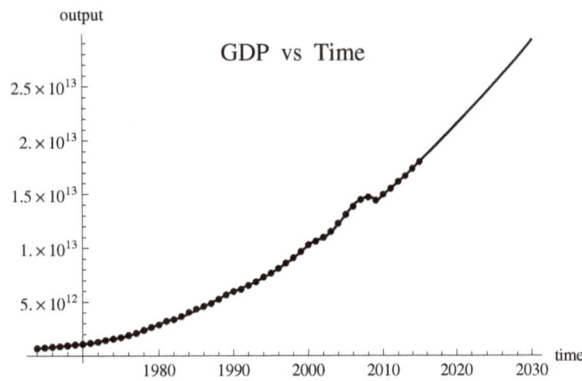

Figure 12.9: Here, we see the output fit to the GDP created using our four-period macroeconomic productivity function for ordinary workers.

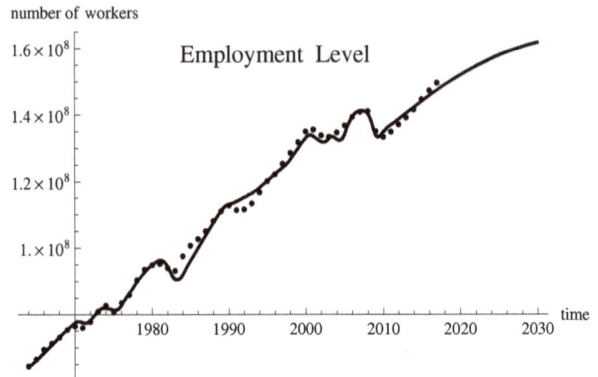

Figure 12.10: In this figure, we plot the fit to the employment level created using our four-period macroeconomic productivity function. We plot the fit over the employment level data.

not because I had any knowledge or intuition about what occurred behind the scene.

We see from Figure 12.10 that our macroeconomic equations have been able to fit the employment level reasonably for the first time. This result is clearly due to the fact that in this fit we now have a productivity expressed in monetary terms that inflates properly with the use of current dollars. Moreover, we see this result resolves the error of my previous interpretation concerning the ever-growing employment level.

Next, we will show the employment rate in Figure 12.11 and the investment-to-GDP ratio in Figure 12.12.

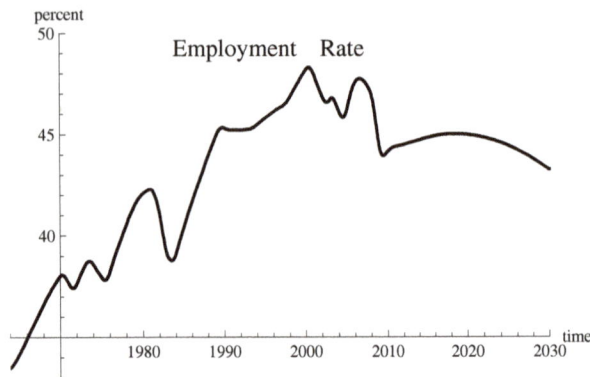

Figure 12.11: Here, we see the employment rate created using our four-period macroeconomic productivity extended through to 2030 for the Federal Reserve no rate hike scenario.

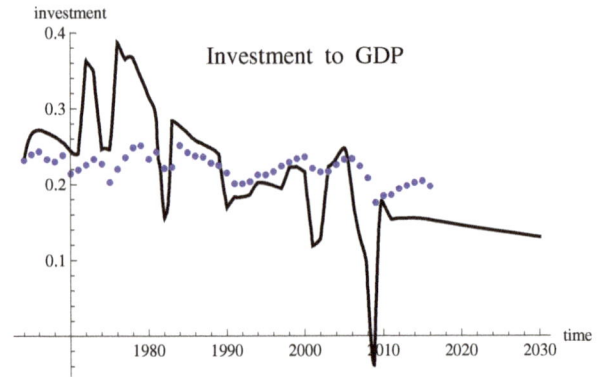

Figure 12.12: Here, we see the investment-to-GDP curve, created using our four-period macroeconomic productivity, plotted over investment-to-GDP data obtained from the World Bank.

We see that the employment rate, as shown in Figure 12.11, grew steadily, but episodically, from 1964 through the year 2000. After the year 2000, we see that the employment rate starts to decline episodically. From the employment level plot, in Figure 12.10, we see that, in about the year 2000, the rate of growth of the employment level suddenly changed to a noticeably slower rate of growth. Presently, we know that a smaller percentage of the potential workforce is employed than has been the case for more than two decades. So, the calculated employment rate is mirroring present-day reality.[1]

In Figure 12.12, we see that just as with the other fits that began in 1964, the investment-to-GDP fit during the period of relatively high inflation, which occurred from the very late 1960s into the early 1980s, is noticeably higher than it should be. Otherwise, the fit seems to be fairly reasonable.

12.2.1 A Digression with Comments

In our discussion of the plot of the exponential growth of the number of workers in the United States, in Figure 11.2 on page 156, we noted that, suddenly in about the year 2000, the growth of the number of workers abruptly diverted from the trend of fifty years and began to follow a dramatically slower growth rate. Earlier, we discussed that this might be because, in about 2000, businesses began, in earnest, to outsource and to offshore their work to peoples in countries whose wage rates were significantly lower than the wage rate in the United States. We then stated:

> *The question is, why would companies in the United States do this? It is a fact that because the workers in the United States are paid much more than the workers in the countries to which the work was outsourced, the companies would make more money and be more profitable. It might seem reasonable that this is the answer. However, this is not the answer. We need another piece of the puzzle before the answer, why, can become clear.*

Since that discussion, we studied macroeconomic productivity and made the connection with the Bivens and Mishel's productivity wage rate separation. Both they and we noticed that this separation did not occur during the period of the 1950s and early 1960s. We made the connection that this period of no wage rate separation between the economic elite and ordinary workers occurred when the top tax bracket's marginal tax rate was very high. We had previously noted that lower marginal tax rates for the top tax bracket had set off periods of economic speculation during the dot-com bubble, the real estate and derivative bubbles leading up to the crisis 2008–9, and for the four-year time period between 1925 and 1929 during which the top marginal tax rate was twenty-five percent before the Stock Market Crash of 1929. Thus, we have seen that a low tax rate in the top marginal tax brackets releases a person's greed.

It is true that if a company outsources and offshores some of its work to people in noticeably lower wage rate countries, then the company will make more profit. However, the real answer to the question is that a low tax rate for the top marginal tax bracket allows the corporate elites to take advantage of their company's newly found profits for their own personal gain. However, when the tax rate is high enough, the economic elite can not do that.

---

[1]This fact is usually obfuscated by quoting the unemployment rate, which has been changed to appear lower than it should be, by deleting "discouraged workers" and hidden, discouraged, potential workers from the calculation.

When the top marginal tax brackets are high enough, then everybody is put into the same economic boat so that all the people move up and down together. This situation means the elites' perspective has to change because for them to do better, everyone has to do better.

The present situation is antithetical to the founding principle of the Country and to the Constitution of the United States. Here we quote part of the second paragraph of the Country's founding document, The Declaration of Independence. However, I will substitute the word people for the word men so that the meaning is not lost on anyone.

> *We hold these truths to be self-evident: That all people are created equal; that they are endowed by their Creator with certain unalienable rights; that among these are life, liberty, and the pursuit of happiness; that, to secure these rights, governments are instituted among people, …*

These simple words are antithetical to how numerous people who claim to want to follow the Country's founding principles believe. For example, many of these people are against gay or transgender marriage. However, one of our unalienable rights is the right to seek happiness, and one of the ways people seek happiness is to couple up. Therefore, when it comes to governance, it is a slam dunk that people have the unalienable right to couple up in any way that they consensually choose.

Moreover, most people who claim to believe in the Country's founding principles think that it is all about liberty. So that when it comes to the economic realm, these people think that it is entirely right and proper to make as much money as they can. No, this is not true. Besides the right to liberty, all people have the right to life. That means that all people have the right to be able to have a job with a livable wage. However, in any year, the output of the Country is limited. So if a few people make too much money from the output of the Country, then there will not be enough money left for all the people to have such a job. Therefore, according to our founding principles, it is incumbent upon the Government to protect this right of the people.

We now know how to set a livable wage and to fund infrastructure jobs which the private sector tends not to do. Therefore, it is the Government's duty to fund such jobs and to set such a wage. Also, because productivity grows at a faster rate than the population, it is the duty of the Government under our founding principles to set immigration policy and the length of the workweek, appropriately, so that all the people in the Country will be able to have a job, preserving their right to life and preserving their right to pursue happiness.

So, it is within the above constraints that people have the liberty to make as much money as they can. Moreover, it is the duty of the Government to set these constraints. For if they do not, it would be like the Government permitting highway robbery or murder.

12.2.2   Back to the Fit

In Figure 12.13, we show the economy debt calculated using our four-period macroeconomic productivity function, and in Figure 12.14, we show the debt-to-GDP plot. Both fits are plotted over the relevant data.

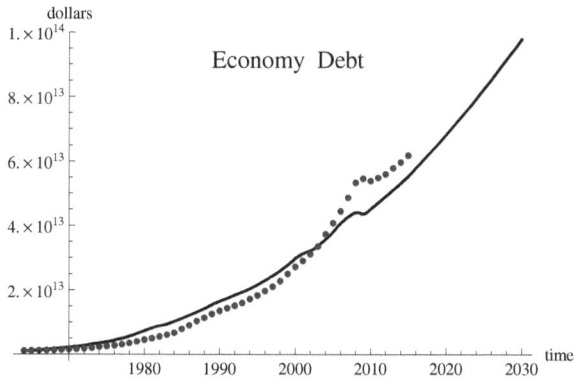

Figure 12.13: This figure shows the total economy debt plotted over the debt data from 1964 through 2017. Compare with Figure 2.4 on page 22 and with Figure 3.4 on page 34.

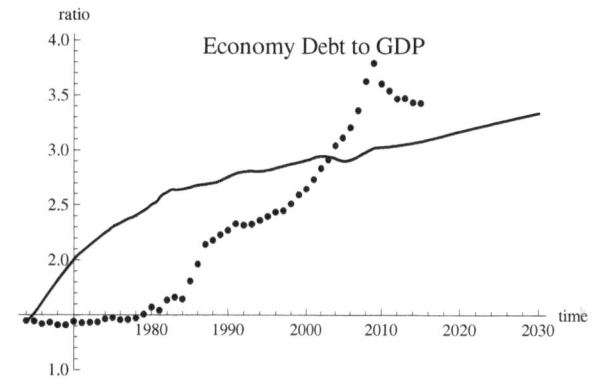

Figure 12.14: Here, we show the plot of the debt-to-GDP ratio calculated using our four-period macro-economic productivity function plotted over the data.

The present economy debt fit shown in Figure 12.13 is very similar to all the other economy debt curves. However, the economy debt-to-GDP curve, shown in Figure 12.14, only looks like the other economy debt-to-GDP plots that start in 1964. In this and the other plots that begin in 1964, the steep rise in the debt-to-GDP ratio starts too early by about fifteen years. This rise contrasts sharply with the fits that start in 1980, all of which begin their steep rise in the debt-to-GDP ratio at most only a couple of years too early.

Previously, we did not display any of the 1980 debt-to-GDP plots. Below in Figure 12.15 and Figure 12.16, the debt-to-GDP curves for Chapter 2 and Chapter 3 are plotted over the debt-to-GDP data.

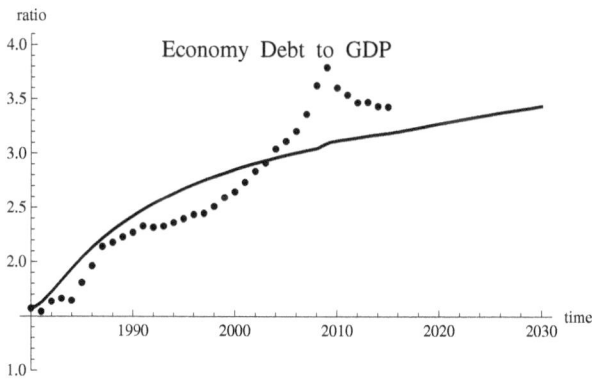

Figure 12.15: In this figure, we display the debt-to-GDP plot for the smooth fit we created in Chapter 2.

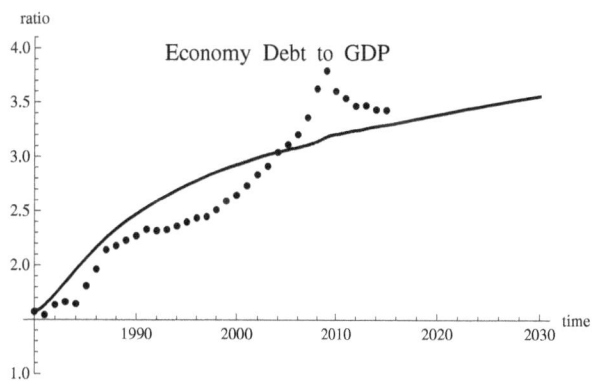

Figure 12.16: Here, we show the plot of the debt-to-GDP ratio for the fit we created in Chapter 3.

12.3 Ordinary Worker Comparison Plots

In Figures 12.17 and 12.18, we show the comparison plots between the Federal Reserve no interest rate hike scenario and the three-quarters of a percent per year rate hike scenario for the GDP and the economy debt plots, respectively.

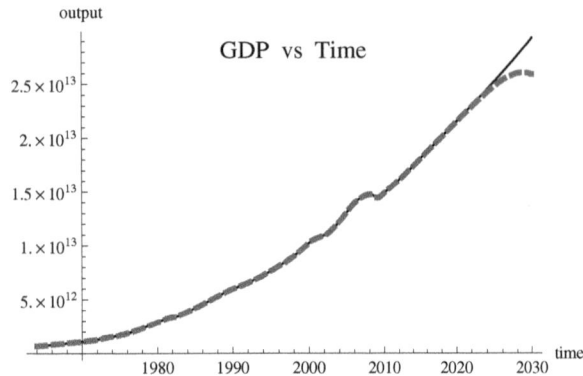

Figure 12.17: Here, we see the GDP versus time graphs constructed from our macroeconomic productivity function, for the Fed no rate hike scenario and the Fed three-quarters of a percent per year rate hike scenario, plotted over each other.

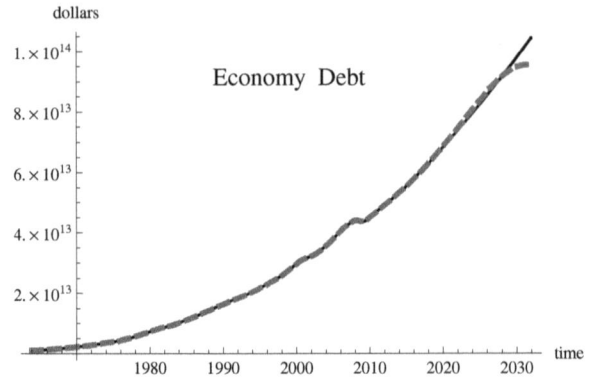

Figure 12.18: Here, we plot the economy debt for both Federal Reserve scenarios. We made both fits using our four-period macroeconomic productivity interpolating function. The thick gray dashed line denotes the interest rate hike scenario.

When we look at Figures 12.17 and 12.18, we see that both the output curve and the economy debt curve look very similar to the other output curves and debt curves produced using our constructed average interest rate function. Just as with our earlier fits, we see that the output curve in the rate hike scenario immediately starts to slowly fall below the no rate hike scenario's output curve, while the debt curve, in the rate hike scenario, at first starts to slowly rise above the no rate hike scenario's debt curve. Furthermore, in all economy debt comparisons, it takes several years after the start of the interest rate hikes for the debt curve to fall below the debt curve in the no rate hike scenario.

However, the timing of when the GDP and the debt will reach their peaks in the Federal Reserves' interest rate hike scenario is quite late. When one checks the numbers, one finds that the peak of the GDP curve occurs at 2028.78, while the peak of the economy debt curve occurs at 2031.35. These dates compare to the fit starting in 1980 using our average interest rate function of 2027.41 for the GDP peak and 2029.95 for the debt peak. Moreover, the fits that start in 1964 and use our average interest rate function produce the values for the timing for the GDP peak at 2026.92 and 2026.97, while they produce timings for the debt peak at 2029.39 and 2029.43. The timing of the peaks in the present fit is significantly later than timings in both the 1980 fits and the 1964 fits.

In part, this results from the non-economist in me. When I was breaking up the productivity into periods, the break up originated only in what I saw in the productivity curve. It was only after and during the breaking up of the curve that I associated them with different economic regimes/periods. The fourth productivity fit seemed to produce a reasonable fit to the productivity data. However later, when I saw the employment level fit, Figure 12.10, produced by the four-period productivity function, I thought the fit looked wrong. Its fourth period looked like it was systematically off.

The last period is critical for projecting the economy forward. The fit's employment level curve looks like a crossing, not a synchronization!

It was then that I realized that there were two distinct economic periods in the fourth period of the four-period macroeconomic productivity function. Outsourcing and offshoring occurred in both periods. However, the first half of the fourth period was ripe with speculation. The second half of that period was a period of trying to hold on and trying somehow to make it back to normal using quantitative easing and zero interest rate policies.

So, I stopped my writing and spent my time, breaking up the fourth period, creating a five-period macroeconomic productivity function and fit. The GDP peak that was produced with this fit occurred at 2026.73, and the peak in the debt curve occurred at 2029.22—more in line with our earlier results. This result puts the values for the peaks of the GDP and the debt very close to the other results starting in 1964 and only about eight months earlier than the 1980 results.

Why am I writing this way? Why don't I just rewrite using the five-period fit, making for a more straightforward text? I have actually done that. However, that resulted in a discussion that missed some delicate points. In addition, I find that I learn from my failures and missteps, as I am sure others learn from theirs. So, if I show my missteps, my hope is that you, the reader, will learn from them, too.

Next, we plot the comparison plots between the two Fed scenarios for the investment, in Figure 12.19, and for the economy profit, in Figure 12.20.

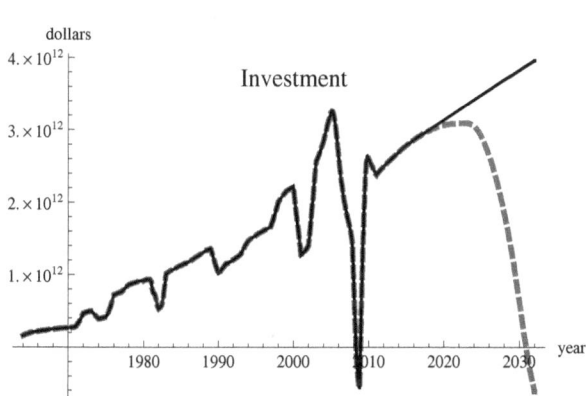

Figure 12.19: In this figure, we display the comparison plots of investment for the Fed's no rate hike scenario—black line—and for the three-quarters of a percent per year interest rate hike—dashed line.

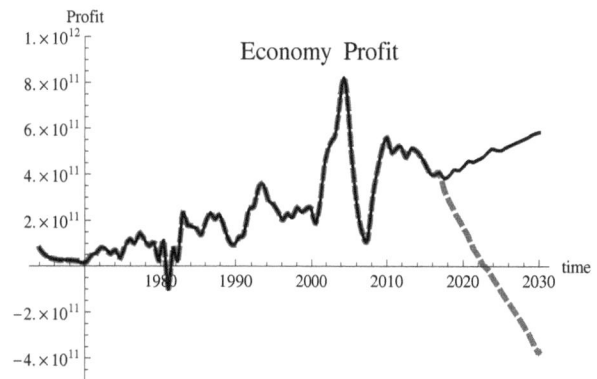

Figure 12.20: Here in this figure, we see the plot of the economy profit in the no rate hike scenario—black line—and the economy profit in the three-quarters of a percent per year Federal Reserve interest rate hike scenario.

The investment comparison curves, which are shown in Figure 12.19, look almost exactly like all the other investment comparison plots in all the other fits we have done. The timing of when investment crashes to zero in the Federal Reserve rate hike scenario is found to be 2030.88 using the four-period macroeconomic productivity function. If we had used the five-period macroeconomic productivity function, we would have found that investment would crash to zero at 2028.70. The previous fits that began in 1964 gave dates for when $I = 0$ of 2028.82 and 2028.86, while the fit that began in 1980, using our average interest rate function, gave a date of 2029.37.

When we look at the economy profit fit shown in Figure 12.20, we see that economy profit dips below zero for a very brief time in about 1980. All the other fits starting in 1964 have shown the same thing. This below-zero dip may be an artifact caused because we have not accounted for inflation in our equations.

The economy profit curve, shown in Figure 12.20, crashes to zero and keeps going down in the Federal Reserve's interest rate hike scenario, just as every other fit has done. The four-period macroeconomic productivity function's profit curve predicted this crash to occur in 2022.88, while the five-period macroeconomic productivity function's fit predicted the crash to zero to occur in 2021.21. These predictions compare to the predictions of 2021.12 for both other fits starting in 1964 and compare to the prediction of 2021.28 for the fit, starting in 1980.

Now, we show the employment level and wage rate comparison plots in Figure 12.21 and Figure 12.22, respectively.

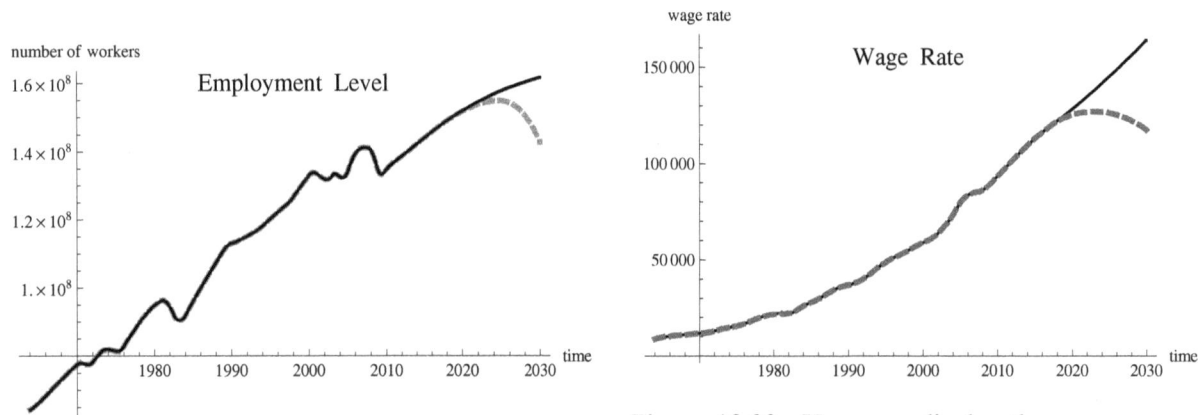

Figure 12.21: In this figure, we display the employment level predictions, created using our four-period macroeconomic productivity function for the no rate hike scenario—black line—and for the three-quarters of a percent per year interest rate hike scenario—thick dashed line.

Figure 12.22: Here, we display the average wage rate for the fit, which was calculated using ordinary worker data, including farmers. In addition, the fit was calculated using the four-period macroeconomic productivity function. The fit was projected forward for the no rate hike scenario—black line—and for the Federal Reserves' interest rate hike scenario—dashed line.

We know from our earlier fit to the employment level that the fit using the four-period macroeconomic productivity keeps the employment level roughly close to the employment level of the workers we are following. The ability of this fit to keep the employment level reasonable is unlike all our previous fits.

In the predictive part of the employment level curve under the assumptions of the Federal Reserve rate hike scenario, we see that the employment level turns over in the middle of the 2020s and then begins to crash. We calculate the date of the peak in the employment level to be 2024.56, while the five-period macroeconomic productivity function fit gives a value for the peak of 2023.77. These values compare to values of the peak for fits starting in 1964 of 2024.23 and 2024.29. The value for the peak of the fit starting in 1980 is 2024.62. These timing results show that the timing of the peak for all the employment level fits produces values that are more randomly scattered than in the other timings, we have compared.

Next, we note that in Figure 12.22, the average wage rate begins to crash under the Federal Reserve's interest rate hike policy in the early 2020s, just as it has for all other fits using the average interest rate function we created in Chapter 7. As we have explained earlier, the timing of the peak of the wage rate occurs when the economy profit crashes to zero.

Using the numbers for the present fit, we calculate that the peak of the average wage rate occurs at 2022.88 for four-period macroeconomic productivity fit, and 2021.21 for the five-period macroeconomic productivity function. For the previous two fits starting in 1964, we found the peak of the average wage rate occurred at 2021.12 and 2021.13, while for the fit starting in 1980, we calculated 2021.28.

Second, for later use, we should note, from Figure 12.22, that the average wage rate of this group of workers is calculated to be noticeably higher than their actual average wage rate. In this regard, it is good to be aware that, as shown in Figure 12.10, this fit is actually tracking the employment level of this group of workers quite well. In the next chapter, we will create a fit using a much larger group of "macroeconomic workers" in order to learn more about the nature of our macroeconomic model of coupled differential equations and the results it produces.

12.3.1 Five Period Macroeconomic Productivity Function

For the curious and for possible future use, we present the five-period macroeconomic productivity function in Figure 12.23. And, in Figure 12.24, we display the fit to the employment level when the five-period macroeconomic productivity function was used in fitting the GDP of the economy.

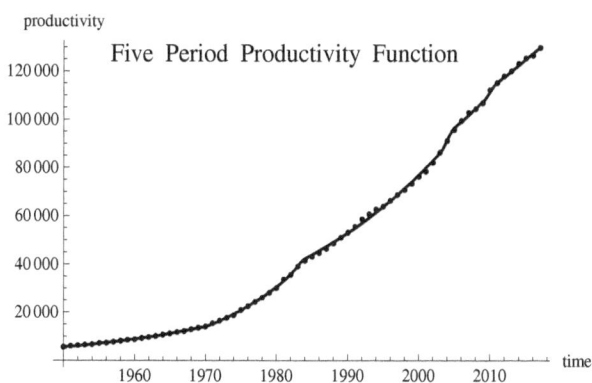

Figure 12.23: Here, we show the five period macroeconomic productivity function's fit to the productivity data.

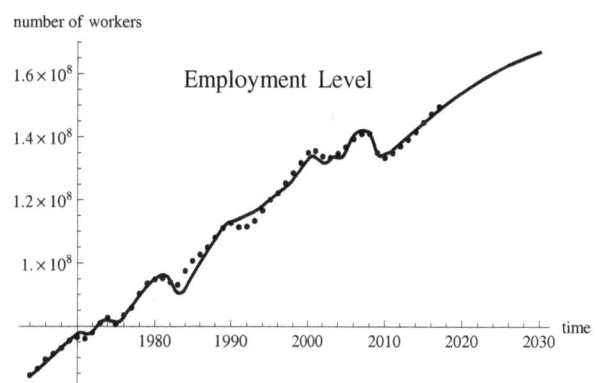

Figure 12.24: Here, we see the fit to the employment level data when the five period macroeconomic productivity function was used in a fit starting in 1964.

When we compare the four-period macroeconomic productivity function's fit, see Figure 12.3, to the five-period, we see that the five-period fit to the productivity data is a bit better, as it should be. However, the four-period fit curve appears to be cutting across the *productivity data* at a very shallow angle.

When we examine the five-period macroeconomic productivity functions use in the fit of the employment level, there appears to be a subtle but critical improvement of its fit to the last few employment level data points. In its fit to the last two data points, the five-period fit curve appears to be below but traveling roughly parallel to the data. However, the employment level curve, which the four-period macroeconomic productivity function helped to generate, appears to be cutting across the trend of the data. See Figure 12.10 on page 176.

Comparing the employment level fits in Figure 12.10 and Figure 12.24, we see that the five-period macroeconomic productivity fit has improved upon the four-period macroeconomic productivity fit. However, when we exam the five-period fit to the *employment level data*, we see that it is a shallow crossing, not a synchronization. Our results indicate that we need to take more care in getting an excellent visual synchronization to the final employment level data in order to create an accurate predictive extension to our fits.

We see from Figure 12.24 that the five-period best fit is still not tracking right down the last critical eight data points that our eyes tell us it could. The last eight data points set a trend line for our eyes that should be matched by the fit curve. If the fit curve is not traveling down the trend line of the data, then we should expect departures from what an ideal fit line would give. Moreover, judging from the discrepancies of the predictions made with the use of the four-period macroeconomic productivity function and the five-period macroeconomic productivity function, the macroeconomic productivity, for ordinary workers, is quite sensitive to departures from the ideal fit line, and therefore to departures from the ideal macroeconomic productivity function that would produce such a line.

It was noticeably easier to match the ideal line that our eyes gave us for the GDP data. We only had to adjust some numerical coefficients, typically c_2 in the investment equation, to find an ideal fit that would enable us to project our macroeconomic model forward in time. However, it is not so easy to find a function that will allow us to match the ideal line that our eyes give us. We might get several best fit lines to try by adjusting the interval endpoints along with the connection points and their connection methods. In addition, we could get a few more best fit lines by adjusting the method by which the best fit is judged.

Chapter 13

Piecewise Continuous Macroeconomic Productivity: Extraordinary "Worker" Model

13.1 Extraordinary Worker Macroeconomic Productivity

In this section, we will investigate what kind of fit we obtain when we consider *all* people who get paid, directly and indirectly, from the businesses that produce something in the economy. This will include people who work for the government, Federal, State, and local. It will include people who work in non-profit organizations. Moreover, it will also include people on welfare, disability, and Social Security, who do no work.

It seems likely to me that the number of "workers" we will be using is systematically short of the actual number of workers. At the time I started writing this chapter (January 15, 2019), I came across a Bureau of Labor Statistics' report of yearly data on the number of workers in the United States Economy that differs consistently from the data I had obtained elsewhere, by ten to twenty million workers. Thus, some government, military, and household workers may have been left out of the other statistics. However, this matters not for our purposes, because what we are after, is determining the effects of using different measures of the employment level on the fitting and predictive ability of our model.

We are including ordinary workers and farmers, but we are also including active-duty military personnel, people on disability, people on welfare, and retired people on Social Security. To create the macroeconomic productivity for this model, we construct a table of macroeconomic productivity by dividing the GDP by the number of these extraordinary "workers" for each year. Then, we plot this productivity data and visually divide it into periods. Finally, we fit each period's data with an exponential function. We show the fit to this macroeconomic productivity in Figure 13.1.

We see in Figure 13.1 that we only used four economic periods in breaking up our productivity data to create our piecewise continuous macroeconomic productivity function. We know that gave problems in our previous fit using ordinary workers plus farmers. However,

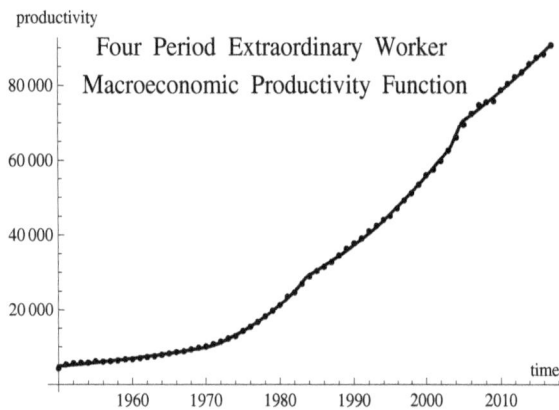

Figure 13.1: In this figure, we display the macro-economic productivity function's fit to the macro-economic productivity data, which we created from our extraordinary set of "workers".

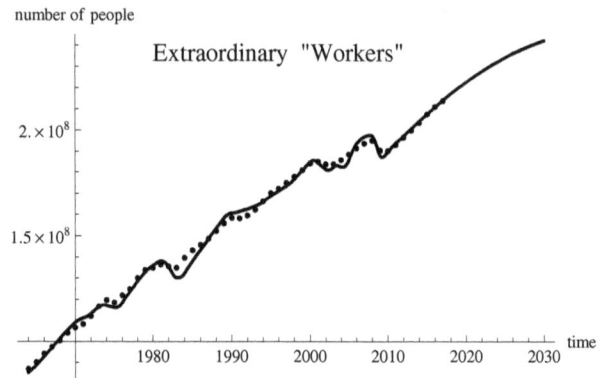

Figure 13.2: Here, we show how well our macro-economic coupled differential equation model produces a fit to employment level when our model uses the four-period macroeconomic productivity function, which we created for extraordinary "workers".

when one looks closely at the fit to the critical last eight data points, which are the data points in the economic period of zero interest rates and quantitative easing, along with offshoring and outsourcing, we see that the fit to these points looks to be extremely good.

In Figure 13.2, we show the fit to the employment level given by the fit of our coupled differential equation macroeconomic model. As we see in the figure, our four-period macroeconomic productivity function produces a good fit to the employment level throughout and a very good to excellent visual fit over the critical last eight employment level data points. The fit is so good in fact, that from our experience, it seems more likely than not that a best-fit function based on only the points from 2010 to 2017 would produce a worse fit to those critical data points—the points that set the trend for a projection of the economy forward in time.

If the reader compares this fit to the employment level over the critical last eight data points, to the results in Figure 12.24 of the previous chapter, one sees that the present four-period macroeconomic productivity function for extraordinary workers helps create a no-ticeably better fit than the five-period macroeconomic productivity function did for ordinary workers plus farmers. This fortuitous result probably has to do with the fact that the present grouping of extraordinary workers is a more stable measure of the employment level because the extraordinary workers all get paid, whether or not they are working, although the pay for some of them may change noticeably depending upon whether they are working or not.

13.2   A Fit Created from the Extraordinary Worker Macroeconomic Productivity

We want to begin the fit that we create from the extraordinary grouping of workers in 1964, and we want to be able to compare it as best we can with the 1980 fit that we created in

Chapter 7. To do this, we will use the average interest rate function we created in Chapter 7. The average interest rate functions we will use are shown in Figure 12.5 on page 174.

In making the present fit, we used the Businessman's Coefficient, c_1, shown in Figure 13.3 and the Banker's Coefficient, c_2, shown in Figure 13.4. Following these plots, we show the output fit curve plotted over the GDP data in Figure 13.5 and the investment-to-GDP curve, in Figure 13.6, that we produced from this fit.

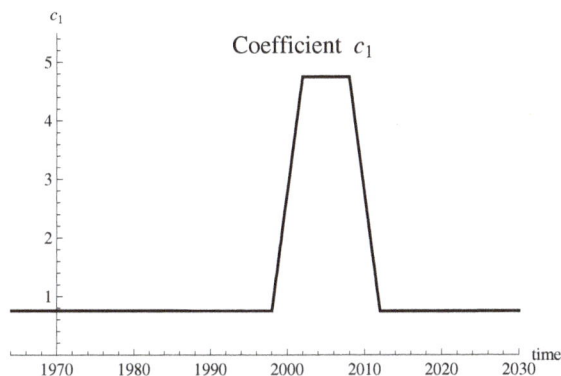

Figure 13.3: Here, we display the coefficient c_1 that helped to make our fit to the United States Economy using the extraordinary workers' group.

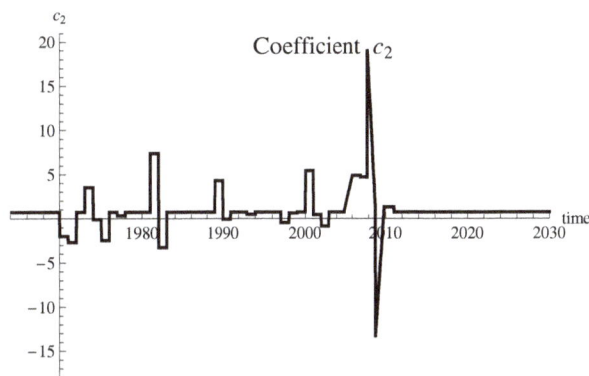

Figure 13.4: In this figure, we display the Banker's Coefficient, c_2, which helped to make the fit to the United States Economy.

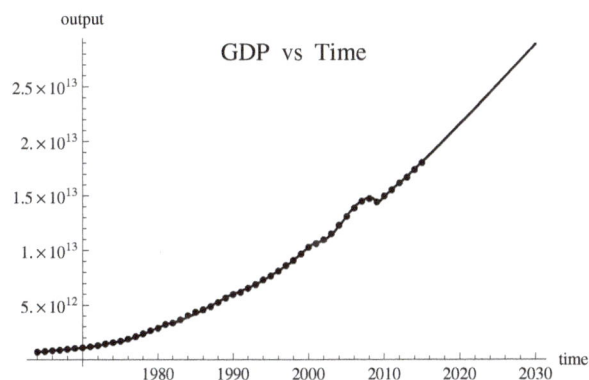

Figure 13.5: Here, we see the results of the output fit to the GDP data using a macroeconomic productivity function created for a grouping of extraordinary workers.

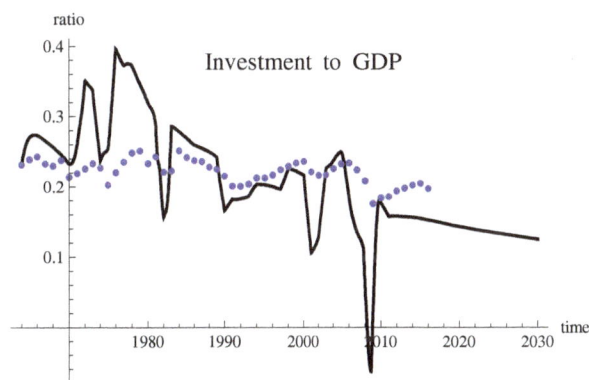

Figure 13.6: Here, we show the investment-to-GDP curve generated using our macroeconomic productivity function, which we created for a grouping of extraordinary workers.

In Figure 13.5, we see that the use of extraordinary workers did not affect the ability of our macroeconomic coupled differential equations to fit the GDP in the United States Economy. In Figure 13.6, we see that the use of our extraordinary grouping of workers did not interfere with the resulting fit of the investment-to-GDP data when we used our macroeconomic coupled differential equations to fit the GDP the United States Economy. Moreover, the investment-to-GDP curve has the same look and scale through the period of high inflation as the other fits that started in 1964.

Next, we look at the graph for the economy debt of the United States in Figure 13.7, and the graph for the economy debt-to-GDP ratio for the United States in Figure 13.8 created by our fit. The curves in both figures are plotted over the appropriate data.

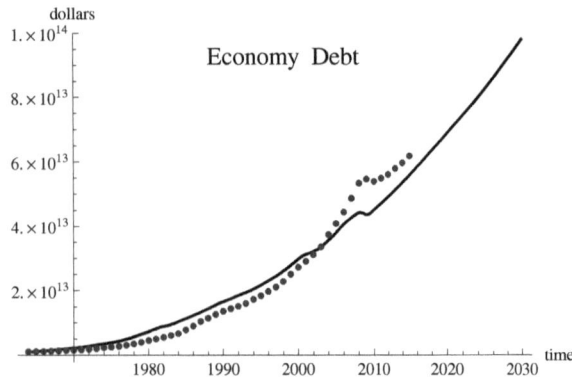

Figure 13.7: In this figure, we show the economy debt curve created using our macroeconomic productivity best fit function to our extraordinary worker group.

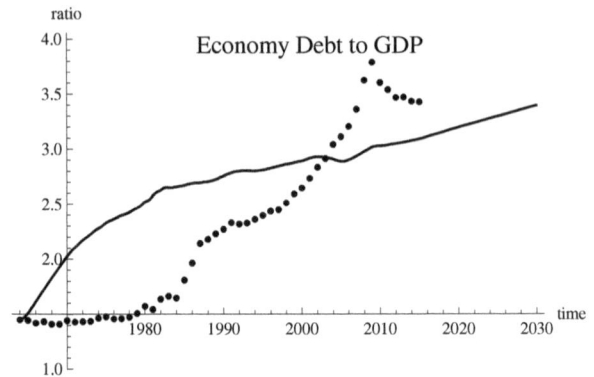

Figure 13.8: Here, we see the graph of the economy debt-to-GDP ratio, which resulted when we used the macroeconomic productivity function created for our extraordinary group of workers.

The economy debt graph in Figure 13.7, created using our extraordinary worker macroeconomic productivity function, looks almost exactly like all the other economy debt graphs that we have created. The much larger extraordinary worker group seems to have had no real affect on the ability of our macroeconomic model to fit the economy of the United States.

In Figure 13.8, we see that in 1965 the fit to the economy debt-to-GDP ratio rises steeply from a debt-to-GDP ratio of about 1.5. This steep rise in the debt-to-GDP ratio looks to be about fifteen years too early when we compare it with the actual rise shown in the data. This early rise is exactly like all the other economy debt-to-GDP graphs for fits that we began in 1964. The use of this much larger sample of people, who are paid directly and indirectly by the businesses that directly produce the GDP output of the country's economy, has so far not seemed to affect our coupled differential equation model's ability to fit the economy of the United States.

13.3   Extraordinary Worker Comparison Plots

In all the comparison fit plots, we will display a table below the plot that shows the timing for a specific event shown in the comparison plot above the table. The table will include entries for all the fits that use the average interest rate function that we created in Chapter 7. We have included the fit that began in 1980 because it will allow us to compare directly the timing of its predictions with all the fits that began in 1964. Note that we have used the five-period fit in Chapter 12 rather than the four-period fit because it is more representative of a fit beginning in 1964.

In Figures 13.9 and 13.10, we show the comparison plots between the Federal Reserve no interest rate hike scenario and the three-quarters of a percent per year, interest rate hike scenario for the output, and the economy debt, respectively. We have also included a table below each figure that gives the timing of the peak in the Federal Reserve's interest rate hike scenario for that fit and the other four fits implied above.

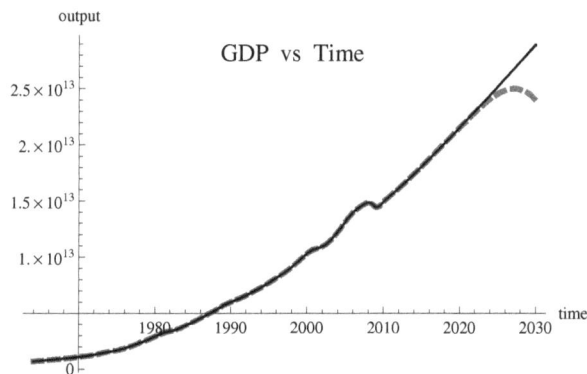

Figure 13.9: Here, we see the comparison of the output graphs, created using the extraordinary worker group, for the Fed no rate hike scenario and for the Fed three-quarters of one percent per year rate hike scenario.

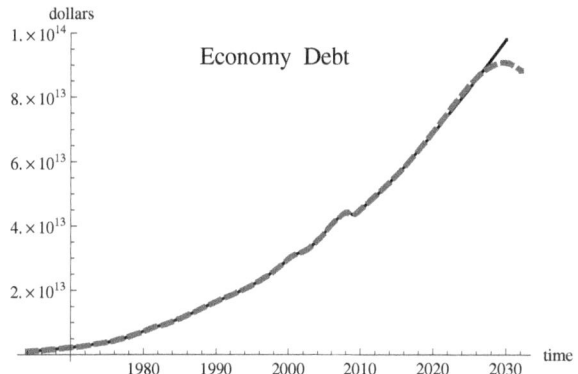

Figure 13.10: In this figure, we display the graphs of the economy debt comparison for the Fed no rate hike scenario, black line, and the three-quarters of a percent per year, interest rate hike scenario, dashed gray line.

GDP Peak	
Fit	Date of Peak
1980	2027.41
1964 with $a_0 = 22276.93$	2026.92
1964 with $a_0 = 11870.02$	2026.97
1964 Five Period	2026.73
1964 Extraordinary Workers	2027.19

Table 13.1: This table presents the dates for the peak in the output predicted by our macroeconomic model using the average interest rate function we constructed in Chapter 7.

Economy Debt Peak	
Fit	Date of Peak
1980	2029.95
1964 with $a_0 = 22276.93$	2029.39
1964 with $a_0 = 11870.02$	2029.43
1964 Five Period	2029.22
1964 Extraordinary Workers	2029.66

Table 13.2: Here, we present a table for the dates for the peak in the economy debt predicted by our macroeconomic model using the average interest rate function we constructed.

Figure 13.9 displays the output comparison plot created using the macroeconomic productivity function, which we constructed from the extraordinary worker group. It looks similar to all the other output comparison plots. In the Federal Reserve interest rate hike scenario, the output peak in the graph occurs at 2027.19. Table 13.1 below the figure displays the predicted timing of the output peak for the various fits that use our constructed average interest rate function. The grouping of predicted times shows the fit that started in 1980 occurs some five to six months later than the average of the group of fits that started in 1964.

Figure 13.10 indicates the peak in the economy debt for the United States Economy occurs in late 2029 or very early 2030, just as all the other fits, using our construct average interest rate function, have shown. The peak in our present fit occurs at 2029.66, some four months earlier than the fit that started in 1980 predicted. Table 13.2 shows that the average timing predicted for the peak in the economy debt for fits starting in 1964 would likely be some five to seven months earlier than predictions from fits starting in 1980.

Next, we show comparison plots for the employment level and the average wage rate in Figures 13.11 and 13.12. We place a table below each figure that shows the timing of the peaks in the rate hike scenario.

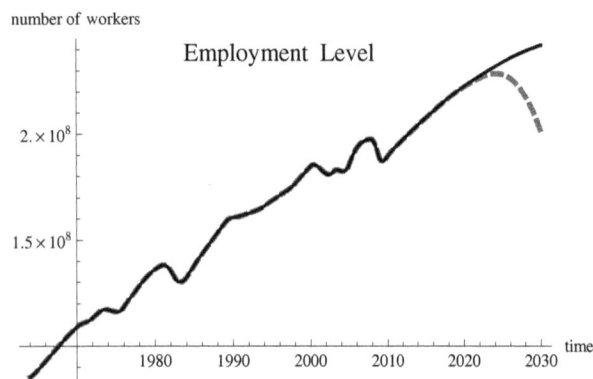

Figure 13.11: Shown in this figure are the employment level graphs for the extraordinary workers in the no rate hike scenario and in the Fed interest rate hike scenario—dashed line.

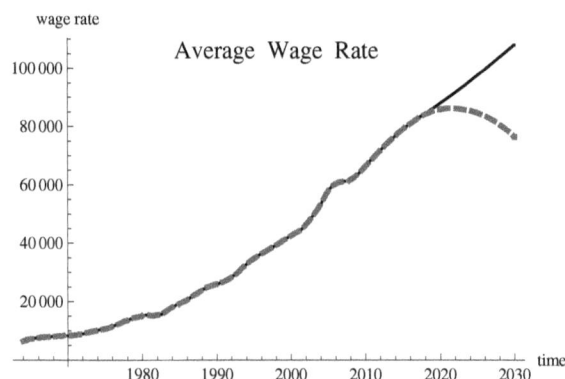

Figure 13.12: Here, we see the average wage rate in the no rate hike scenario—black line—and in the interest rate hike scenario—gray dashed line—using the average interest rate function we created.

Employment Level Peak	
Fit	Date of Peak
1980	2024.62
1964 with $a_0 = 22276.93$	2024.23
1964 with $a_0 = 11870.02$	2024.29
1964 Five Period	2023.77
1964 Extraordinary Workers	2024.12

Table 13.3: This table presents the dates of the peak in the employment level predicted by our macroeconomic model using the average interest rate we constructed in Chapter 7.

Wage Rate Peak	
Fit	Date of Peak
1980	2021.28
1964 with $a_0 = 22276.93$	2021.12
1964 with $a_0 = 11870.02$	2021.13
1964 Five Period	2021.21
1964 Extraordinary Workers	2021.46

Table 13.4: Here, we present a table for the dates for the peak in the average wage rate predicted by our macroeconomic model using the average interest rate we constructed.

In Figure 13.11, we see that employment level stays under the population of the United States, using our macroeconomic productivity function, just as it did with the macroeconomic productivity function we created for ordinary workers plus farmers. We also see that the employment level in the Federal Reserve increases interest rates at three-quarters of a percent per year turns over and begins to fall in the early to mid-2020s, just as it did for all the fits, which used the average interest rate that we constructed in Chapter 7. Table 13.3, below Figure 13.11, shows that the date of the employment level peak predicted by those fits, which used our average interest rate and began in 1964, would likely be some five to seven months earlier than the average for fits that start in 1980.

Figure 13.12 shows us that the average wage rate is predicted to peak in the early 2020s, just as did in all the other fits that used the average interest rate function we created. Table 13.4 indicates that the average predicted time of the wage rate peak for the fits starting in 1964 would likely be consistent with the average for the fits starting in 1980. However, the distribution of the predicted times indicates the possibility that the peaks for fits starting in 1964 might be up to about a month earlier than for fits beginning in 1980.

Next, we present a comparison of the trajectories under the two Fed scenarios for investment, in Figure 13.13, and for the total economy profit, in Figure 13.14. Tables 13.5 and 13.6, which show the times when investment and economy profit crash to zero in the Federal Reserve interest rate hike scenario, are displayed below their respective figures.

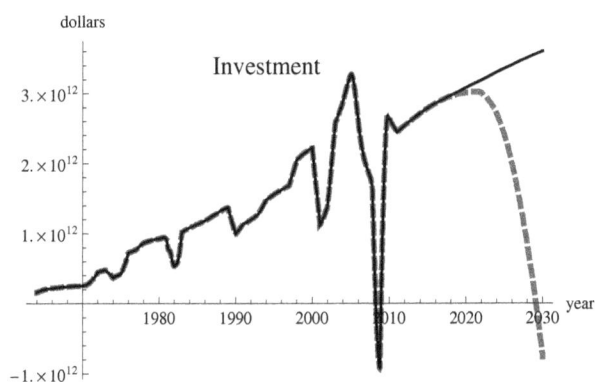

Figure 13.13: Presented here is the investment graph for the extraordinary workers in the Fed no rate hike scenario–black line—and the investment graph for the three-quarters of a percent per year, interest rate hike scenario—gray dashed line.

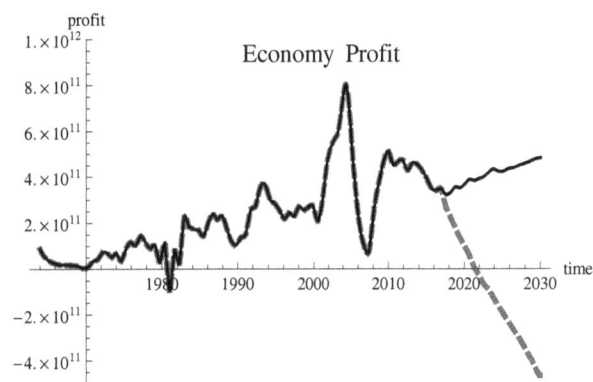

Figure 13.14: Here, we show the economy profit in the no rate hike scenario—black line—and in the interest rate hike scenario—thick dashed line—both using the macroeconomic productivity function we created for the extraordinary workers.

Investment Zero Intercept	
Fit	Date of Zero Intercept
1980	2029.37
1964 with $a_0 = 22276.93$	2028.82
1964 with $a_0 = 11870.02$	2028.86
1964 Five Period	2028.70
1964 Extraordinary Workers	2029.14

Table 13.5: This table presents the date of the zero intercept for investment as predicted by our macroeconomic model using the average interest rate we constructed in Chapter 7 and particular choices for our macroeconomic productivity function.

Economy Profit Zero Intercept	
Fit	Date of Zero Intercept
1980	2021.28
1964 with $a_0 = 22276.93$	2021.12
1964 with $a_0 = 11870.02$	2021.12
1964 Five Period	2021.21
1964 Extraordinary Workers	2021.46

Table 13.6: Here, we present a table for the date of the zero intercept of the economy profit predicted by our macroeconomic model using the average interest rate we constructed and using a particular choice for our macroeconomic productivity function.

In Figure 13.13, we see that the investment within the economy climbs steadily in time, interrupted roughly every ten years with a downward spike. During the Federal Reserve Scenarios, which start in 2017, we see the three-quarters of percent per year, interest rate hike scenario slowly begins to underperform relative to the no rate hike scenario. Then the interest rate scenario turns over and begins to crash rapidly. This behavior is typical of all fits. In this fit, we see that investment crashes through zero near 2029. Table 13.5 states that this occurs at 2029.14. Table 13.5 also indicates that all other fits using our average interest function also crash through zero at times, not far from this time. However, again, on average, the fits starting in 1964 would likely be four to six months earlier that the average for fits starting in 1980.

In Figure 13.14, we see that the economy profit reacts quickly to the rise in interest rates, with the rate hike scenario beginning to fall away from the no rate hike trajectory, and within about one year, it begins to crash. In this fit, the economy profit is predicted to crash through zero in 2021.46, assuming no changes in economic conditions. Table 13.6 indicates that all the fits, using the average interest rate we constructed in Chapter 7, predict a relatively tight grouping for the time when the economy profit crashes through zero.

We have seen that some results are systematically off for fits starting in 1964 when compared to the results for fits that start in 1980. The predicted investment-to-GDP ratio is systematically too high during the period of high inflation during the 1970s. The sudden and fast rise in the debt-to-GDP ratio, which starts when the debt-to-GDP ratio is about 1.5 and continues until the debt-to-GDP ratio is above 2.5, starts about fifteen years too early in the fits that begin in 1964. Moreover, as we have just seen, the predictions of the fits that begin in 1964 are typically, systematically too early when compared to the predictions made by the fit that begins in 1980.

So far, we have not considered inflation in our macroeconomic coupled differential equation model. If we develop a function based on the yearly inflation rate to add to the output equation, can we fix some or all of these systematic discrepancies? We will attempt this, now, before passing on this monograph as finished. However, because we are pressed for time due to this Country's economic and political situation and that of the World, we can only give a very limited amount of time to this effort before we have to throw in the towel and leave that effort for another day. Time is of the essence.

Success!! A crude method of modeling high inflation and adding it into our coupled differential equation macroeconomic model was found. Therefore, we can complete our discussion.

Chapter 14

Inflation and Our Macroeconomic Model

In our economic modeling, we found that we were effortlessly able to form smooth fits that began in 1980, which would cruise through long periods of time without us having to adjust the Businessman's and Banker's Coefficients, c_1 and c_2. See our first smooth fit in Section 2.1, and the accompanying values for the coefficients c_1 and c_2 shown in Figure 2.1 and Figure 2.2 on page 20.

However, it was impossible to find a smooth fit going from 1964 to 1980 for any of the fits that we started in 1964. Look, for instance, at the GDP versus time fit in Figure 10.3 on page 150. This output curve between 1964 and 1980 is quite smooth. Nonetheless, look at the manipulations we needed to make in the Banker's Coefficient, c_2, shown in Figure 10.2 on page 149, in order to create that fit. Making that fit was a struggle.

14.1 A Crude Model of Inflation

We saw in Figure 10.6 on page 150 that high yearly inflation was happening in the United States during this time. We have repeated an expanded view of this inflation in Figure 14.1.

From Figure 14.1, we see that there was a steep upward climb in inflation between 1964 and 1980. In addition, we see that the economy had to traverse three mountainlike spikes in inflation during that time.

However, when we compare this to the inflation that the economy had to traverse starting from 1980 onward, we see that, after 1980, inflation had a general downward trend, quick at first, then changing to a long slow downward slope. We note that the ups and downs in inflation are there, as they were in the upward trek from 1964 to 1980, but the ups and downs were smaller and less sharp.

What do we take away from all this? First, there is a certain level of inflation that our economy will be able to respond to naturally without really getting out of balance. Second, we know that humans usually take some time to respond and that humans also anticipate. Thus, we might expect that the human societal response to sharp ups and downs in inflation would likely be less sharp because we anticipate in the front end and take time to respond

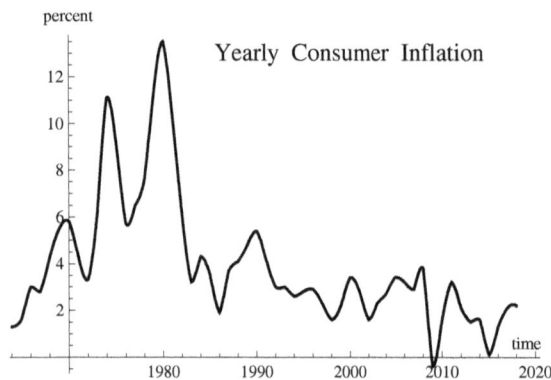

Figure 14.1: This figure shows the yearly consumer inflation rate from 1964 to 2018.

Figure 14.2: Here, we show the coefficient, which, when multiplied by the output gives us our estimate for the amount of money that businesses in the economy will receive from their price increases in lieu of investment, during periods of high inflation.

in the back end. Furthermore, because our responses tend to be stretched out in time, the amplitudes of our response will tend to be of a more moderated amplitude than the inflation stimulus we are responding to.

Our model will take into account that there is a certain level of inflation that the United States Economy responds to naturally. Then, without taking into account the stretching out and the moderation of the response, a simple crude model of inflationary price increases presents itself.

We will assume that the amount of money due to price increases that can be used by business in lieu of investment money obtained by borrowing is given by subtracting the amount of inflation that can be handled naturally by the economy, Ci_0, from the yearly inflation rate, Δ_{cpi}, and then multiplying this quantity by the output. That is, the amount of money added to businesses in place of investment money is $(\Delta_{cpi} - Ci_0) * Y$.

The question then becomes: How and where do we add this quantity into our coupled differential equation model? This money will go directly into the output equation because it is directly added to businesses in current (inflated) dollars. However, it is not new money added to the economy. Therefore, it will not go where investment money goes. This term is just directly added to the output equation because it adds directly to businesses' ability to create output. Thus, our new modified, output equation that takes into account inflation is:

$$\frac{dY}{dt} = \frac{I}{v} - \gamma * Y + c_{Inf} * Y,$$

$$\text{where } c_{Inf} = \begin{cases} \Delta_{cpi} - Ci_0 & \text{if } \Delta_{cpi} - Ci_0 > 0 \\ 0 & \text{otherwise.} \end{cases} \tag{14.1}$$

The constant c_{Inf} is shown in Figure 14.2, and the value for the constant Ci_0 that we used in this fit is 0.035. That is, we are assuming that the economy would handle naturally a three and one-half percent yearly inflation rate.

14.2 A Fit that Accounts for Inflation

The fit of this section is essentially the same fit that we performed in Chapter 10. In particular, this sister fit was the fit that used a productivity function with a constant growth rate that was not defined in relation to a 1980 fit. Both fits use the average interest rate that we constructed. All the initial parameters are the same. The only difference is that we are using the modified output equation, Equation 14.1, in order to include the influence of inflation into our fit. While the initial and predictive values are the same as those used in the fit of Chapter 10, the values of c_1 and c_2 needed to be changed during the fitting period, itself, in order to create the fit. The values of c_1 and c_2, which we used in the fit, are shown in Figure 14.3 and Figure 14.4, respectively.

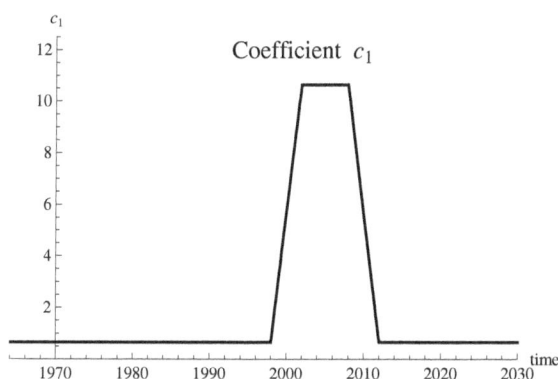

Figure 14.3: This figure shows a plot of the values used for the coefficient c_1 in the investment equation that allowed us to fit the United States Economy's output while taking into account high inflation.

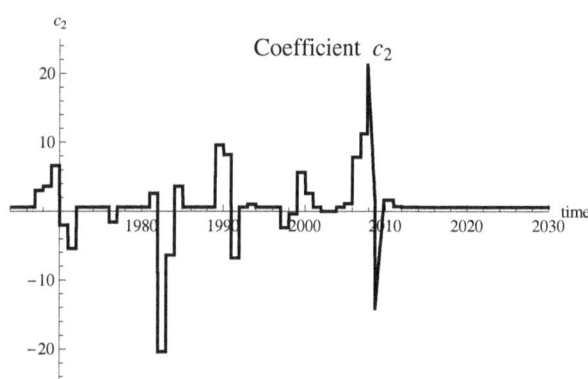

Figure 14.4: Here, we display a graph of the values of the Banker's Coefficient, c_2, which allowed us to make the fit that takes into account the influence of high inflation during the 1970s and early 1980s.

When we compare Figure 14.3 with the plot of c_1, shown in Figure 10.1 on page 149, we see that they look very similar. The height of the peak in this fit is about one unit lower, while the beginning and end values are 0.65 in both fits.

When one compares the coefficient c_2 in the previous fit with the coefficient c_2 in Figure 10.2 on page 149, one observes that fit's Banker's Coefficient is very bottom-heavy in values compared with our present fit. This means that the sister fit was stimulating lending for investment to a much greater extent than our present fit over the time interval of high inflation from about 1968 to 1982. The beginning and ending value of the Banker's Coefficient, c_2, is 0.6 in both fits.

We can also see that the sister fit through the period from 1997 to 2007 was a smooth fit, while in the present fit, we resorted to a refined fit. The present refined fit is a somewhat unfortunate choice because it will not allow as clean of a comparison between the timing of predicted events as some might like. However, as we saw earlier, the comparison of the timing of events between the refined fits and the smooth fits produced results that were very close to one another—noticeably closer than the results for the fits that begin in 1964 as compared with those fits that begin in 1980.

Next, for the present fit, in order to keep clear exactly which version of our average interest rate function we are using in the present fit and its sister fit, which we presented in Chapter 10, we show the average interest rate functions used in both fits in Figure 14.5. We show the output curve that the present fit creates with the GDP data plotted over it, in Figure 14.6.

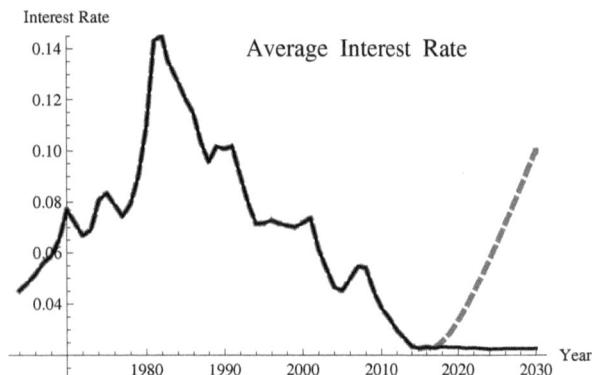

Figure 14.5: This figure shows the average interest rate interpolating functions used in the present fit, which was projected forward in the two Federal Reserve interest rate scenarios.

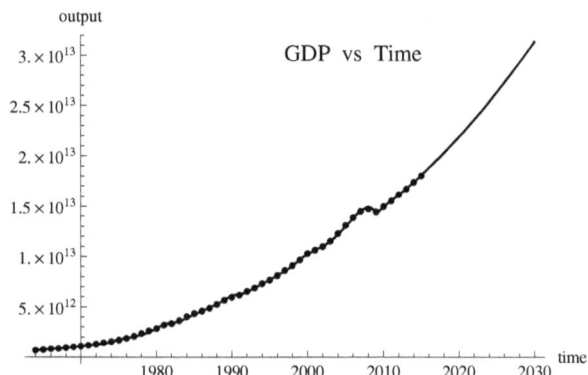

Figure 14.6: Here, we display the output curve for the present fit, which takes into account the high inflation of the 1970s and early 1980s, plotted over the GDP data.

If we compare the average interest rate interpolating function used in our present fit with the average interest rate function, shown in Figure 9.3 on page 144, used in our present fit's sister fit of Chapter 10, we see that they are exactly the same. This average interest rate function was also used with the fit in Chapter 9. However, when we compare it with the average interest rate interpolating function used in the fits that were created with our macroeconomic productivity functions, we see that it is slightly smoother than the interpolating function version used in those fits. See Figure 12.5 on page 174.

We see from Figure 14.6 that the present fit has been created by making a very nice fit to the GDP data.

Next, we present in Figure 14.7, the investment-to-GDP curve for the present fit plotted over the investment-to-GDP data. Beside it, in Figure 14.8, we present the function that we added to the output equation in order to correct for periods high inflation. We express the correction in current dollars. We do this so that the reader will be aware of the actual dollar amounts we are talking about. Furthermore, we will want to have the figure right in front of us because we will be making some subtle observations and comparisons that becomes more difficult when a person has to keep flipping pages to make them.

We see from Figure 14.7 that the crude function we created in order to correct for high inflation has worked. In this figure, we see that the investment-to-GDP trajectory, created by the fit, travels through the fit data from 1964 to 1980. No other fit that we began in 1964 has done this! All the other investment-to-GDP fit curves have traveled well above the data from 1964 to 1980. See Figure 9.6 on page 144, Figure 10.5 on page 150, Figure 12.12 on

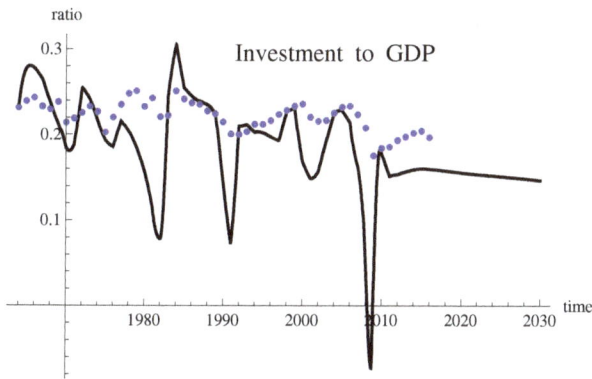

Figure 14.7: In this figure, we plot the investment-to-GDP curve generated by the present fit. We plot the curve over the investment-to GDP-data for the United States.

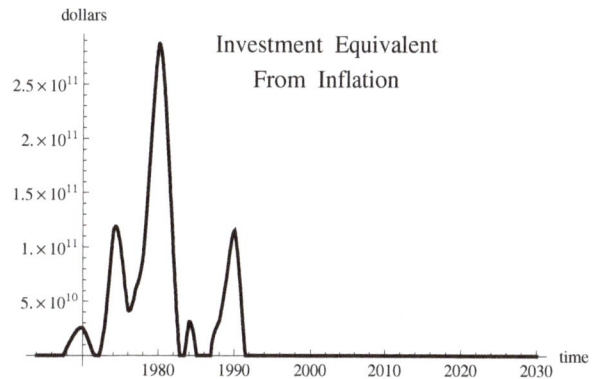

Figure 14.8: Here in this figure, we present, in current dollars, our crude model's change to the output equation that takes into account the influence of high inflation.

page 176, and Figure 13.6 on page 187.

We also see from Figure 14.7 that our crude correction for high inflation has resulted in too spiky a response, just as we thought it might. This is particularly evident in the response to the sharpest and biggest spikes centered over 1980 and 1990 in Figure 14.8. In this regard, we see our algorithm caused too much of the money received from the price increase spikes to be spent in lieu of investment at the time of the spikes. The money was not spread out more evenly, as businesses would likely have done. Also, some of the excess money, in the spikes, probably would have been siphoned off into wage increases for the business elite. This likelihood is increased because significant tax cuts occurred at or just before those spikes. See the plot of the maximum tax brackets, which is shown in Figure 11.11, on page 166.

We also observe, as we observed earlier, that investment-to-GDP data starts to rise above the investment-to-GDP fit curves beginning in the late 1990s. This rise is probably due to the fact that banking regulations were significantly weakened back then. Ultimately, in 1999, Glass-Steagal was repealed. These changes in banking regulations allowed all banks to deal in speculation. Consequently, some credit issued for speculative purposes probably has been mixed with the data for credit issued into the real economy.

Finally, we should note in Figure 14.8 that our crude algorithm does not create any money from high inflation to be used in place of investment from 1964 to about December of 1967. However, Figure 14.7 suggests that there may have been an in lieu of investment source of money during this period. Figure 14.7 makes this suggestion because the investment-to-GDP curve bubbles above the investment-to GDP-data by about two percent there. In current dollars, this would suggest a ten to twenty billion dollar in lieu of investment source might have been at play during the period from 1964 to 1968.

When one looks at the plot of the yearly consumer price inflation shown in Figure 14.1, one sees that there is a sharp spike in inflation that runs all the way from 1964 through to 1970. There also appears to be a hint in that figure that inflation flattens out (going backward in time) at the very beginning of 1964. Looking at the wider in time plot of the yearly inflation rate, shown in Figure 11.9 on page 164, we see that the yearly inflation rate held at a very low level from 1959 to 1964. This leaves open the possibility that the sharp, abrupt inflation spike could have acted as an in lieu of investment money source during the period from 1964 through 1968 even though over this period, the yearly inflation rate had not yet reached the three and one-half percent level of our algorithm.

The President Kennedy and President Johnson tax cuts, which went from ninety-one percent in 1963 to seventy percent in 1965, might also have been a source of in lieu of investment money. President Kennedy's Council of Economic Advisers had predicted that a tax cut from ninety-one percent to sixty-five percent would have resulted in a loss of 10 billion dollars of tax revenues, but subsequently would have resulted in a 20 billion dollar increase in yearly GDP due to the stimulation of the economy (Cooper and John, 2012, Chapter 12). Cooper and John's textbook calculation estimated a 9.3 billion dollar tax loss and a 21.4 billion dollar yearly GDP gain.

Therefore, because of the unique situation described above, there probably was a ten to twenty billion dollar source of "free" investment money that increased the growth of the GDP during the three years between 1965 and 1968. If the source had been included in our model, this would have caused the investment-to-GDP curve to be lowered closer to the investment-to-GDP data.

Next, in Figure 14.9, we display how adding a term to the output equation, which crudely takes high inflation into account, modifies the economy debt curve's fit of our coupled macroeconomic differential equation model. In Figure 14.10, we display how this change modifies the economy debt-to-GDP fit.

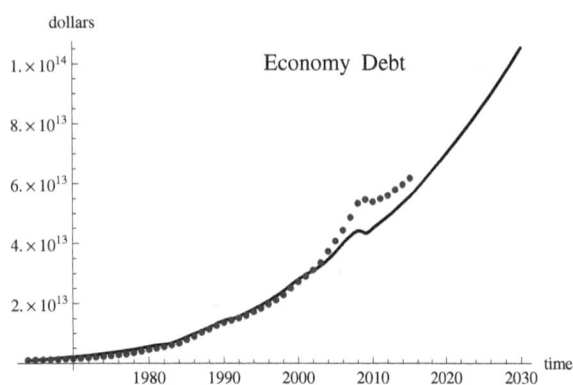

Figure 14.9: In this plot, we show the fit to the economy debt data when our macroeconomic model's output equation is modified to include the influence of high inflation.

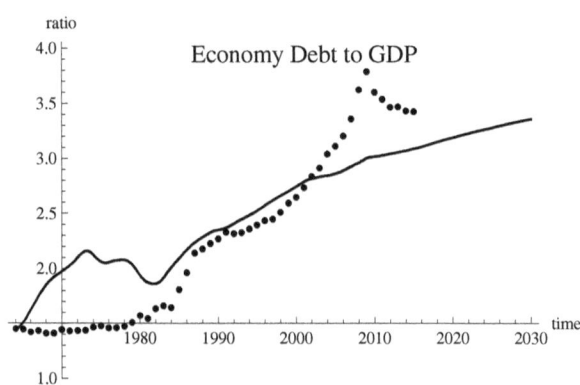

Figure 14.10: Here, we display how the debt-to-GDP curve of our macroeconomic model matches the debt-to-GDP data when our model includes a term that tries to account for high inflation.

We see in Figure 14.9 that the economy debt curve is a very tight fit to the total economy debt in the real economy of the United States up through and just past the year 2000. In fact, it is a noticeably closer fit to the data during this period than all the other economy debt fits, which were started in 1964. Moreover, it is even a slightly better fit to the economy debt data than the fits that were begun in 1980.

Also, we see clearly that the debt data starts to rise quickly above the total economy debt of the real economy fit curve just after the year 2000. This divergence is very likely due to speculative debt and investment data having been merged with the real economy debt and investment data, which probably occurred after the bank deregulation and the repeal of Glass-Steagall in the late 1990s.

When we compare the debt-to-GDP plot of the present fit, shown in Figure 14.10, with its sister plot, which uses the same productivity function and initial values, we see that the debt-to-GDP curve has been shifted dramatically to the right. However, we also notice that the very beginning of the economy debt-to-GDP curve has not been shifted to the right. This lack of an early shift is almost surely because our algorithm to take into account high inflation is not sophisticated enough to include a steep rise in inflation after a relatively long period of low inflation. In addition, our modeling equations have not taken into account the change in the tax structure that effectively started in 1965. Both impacts, if modeled for, would have almost certainly shifted the beginning of the fast rise in the debt-to-GDP fit curve to the right, just as the in lieu of investment, inflation-induced price rise money did.

14.3 Comparison Plots for an Inflation Corrected Fit

Next, we will present the comparison plots showing what is predicted to occur in the Federal Reserve no interest rate hike scenario and in the Fed raises interest rates at three-quarters of a percent per year scenario. Below each of the comparison plots, we will present a table that shows when a significant event in the interest rate hike scenario occurs. This table will include the fit that begins in 1980; the sister scenario, which begins in 1964 with the same value for all the parameters; and the present fit, which has included a crude algorithm that inputs the influence of high inflation into our coupled macroeconomic differential equations. We begin the series of comparison plots with GDP in Figure 14.11 and with the economy debt in Figure 14.12.

From Figure 14.11 and Figure 14.12, we see that both the GDP comparison plot and the economy debt comparison plot have the same visual form as all the other GDP and economy debt comparison plots that we have calculated previously. However, when we look at the GDP peak in the Federal Reserve's three-quarters of a percent per year, interest rate hike scenario, we find, in Table 14.1, that the fit beginning in 1964, which uses our inflation reconciliation algorithm, is consistent in the timing of the GDP peak with the fit that started in 1980. Previously, all the fits starting in 1964 were seen to be inconsistent with the 1980 fit by some five to six months. Using our algorithm, which endeavors to take high inflation into account when doing a fit, has extended the time of the GDP peak by about six months. This is not an apple to orange comparison because the 1964 fit being compared is its sister fit, which has the same constants, average interest rate, and the same initial parameters. The only thing that is different between the two fits is that one fit uses a crude algorithm that takes high inflation into account during its calculations.

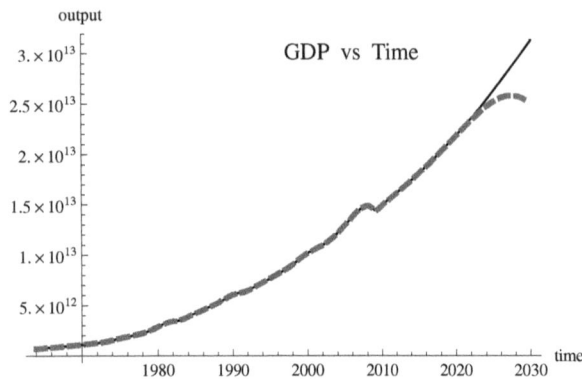

Figure 14.11: In this figure, we display the GDP fit, adjusted for high inflation, that is run for the Fed no rate hike scenario—black line—and for the three-quarters of a percent per year, interest rate hike scenario—dashed line.

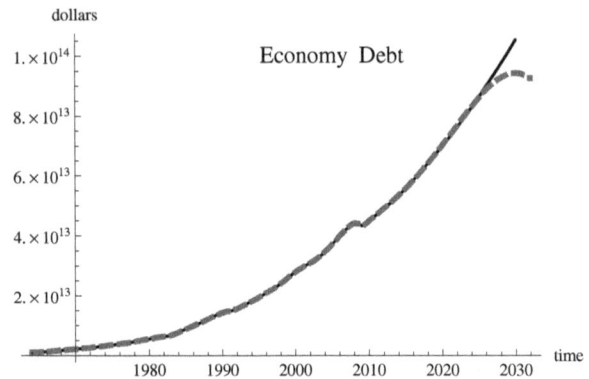

Figure 14.12: Here, we present the economy debt curve propagated forward for the no interest rate hike scenario—black line—and for the Federal Reserve increases interest rates by three-quarters of a percent per year scenario—dashed gray line.

GDP Peak	
Fit	Date of Peak
1980	2027.41
1964 with $a_0 = 11870.02$	2026.97
1964 inflation-adjusted	2027.49

Table 14.1: In this table, we present the date of the peak in the output predicted by our macroeconomic model using the average interest rate we constructed in Chapter 7 for the particular fit choices described above.

Economy Debt Peak	
Fit	Date of Peak
1980	2029.95
1964 with $a_0 = 11870.02$	2029.43
1964 inflation-adjusted	2030.03

Table 14.2: Here, we present a table for the date of the peak in the economy debt predicted by our macroeconomic model using the average interest rate we constructed for the particular fit choices described in the text.

The economy debt comparison shows precisely the same result. The present fit using our inflation correction term, $(\Delta_{cpi} - Ci_0) * Y$, in the output equation has extended the time until the occurrence of the peak in economy debt by five months over its sister fit's time. As shown in Table 14.2, our inflation algorithm has made the time when the economy debt peak occurs consistent with the time when the peak occurs in the fit that began in 1980.

Next, we present the comparison plots for the employment level and the average wage rate in Figure 14.13 and Figure 14.14.

We see from Figure 14.13 and Figure 14.14 that the fits, using our algorithm correcting for high inflation, project forward both the employment level and the average wage rate so that their trajectories have the same form when projected forward in time as all the other fits do.

In addition, when we consult Table 14.3, we see that our macroeconomic model, to which we have added our algorithm that corrects for high inflation, has shifted the peak in the em-

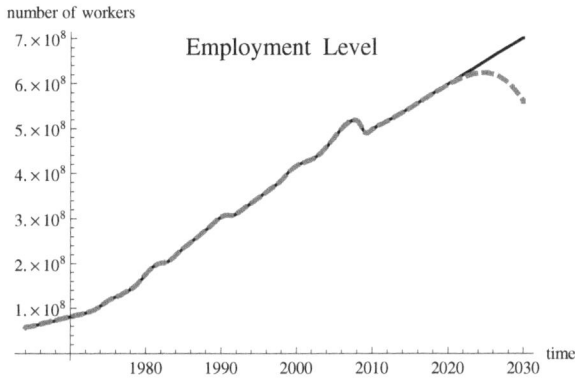

Figure 14.13: In this figure, we display the plot of the employment level for the no rate hike scenario— black line—and for the Federal Reserve's rate hike scenario—dashed line—calculated using the inflation reconciliation algorithm.

Figure 14.14: In this figure, we present the average wage rate curves as calculated using our inflation correcting algorithm. The projection forward includes the no rate hike Fed scenario—black line— and the interest rate hike scenario—dashed line.

Employment Level Peak	
Fit	Date of Peak
1980	2024.62
1964 with $a_0 = 11870.02$	2024.29
1964 inflation-adjusted	2024.69

Average Wage Rate Peak	
Fit	Date of Peak
1980	2021.28
1964 with $a_0 = 11870.02$	2021.13
1964 inflation-adjusted	2021.31

Table 14.3: This table presents the date of the peak in the employment level predicted by our macroeconomic model for the particular choices described above. The fits use the average interest rate we constructed in Chapter 7.

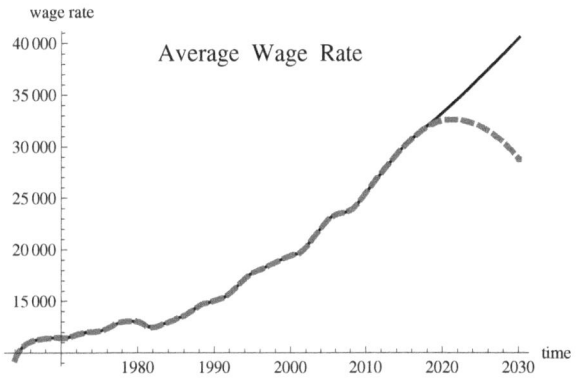

Table 14.4: In this table, we display the date of the peak in the average wage rate predicted by our macroeconomic model, using the average interest rate function we constructed, for the three particular fit choices described in the text.

ployment level, under the Federal Reserve's rate hike scenario, so that it becomes consistent with the timing of the peak in a fit that begins in 1980. In effect, it has shifted the employment level peak of its sister fit by 146 days or just under five months.

From the results shown in Table 14.4, we see that our inflation correction term has added about sixty-six days to the time when the present fit's sister fit predicts that the average wage rate will peak in the Federal Reserve's three-quarters of a percent per year, interest rate hike scenario. This inflation correction has pushed the time of the peak about eleven days past the time of the average wage rate peak predicted by the fit that begins in 1980. This makes the present fit's timing securely consistent with the predicted timing of the 1980 fit.

Next, we present the comparison plots for investment and economy profit in Figure 14.15 and Figure 14.16, along with their accompanying tables.

In Figure 14.15 and Figure 14.16, we see that investment in the real economy and economy profit have the same general form that we have seen in all the other fits.

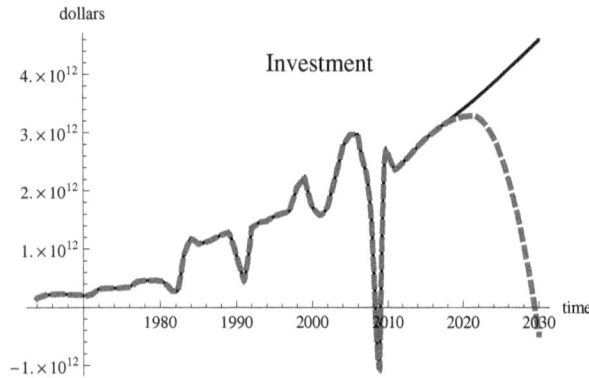

Figure 14.15: Here, we display the investment comparison plots of the present fit for the Fed's no rate hike scenario—black line—and the three-quarters of a percent per year, interest rate hike scenario.

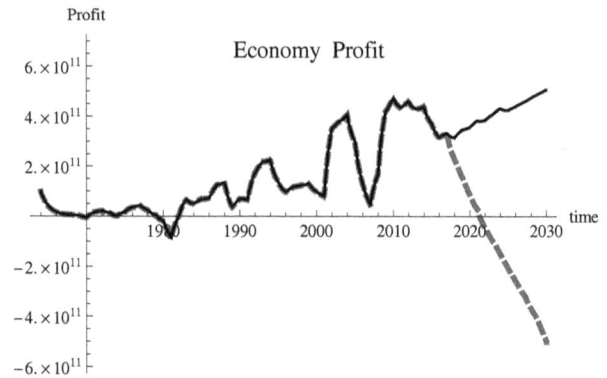

Figure 14.16: This figure displays the high inflation corrected fit's graph of the economy profit in the no interest rate hike scenario and in the interest rate hike scenario—dashed line.

Investment Zero Intercept	
Fit	Date of Zero Intercept
1980	2029.37
1964 with $a_0 = 11870.02$	2028.86
1964 inflation-adjusted	2029.47

Table 14.5: This table presents the time when investment crashes to zero that is predicted by our macroeconomic model when it uses the average interest rate we constructed in Chapter 7 for the particular fit choices described above.

Economy Profit Zero Intercept	
Fit	Date of Zero Intercept
1980	2021.28
1964 with $a_0 = 11870.02$	2021.12
1964 inflation-adjusted	2021.31

Table 14.6: Here, in this table, we present the date when the economy profit crashes to zero as predicted by our macroeconomic model using the average interest rate we constructed for the three particular fit choices described in the text.

Table 14.5 displays the time that the present fit predicts that investment will crash to zero under the Federal Reserve's three quarters of a percent per year, interest rate hike scenario. It also displays the sister fit's prediction along with the predicted time for the fit that began in 1980. From this display, we see that the crude algorithm which accounts for high inflation has corrected the sister fit's predicted time so that it becomes consistent with the time the fit that begins in 1980 predicts for the moment the investment will crash to zero in the Federal Reserve's interest rate hike scenario.

Table 14.6 displays the time the present fit predicts the economy profit will crash to zero. From the table's display, we see that the fit that starts in 1964 and uses the algorithm that adjusts for high inflation is consistent with the time predicted by the fit that began in 1980.

This chapter has shown us that any fit created by our macroeconomic coupled differential equation model that follows our fitting procedures can be made entirely consistent with the results from our model starting in 1980 as long as the fit properly takes inflation into account. Therefore, this result means that any fit that begins in 1980 is a valid fit for the United States

Economy because the fits starting in 1980 are consistent with one another.

More importantly, this means that the fix to the United States Economy that we created in Chapters Five and Six is valid and would work. The same would be true for any other fix that might be created using our coupled macroeconomic differential equation model as long the solution includes a livable minimum wage and high top tax brackets such as those that existed during the 1950s and early 1960s.

Chapter 15

Odds and Ends

15.1 Employment Level and Average Wage Rate

Figure 15.1 displays some of the employment levels that have occurred in constructing our fits.

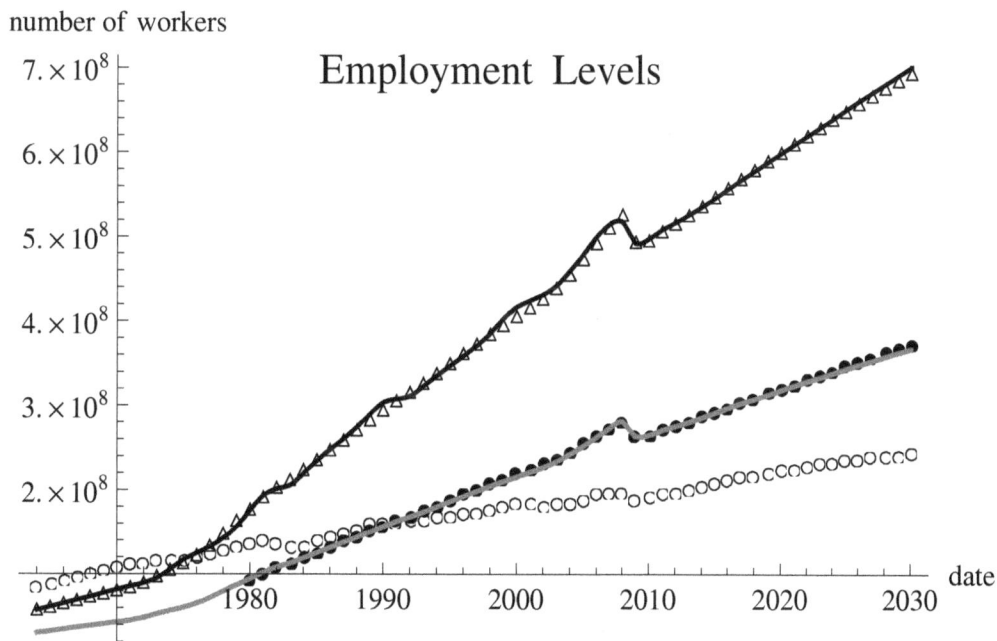

Figure 15.1: Here, we show the employment levels in the no rate hike scenario for five fits that we presented, which were calculated using the average interest rate function we constructed. These fits include the 1980 fit that used a productivity of $a_0 = 30,727.3$—black circular disks—and its 1964 brother fit, whose productivity growth rate equals that of the 1980 fit and in addition, has an initial productivity value such that its 1980 value will equal the initial value of the 1980 fit's productivity—gray line. We have also included the inflation corrected 1964 fit—black line—and its sister fit, whose productivity was chosen to reproduce the initial employment level in 1964—open triangles. We also show the fit that uses our macroeconomic productivity, $\hat{a}(t)$, which was chosen to fit the extraordinary or unusual class of "workers", such as Social Security recipients, who, in effect, get paid by the output of the real economy, but ordinarily do no work—open circles.

When we look at Figure 15.1, we see that there is a very wide range in the employment levels, which we created in our fits of the United States Economy. We also see, because of the clear difference in slopes of the employment level curves, that there are very different instantaneous growth rates in the various employment levels we have used in creating fits to the United States Economy. However, even with all the variations in the employment levels used to create fits, we have been able to fit the gross domestic product, the total investment, the economy profit, and the total debt in the real economy. Moreover, the predictions made by projecting these various fits forward in time are essentially the same. How is this possible? How can it be that employment levels can be so divergent, and yet the results of a fit so similar?

Our coupled macroeconomic differential equation model has three equations that involve the employment level, L. They are the definition of the productivity equation, the wage equation, and the economy profit equation. They are displayed below:

$$a = \frac{Y}{L},$$

$$\frac{dw}{dt} = m\frac{\Pi}{L}, \quad \text{and}$$

$$\Pi = Y - w * L - r * D.$$

We see from the productivity equation that the employment level is given by Y/a. Both the output and the productivity grow approximately exponentially so that the employment level is given approximately as

$$\frac{Y_0}{a_0}e^{(\eta-\alpha)(t-t_0)},$$

where η is the exponential growth rate of the output, and α is the exponential growth rate of productivity.

Now, output grows exponentially as the sum of the exponential growth rates of population, productivity, and inflation, while macroeconomic productivity grows exponentially as the sum of the exponential growth rates of productivity plus inflation. Therefore, a fit that uses the macroeconomic productivity, the open circle fit in Figure 15.1, should be expected to grow roughly at the rate at which the population grows.

However, when a fit uses the productivity to create the fit, that fit's productivity does not take into account inflation. Productivity is defined in terms of the physical or intellectual output per hour of worker time. The monetary value of the thing, which is output, is not part of the definition. Thus, when a fit uses productivity to create the fit, the black disks and open triangles in Figure 15.1, the employment level grows exponentially at roughly the sum of exponential growth rates of population plus inflation.

Both the black disk and the open triangle fits have the same exponential growth rate. However, the open triangle fit begins with a greater initial value than the gray line associated with the black disk fit. Therefore, in 1964, the slope of the open triangle fit is greater than the slope of the gray lined fit associated with the black disk fit.[1] Thus, the difference in value between the open triangle fit and the black disk fit is growing in time. This reasoning explains what we see in Figure 15.1, but it does not explain why fits in our model with such divergent employment levels work.

As we saw earlier in Figure 7.17 on page 121, the economy profit and output of the economy grow on average at the same rate. So, looking at the wage equation, $dw/dt = m * \Pi/L$, we see that

$$\frac{dw}{dt} = m\frac{\Pi}{Y} * a, \text{ because } L = Y/a,$$

where a can be either the productivity or the macroeconomic productivity. This means, on average, the average wage rate grows as the productivity. Moreover, because the productivity's growth rate is exponential, then it is possible that the average wage rate, itself, after a while, is approximately proportional to the productivity.

We see that the average wage rate and the employment level only couple to the other equations of our macroeconomic coupled differential equation model through the economy profit equation, $\Pi = Y - w * L - r * D$, through the term $w * L$. Looking at the term $w * L$, assuming the wage rate is proportional to productivity, we find:

$$\begin{aligned} w * L &\propto m\frac{\Pi}{L} * L \\ &\propto m\Pi. \end{aligned}$$

Thus, the average wage rate times the employment level, $w * L$, would be roughly proportional to GDP because, on average, economy profit grows as output. That is, $w * L \approx k * Y$, where the constant, k, may slowly vary over time as the nature of economic conditions change.

Let us test this out. To do so, in Table 15.1, we display the GDP and the corresponding value of $w * L$ in the no rate hike scenario for the five fits that appear in Figure 15.1.

We see from Table 15.1 that all the fits eventually became synchronized so that their values for $w * L$ were consistent to within three significant digits. By the time the output reached 15.0×10^{12} dollars in the calculated fits, just after the beginning of 2010, the values of $w * L$ agree to three significant digits. This synchronization is kept by all fits beyond 2015 and throughout the projection forward of the Federal Reserve's no rate hike scenario.

By the time the output of the fits reached five trillion dollars, about the beginning of May in 1987, only the inflation-corrected fit starting in 1964 had synchronized up with the fit beginning in 1980. In May of 1987, $w * L$ of the other fits were about thirty percent less than the 1980 fit's value for $w * L$. When the output reached eight trillion dollars per year,

---

[1]For an exponential function, $x(t) = x(t_0)e^{\epsilon(t-t_0)}$, the slope is given by $dx/dt = x(t_0)\epsilon e^{\epsilon(t-t_0)}$. Therefore, the bigger the initial value, $x_0 \equiv x(t_0)$, the greater the slope.

			Wage Rate Employment Level GDP Relation		
GDP	1980 Fit $w * L$	1964 Fit $a_0 = 22276.93$ $w * L$	1964 Fit $a_0 = 11870.02$ $w * L$	1964 Fit unusual workers $w * L$	1964 Fit inflation corrected $w * L$
5×10^{12}	3.77×10^{12}	3.31×10^{12}	3.31×10^{12}	3.41×10^{12}	3.74×10^{12}
6×10^{12}	4.50×10^{12}	4.09×10^{12}	4.09×10^{12}	4.19×10^{12}	4.51×10^{12}
7×10^{12}	5.38×10^{12}	5.05×10^{12}	5.04×10^{12}	5.13×10^{12}	5.46×10^{12}
8×10^{12}	6.37×10^{12}	6.09×10^{12}	6.09×10^{12}	6.14×10^{12}	6.41×10^{12}
10×10^{12}	7.90×10^{12}	7.61×10^{12}	7.62×10^{12}	7.67×10^{12}	7.95×10^{12}
12×10^{12}	9.91×10^{12}	9.77×10^{12}	9.77×10^{12}	9.58×10^{12}	9.96×10^{12}
14×10^{12}	11.8×10^{12}	11.6×10^{12}	11.6×10^{12}	11.7×10^{12}	11.8×10^{12}
15×10^{12}	12.8×10^{12}	12.7×10^{12}	12.7×10^{12}	12.8×10^{12}	12.8×10^{12}
18×10^{12}	16.3×10^{12}	16.3×10^{12}	16.3×10^{12}	16.3×10^{12}	16.4×10^{12}
22×10^{12}	20.0×10^{12}	19.9×10^{12}	19.9×10^{12}	20.0×10^{12}	20.0×10^{12}
30×10^{12}	27.2×10^{12}	27.1×10^{12}	27.1×10^{12}	27.2×10^{12}	27.2×10^{12}

Table 15.1: In this table we display the value of $w * L$ when the output of a fit in the no rate hike scenario reaches the GDP shown in the far left-hand column for each of the five fits shown in Figure 15.1.

just before the beginning of October in 1995, the inflation uncorrected 1964 fits' values of $w * L$ had closed the gap so that the 1980 fit's value of $w * L$ was only about 4.4 percent higher. However, the inflation uncorrected fits did not become fully synchronized until those fits began to get serious about matching up their fits with the data either during the crisis of 2008–9 or during the lead-in to that crisis. This result adds support to our discussion concerning the macroeconomic dynamics of the economy in Chapter 8.

What has become clear from the discussion is that fits, which are begun in 1980, eventually get their timing right when projecting the economy forward if they synchronize with the data after the crisis in 2008–9. Also, it is clear the fits that begin in 1964, which take into account high inflation, also eventually get *all* their timing right if their fits synchronize with the data after the crisis of 2008–9.

In the last two chapters, we have shown the generality of the fits to the United States Economy that begin in 1980. Therefore, our discussion in Chapter 5 and Chapter 6, on how to fix the United States Economy, has not been corrupted because we used fits beginning in 1980 to determine a method to fix the economy. Furthermore, we have seen that the fix to the United States Economy would not have been corrupted because the productivity we used in the modeling equations produced the wrong employment level. Accordingly, we have a firmer knowledge that the solution to fix the United States Economy, which we came up with, will fix the United States Economy.

15.1.1 Wage Rate and Employment Level Part of the Economy

Looking, for example, at the ratio of the product of the wage rate and employment level, $w * L$, to the GDP shown in Table 15.1 for the 1980 fit, we notice that

$$\frac{4.5 \times 10^{12}}{6 \times 10^{12}} = 0.75,$$

$$\frac{7.9 \times 10^{12}}{10 \times 10^{12}} = 0.79,$$

$$\frac{12.8 \times 10^{12}}{15 \times 10^{12}} = 0.85, \text{ and}$$

$$\frac{16.3 \times 10^{12}}{18 \times 10^{12}} = 0.91.$$

Thus, we can see from Table 15.1 that the monetary fraction of the average wage rate times the employment level part of the economy in the no rate hike scenario steadily increased up through 2015. It then held steady to 2017 and then started to decline slowly because interest rate hikes were taking a growing slice of the output for the financial institutions.

We should note that, after a while, when the fits synchronize, they all show that the wage rate times the employment level, $w * L$, become equal. Also, we should take note that the average wage rate times the employment level in the economy is the total income in the real economy. These connections mean that when we synchronize the economy, we are synchronizing the total income in the economy, not the employment level or the average wage rate.

Now, if we write the economy profit equation as

$$Y = w * L + r * D + \Pi,$$

we see that Table 15.1 is telling us that the total income in the economy would have been a growing percentage of the proceeds from the output of the economy up until the beginning of 2017.

However, we know from the work of Bivens and Mishel (Bivens and Mishel, 2015) and Emmanuel Saez (Saez, 2016) that the economic elites are taking a bigger and bigger fraction of the output of the economy compared to the ordinary worker. Furthermore, we saw, in Figure 11.2 on page 156, that the rate of growth in the employment level became drastically lower in about the year 2000, so that a greater and greater fraction of the population has come to be out of work.

Taken together, this means that the economic elites are stealing the wealth created by all of us. It is occurring with as much effect as if it were occurring in feudal times by an invading force. If it had occurred with the pain and the abruptness of an invasion, we would have fought back, just as a lobster struggles when you thrust it into a pot of boiling water.

It has taken a long time for us to get into this situation. We were not aware that what was happening in the economic world around us would lead to our present situation. Even the actors who were initiating the changes that were slowly creating the present economic situation were not aware of the ramifications of what they were doing. However, we now find ourselves in a pot of hot water. We sense the situation is bad. Our situation has developed slowly, just as it would have if we placed the lobster into a pot of cold water and slowly heated it. By the time the lobster realizes something bad is happening, it has become pacified and seemingly unable to act. Can we learn, and can we act to pull ourselves out of the pot?

We now know how to do it. We know how to fix our economy and keep it fixed. But! will we do it?

15.2   The Bankers' Share of the Economy

The economy profit equation, $\Pi = Y - w * L - r * D$, helps to lay bare the monetary importance of various elements within the economy. We have seen that our limited set of equations makes it challenging to get a good handle on the average wage rate and the employment level within the economy because we do not know either quantity well. However, we do seem to know their product reasonably well.

We should also be able to know the debt repayment term, $r * D$, rather well. I have seen data from back in the 1930s that provide this simple data by the Federal Reserve Bank in St. Louis. The data they provide is the volume of debt outstanding, the interest repayable during the year, and the average interest rate for the year. The latter is a simple calculation from the first two quantities because

$$r = \frac{r * D}{D}.$$

They provide this data from 1929 to 1941. However, I have not seen this data for any other years. Sometimes simple data is better because it is all that one needs. Moreover, because we do not have a way of calculating the average interest rate directly from the data they provide, we have had to try to estimate it.

However, our calculated average interest rate seems to provide us reasonable values for our investment-to-GDP calculations and our debt calculations. So, we will use our average interest rate function back to 1957. We also have total economy debt data back to 1947.

Therefore, we can directly calculate yearly values for the interest payment term, $r * D$, from 1957 to 1963. Then, we can add these directly calculated yearly values to a table of the yearly values of $r * D$ taken from the calculations of the inflation-corrected fit that begins in 1964. Creating an interpolating function from this yearly table of values of the repayment term $r * D$ should provide us with a reasonable estimate of the banking system's monetary share in the economy as a function of time. We use the Federal Reserve no rate hike scenario in our estimate of the bankers' share in the economy in order to give us a base reference. We display our estimate of the bankers' share in the economy in Figure 15.2.

We see from Figure 15.2 that the bankers' share of the economy during the late 1950s and early 1960s, when the economy was running well, was about five to six percent. Then,

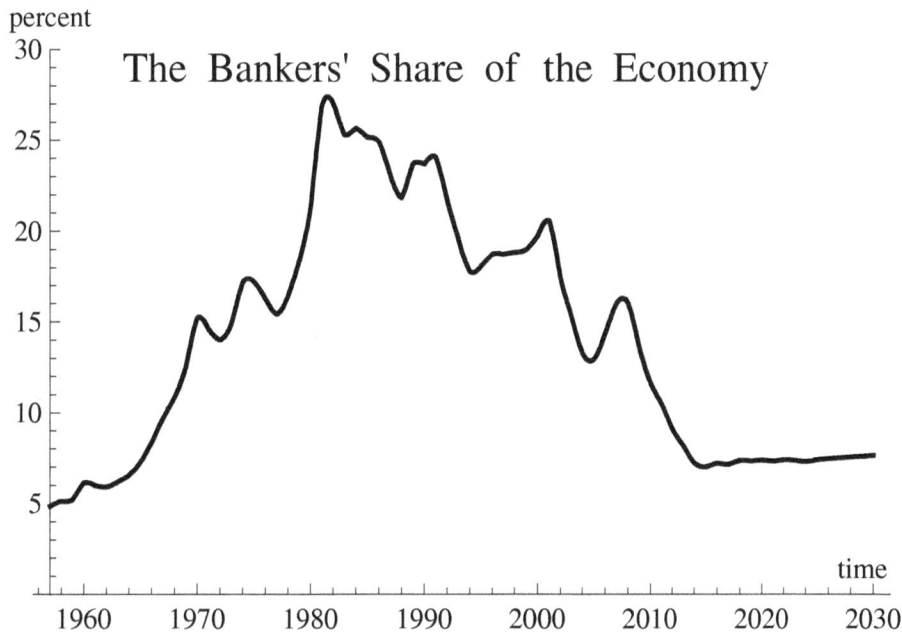

Figure 15.2: Here, we display a graph showing the percent of the GDP of the United States Economy that is received by the banks as interest payments each year from 1957 to 2030 as calculated in the Federal Reserve's no interest rate hike scenario.

as the Government ramped up the Vietnam War and as inflation took hold, the bankers' share of the economy steadily climbed to better than twenty-five percent of the economy. Finally, in the early 1980s, when we got inflation under control—see Figure 14.1 on page 194—and as interest rates began to decline—see Figure 12.5 on page 174—the banker's share of the economy declined moderately slowly into the mid-teens, percentage-wise.

In the crisis of 2008–9, the bankers' share dropped quickly from something above sixteen percent to about ten percent. Their share continued to drop to about seven percent by 2015. Since then, under the Federal Reserve's no rate hike scenario, the bankers' share has been rising inexorably, but very very slowly. Even though the average interest rate is barely above two percent in the no rate hike scenario, the bankers' share of the economy has been able to rise because the debt in the economy is so high. By 2030, the bankers' share would have risen to about 7.65 percent in the no rate hike scenario.

Presently, as of January 2019, in the Federal Reserve's three-quarters of a percent per year, interest rate hike scenario, the bankers' share is about 9.2 percent of the economy and rising. See Figure 15.3 below. Furthermore, as we see in Figure 15.4, the bankers' increasing share is just starting to push down the total income part of the economy, $w * L$. This shows how delicately balanced the economy is at present because there is virtually no leeway left to let the profit within the economy absorb the shock of interest rate rises.

At this point, the Federal Reserve's desire to raise interest rates is not so much out of greed but is out of their interest in self-preservation. The financial system worldwide is presently in a very dire financial state. At this point, it would not be wise to let them fail, as

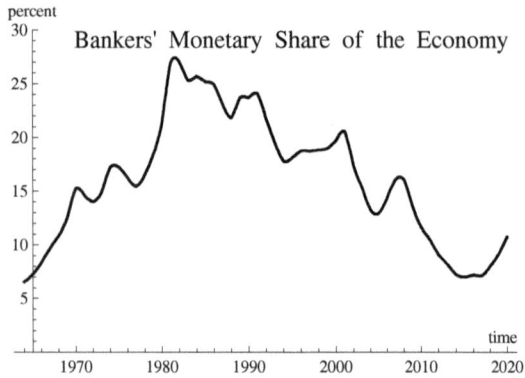

Figure 15.3: Here, we show the bankers' monetary share of the economy in the Federal Reserve's rate hike scenario.

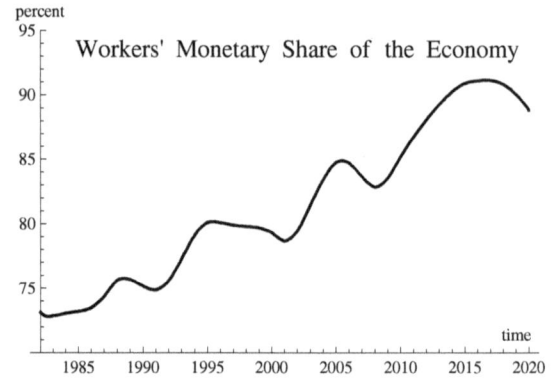

Figure 15.4: This figure displays the workers' monetary share of the economy in the Federal Reserve's interest rate hike scenario.

they would in a free market because the Government is not prepared to step in to prevent the real economy from failing should the financial system fail. The real economy is in somewhat better shape than the financial system so that we can give them a little leeway. If the financial system fails now, we fail. Moreover, this failure is likely to lead to a depression such as the World has never seen before.

It is our job, therefore, to show Our Country and the World how we can fix the enormous debt problem that we all face and to convince our governments that we can salvage the situation. And then support them in their efforts to put together a policy that will work. It is our job, and it is our duty, because we are the ones who know how to fix the problem and keep it fixed.

Bibliography

ANDERSON, SARAH (2016), The Wall Street Bonus Pool and Low-Wage Workers, *Institute for Policy Studies*, March 8, 2016.

BIVENS, JOSH AND MISHEL, LAWRENCE (2015), Understanding the Historic Divergence Between Productivity and a Typical Worker's Pay, *Economic Policy Institute Briefing Paper*, **406**, September 2, 2015. Available online at: www.epi.org/publication/understanding-the-historic-divergence-between-productivity-and-a-typical-workers-pay-why-it-matters-and-why-its-real/

CHAMBERLAIN, ANDREW (2013), Federal Individual Income Tax Rates History, *Tax Foundation*, Available online at: https://www.taxfoundation.org.

COOPER, RUSSELL AND JOHN, ANDREW (2012), *Macroeconomics: Theory through Applications*, Saylor Foundation, Available online at: https://saylordotorg.github.io/text_macroeconomics-theory-through-applications/s16-02-the-kennedy-tax-cut-of-1964.html.

CORBETT, MICHAEL F. (2004), The Outsourcing Revolution, *getAbstract*, 2004.

DUNGAN, ADRIAN (2015), Individual Income Tax Shares, 2012, *Statistics of Income Bulletin*, Spring 2015, Available online at: https://www.irs.gov/pub/irs-soi/soi-a-ints-id1506.pdf.

EVANS, PAUL (1982), The Effects of General Price Controls in the United States during World War II, *Journal of Political Economics,* **90 No. 5**, (October, 1982), 944–966, Available online at: https://www.jstor.org/stable/1837127.

GOODWIN, R. M. (1965), A Growth Model, *Presented at the First World Congress of the Econometric Society, held in Rome, 1965*, Published 2014, by *Semantic Scholar*, Available online at: https://pdfs.semanticscholar.org/dd29/697eeb31a2d05e7927ad207899ecd70cf8f7.pdf.

THE HUFFINGTON POST (11/04/2012), Bill Clinton's True Legacy: Outsourcer-in-Chief, Available online at: https://www.huffingtonpost.com/jane-white/bill-clintons-true-legacy-b-1852887.html.

KEEN, STEVE (2010), Solving the Paradox of Monetary Profits, *Economics: The Open-Access, Open Assessment E-Journal*, **4**, 2010–31.

KEEN, STEVE (2011), *Debunking Economics: The Naked Emperor Dethroned*, London, UK: Zeb Books Ltd.

KEEN, STEVE (2013), A Monetary Minsky Model of the Great Moderation and the Great Recession, *Journal of Economic Behavior & Organization*, **86**, 221–235.

KUMHOF, MICHAEL AND ZOLTÁN, JAKAB (2016), *Finance & Development*, **53**, March 2016, No. 1.

MINSKY, HYMAN (1982), *Can "It" Happen Again*, New York, NY: Routledge (Routledge Classics, 2016).

MINSKY, HYMAN P. (2008), Stabilizing an Unstable Economy, New York, NY; McGraw-Hill.

MOTHER JONES (02/2005), Exporting America: An Interview with Lou Dobbs, https://www.motherjones.com/politics/2005/02/exporting-america-interview-lou-dobbs/.

SAEZ, EMMANUEL (2016), Striking it Richer: The Evolution of Top Incomes in the United States (Updated with 2015 Preliminary Estimates), UC Berkeley, Spring 2016.

SOCIAL SECURITY ADMINISTRATION (2018), Wage Statistics for 2012, March 12, 2018, Available online at: https://www.ssa.gov/netcomp.cgi?year=2012.

US DEPARTMENT OF COMMERCE AND BUREAU OF THE CENSUS (1954), Family Income in the United States: 1952, **P-60, No. 15**, April 27, 1954.

US DEPARTMENT OF COMMERCE AND BUREAU OF THE CENSUS (1963), Average Family Income up 4 Percent in 1962, **P-60, No. 40**, June 26, 1963.

US DEPARTMENT OF COMMERCE AND BUREAU OF THE CENSUS (1965), Median Family Income up about 5 Percent in 1965, **P-60, No. 49**, August 10, 1966.

US DEPARTMENT OF COMMERCE (1969), Household Income in 1966 and Selected Social and Economic Characteristics of Households, **P-60, No. 65**, October 31, 1969.

US DEPARTMENT OF COMMERCE AND BUREAU OF THE CENSUS (1980), Money Income in 1978 of Households in the United States, **P-60, No. 121**, February 1980.

US DEPARTMENT OF COMMERCE AND BUREAU OF THE CENSUS (1984), Money Income of Households, Families, and Persons in the United States: 1982, **P-60, No. 142**, February 1984.

US DEPARTMENT OF COMMERCE AND BUREAU OF THE CENSUS (1993), Money Income of Households, Families, and Persons in the United States: 1992, **P-60, No. 184**, September 1993.

UNITED STATES CENSUS BUREAU (2017), Table H-3. Mean Household Income Received by Each Fifth and Top 5 Percent, All Races: 1967 to 2016, Available online at: https://www.census.gov/data/tables/time-series/demo/income-poverty/historical-income-households.html.

www.ingramcontent.com/pod-product-compliance
Lightning Source LLC
Chambersburg PA
CBHW052349210326
41597CB00038B/6310